# Real Estate Appraisal

*First Edition, Third Printing*

Roy K. Bottger

Dwight E. Norris

Eric Sharkey

ASHLEY CROWN SYSTEMS, INC.

# Real Estate Appraisal

This publication is designed to provide accurate and current information regarding the subject matter covered. The principles and conclusions presented are subject to local, state and federal laws and regulations, court cases and revisions of same. If legal advice or other expert assistance is required, the reader is urged to consult a competent professional in the field.

**Director of Publishing & Course Development**
Lars Jentsch

**Real Estate Publisher**
Leigh Conway

**Writer/Copyeditor**
Sue Carlson

**Technical Writer**
Ben Hernandez

**Senior Technical Writer**
Judy Moyer

**Copyeditor**
Emily Rehkopf

**Administrative Assistant**
Stephanie Pratap

**Production Coordinator**
Judy Hobbs

**Graphic Design**
Kellee LaVars
Susan Mackessy
Rey Dulay

Published by
Ashley Crown Systems, Inc.
22952 Alcalde Drive
Laguna Hills, California 92653

Printed in the United States of America

ISBN: 0-934772-19-3

# Contents

# PREFACE

Appraisal plays a crucial role in hundreds of thousands of real estate transactions every year. Appraisers rely on their knowledge of real estate and economics to determine the property values for their clients—from lenders to lawyers. *Real Estate Appraisal* introduces the beginner to the key concepts of the real estate appraisal profession.

*Real Estate Appraisal* combines theoretical concepts with practical examples to produce a concise, accurate, and easy-to-understand text. Each chapter begins with learning objectives to help the student identify the most important information. Relevant forms, data charts, and illustrations abound throughout the chapters, making the text visually appealing. Chapters then conclude with summary and review questions that not only test comprehension, but also reinforce knowledge. Answers and detailed explanations are provided in the back of the book.

*Real Estate Appraisal* has been written and organized to meet the 2008 licensing requirements as established by the Appraiser Qualifications Board of the Appraisal Foundation. This book explores all the required subtopics of basic appraisal principles and procedures and provides students with a comprehensive overview of appraisal fundamentals and general real estate principles.

The concepts and techniques provided in *Real Estate Appraisal* are useful for students in any field of real estate, but naturally focus on the individual who is seeking state licensure in real estate appraisal.

# ABOUT THE AUTHORS

### ROY K. BOTTGER

Roy Bottger has over twenty years experience in California real estate appraisal, and has published several articles on real estate in national publications. As an expert real estate witness, he has performed forensic appraisals for legal litigation on construction defects, condemnation, and other stigmatized properties.

Mr. Bottger has a Bachelor of Science Degree in Business Administration with a real estate emphasis from San Diego State University. He is currently a California Certified General Real Estate Appraiser and AQB Certified USPAP instructor.

### DWIGHT E. NORRIS

Dwight Norris has been involved in real estate since 1979, and is the author of *Property Management* published by Ashley Crown Publications, Inc. He has been active in the California real estate profession for over twenty years, and is an experienced Certified Residential Appraiser.

Mr. Norris has a Bachelor of Arts and a Masters Degree in Communications from Pepperdine University. He is currently a real estate broker and instructor in California.

### ERIC T. SHARKEY

Eric Sharkey is a licensed appraiser and a certified instructor for the California Bureau for Private Postsecondary and Vocational Education. He has a Bachelor of Arts Degree in English from Seattle University. Mr. Sharkey has personally assisted many students in attaining their appraisal licenses in California, Washington, Louisiana, and Virginia.

# The Appraisal Industry

## Introduction

The most frequently asked question in real estate is probably, "How much do you think my property is worth?" Anyone in the real estate industry is likely to be asked this question by friends and family.

Most homeowners know, within a range, the value of their home. Without realizing it, they often use some of the same techniques as a professional appraiser.

> Example: Joe and Mary know the selling price of their neighbors' house and the selling price of the house down the street. Based on amenities, location, and condition, they have added to –- or subtracted from — those selling prices, to come up with a fairly accurate value for their own house.

This textbook will examine the appraisal process and the methods used to determine property values so that you can answer when a client asks the question, "How much do you think my property is worth?"

## Learning Objectives

After reading this chapter, you will be able to:

- define appraiser and appraisal.

- identify the difference between retrospective and prospective appraisals.

- distinguish the difference between value, cost, and price.

- recognize FIRREA and the reason for its enactment.

- recognize the different appraisal-related committees: TAF, ASB, AQB, and ASC.

- distinguish the differences between license levels.

**Figure 1.1** People want to know how much their property is worth.

## Definition of Appraisal

Appraisal is a general term used to identify the appraisal industry. More specifically, an **appraisal** is an unbiased estimate or opinion of a specific property's value on a given date. An **appraiser** is a person who is expected to value property in a competent, objective, and impartial manner. An appraiser gives his or her opinion of value in a written statement called an **appraisal report**. It is the conclusion of the appraiser's research and analysis of all relevant data regarding the subject property.

**Figure 1.2** Real estate appraisal is performed
by people from different backgrounds.

The majority of appraisals are performed for companies involved in real estate financing.   Almost everyone who purchases a single-family residence takes out a loan to cover the majority of the cost of the house.   Lenders need to be sure that the value of the real estate being used as collateral is sufficient to cover the amount of the loan.   **Collateral** is property pledged to secure a loan.   Lenders can take ownership of the property if the debt is not paid.

**Figure 1.3** Property ownership can be forfeited
to a lender if the debt is not paid.

With over eight million sales of single-family residences in the last year, there are plenty of opportunities for appraisers. In fact, appraisals are used in a wide variety of situations.

Appraisals are usually required whenever property is bought, sold, refinanced, assessed, taxed, condemned, insured, or mortgaged. They may be required for divorce settlements, when business partnerships are dissolved, or when property is listed as a business asset.

Not only are appraisals required for different reasons, appraisals can also look at different time periods. Most appraisals are used to determine a property's current value, but there are other possibilities. **Retrospective appraisals** are ones that look at the value of a property at a point of time in the past.

For example, a retrospective appraisal could be used for insurance purposes to find the value of a house that has since burned down.

**Figure 1.4** The value of a house destroyed by fire is
an example of retrospective appraisal.

A **prospective appraisal** looks at the value of a property at a future point of time.

> For example, a lender who is providing a construction loan might ask an appraiser to determine if houses should be built for sale in a particular area. Part of the appraiser's work would be to value the houses as if they were finished.

**Figure 1.5** An appraiser's job may include evaluating houses under construction in a specific area to determine if the houses should be built in that area.

## Definition of Value

**Value** is defined as the monetary worth of a property, good, or service to buyers and sellers at a given time. It is important to note that people create value. Value is not built into an item. An item is valuable because people perceive it has worth.

Depending on the purpose of the appraisal, appraisers are asked to find different types of value. The focus of most real estate appraisal assignments is determining the market value of a specified property. **Market value** is usually defined as the most probable price a property would bring in normal market conditions.

Remember that the price or cost of a property is not always the same as its value. **Price** is the amount of money requested or paid for a property. To an appraiser, **cost** is the amount of money it takes to build a structure.

## The Appraiser's Role

In real estate transactions, an objective, third-party opinion is often needed to determine the value of real property. The professional appraiser, because of training, experience, and ethics, is responsible for giving clients an objective opinion of value, reached without bias. An appraiser has a serious responsibility to be correct in evaluating data and not to allow other factors to influence evaluation of a property. The appraiser must remember to be a neutral party, responding only to the forces affecting value and not to people with special interests who might want to influence his or her judgment.

# Industry Regulation

Appraisal services have been a part of the real estate industry for a very long time. Over time, real estate appraisal has become its own structured industry as professional associations have developed and national standards and laws have been created to regulate the industry.

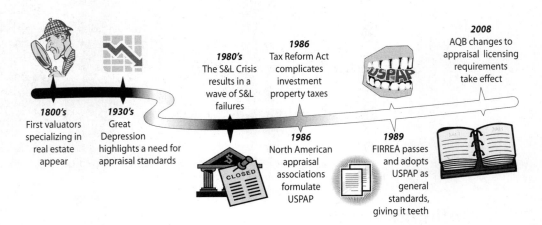

**1800's**
First valuators specializing in real estate appear

**1930's**
Great Depression highlights a need for appraisal standards

**1980's**
The S&L Crisis results in a wave of S&L failures

**1986**
Tax Reform Act complicates investment property taxes

**1986**
North American appraisal associations formulate USPAP

**1989**
FIRREA passes and adopts USPAP as general standards, giving it teeth

**2008**
AQB changes to appraisal licensing requirements take effect

**Figure 1.6**  Time line chart

# Professional Associations

Individuals and firms first began specializing in real estate valuation during the 1800s. Their services were connected primarily with brokerage and insurance underwriting at that time. Chaos in the economy during the era of the Great Depression in the 1930s highlighted the need for professionalism and standards in the real estate appraisal industry. During that time, the first formally organized groups of professional appraisers appeared.

Appraisers with membership in these groups educated themselves through classes and written materials, with the more experienced members teaching the newer appraisers. The associations offered designations or titles for different levels of expertise, and their members were bound to a code of ethics regulating professional behavior.

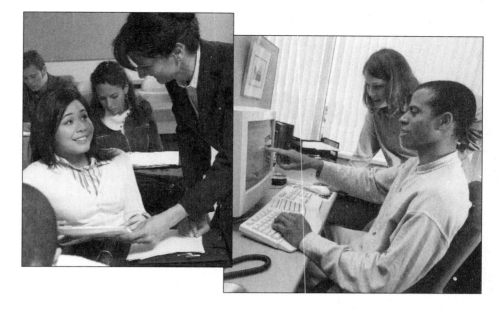

**Figure 1.7** Associations, real estate schools, and community colleges offer appraisal courses in classrooms or through distance education.

In 1986, the major North American-based appraisal associations formulated a set of written standards defining the ethical and competent behavior for appraisers. The stated purpose for these standards was to promote and maintain a high level of public trust and confidence in professional appraisal practice. This document was called the **Uniform Standards of Professional Appraisal Practice (USPAP)**.

## The Appraisal Foundation

A year later, the eight U.S.-based associations that had helped create USPAP founded a private, non-profit organization called **The Appraisal Foundation (TAF)**. The Appraisal Foundation includes two independent boards: the Appraiser Qualifications Board (AQB), and the Appraiser Standards Board (ASB).

The **Appraiser Qualifications Board (AQB)** is made up of five appraisers who are appointed by TAF's Board of Trustees for three-year terms. Among other things, the AQB establishes the minimum education, experience, and examination requirements an individual must meet in order to become a licensed or certified appraiser.

The **Appraisal Standards Board (ASB)** is made up of six appraisers who are appointed by TAF's Board of Trustees for three-year terms. The ASB develops, publishes, interprets, and amends the Uniform Standards of Professional Appraisal Practice.

Since TAF is a private entity, neither TAF nor its Boards have any legal authority of their own.

## The Savings & Loan Crisis

The **Savings and Loan Crisis (S&L Crisis)** of the 1980s was a wave of savings and loan failures caused by mismanagement, failed speculation, and, in some cases, fraud. The **Tax Reform Act of 1986** also caused problems when it changed the tax implications associated with many investment properties. These things, along with other economic issues at the time, combined to cause serious adverse economic consequences. When the economy declined, many property owners defaulted on their loans resulting in huge losses for lenders.

**Figure 1.8** The savings and loans crisis resulted in a decline in the economy. When the economy declined, many property owners defaulted on their loans.

The causes and consequences of these problems have been examined, and it has been found that in a large percentage of cases, the loans that were defaulted on had been based on inflated real estate values. In some cases, this overvaluation was apparently due to appraiser incompetence, and in other cases, it seemed to be a result of appraisers yielding to pressure from lenders or developers to manufacture values high enough to make the loan work.

All of this led to the realization that credible appraisal reports, performed by ethical and competent appraisers, are necessary to the country's economic well-being. Since only a small portion of practicing appraisers had memberships in the generally recognized appraisal organizations at that time, most appraisers were not bound to any one set of qualifications, standards, or ethics rules. This was a deficiency in the real estate appraisal industry that needed to be addressed.

## Financial Institutions Recovery, Reform, and Enforcement Act

As a response to the Savings & Loan crisis, Congress passed the **Financial Institutions Reform, Recovery, and Enforcement Act** (also known as FIRREA or the "S&L Bailout Bill") in 1989. Among other things, FIRREA adopted USPAP as the generally recognized standards of practice in the appraisal profession. This is the law that gave USPAP "teeth" and enforced a set of standards and ethics on the real estate appraisal profession.

**Figure 1.9** The Financial Institutions Reform, Recovery, and Enforcement Act (FIRREA) was created by the federal government.

FIRREA required all states to license and certify real estate appraisers. In addition, FIRREA required that federally related transactions with a transaction value greater than $250,000 be performed by a licensed or certified appraiser. If the transaction is a business loan, a licensed or certified appraiser must be used if the transaction value is greater than $1 million. A **federally related transaction** is any real estate-related financial transaction which a federal financial institution's regulatory agency engages in, contracts for, or regulates, and which requires the services of an appraiser. The **transaction value** is either the loan amount or the market value of the property involved.

Since lending institutions are federally regulated and because the financial world is so interconnected, almost every real estate-related financial transaction ends up being federally related, so this limitation is almost universal. Some states have stricter legislation that requires an appraisal license or certification regardless of transaction value. Regulations change periodically, so individuals pursuing an appraisal license should check with their state's agency to find the most current requirements.

### *Appraisal Subcommittee*

FIRREA also established the **Appraisal Subcommittee (ASC)** which, among other things, maintains the official registry of state licensed and certified appraisers and oversees both the individual state agencies and The Appraisal Foundation.

The Appraisal Subcommittee's mission is to ensure that real estate appraisers are sufficiently trained and tested since real estate appraisers play such an important role in the economy. This helps to guarantee that appraisals are competently performed and that they are based on unbiased, independent judgment.

## State Agencies

In response to FIRREA's mandate, all states have set up real estate appraiser licensing and regulatory agencies. These agencies issue licenses or certifications based upon the appraiser's education, experience, and qualifications. The state agencies are the ones who enforce compliance with USPAP. They receive and investigate complaints against licensees and administer discipline where appropriate.

**Figure 1.10**  Each state is required by FIRREA to set up real estate appraiser licensing and regulatory agencies.

You can also check The Appraisal Foundation's website for a current list (of all the state agencies and their contact information): www.appraisalfoundation.org.

## License Levels

Although appraisal licensing and certification is regulated by each state, FIRREA gave the Appraiser Qualifications Board (AQB) authority to establish the minimum education, experience, and examination requirements that an appraiser must meet in order to obtain a state certification.

Most states have the following four levels of real estate appraiser licensing, although some states do not have the trainee license level:

1. Trainee License
2. Residential License
3. Certified Residential
4. Certified General

Officially, the AQB only has authority to regulate the Certified Residential and Certified General levels, but most states choose to follow their guidelines for the Trainee License and Residential License levels as well.

See the chart on the next page for a summary of the typical education, experience, examination, and continuing education requirements for each level. The chart also shows that an appraiser's classification level affects what properties he or she can appraise.

Legally, when working with a federally related transaction, all appraisers, regardless of license level, must follow USPAP. This means that even Certified General appraisers whose classification level technically allows them to appraise any property must still follow USPAP's requirement that requires necessary knowledge and experience to complete the assignment with competence.

The AQB has decided to make significant changes to some license requirements. The new requirements take effect on January 1, 2008. The AQB's changes are indicated on the second chart.

Changing the requirements for who can supervise trainees is one change that will affect beginning appraisers. Currently, trainees can work under the supervision of an appraiser with any of the three higher qualification levels. There is no limit to the number of appraisers a trainee can work for or the number of trainees an appraiser can supervise. Under the new requirements, only certified residential or certified general appraisers will be able to supervise trainees, and they will be able to supervise a maximum of three trainees at one time.

# EDUCATION, EXPERIENCE, EXAMINATION, AND CONTINUING EDUCATION REQUIREMENTS

|  | Trainee License | Residential License | Certified Residential | Certified General |
|---|---|---|---|---|
| Scope | Must be directly supervised by a state licensed or certified appraiser. May appraise any property that the supervising appraiser is permitted to appraise. | May appraise any non-complex 1-4 unit residential property up to a transaction value of $1 million and complex 1-4 unit residential property[1] up to $250,000. | May appraise any 1-4 unit residential property. | May appraise any property. |
| Education | 75 hours (including 15 hours of USPAP). | 90 hours (including 15 hours of USPAP). | 120 hours (including 15 hours of USPAP). | 180 hours (including 15 hours of USPAP). |
| Experience | None required. | 2,000 hours. | 2,500 hours during at least two years. | 3,000 hours during at least two-and-a-half years. |
| Exam | None required. | Licensed Real Property Appraiser Examination | Certified Residential Real Property Appraiser Examination | Certified General Real Property Appraiser Examination |
| Continuing Education | 14 hours per year including 7 hours of USPAP once every two years. | 14 hours per year including 7 hours of USPAP once every two years. | 14 hours per year including 7 hours of USPAP once every two years. | 14 hours per year including 7 hours of USPAP once every two years. |

[1] **Complex 1-4 unit residential property** means that the property being appraised, the form of ownership, or the market conditions are atypical.

## EDUCATION, EXPERIENCE, EXAMINATION, AND CONTINUING EDUCATION REQUIREMENTS

| Starting **January 1, 2008** | **Trainee License** No changes. | **Residential License** See italicized requirements. | **Certified Residential** See italicized requirements. | **Certified General** See italicized requirements. |
|---|---|---|---|---|
| Scope | Must be directly supervised by a state certified appraiser. May appraise any property that the supervising appraiser is permitted to appraise. | May appraise any non-complex 1-4 unit residential property with a transaction value of less than $1 million and complex 1-4 unit residential property less than $250,000. | May appraise any 1-4 unit residential property. *May supervise up to 3 trainees.* | May appraise any property. *May supervise up to 3 trainees.* |
| Education | *75 hours* (including 15 hours of USPAP). | *150 hours* (including 15 hours of USPAP). | *200 hours* (including 15 hours of USPAP). *An associate's degree or 21 units in specified college courses.* | *300 hours* (including 15 hours of USPAP). *A bachelor's degree or 30 units in specified college courses.* |
| Experience | None required. | 2000 hours *during at least one year.* | 2,500 hours during at least two years. | 3,000 hours during at least two-and-a-half years *including at least 1,500 hours of non-residential appraisal work.* |
| Exam | None required. | Licensed Real Property Appraiser Examination | Certified Residential Real Property Appraiser Examination | Certified General Real Property Appraiser Examination |
| Continuing Education | 14 hours per year including 7 hours of USPAP once every two years. | 14 hours per year including 7 hours of USPAP once every two years. | 14 hours per year including 7 hours of USPAP once every two years. | 14 hours per year including 7 hours of USPAP once every two years. |

# Summary

An **appraisal** is an unbiased estimate or opinion of a specific property's value on a given date.   An **appraiser** is a person who is expected to value property in a competent, objective, and impartial manner. An appraiser gives his or her opinion of value in a written statement called an **appraisal report**.   There are many different types of real estate-related financial transactions that may require an appraisal. The majority of the appraiser's work comes from lenders, who require appraisals to justify their loans.

**Value** is defined as the present worth of rights to future benefits that come from property ownership.   Depending on the purpose of the appraisal, appraisers are asked to find different types of value.   The focus of most real estate appraisal assignments is determining the market value of a specified property.   **Market value** is usually defined as the most probable price a property would bring in a competitive and open market.

Because appraisals play such an important role in real estate-related financial transactions, an appraiser has a serious responsibility to be correct in evaluating data and not to allow other factors to influence evaluation of a property.

Over time, real estate appraisal has become its own structured industry as professional associations have developed and national standards and laws have been created to regulate the industry.   The **Uniform Standards of Professional Appraisal Practice (USPAP)** was created by a group of several different professional appraisal associations. Their goal was to formulate a set of written standards defining ethical and competent behavior on the part of appraisers.   They also founded a private, non-profit organization called **The Appraisal Foundation (TAF)**.   The Appraisal Foundation includes two independent boards: the **Appraiser Qualifications Board (AQB)** and the **Appraiser Standards Board (ASB)**.

The **Savings and Loan Crisis** in the 1980s played a major role in increasing regulation of the appraisal industry.   As a response to the Savings & Loan Crisis, Congress passed the **Financial Institutions Reform, Recovery, and Enforcement Act (FIRREA)** in 1989.   This law enforced a set of standards and ethics on the real estate appraisal profession.

One of FIRREA's requirements was that all the states set up real estate appraiser licensing and regulatory agencies.   These state agencies issue licenses or certifications based upon the appraiser's education, experience, and qualifications, and they enforce compliance with USPAP.

The **Appraisal Subcommittee (ASC)**, which was also established by FIRREA, maintains the official registry of state licensed and certified appraisers and oversees both the individual state agencies and The Appraisal Foundation.

In most states, a beginner in the appraisal industry starts by obtaining a trainee license and working under a certified or licensed appraiser. With additional education and experience as well as successful completion of the applicable exams, the trainee can obtain a residential license or become a certified residential or certified general appraiser.

## Review Exercises

### *Matching Exercise*

**Instructions:** Look up the meaning of the terms in the Glossary, then write the letter of the matching term on the blank line before its definition. Answers are in Appendix B.

### Terms

A. appraisal

B. appraisal report

C. Appraisal Standards Board (ASB)

D. Appraisal Subcommittee (ASC)

E. appraiser

F. Appraiser Qualifications Board (AQB)

G. collateral

H. complex 1-4 unit residential property

I. cost

J. federally related transactions

K. Financial Institutions Reform, Recovery, and Enforcement Act (FIRREA)

L. market value

M. price

N. prospective appraisal

O. retrospective appraisal

P. Savings and Loan Crisis (S&L Crisis)

Q. Tax Reform Act of 1986

R. The Appraisal Foundation (TAF)

S. transaction value

T. Uniform Standards of Professional Appraisal Practice (USPAP)

U. value

### Definitions

1. _____ A person who is expected to value property in a competent, objective, and impartial manner.

2. _____ The written statement where an appraiser gives his or her opinion of value.

3. _____ Property pledged to secure a loan.

4. _____ An appraisal that looks at the value of a property at a point of time in the past.

5. _____ The present worth of rights to future benefits that come from property ownership.

6. _____ The most probable price a property would bring in normal market conditions.

7. _____ The amount of money paid for a property.

8. _____ A set of written standards defining ethical and competent behavior on the part of appraisers.

9. _____ The board that develops, publishes, interprets, and amends the Uniform Standards of Professional Appraisal Practice.

10. _____ A wave of savings and loan failures in the 1980s caused by mismanagement, failed speculation, and, in some cases, fraud.

11. _____ Adopted USPAP as the generally recognized standards of practice in the appraisal profession and gave USPAP "teeth."

12. _____ Any real estate-related financial transaction which a federal financial institutions regulatory agency engages in, contracts for, or regulates and which requires the services of an appraiser.

13. _____ Either the loan amount or the market value of the property involved.

14. _____ An agency created by FIRREA which maintains the official registry of appraisers and oversees the state agencies and The Appraisal Foundation.

15. _____ The board that establishes the minimum education, experience, and examination requirements an individual must meet in order to be a licensed or certified appraiser.

## *Multiple Choice Questions*

**Instructions:** Circle your response and go to Appendix B to read the complete explanation for each question.

1. An appraisal is:
   a. a person who values property in a competent, objective, and impartial manner.
   b. a biased estimation of value.
   c. the work performed by an appraiser.
   d. a written statement depicting the appraiser's opinion.

2. Why do lenders usually use the services of an appraiser?
   a. To ensure that the property value is high enough to cover the loan amount
   b. Because of a legal contract between The Appraisal Foundation and FNMA
   c. For income tax reasons
   d. None of the above

3. A prospective appraisal looks at the:
   a. amount of money paid for a property.
   b. value of a property as if additional modifications had already been completed.
   c. value of a property at a point of time in the past.
   d. value of a property at a future point in time.

4. The money, labor, and material are the _____ to build a property:
   a. collateral
   b. cost
   c. price
   d. value

5. Who or what created The Appraisal Foundation?
   a. The Appraisal Qualifications Board
   b. The eight U.S.-based appraisal associations that had helped create USPAP
   c. The Appraisal Standards Board
   d. FIRREA

6. Appraisers' overvaluation of real estate helped cause the:
    a. Great Depression.
    b. Savings and Loan Crisis.
    c. Tax Reform Act of 1986.
    d. change to stricter licensing requirements in 2008.

7. The mission of the Appraisal Subcommittee is to:
    a. develop, publish, interpret, and amend USPAP.
    b. establish the minimum education, experience, and examination requirements for appraisers.
    c. ensure that real estate appraisers are sufficiently trained and tested.
    d. promote and maintain a high level of public trust and confidence in professional appraisal practice.

8. Which of the following is **not** a license level?
    a. Trainee License
    b. Residential License
    c. Certified Trainee
    d. Certified Residential

9. Under the current requirements, how many hours of experience are needed to obtain a trainee license?
    a. 2,000 hours
    b. 3,000 hours
    c. At least two years
    d. No experience is required.

10. Starting on January 1, 2008, a bachelor's degree is required to obtain which of the following license levels?
    a. Trainee License
    b. Residential License
    c. Certified Residential
    d. Certified General

# Real Property Concepts and Characteristics

## Introduction

When starting on an appraisal, it is critical for the real estate appraiser to know what exactly he or she is appraising. The appraiser must know what is included in the appraisal and how to describe it. This chapter introduces the definitions of real property and personal property and the three types of legal descriptions the appraiser will encounter.

## Learning Objectives

After reading this chapter, you will be able to:

- define real property.
- distinguish between real property and personal property.
- identify the five legal tests of a fixture and explain each legal test.
- identify the different types of legal descriptions.
- find the area of a property based on its legal description.

# Property

**Property** is anything that may be owned and gained lawfully. Property can be real or personal.

When buying real estate, you might think you are buying the property, but what you are really buying are the rights to that property. Property rights are the rights someone has in something and are known collectively as the **bundle of rights**. This important package includes the right to own, possess, use, enjoy, borrow against, and dispose of real property. An owner may choose to sell or give away one of the rights and keep the rest. For example, under a lease agreement, an owner may give away to a tenant the right of use for a period of time.

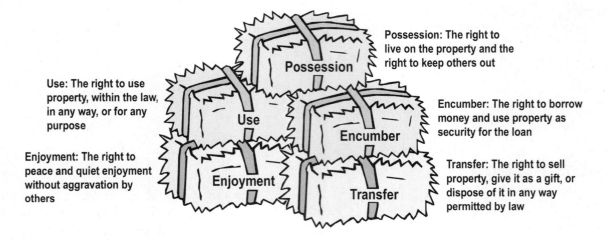

Possession: The right to live on the property and the right to keep others out

Use: The right to use property, within the law, in any way, or for any purpose

Encumber: The right to borrow money and use property as security for the loan

Enjoyment: The right to peace and quiet enjoyment without aggravation by others

Transfer: The right to sell property, give it as a gift, or dispose of it in any way permitted by law

**Figure 2.1** Bundle of Rights: All the legal rights attached to real property ownership.

# Real Estate

**Real estate** is sometimes distinguished from **real property**. At one time, the term "real estate" was used to describe the physical object owned, the land. "Real property" was used to describe the rights gained by owning the land. This distinction is not commonly used anymore, and the terms are used interchangeably throughout this book.

As it is described now, real property includes four things: the land, anything permanently attached to the land, anything appurtenant to the land, and anything immovable by law. Real property is immovable and is usually transferred or sold by a deed. Anything that is not real property is personal property. When real property is sold, anything that has become attached to it goes to the buyer as part of the sale unless other arrangements have been made.

## Land

**Land** includes airspace, surface rights, mineral rights, and water rights.

**Airspace** is considered real property to a reasonable height. An owner or developer of high-rise condominiums may sell the airspace as real property.

**Surface rights** are the rights to use the surface of land, including the right to drill or mine through the surface when subsurface rights are involved.

**Minerals** are owned as real property unless they are non-solid, migratory minerals such as oil or gas. These may not be owned until taken from the ground and then they become the personal property of whoever removed them.

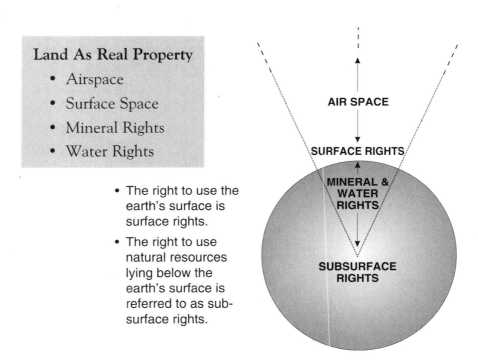

**Land As Real Property**
- Airspace
- Surface Space
- Mineral Rights
- Water Rights

- The right to use the earth's surface is surface rights.
- The right to use natural resources lying below the earth's surface is referred to as subsurface rights.

AIR SPACE

SURFACE RIGHTS

MINERAL & WATER RIGHTS

SUBSURFACE RIGHTS

**Figure 2.2**  Land includes airspace, surface rights, mineral rights, and water rights.

**Water** on the surface, flowing in a stream, or underground is real property. If it is taken and bottled, then it becomes personal property.

Certain water rights go with the land and are considered real property. The owner of property bordering a stream or river has **riparian rights,** which include the rights of irrigation, swimming, boating, and fishing among others. Owners of land bordering a lake possess **littoral rights.** Littoral property owners generally own to the average low water mark or the edge of the lake. The boundary line of land touching the ocean is the ordinary high-tide mark.

**Figure 2.3**  Riparian Rights

## Anything Permanently Attached to the Land

Items permanently attached to the land are real property and belong to the owner. Improvements such as houses, garages, fences, or swimming pools are owned as a part of the property. Anything permanently attached to the building, such as a fixture, is owned as real property. A **fixture** is real property that used to be personal property. It has become a fixture because it is permanently attached to real property. In addition, growing things attached by roots, such as trees, shrubs or flowers, are real property. Emblements are an exception to this rule, however, since they are considered personal property. **Emblements** are crops that are cultivated annually for sale and fruit from orchards in a commercial grove.

**Figure 2.4**  Emblements

## Anything Appurtenant to the Land

An **appurtenance** is anything that belongs to a particular piece of land and is used for its benefit. Typical appurtenances are easements, water rights, mineral rights, and property improvements. These items pass to the new owner when title transfers, whether or not they are mentioned in the deed. However, most deeds describe the property being transferred and then state that the property is being transferred "together with all appurtenances."

## Anything Immovable by Law

There are some items that are considered immovable by law and must be sold with the property. Established trees are an example of this. A seller may not sell the property and exclude the orange grove from the sale. The seller may have sold the crop resulting from the trees as personal property, but the trees themselves remain real property and may not be excluded from the sale.

**Figure 2.5** Established trees are considered immovable by law.

# Personal Property

**Personal property**, sometimes known as **chattel** (from "cattle," an early form of personal property), is movable and transferred or sold using a bill of sale. Personal property includes money, movable goods such as trade fixtures, evidences of debt such as a promissory note, and some growing things such as crops.

Real and personal property can change from one to the other.

For example, a tree is real property until it is cut as timber, then it becomes the personal property of whoever cut it. If that timber is milled into lumber, sold and used to build a house, it becomes real property. Over time, the house ages and deteriorates. When it is torn down and hauled away as scrap lumber, it becomes personal property once again.

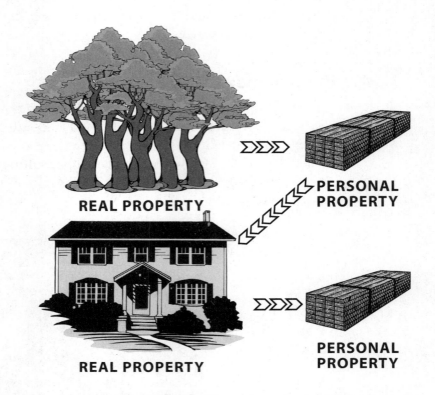

REAL PROPERTY

PERSONAL PROPERTY

REAL PROPERTY

PERSONAL PROPERTY

**Figure 2.6** Property can be real or personal.

In the sale of real estate, the personal property goes with the seller rather than staying with the real property belonging to the buyer. The appraiser must identify which items are considered personal property, since personal property does not contribute any value to the real property being appraised.

## Fixtures

Disputes about real and personal property have caused the courts to adopt a set of tests to help them decide ownership rights when the buyer and seller disagree. The five tests to determine a fixture are: (1) method of attachment, (2) adaptation, (3) relationship of the parties, (4) intent of the parties, and (5) agreement of the parties.

## (1) Method of Attachment

How is the disputed item attached to the property? If it is permanently attached, it is real property. A chandelier wired into the electrical system becomes a fixture, or real property. It would be included in the sale of the house as something attached or affixed to the land unless the sellers specifically mentioned they wanted to take it with them.

## (2) Adaptation

Has the item been made especially for the property? For example, have the drapes been custom-made for the windows? Has the carpet been cut especially to fit the rooms? Is the stove built into the counter? If so, each has become a fixture and has lost its status as personal property.

## (3) Relationship of the Parties

In a dispute about fixtures, when there is no convincing evidence of the right of one party, courts will look at whether the parties are landlord-tenant, lender-borrower, or buyer-seller. The court then makes a decision based on the relationship of the parties in the case. Usually the court will favor the tenant over the landlord, the lender over the borrower, and the buyer over the seller.

## (4) Intention of the Parties

If apparent, either in writing or by the actions of either party involved, intention is considered the most important test of a fixture. Let's look at the tenant who wired special cosmetic lights into the bathroom wall, telling the landlord he intended the lights to remain his personal property. He said he would repair the wall when he moved and would take the lights with him. This was a clear case of a tenant's intention to keep the lights as his personal property. A fixture may remain personal property if all parties are informed. Intention should always be put in writing.

## (5) Agreement of the Parties

When there has been a clear agreement between the parties in a dispute about fixtures, the courts will apply this test to determine who is in the right.

### Trade Fixtures

**Trade fixtures** are items of personal property, such as shelves, cash registers, room partitions, or wall mirrors, used to conduct a business. Tenants retain ownership of the items as personal property when they vacate the premises, but are responsible for repairing any damage that results from placing or removing the trade fixtures.

# Legal Descriptions

Once the appraiser has identified the property included in the appraisal, the next step is to describe it accurately. Property descriptions in the U.S. have evolved over the years. As pioneers moved west and improved the land on which they settled, they created a need for systematic property descriptions. A street address was adequate for social contacts and for delivering mail, but it was not precise enough to identify a particular property.

Today, a legal description is required before a deed can be recorded to transfer title to a new owner. Appraisers include the legal description in the appraisal report, and it is a critical part of identifying the subject property. There are three common ways to describe property: (1) lot, block, and tract, (2) government survey, and (3) metes and bounds.

## Lot, Block and Tract

Other names for the **lot, block, and tract system** are **lot and block system, subdivision system,** or **recorded map system.** It is the most convenient and easily understood method of land description and is most common for metropolitan use. When developers divide parcels of land into lots, they prepare and record a **subdivision map** or **plat map.** The subdivision map shows the location and boundaries of each new lot in the subdivision, and must be recorded in the county recorder's office. After the subdivision map has been filed or recorded, it is public record and is available to anyone. Each lot in a subdivision is identified by number, as is the block in which it is located; each lot and block is in a referenced tract. Recorded map descriptions of land are most likely to be found in cities where developers have planned communities and commercial growth areas.

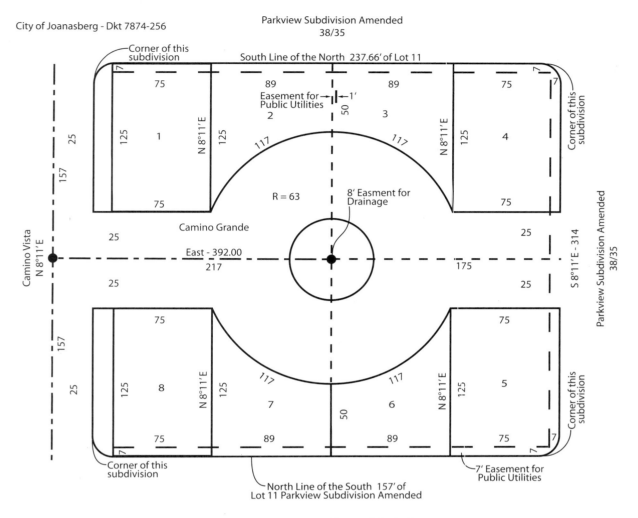

**Figure 2.7** A plat map

This type of legal description refers to the recorded map. A lot, block, and tract description might read something like this: Lot 5 of Block B of Lake Forest Estates, Tract 4312, as recorded November 18, 1955, in Book 17 of Maps, Page 211, official records of Anywhere County.

## Government Survey

By the late 19th Century, the U.S. government had established a system of land description for new territories, states and other public lands. The **government survey system**, also known as the **rectangular survey system** or **U.S. Government Section and Township Survey**, uses imaginary lines to form a grid to locate land. North-south longitude lines, called **meridians**, and east-west latitude lines called **baselines**, intersect to form a starting point from which distances are measured.

After establishing a starting point at the intersection of a chosen principal meridian and baseline, the government surveyors drew imaginary vertical lines called **range lines** every six miles east and west of the meridian to form columns called **ranges**. Each range was numbered either east or west of the principal meridian.

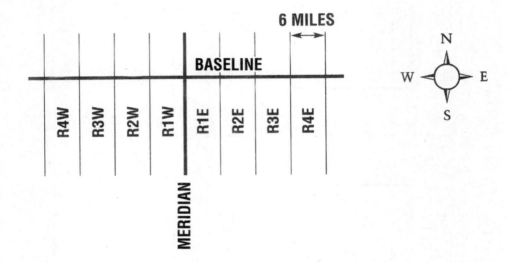

**Figure 2.8** Range Lines

For example, the first range east of the meridian was called Range 1 East (R1E), and the first range west of the meridian was called Range 1 West (R1W).

Imaginary **township lines** were drawn every six miles north and south of the baseline to form a horizontal row or **tier of townships**. Then these rows were numbered according to their distance from the baseline.

For example, the first row of townships north of the baseline was called Township 1 North (T1N) and the first row of townships south of the base-line was called Township 1 South (T1S).

Thus, a grid of squares, called **townships** appears. Each township is six miles by six miles (36 square miles). Each township is described by its location, relative to the intersection of the baseline and meridian.

For example, a township in California in the fourth tier north of the baseline and in the third range west of the meridian — with "T" for township and "R" for range — would be described as follows: T4N, R3W, San Bernardino Baseline and Meridian. The way to locate T4N, R3W is to start at the intersection of the baseline and meridian and count up — or north — four rows and then count to the left — or west — three rows.

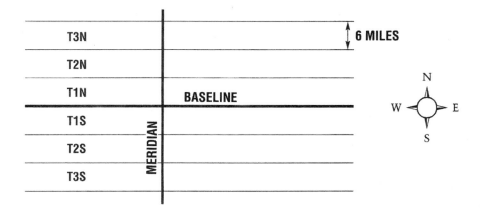

**Figure 2.9** Township Lines

Within a township, there are 36 sections — each measuring one mile by one mile. The sections are numbered, starting with section 1 in the northeast corner, and continuing in a snake-like manner to section 36 in the southeast corner. Each section is one mile by one mile and contains 640 acres.

A section may then be divided further into quarter sections containing 160 acres each, and then divided into smaller and smaller parcels. These parcels are identified by their compass direction (NE, SE, NW, and SW). Armed with this knowledge, a student may locate any size parcel, no matter how large or small, by simply dividing the section.

Using the government survey system, a particular piece of property could be described as the Northeast quarter of the Southeast quarter of section 22, Township 1 North, Range 1 East. It is normally expressed as a legal description in abbreviated form: NE $\frac{1}{4}$ of the SE $\frac{1}{4}$ of section 22, T1N, R1E. The quickest way to calculate the acreage contained within this description is to multiply the fractions by 640 acres (acres within a section). $\frac{1}{4} \times \frac{1}{4} \times 640 = 40$ acres.

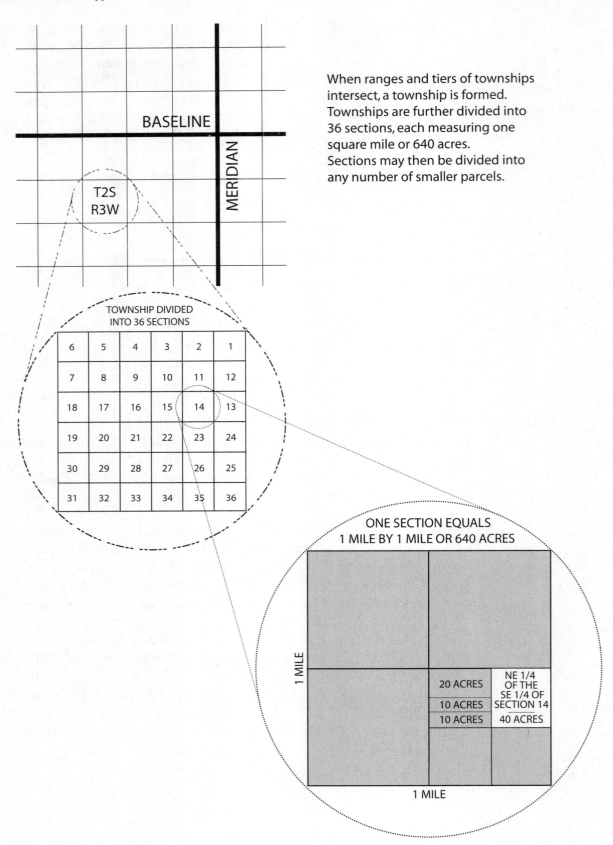

When ranges and tiers of townships intersect, a township is formed. Townships are further divided into 36 sections, each measuring one square mile or 640 acres. Sections may then be divided into any number of smaller parcels.

**Figure 2.10**  Government survey system

**Figure 2.11**  The government survey system is used for large rural tracts of land (farms).

# Metes and Bounds

A **metes-and-bounds** description of land delineates boundaries and measures distances between landmarks to identify property. Landmarks (trees, boulders, creeks, fences, etc.) are called **monuments**. This is a method of land description in which the dimensions of the property are measured by distance and direction. Land that is irregular in shape or cannot be described using either of the two other methods may have a metes-and-bounds description.

Think of measuring when you think of metes and bounds. Metes are measures of length: feet, yards, etc. and bounds are measures of boundaries, both natural and manmade: e.g., rivers and roads. Generally, you will only need to recognize this type of description when you see it. A surveyor will measure the distances and establish the legal description.

A metes-and-bounds description starts at a well-marked point of beginning (POB), and — following the boundaries of the land — measures the distances between landmarks, then returns to the beginning.

Here is a description of an uneven, hilly parcel of land with a walnut grove in Anytown:

Beginning at the intersection of the east line of Buena Creek Road and the south line of Cleveland Trail; thence east along the south line of Cleveland Trail 300 feet; thence south 657.5 feet to the center line of Buena Creek; thence northwesterly along the center line of Buena Creek to its intersection with the east line of Buena Creek Road; thence north 325 feet along the east line of Buena Creek road to the place of beginning.

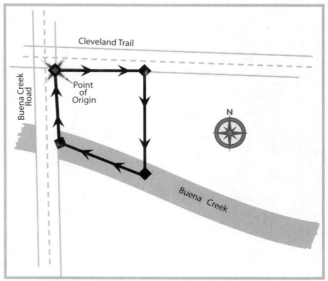

**Figure 2.12** Diagram showing metes and bounds.

Real estate appraisers are not required to be an expert in any of the three land-description methods. However, they find it helpful to be adequately informed about which method is used for the type of property they most frequently appraise.

| Methods of Land Description | |
|---|---|
| **Method** | **Typical Use** |
| Lot and Block | Urban areas, cities |
| Government Survey | Rural, undeveloped areas |
| Metes and Bounds | Irregular parcels of land |

# Summary

**Property** is an umbrella term that describes both **personal** and **real property**. Real estate appraisers are, of course, principally concerned with real property, which has a multi-faceted definition. This complex phrase includes not only the **land**, but also tenant's rights, airspace, and surface rights, among other things.

Before valuing real property, the appraiser must be able to identify correctly the land that he or she is appraising. This is done through three commonly used types of **legal descriptions**. For the residential appraiser, the **lot, block, and tract system** will be the most widely used. The **government survey system** is ideal for large tracts of rural land and the **metes-and-bounds** description works best for odd shaped lots that are difficult to identify with the other two.

# Review Exercises

## Matching Exercise

**Instructions:** Look up the meaning of the terms in the Glossary, then write the letter of the matching term on the blank line before its definition. Answers are in Appendix B.

### Terms

A. appurtenance

B. baselines

C. bundle of rights

D. emblements

E. fixture

F. government survey system

G. littoral rights

H. lot and block system

I. meridians

J. metes and bounds

K. monuments

L. plat map

M. property

N. range lines

O. ranges

P. real estate

Q. real property

R. riparian rights

S. tier of townships

T. township

U. township lines

### Definitions

1. _____ Includes the right to own, possess, use, enjoy, borrow against and dispose of real property.

2. _____ Anything that may be owned, whether real or personal.

3. _____ Personal property that has become permanently attached to the land.

4. _____ Cultivated crops for annual sale.

5. _____ Something that belongs to a particular piece of land that is used for its benefit.

6. _____ Another name for subdivision map.

7. _____Legal description that uses imaginary lines to form a grid.

8. _____Latitude lines.

9. _____Columns that are six miles wide.

10._____Imaginary horizontal lines that are six miles apart.

11._____Six mile, by six mile square composed of intersecting ranges and tiers.

12._____Legal description that uses landmarks.

13._____Synonym for landmark.

## *Multiple Choice Questions*

**Instructions:**   Circle your response and go to Appendix B to read the complete explanation for each question.

1. A property owner's bundle of rights includes all of the following **except**:
   a.  the right to enjoy the property.
   b.  the right to borrow against the property.
   c.  the right to dispose of real property.
   d.  the right to build any structure desired on the property.

2. Real property includes:
   a.  the land, anything immovable by law, the airspace, anything permanently attached to the land.
   b.  anything permanently attached to the land, anything appurtenant to the land, the land, the airspace.
   c.  anything appurtenant to the land, the land, the airspace, anything immovable by law.
   d.  anything immovable by law, anything appurtenant to the land, anything permanently attached to the land, the land.

3. Land does not include:
   a.  airspace rights.
   b.  water rights.
   c.  riparian rights.
   d.  mineral rights.

4. What is the difference between riparian and littoral rights?
   a. Littoral property owners own to the average low water mark.
   b. Littoral refers to land bordering a lake and riparian refers to land bordering a river.
   c. Riparian property owners have reasonable use of flowing water.
   d. Riparian refers to land bordering an ocean and littoral refers to land bordering a lake.

5. A tree purchased at a nursery and then planted in a backyard is not considered:
   a. real property.
   b. immovable by law.
   c. chattel.
   d. a fixture.

6. A commercial orange grove is sold one week before the harvest. What happens to the orange crop?
   a. The new owner takes possession.
   b. The previous owner retains possession.
   c. It is up to a court to decide.
   d. The new owner must split the proceeds from this crop with the seller.

7. Teresa rents a condominium to three college kids. While tenants, they install a custom sprinkler system in the lawn and garden. There is no agreement. When they move out the sprinklers are:
   a. Teresa's because of the sprinklers' method of attachment.
   b. the tenants' unless specified in writing.
   c. the tenants' because of the sprinkler's adaptation.
   d. Teresa's because of the relationship of the parties.

8. The following legal description, the SW ¼ of the S ½ of the E ½ of Section 27 in T7S, R8E, contains how many acres?
   a. 40
   b. 60
   c. 90
   d. 160

9. Which type of legal description does the following refer to:

   Starting from the south west corner of Smyth Street and Barney Avenue, traveling north 158 yards, thence north easterly for 91 yards until the great pine tree, thence directly south 167 yards to the south east corner of Smyth Street and Westin Lane, thence along the southern border of Smyth Street to the point of beginning.

   a. Lot and block

   b. Metes and bounds

   c. Rectangular survey

   d. Recorded map

10. While appraising in a metropolitan area, which type of legal description is an appraiser most likely to encounter?

    a. Government Survey System.

    b. Metes and Bounds.

    c. Rectangular Survey System.

    d. Recorded Map System.

# *Legal Considerations in Appraisal*

## Introduction

Owning real estate is considered a basic right in our culture, and each owner of real estate acquires certain rights along with property ownership. In fact, ownership of real estate is legally described in terms of these rights and not in terms of what is owned.

Historically, the question has been, "Who owns this property, and what is their interest in it?" To appraise property, the appraiser must know the ways property may be owned, what kind of ownership may be taken, how ownership is measured, how long ownership lasts, and how much is owned. This chapter answers these questions about titles and estates.

### Learning Objectives

After reading this chapter, you will be able to:

- identify freehold estate and less-than-freehold estate characteristics.

- identify different forms of ownership.

- recognize types of encumbrances.

- identify different types of deeds and describe the process of recording evidence of title or interest.

- list the necessary elements of a contract.

# Types of Estates

After identifying the property, the appraiser determines what type of ownership interest is being appraised. An **interest in property** is a legal share of ownership in property. Another term used interchangeably is "estate." An **estate** is the ownership interest or claim a person has in real property. The extent of ownership or interest in property determines the rights that go along with the property.

The rights that typically go along with property ownership are referred to as the bundle of rights. The bundle of rights includes the right to own, possess, use, enjoy, borrow against, and dispose of real property.

> For example, if Joe is leasing property from Sally, his interest in the property is described as a partial interest because he does not have all the rights that typically go along with ownership of property. In Joe's case, he has the right to use the property, but he does not have the right to sell it.

Rights affect value because they set the limits within which the property may be used, so the appraiser must know how the property is owned in order to determine its value under that type of ownership. If there are restrictions on the property use, it will not be worth as much as a property that is owned without restriction.

> In the example above, the value of Joe's interest in the property is less than it would be if he had full ownership of the property.

Ownership interests or estates are divided into two categories: freehold and less-than-freehold. A **freehold estate** is an estate of indefinite duration and can be sold or inherited. A **less-than-freehold estate** is an estate owned by a tenant who rents real property. The type of estate determines the extent of the claim. Each type of estate is described in terms of its duration and rights.

## Freehold Estates

The freehold estate is a real property estate of an owner, whose *hold* on the estate is *free* of anyone else's restrictions. Freehold estates are real property estates of ownership. They are the most complete form of ownership, and include the most rights. The two types of freehold estates are fee estates and life estates.

### Fee Simple Estates

A **fee simple estate**, sometimes known as a **fee estate** or **estate in fee,** is the most complete form of ownership. Since an owner of a fee simple estate may dispose of it in his or her lifetime or after death by will, it is also known as an **estate of inheritance** or a **perpetual estate**. This is the kind of estate that is transferred in a normal real estate transaction. If the property is transferred or sold with no conditions or limitations on its use, it is known as an estate in **fee simple absolute**.

A property owner may impose qualifications, conditions, or restrictions when transferring title to property. Property restrictions are created by deed or written agreement. If a seller imposes qualifications or conditions that the buyer must do or not do, this is known as a **fee simple qualified** or **fee simple defeasible** estate. This is a fee simple estate with conditions that control certain aspects of the owners' use of the property. If the owners violate these conditions, they will lose title to the property, based on a forfeiture clause in the granting of title.

A high-profile example of this occurred with Griffith Park in Los Angeles. Many acres were donated to the city for a park. One of the conditions in granting this land was that the city must always allow admission to the park free of charge. The city officials (several generations removed) were unaware of the condition and were planning to begin charging an admission fee. This would have been a windfall for the heirs of the Griffith family, as it would have caused the city of Los Angeles to forfeit all of that land to them. Nevertheless, fortunately for the people of Los Angeles, some city attorneys were doing their job reading the small print, and at the last minute, advised the city not to make that change.

If a condition in the granting of title were so restrictive that it limited the use of the property and caused it to be less desirable in the marketplace, such a condition would have an impact on value and would have to be taken into consideration by the appraiser.

## Life Estates

A **life estate** is one that is limited in duration to the life of its owner or the life of another designated person. Since a life estate is a type of freehold, or fee estate, the holder of a life estate has all the rights that go with fee ownership except disposing of the estate by will. Life estate holders must pay the taxes and maintain the property. They may collect all rents and keep all profits for the duration of the life estate. They may encumber the property or dispose of it in any way except by will. Any interest the life estate holders may create in the property — extending beyond the life of the person used to measure the estate — will become invalid when that designated person dies.

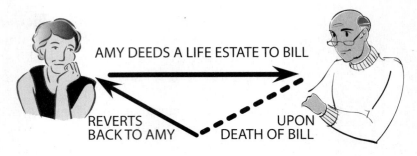

**Figure 3.1** Estate in Reversion

Life estates are normally used in certain types of situations. Consider the example of an elderly husband and wife who own their own home. They are still in good enough health to maintain themselves and the home. They know that when they die, they want their children to own the home, and they would like to help the children avoid the time and expense of probate. Therefore, they grant title of the home to the children now, and the children grant back to them a life estate. The parents are now the life tenants. They have the right to use, occupy, and control the property. They also are the designated persons, upon whose lifetimes the duration of the estate is based. When the designated persons die, the estate terminates and reverts to the grantors, the couple's children. This is referred to as an **estate in reversion**, and it is the simplest type of life estate.

Such an ownership arrangement presents an unusual appraisal problem. The estate will endure for an indefinite period of time, so the time period has to be estimated using actuarial tables, based on the age and life expectancy of the designated persons. The value of the estate then has to be estimated based on capitalization or comparison, and reconciled with its expected duration.

## Less-Than-Freehold Estates

A **lease** is a written or unwritten agreement that gives temporary rights in a real property estate to the renter or tenant. A lease creates two types of estates. The owner's fee estate becomes a **leased fee estate** when the property is leased. The tenant now owns a **less-than-freehold estate**, which is also known as a **leasehold estate**.

The owner of the leased property is called the **lessor**, and the tenant is called the **lessee**. The owner of the leasehold estate (the lessee) has exclusive possession and use of the rented property for a fixed period of time. The owner of the leased fee estate (the lessor) maintains the rights to take out a loan on the property and to sell it or give it away.

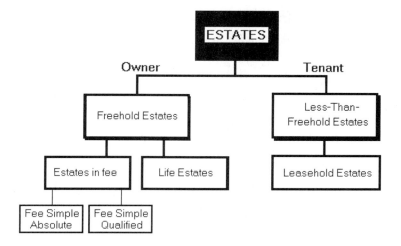

**Figure 3.2**  Types of Estates

## Types of Leaseholds

There are four types of leaseholds that are distinctive because of differences in their duration.

### Estate for Years

An **estate for years** is for a fixed term.  It does not have to be for only a year, but a definite end date is stated.  The lease of office space or a commercial center is commonly an estate for years.  An apartment lease mentions an end date; it is considered an estate for years, too.  It is not automatically renewable and does not require notice to quit at the end of the lease (must be renegotiated.)

### Estate from Period to Period

Another kind of lease or rental agreement, probably the most common for residential use, is the **estate from period to period**, also known as periodic tenancy.  This is the typical month-to-month tenancy that requires 30 days notice to quit.  It automatically renews itself unless terminated by the owner or tenant.

### Estate at Will

When there is no written agreement between the owner and tenant, the tenancy is known as an **estate at will**.  The tenancy may be ended by the unilateral decision of either party.  There is no agreed-upon termination date, however, and either party must give 30 days notice before ending the tenancy.  A property manager living on the property for free as part of the employment agreement possesses an estate at will.

### *Estate at Sufferance*

An **estate at sufferance** occurs when a tenant occupies the property without paying rent and without the permission of the owner. Typically, if this occurs, it would be after a lease had expired.

## Lease Provisions

Through a lease agreement, the owner temporarily transfers certain rights to the tenant, and the tenant compensates the owner. Methods of compensation to the owner are varied and flexible. The ideal compensation plan maximizes income to the owner, while at the same time benefiting the tenant.

A lease may be set up as a gross lease or a net lease. A **gross lease** means that the tenant pays a fixed amount of rent, and the owner pays all the expenses of ownership, such as maintenance, insurance, taxes, and assessments. This is the type of lease that is typically used with residential property. A **net lease** means that the tenant pays rent plus at least some of the ownership expenses. This type of arrangement is more common with commercial property.

Net leases vary from single-net leases, to double-net leases, to triple-net leases. A **triple-net lease,** also known as a net-net-net lease or absolute-net lease, indicates the tenant is paying rent and virtually all of the expenses. In this situation the owner does not have to put any of the rental income back into the property.

Another issue to be decided is how to determine the amount of the rent. The most basic form of payment is a flat monthly rent. However, when renting commercial property, like a strip mall, the owner wants to maximize his or her income from the property. If the tenant is doing extremely well in business, part of that success can be attributed to the location and facilities provided by the owner. In a **percentage lease,** the tenant pays a minimum monthly amount plus a percentage of the gross receipts from the business. The amount over the minimum that the tenant pays is called **overage rent.**

Another alternative is to establish a **graduated lease** that contains an **escalator clause** that allows for increases in rent based on increases in the Consumer Price Index (CPI) or some other economic indicator.

Establishing a pattern of increases like this makes sense, because the tenant can afford to pay. If the owner tries to increase the rent regardless of the well-being of the tenant, that could be the last straw and force the tenant out.

# Ownership of Real Property

All property has an owner, whether the government, a private institution, or an individual.  **Title** is the evidence that the owner of land is in lawful possession; it is the proof of ownership.  **Tenancy** refers to a mode or method of ownership or holding title to property.  Separate ownership and concurrent ownership are the two ways a person or other entity can take title to or own real estate.

## Separate Ownership

Separate property means ownership by one person or one entity, such as a city or corporation.  Property owned by one person or entity is known as sole and separate ownership or **ownership in severalty.** With separate ownership, the ownership rights are "severed" from everyone else.

**Figure 3.3**  Ownership by one entity (ABC Company) or one person.

## Concurrent Ownership

When property is owned by two or more persons or entities at the same time, it is known as **concurrent ownership**, or co-ownership. Concurrent ownership comes in several forms such as joint tenancy, tenancy in common, community property, tenancy by the entirety, and tenancy in partnership.

### Tenancy in Common

A **tenancy in common** exists when two or more persons are owners of an undivided interest in a single estate.  **Undivided interest** means that, although their ownership interests are not necessarily equal (one party may have one-half interest, one-fourth interest, etc.), they each have the right to use the whole property.  None of the owners may exclude any co-owner from the property, nor claim any portion of the property for exclusive use.

**Figure 3.4** This is an example of tenancy in common —
have equal possession.

Whenever there are co-owners and some other form of ownership is not mentioned specifically, title is assumed to be a tenancy in common.

## Joint Tenancy

When two or more parties own real property as co-owners, with the right of survivorship, it is called **joint tenancy**. The **right of survivorship** means that if one of the joint tenants dies, the surviving joint tenant automatically becomes sole owner of the property. Due to the right of survivorship, a joint tenant may not will his or her share like in a tenancy in common. The deceased's share becomes the property of the co-tenant without becoming involved in probate. In addition, the surviving joint tenant is not liable to creditors of the deceased who hold liens on the joint tenancy property.

**Figure 3.5** This is example of joint tenancy.

In order to have a joint tenancy, there are four unities that must be in existence: (1) time, (2) title, (3) interest, and (4) possession. This means all joint tenants must take title at the same time, with each tenant receiving equal interest in the property with the right of possession. If any one of the unities is missing, a tenancy in common is created.

Co-owners may sell their interest, give it away, or borrow money against it, without consent of the other joint tenants. However, all four unities must occur to have a joint tenancy, so joint tenancy is terminated when any one of the four unities ends. Joint tenancy can be terminated by sale, gift or by mutual agreement. For example, a joint tenant may sever his or her interest in the joint tenancy by selling it. The new co-owner would become a tenant in common with the remaining joint tenants. A joint tenancy is not severed if a lien is put against the interest of one of the co-owners. However, a foreclosure on the lien would sever that interest from the joint tenancy.

## Marital Property

Married people may have a special status as property owners. Forms of marital property ownership vary from state-to-state. The two most common forms are community property and tenancy by the entirety. When appraisers are determining the ownership interest, this is an issue they have to consider.

### *Community Property*

Nine states — Arizona, California, Idaho, Louisiana, Nevada, New Mexico, Texas, Washington, and Wisconsin — use the community property system to determine the interest of a husband and wife in property acquired during marriage.

In these states, there are two classifications: (1) **separate property** — property either spouse owned before marriage, and property either spouse acquires by gift or inheritance during marriage; and (2) **community property** — all other property acquired by either spouse during a valid marriage. Community property has one unity, equal interest, with each spouse owning 50%.

**Figure 3.6** Interest is equal (50/50) in community property.

Each spouse's income is also considered community property, unless it is income derived from separate property. Income derived from separate property must be kept separate, or it becomes community property. If separate income is used to purchase property, that property is also separate property.

Community property cannot be sold or encumbered by only one of the partners. Either spouse may lease community property for up to one year. Either husband or wife may sign a listing agreement to put community property "on the market," and the listing agreement would be enforceable. However, both spouses must accept and sign any contract for the transfer of community property to a new owner to transpire.

Either husband or wife may buy real or personal property without the consent of the other, and both spouses are bound by the contract made by either one. This does not apply if the new property is bought specifically as separate property, with funds from a separate property account.

## Tenancy by the Entirety

**Tenancy by the entirety** is another form of marital property ownership. It is a special joint tenancy between spouses in which each spouse has an undivided interest in the entire property and the right of survivorship. Tenancy by the entirety is used in the following states: Alaska, Arkansas, Delaware, Florida, Hawaii, Indiana, Kentucky, Maryland, Massachusetts, Michigan, Mississippi, Missouri, New Jersey, New York, North Carolina, Ohio, Oklahoma, Oregon, Pennsylvania, Tennessee, Vermont, Virginia, Wyoming, and the District of Columbia.

Like community property, property owned by spouses as tenants by the entirety cannot be sold or encumbered by only one of the partners. In fact, any document relating to property held in a tenancy by the entirety must be signed by both spouses.

## Tenancy in Partnership

A **tenancy in partnership** is a form of co-ownership that may be used by two or more persons who have formed a partnership for business purposes. The rights of each of the partners are subject to a partnership agreement and are described in that agreement. All partners have equal interest in the property and equal rights to enjoy, possess, and use the property for partnership purposes.

### Concurrent Ownership

| | Joint Tenancy | Tenancy in Common | Community Property and Tenancy by Entirety | Partnership |
|---|---|---|---|---|
| Parties | Any number | Any number | Spouses only | Any number |
| Interest | Must be equal | Equal or unequal | Must be equal | Mutual consent |
| Possession | Equal right | Equal right | Equal right | Equal right |
| Death | Survivorship | No survivorship | Varies | No survivorship |

**Figure 3.7**

# Special Ownership Forms

There are other types of ownership that blend separate and concurrent ownership.

## Undivided Interest

In an undivided interest, the land itself is not divided but the ownership is. The buyer receives an undivided interest in a parcel of land as a tenant in common with all the other owners. All owners have the nonexclusive right to the use and occupancy of the property. A recreational vehicle park with campground and other leisure-time amenities is an example.

## Common Interest Developments

A **common interest development** (CID) combines the individual ownership of private dwellings with the shared ownership of common facilities of the entire project. The common facilities can range from roads and water systems to clubhouses, swimming pools, golf courses and even stables and private airport facilities. The CID provides a system of self-governance through a community association, sometimes called a homeowners' association. The association has the authority to enforce community rules and to raise money through regular and special assessments.

Common interest developments vary in both physical design and legal form. The following CIDs are all considered subdivisions and under the control of the subdivision laws:

## Condominiums

A **condominium** consists of a separate fee interest in airspace and everything contained within (the unit), plus an undivided interest in all common or public areas of the development. All owners are allowed to use any of the facilities in the common area. Unit owners each have a deed, they each obtain separate financing, and they each pay the property taxes for their unit but have no interests in the land beneath their unit.

## Planned Developments

A **planned unit development (PUD)** is a planning and zoning term describing land not subject to conventional zoning requirements. It allows clustering of residences or other characteristics of the project that differ from normal zoning. In a planned development subdivision, the owner has title to the unit and land under it, together with membership in an association that owns common areas, which can include private roadways, water systems, septic systems, parks, open spaces, ponds and lakes, airport-landing strips, trails and ocean access. Some planned developments even share the ownership of forests and agricultural lands, which produce income for the community. Sometimes the owners of separate interests also have an undivided interest in the common area.

**Figure 3.8** A planned development allows clustering of residences or other characteristics of the project which is different from normal zoning.

## Cooperatives

A corporation formed for the purpose of owning property is known as a **stock cooperative**. Each stockholder is given the use of a living unit and any amenities and community recreational facilities, with the building being owned by the corporation.

### *Time-shares*

Ownership of a **time-share** is an interest in a building with the right to occupy limited to a specific time period. This type of ownership is popular in resorts and other desirable areas where people like to vacation once or twice a year, but do not need the right of possession the rest of the time.

**Figure 3.9** Time-shares are frequently purchased as a vacation investment because the cost of owning a good time-share is less than renting comparable hotel accommodations year after year.

# Limitations on Real Estate Ownership

An **encumbrance** is an interest in real property that is held by someone who is not the owner. Anything that burdens or affects the title or the use of the property is an encumbrance. A property is encumbered when it is burdened with legal obligations against the title. Most buyers purchase encumbered property.

# Money Encumbrances (Liens)

Encumbrances that create a legal obligation to pay are known as **liens**. A lien uses real property as security for the payment of a debt. Liens can be categorized as voluntary or involuntary, specific or general, and private or public.

A lien may be voluntary or involuntary. An owner may choose to borrow money, using the property as security for the loan, creating a voluntary lien. Typical voluntary liens include trust deeds and mortgages. On the other hand, if the owner does not pay taxes or the debt owed, a lien may be placed against his or her property without permission, creating an involuntary lien. Typical involuntary liens include mechanic's liens, judgments, tax liens, and attachments.

A lien may also be specific or general. A specific lien is one that is placed against a certain property, such as a mechanic's lien, trust deed, attachment, property tax lien, and lis pendens. A general lien affects all property of the owner such as federal or state income tax liens, or a judgment lien.

## Private Liens

Private liens are created by the property owner or another private party.

### Trust Deeds and Mortgages

The most common liens are trust deeds and mortgages. They are both instruments used in real estate financing to create private, voluntary, or specific liens against real property. They will be discussed in detail in Chapter 5.

### Mechanic's Liens

A **mechanic's lien** may be placed against a property by anyone who supplied labor, services, or materials used for improvements on real property and did not receive payment for the improvements. Therefore, a contractor, subcontractor, laborer, or any person who furnished materials such as lumber, plumbing, roofing, or services such as an architect, engineer, teamster, or equipment lessor is eligible to file a mechanic's lien. This type of lien is a private, involuntary, specific lien.

## Public Liens

The government's power to tax real property and its authority to resolve lawsuits can result in certain types of liens.

### Property Taxes and Special Assessments

If any government taxes are not paid, they become a tax lien against the property. Special assessments are levied against property owners to pay for local improvements, such as underground utilities, street repair, or water projects. Payment for the projects is secured by a special assessment that becomes a lien against real property. Property taxes and special assessments are specific liens, whereas other government taxes (e.g., income taxes) are general liens.

### Attachment Liens

An **attachment lien** or **writ of attachment** is used by the court to hold the real or personal property of a defendant as security for a possible judgment pending the outcome of a lawsuit. An attachment lien is a public, involuntary, specific lien.

A **lis pendens** (also called a pendency of action) is a recorded notice that indicates pending litigation affecting the title on a property. It clouds the title, preventing the sale or transfer of the property until the lis pendens is removed, the action dismissed, or final judgment rendered. The lis pendens is not a lien but occurs before an attachment lien and warns potential buyers.

### Judgments

A **judgment** is the final determination by the court of the rights of the parties in a lawsuit. A judgment does not automatically create a lien. A summary of the court decision, known as an abstract of judgment, must be recorded with the county recorder. When the abstract of judgment is recorded, it creates a public, involuntary, general lien on all non-exempt property owned or acquired by the judgment debtor in the county in which the abstract is filed. The court may force a sale of the property to satisfy the judgment by issuing a writ of execution. The sale is called an execution sale.

## Non-Money Encumbrances

A non-money encumbrance affects the use of property such as an easement, a building restriction, an encroachment, or a lease.

### Private

The following are non-money encumbrances that are created by the property owner or another private party.

### Deed Restrictions

A **restriction** is a limitation placed on the use of property and may be placed by a private owner, a developer, or the government. Restrictions are commonly known as covenants, conditions and restrictions or **CC&Rs**. They are usually placed on property to assure that land use is consistent and uniform within a certain area. Private restrictions are created in the deed at the time of sale or in the general plan of a subdivision by the developer. For example, a developer may use a height restriction to ensure views from each parcel in a subdivision.

A **covenant** is a promise to do or not do certain things. The penalty for a breach of a covenant is usually money damages or a court order forcing compliance with the covenant. An example of a covenant might be that the tenant agrees to make some repairs, or that a property may be used only for a specific purpose.

A **condition** is much the same as a covenant, a promise to do or not do something (usually a limitation on the use of the property), except the penalty for breaking a condition is the return of the property to the grantor. There are two types of conditions:

(1) A **condition subsequent** is a restriction placed in a deed at the time of conveyance, upon future use of the property and comes into play subsequent to the transaction. Upon breach of the condition subsequent, the grantor may take back the property. As an example, imagine that a wealthy philanthropist donates a piece of property to his or her church with the condition that no alcohol is to be sold on the property. If this condition is ever broken, the property will revert to the grantor, i.e., the philanthropist.

(2) A **condition precedent** requires that a certain event, or condition, occur before title can pass to the new owner. The condition must be taken care of preceding the transaction. An example would be a clause in a contract that requires the buyer to obtain mortgage insurance before the title transfers.

Appraisers generally do not read the CC&Rs of the subject property nor of the comparable sale properties. However, appraisers must take into account any restrictions present that make an impact on the property's value.

## Leases

Leases were discussed earlier as an instrument that creates two different estates. A lease is also a type of non-money encumbrance since it affects how the property can be used. This, in turn, can affect the value of the property.

## Easements

An **easement** is the right to enter or use someone else's land for a specified purpose. The holder of an easement can use it only for the purpose intended and may not exclude anyone else from using it. There are many ways that easements can be established and terminated, but the important thing for appraisers to determine is what impact the easement has on value.

**Page 3.10** This is an example of an easement.  Neighbors use the same pathways on private land to enter (ingress) and exit (egress).

### Easement Appurtenant

An **easement appurtenant** is an easement that is connected to a particular property and is transferred along with that property.  Each easement appurtenant involves two properties: (1) The **servient tenement** - the land one person owns that is being used by someone else.  The servient tenement is encumbered by the easement. (2) The **dominant tenement** - the other person's land receiving the benefit of the easement.  An easement appurtenant automatically goes with the sale of the dominant tenement.  The typical easement appurtenant is the right to cross over the land of the servient tenement to get to the land of the dominant tenement as with a driveway or a path to a river or lake.

**Figure 3.11** Easement Appurtenant

Appurtenant easements can also be classified as affirmative or negative.  An **affirmative easement** is one that requires the owner of the servient estate to do something to benefit the dominant estate.  An easement is called a **negative easement** if it prohibits a property owner from doing something on his or her estate because of the effect it would have on the dominant estate.

### Easement in Gross

Easements that are not appurtenant to any one parcel are known as **easements in gross**. These are typically owned by utility companies. With an easement in gross, there is only a servient tenement. Easements in gross are the most common type of easement.

### Prescriptive Easements

A **prescriptive easement** is created by using someone else's property without his or her permission. To create this type of easement, the following conditions must be met: The use must be open and notorious (meaning that the present owner can observe the other party's use of his or her land). It must be against the present owner's wishes. There has to be some reasonable right to a claim of adverse possession. Use must be continuous and uninterrupted for a time period specified by law, which will vary in different states. The person using the easement must exclude the property owner and all others from using it.

### Other Easements

Other types of easements may occur in special situations. For example, an **avigation easement** is an easement over private property near an airport that limits the height of structures and trees in order to keep the take off and landing paths of airports clear.

## *Encroachments*

Placing a permanent improvement such as a fence, wall, driveway or roof, so that it extends over the lot line into adjacent property owned by another, is known as an **encroachment**. This unauthorized intrusion on the adjoining land can limit its use and reduce it in size and value. The property owner has a certain time period (determined by local laws) in which to take legal action to have the neighbor remove the unauthorized encroachment. After that time period, the encroachment can become a permanent prescriptive easement.

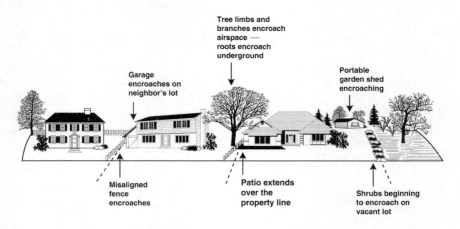

**Figure 3.12** Common Encroachments

## Public Restriction

As discussed earlier, the government power of taxation can create money encumbrances. The government's police power can create non-money encumbrances. **Police power** is the authority of the state to enact laws within constitutional limits to promote the order, safety, health, morals, and general welfare of our society. Police power does not give the state legislature authority to issue arbitrary laws that force unreasonable or unnecessary burdens on people or their property.

### *Zoning*

The regulation of structures and uses of property within selected districts is known as **zoning**. Zoning ordinances are exercises of a city's or county's police power and are upheld as long as they reasonably protect the public health, safety, and general welfare of an area.

Most cities and counties have ordinances that create land use districts or zones. Each zone has a specific set of regulations that control the use of land, lot sizes, types of structures permitted, building heights, building setbacks and density. There are zones for single-family residences, multi-family dwellings, commercial uses, industrial uses, and open space or agriculture land.

### Zoning Symbols

- A — Agricultural
- C — Commercial
- M — Manufacturing
- P — Parking lots and parks
- R — Homes, other residences
- R1 — Single-family home
- R2 — Duplex
- R3 — Multiple residential units
- R4 — Four units or higher-density dwellings

Under an area's existing zoning, there are two different types of uses allowed: (1) permitted uses and (2) conditional uses. **Permitted uses** meet the current use requirements within the district. **Conditional uses** do not meet the current use requirements but may be allowed by obtaining a special permit.

A — Agricultural

C — Commercial

M — Manufacturing

P — Parking lots and parks

R — Homes, other residences

R1 — Single-family home

**Figure 3.13** Each zone has a specific set of regulations.

R3 — Multiple residential units                 R4 — Four units or higher-density dwellings

A **conditional-use permit** or **special-use permit** allows a land use that may be incompatible with other uses existing in the zone.  The use is allowed as long as the project owner complies with the conditions specified in the permit.  If the owner does not comply with the conditions, the permit may be revoked.  A conditional-use permit runs with the land and its provisions still apply even if there is a change in ownership.  Hospitals, fire stations, or schools that are located in residential zones are examples of conditional uses.

### Zoning Changes

Changes in zoning may be initiated by a single property owner, developer, or government entity.  If a person wants to use property in a way that is currently prohibited by zoning laws, he may petition to rezone the entire area or petition for a variance for the single piece of land.

When an entire area is rezoned, commonly zoning is changed from a high-density use to a lower-density use, such as from residential to conservation.  This is called **downzoning.**  Sometimes developers ask for higher density, such as changing from low-density residential (R-1) to high-density (R-3) in order to build condominiums.

Rezoning an area can create **nonconforming uses**.  For example, if farmland is rezoned for residential use, all new structures must conform to the new zoning and be for residential use.  Existing farms are now nonconforming properties.  However, they may continue to operate because a grandfather clause allows an owner to continue to use structures that are now nonconforming within the new zoning laws.

A **variance** occurs when a city or county allows a structural design or land use that is expressly prohibited by the current zoning laws.  The city or county will typically only allow the variance under unique circumstances.  For example, if a lot's irregular shape makes it difficult to meet the standard zoning for a side-yard setback, the owner is at a disadvantage when trying to develop the property. The owner may ask the city or county for a zoning variance that allows the property to be developed closer to the property line than the zoning laws would normally allow.

### Special Types of Zoning

There are several different types of zoning, each with a specific purpose:

**Aesthetic zoning** regulates the appearance of buildings in the area. For example, aesthetic-zoning laws may require that new buildings conform to specific types of architecture.

**Historic zoning** helps protect historic buildings within a specified area referred to as a historic district. Within historic districts, cities typically provide incentives for meeting requirements that are additional to the existing zoning rules for that area.

**Cumulative zoning** allows so-called higher uses (residential) to exist in lower use zones (industrial), but not vice versa.

**Bulk zoning** controls density and prevents overcrowding. Bulk zoning regulates setbacks, building height, and percentage of open area.

**Incentive zoning** is more flexible than traditional zoning laws. It allows a developer to exceed the limitations set by a zoning law if the developer agrees to fulfill conditions specified in the law. For example, the developer may be allowed to exceed height limits by a specified amount in exchange for providing open spaces adjacent to the building.

# Transfer of Ownership

Real estate can be acquired and conveyed by will, succession, accession, occupancy, and transfer. Beginning real estate appraisers almost invariably deal with properties that are being acquired by transfer. Property is acquired by **transfer** when, by an act of the parties or of law, title is transferred from one person to another by means of a written document. The transfer may be voluntary, such as the sale of a home, or involuntary by act of law, such as a foreclosure sale. Real property may be transferred by private grant, public grant, public dedication, or operation of law (court action).

## Private Grant

When property is transferred by **private grant,** its title is transferred from one person to another and a written instrument is used. An **instrument** is a formal legal document such as a contract, deed or will. The following kinds of deeds differ primarily in the warranties given by the seller. A **warranty** is a guaranty by the seller regarding the property being transferred.

### Grant Deed

The **grant deed** is the most frequently used instrument to transfer title. The parties involved in the grant deed are the grantor and grantee. The **grantor** is the person conveying the property, and the **grantee** is the person receiving the property or to whom it is being conveyed.

A grant deed contains two implied warranties by the grantor. One is that the grantor has not already conveyed title to any other person, and the other is that the estate is free from encumbrances other than those disclosed by the grantor.

The grantor also promises to deed any rights he or she might acquire to the property after conveying it to the grantee. This is called after-acquired title, which means any benefits that come to the property after a sale must follow the sale and accrue to the new owner. For example, oil or mineral rights might revert to the property at some time in the future, after the present owner has sold the property.

### Quitclaim Deed

A **quitclaim deed** contains no warranties and transfers any interest the grantor may have at the time the deed is signed. It is often used to clear a cloud on the title (any condition that affects the clear title of real property) or any minor defect in the chain of title that needs to be removed. A quitclaim deed is frequently used to transfer interests between husband and wife or to terminate an easement. If a buyer defaults on a loan carried back by the seller, the fastest way to clear title would be for the defaulting buyer to sign a quitclaim deed to the seller.

### Other Deeds

A **gift deed** is used to make a gift of property to a grantee, usually a close friend or relative.

A **warranty deed** is a document containing express covenants of title. As title companies take over the role of insuring title to property, this type of deed is being used less frequently.

A **deed of trust** and its opposite, a **deed of reconveyance,** are primarily financing instruments and will be discussed in greater detail in Chapter 5.

## Public Grant

Real property can be transferred by **public grant**, which is the transfer of title by the government to a private individual. A **patent** is the document used by the government to transfer title to land.

## Public Dedication

When real property is intended for public use, it may be acquired as a **public dedication**. There are three means of public dedication: (1) common law dedication, (2) statutory dedication, and (3) deed.

In a common law dedication, a property owner implies through his or her conduct the intent that the public use the land. In order to be effective, the dedication must be accepted by public use or local ordinance.

A statutory dedication is a dedication by a private individual to the public. It is commonly used by developers to dedicate streets and common areas to the public.

A deed is a formal transfer by a private individual as in a gift deed where there is no consideration.

## Operation of Law

Sometimes property is transferred by the operation of law. It is usually an involuntary transfer involving foreclosure or is the result of a judgment or some other lien against the title. There are a variety of situations in which courts establish legal title regardless of the desires of the record owners.

### Foreclosure

**Foreclosure** is a public sale after default on a loan occurs and after the statutory time requirements have been met.

### Bankruptcy

**Bankruptcy** is a court proceeding to relieve a person's or company's financial insolvency. A person whose debts exceed their assets and is unable to pay current debts is financially insolvent.

## *Quiet Title Action*

**Quiet title action** is a court proceeding to clear a cloud on the title of real property.  It is frequently used to clear tax titles, titles based on adverse possession, and the seller's title under a forfeited, recorded land contract.

## *Partition Action*

**Partition action** is a court proceeding to settle a dispute between co-owners (joint tenants or tenants in common) about dividing their interests in real property.  The court can physically divide either the property or the money derived from its sale.

**Figure 3.14** Partition action is a court proceeding to settle a dispute between co-owners (joint tenants or tenants in common) about dividing their interests in real property.

## *Execution Sale*

**Execution sale** is a forced sale of property under a "writ of execution" with the proceeds used to satisfy a money judgment.  A sheriff's deed is given to a buyer when property is sold through court action in order to satisfy a judgment for money or foreclosure of a mortgage.

## *Escheat*

**Escheat** is a legal process in which property reverts to the state because the owner dies intestate, or with no will or legal heirs.  The state must wait a specified time period (five years in most states) before trying to claim the property.

### *Eminent Domain*

**Eminent domain** is the power of the government to take over private property for the public good after paying just compensation to the owner. **Condemnation** is the process by which the government acquires private property for public use, under its right of eminent domain.

The condemnation process starts with an appraisal performed on behalf of the government agency acquiring the property. The owner is contacted by the agency and notified of the impending acquisition as well as the price to be paid based on the appraisal. If the property owner feels the price to be inadequate, he or she is entitled to obtain an independent appraisal and challenge the offer in court.

States, cities, counties, improvement districts, public utilities, public education institutions, and similar public and semi-public bodies can all exercise the power of eminent domain. They almost always succeed in obtaining the private property they want for public use after paying just compensation. Examples of public uses include streets, off-street parking, railroads, irrigation, electric power facilities, sewers, public housing, libraries, parks, schools, and universities.

**Inverse condemnation** is the opposite of the eminent domain process. With inverse condemnation, a private party forces the government to pay just compensation if the property value or use has been diminished by a public entity. For example, if part of a farmer's land is condemned for freeway construction, leaving an unusable piece that is cut off from the rest of the farm, the farmer could sue for inverse condemnation since the unusable piece has been effectively taken without just compensation.

# Recording a Deed

The transfer of property is made formal when the deed is recorded. The recording process consists of copying the instrument to be recorded in the proper index, and filing it in alphabetical order, under the names of the parties. The document must be recorded by the county recorder in the county where the property is located. The purpose of recording a deed is to protect the chain of title. This is a sequential record of changes in ownership showing the connection from one owner to the next. A complete chain of title is desirable whenever property is transferred and is required by title insurance companies if they are writing a policy on a property. Deeds and other information that might influence ownership, such as liens and other encumbrances, can be recorded.

# Acknowledgement

**Acknowledgement** is a formal declaration before a notary public or certain public officials, by the grantor who signed the deed that he or she did in fact sign the document. Acknowledgement is necessary before recording any instrument or judgment affecting the title to real property. Acknowledgement acts as a safeguard against forgery and once acknowledged, a deed can be accepted as evidence in court. A deed does not have to be acknowledged to be valid, but must be acknowledged to be recorded.

# Priorities in Recording

Recording laws are meant to protect citizens against fraud and to give others notification of property ownership. Whether it is a grant deed, trust deed or some other evidence of a lien or encumbrance, the priority is determined by the date stamped in the upper right-hand corner of the document by the county recorder. To obtain priority through recording, a buyer must be a good faith purchaser and record the deed first. The first valid deed that is recorded determines the owner, unless that person had either actual or constructive notice of the rights of others prior to recording. For this reason, it is important that recording be done without delay.

There are certain instruments not affected by the priority of recording rule. Certain liens, such as tax liens, and mechanic's liens take priority even though they are recorded after a deed.

# Real Estate Contracts

A **contract** is a legally enforceable agreement made by competent parties, to perform or not perform a certain act.

## Basic Elements of Contracts

In order for a contract to be legally binding and enforceable, there are four requirements: (1) legally competent parties, (2) mutual consent between the parties, (3) sufficient consideration, and (4) lawful object.

### Legally Competent Parties

Parties entering into a contract must have legal capacity to do so. To be considered legally competent, a person must be at least 18 years of age, unless married, in the military, or declared emancipated by the court.

A minor is not capable of appointing an agent, or entering into an **agency** agreement with a broker to buy or sell. Brokers dealing with minors should proceed cautiously and should seek an attorney's advice.

When it has been determined judicially that a person is not of sound mind, the contract made by the incompetent person is terminated. If it is obvious that a person is completely without understanding there can be no contract. In the case of an incompetent, a court-appointed guardian would have legal capacity to contract.

A contract made by a person who is intoxicated or under the influence of legal or illegal drugs can be cancelled when the individual sobers up. Alternatively, the individual may choose to **ratify** (approve after the fact) the contract.

Any person may give another the authority to act on his or her behalf. The legal document that does this is called a **power of attorney**. The person holding the power of attorney is an **attorney-in-fact.** When dealing with real property, a power of attorney must be recorded to be valid, and is good for as long as the principal is competent. A power of attorney can be cancelled by the principal at any time by recording a **revocation**. A power of attorney is useful, for example, when a buyer or seller is out of town and has full trust in that agent to operate in his or her behalf.

## Mutual Consent

In a valid contract, all parties must mutually agree. **Mutual consent** (or mutual assent) is sometimes called a **"meeting of the minds."** It is an offer by one party and acceptance by the other party. Both parties must genuinely consent to the contract.

### *Offer*

An **offer** shows the contractual intent of the **offeror,** or the person making the offer, to enter into a contract. That offer must be communicated to the **offeree**, the person to whom the offer is being made, and the offer must be definite and certain in its terms.

### *Acceptance*

One party must offer and another must accept without condition. An acceptance is an unqualified agreement to the terms of an offer. The offeree must agree to every item of the offer for the acceptance to be complete. Acceptance of an offer must be communicated to the offeror, in the manner specified, before a contract becomes binding between the parties. The seller may rescind an offer prior to acceptance. Silence is not considered to be acceptance.

If the original terms change in any way in the acceptance, the offer becomes a **counteroffer**, and the first offer terminates. The person making the original offer is no longer bound by that offer, and may or may not accept the counteroffer. The counteroffer becomes a new offer, made by the original offeree.

## *Genuine Assent*

A final requirement for mutual consent is that the offer and acceptance be genuine and freely made by all parties. Genuine assent does not exist if there is fraud, misrepresentation, mistake, duress, menace, or undue influence involved in reaching an agreement.

### Fraud

An act meant to deceive in order to get someone to part with something of value is called **fraud.** An outright lie, or making a promise with no intention of carrying it out, can be fraud. Lack of disclosure — causing someone to make or accept an offer — is also fraud. For example, failure to tell a prospective buyer who makes an offer to purchase on a sunny day that the roof leaks is fraud. It can make the contract voidable.

### Innocent Misrepresentation

When the person unknowingly provides wrong information, **innocent misrepresentation** occurs. Even though no dishonesty is involved, a contract may be rescinded or revoked by the party who feels misled.

### Mistake

In contract law, **mistake** means an agreement was unclear or there was a misunderstanding in the facts. Mistake does not include ignorance, incompetence, or poor judgment.

There are times when ambiguity creates a misunderstanding, and ultimately one party chooses to void the contract. For instance, Alex and Anita were given directions to a friend's beach house, went there on their own, and fell in love with the home. They immediately made an offer, which was accepted, only to discover they had gone to the wrong house. Because they thought they were purchasing a different property than the one the seller was selling, this "mistake" is a "major misunderstanding of a material fact," and therefore would void any signed contract.

### Duress and Undue Influence

Use of force, known as **duress** or **menace**, which is the threat of violence, cannot be used to get agreement. **Undue influence** or using unfair advantage is also unacceptable.

## Consideration

Legally, all contracts require sufficient consideration or payment. Several types of consideration can be used in a contract, and they can be categorized as "valuable" or "good." **Valuable consideration** is something of value such as money, property, or personal services. A promise of future payment, forgiving a debt or obligation, or giving up an interest or right can also qualify as valuable consideration. Gifts of love and affection are called **good consideration**.

In some contracts, a promise by one party is consideration for the promise by the other party. For example, in the sale of real property, the buyer promises to pay a certain amount and the seller promises to transfer title.

## Lawful Object

Even though the parties are capable, and mutually agreeable, the object of the contract still must be lawful. A contract requiring the performance of an illegal act would not be valid, nor would one where the consideration was stolen.

The contract also must be legal in its formation and operation. For example, a note bearing an interest rate in excess of that allowed by law would be void. Contracts contrary to good morals and general public policy are also unenforceable.

# Contracts that Must be in Writing

The Statute of Frauds, a law in every state, requires that certain contracts be in writing to prevent fraud in the sale of land or an interest in land. Included in this are offers, acceptances, loan assumptions, land contracts, deeds, escrows, and options to purchase. Trust deeds, promissory notes, and leases for more than one year must also be in writing to be enforceable.

**Figure 3.15** Contracts that must be in writing.

## Parol Evidence Rule

When two parties make oral promises to each other, and then write and sign a contract promising something different, the written contract will be considered the valid one.  Parol means "oral," or by "word of mouth." The **parol evidence rule** extends this meaning to include any evidence that is not in written form.  It prohibits introducing any kind of outside evidence to vary or add to the terms of deeds, contracts or other writings once executed.  Under the parol evidence rule, when a contract is intended to be the parties' complete and final agreement, no further outside promises, oral or written, are allowed.

Occasionally, a contract is ambiguous or vague.  In such cases, the courts will allow use of prior agreements to clarify an existing disputed contract.

## Preprinted Forms

Often, the question arises as to whether or not changes can be made to a preprinted form.  If the parties involved want to make handwritten changes and initial them, those changes control the document.

Generally, when using preprinted forms:

- specific information takes precedence over general information.
- typed clauses and insertions take precedence over the preprinted material.
- handwritten clauses and insertions take precedence over the typed and preprinted material.

**Figure 3.16** Many real estate forms are now electronic
and can be downloaded.

# Describing Contracts

Contracts can be categorized in many different ways: express or implied, bilateral or unilateral, executory or executed, and void, voidable, unenforceable, or valid.

## Express or Implied

A contract is considered an **express contract** when the parties declare the terms and put their intentions in words, either oral or written. A lease or rental agreement, for example, is an express contract. The landlord agrees to allow the tenant to live in the apartment and the renter agrees to pay rent in return.

On the other hand, a contract may be an **implied contract** in which agreement is shown by act and conduct rather than words. When we go into a restaurant and order food, go to a movie or have a daily newspaper delivered, we create a contract. By showing a desire to use a service, we imply that we will pay for it.

## Bilateral or Unilateral

A **bilateral contract** is an agreement in which each person promises to perform an act in exchange for another person's promise to perform. In other words, both parties must keep their agreement for the contract to be completed. An example might be a promise from a would-be pilot to pay $2,500 for flying lessons, and a return promise from the instructor to teach him or her to fly.

A **unilateral contract** is a contract where a party promises to perform without expectation of performance by the other party. The second party is not bound to act, but if he or she does, the first party is obligated to keep the promise. An example might be a radio station offering $1,000 to the 100th caller. Some lucky person makes the call and the station pays the money. An option is another example of a unilateral contract.

## Executory or Executed

A contract may be executory or executed. In an **executory contract**, something remains to be performed by one or both parties. An escrow that is not yet closed or a contract not signed by the parties are examples of executory contracts. In an **executed contract**, all parties have performed completely. One of the meanings of execute is to sign, or complete in some way. An executed contract may be a sales agreement that has been signed by all parties.

## Void, Voidable, Unenforceable, or Valid

Contracts may be void, voidable, unenforceable, or valid.

A **void contract** is no contract at all or has no legal effect.  If one of the parties to the contract is not of sound mind or if the contract does not have a legal object, it is considered void.

A **voidable contract** is valid and enforceable on its face, but may be rejected by one or more of the parties.  For example, a contract with a minor is considered voidable by the minor.  A contract is also voidable if one party was acting under duress.

An **unenforceable contract** is valid, but for some reason cannot be proved by one or both of the parties.  For example, an oral agreement that should have been in writing because of the Statute of Frauds is unenforceable.

A **valid contract** is binding and enforceable and has all the basic elements required by law.

# Discharge of Contracts

**Discharging** a contract refers to the cancellation or termination of a contract.   Contracts are discharged by performance, release, assignment, novation, and breach.

## Performance

Commonly, the discharge of a contract occurs when the contract has been fully performed.

## Release

The person in the contract to whom an obligation is owed may release the other party from the obligation to perform the contract.  This discharges the contract.  A **mutual rescission** occurs when all parties to a contract agree to cancel the agreement.

## Assignment

An **assignment** will transfer an interest in property or a right of one party to someone else.  The **assignor** transfers his rights, remedies, benefits, and duties in the contract to the **assignee**.  In this situation, the assignor is not completely released from the obligations for the contract and remains secondarily liable.

## Novation

If the assignor wants to be released entirely from any obligation for the contract, it may be done by **novation**. That is the substitution, by agreement, of a new obligation for an existing one, with the intent to extinguish the original contract. For example, novation occurs when a buyer assumes a seller's loan, and the lender releases the seller from the loan contract by substituting the buyer's name on the loan.

## Breach

Occasionally, a breach of contract occurs. A **breach of contract** is a failure to perform part or all of the terms and conditions of a contract. A person harmed by non-performance can accept the failure to perform or has a choice of three remedies: (1) unilateral rescission, (2) lawsuit for money damages, or (3) lawsuit for specific performance.

By law, any person seeking remedy for a breach of contract must do so within the guidelines of the **statute of limitations**. This set of laws establishes the period after an incident occurs within which a lawsuit may be filed regarding the incident.

### Unilateral Rescission

**Unilateral rescission** is available to a person who enters a contract without genuine assent because of fraud, mistake, duress, menace, undue influence, or faulty consideration.

If one of the parties has been wronged by a breach of contract, that innocent party can stop performing all obligations as well, thereby unilaterally rescinding the contract. It must be done promptly, restoring to the other party everything of value received as a result of the breached contract on condition that the other party shall do the same.

### Lawsuit for Money Damages

When a party is a breach-of-contract victim, a second remedy is a **lawsuit for money damages**. If damages to an injured party are expressed in a dollar amount, the innocent party could sue for money damages, that might include, for example, the price paid by the buyer, the difference between the contract price and the value of the property, title and document expenses, consequential damages, and interest.

### Lawsuit for Specific Performance

A third remedy for breach of contract is a **lawsuit for specific performance**. This is an action in court by the injured party to force the breaching party to carry out the remainder of the contract according to the agreed-upon terms, price, and conditions. Generally, this remedy occurs when money cannot restore an injured party's position. This is often the case in real estate because of the difficulty in finding a similar property.

# Summary

Since owners of real estate acquire more than a piece of land, the appraiser must identify the type and extent of property ownership in addition to identifying the physical parcel.

A **freehold estate** is of **indefinite duration**, and can be sold or inherited. The most complete form of ownership interest is a **fee simple estate**, a type of freehold estate. A **less-than-freehold estate** is created when property is leased. There are four types of leaseholds and numerous lease provisions, all of which can have a direct bearing on a property's value.

Property ownership can be separate, concurrent, or in a special form of ownership which blends the two. In most states, married people can have a special status as property owners.

Any form of ownership can be encumbered in some way. There are private encumbrances, such as mortgages and deed restrictions, and public encumbrances like liens, assessments, and zoning, all of which affect property value to some degree.

Property ownership can be transferred by **private grant**, **public grant**, **public dedication**, or **operation of law**. When it is transferred by private grant, there are several different types of deeds that can be used. Then, the deed is recorded in order to protect the chain of title and make it clear who rightfully owns the property.

In real estate, as with any type of contract, contracts must involve **legally competent parties, mutual consent between the parties, sufficient consideration**, and **lawful object** in order to be valid. Most real estate contracts must also be in writing to be enforceable.

# Review Exercises

## *Matching Exercise*

**Instructions:** Look up the meaning of the terms in the Glossary, then write the letter of the matching term on the blank line before its definition. Answers are in Appendix B.

### Terms

A. bilateral contract

B. bundle of rights

C. Common Interest Development (CID)

D. concurrent ownership

E. condemnation

F. conditional use

G. conditions, covenants, and restrictions (CC&Rs)

H. condominium

I. contract

J. dominant tenement

K. duress

L. easement

M. easement appurtenant

N. easement in gross

O. eminent domain

P. encroachment

Q. encumbrance

R. escalator clause

S. escheat

T. estate

U. executed contract

V. executory contract

W. express contract

X. fee simple estate

Y. fraud

Z. grantee

AA. grantor

BB. implied contract

CC. joint tenancy

DD. less-than-freehold estate

EE. lien

FF. life estate

GG. mutual consent

HH. nonconforming use

II. overage rent

JJ. ownership in severalty

KK. police power

LL. planned unit development

MM. ratify

NN. right of survivorship

OO. servient tenement

PP. tenancy

QQ. tenancy in common

RR. unilateral contract

SS. unilateral rescission

TT. variance

UU. void contract

VV. voidable contract

WW. warranty

XX. zoning

## Definitions

1. _____ The ownership interest or claim a person has in real property.

2. _____ The rights that typically go along with property ownership including the rights to own, possess, use, enjoy, borrow against, and dispose of real property.

3. _____ The most complete form of ownership.

4. _____ An estate that is limited in duration to the life of its owner or the life of another designated person.

5. _____ The type of estate the renter of a leased property holds.

6. _____ The amount over the minimum rent that a tenant pays.

7. _____ A provision in a lease that provides for increases in rent based on increases in the consumer price index or some other economic indicator.

8. _____ A mode or method of ownership or holding title to property.

9. _____ Property owned by one person or entity.

10. _____ Property owned by two or more persons or entities.

11. _____ When one of the joint tenants dies, the surviving joint tenant automatically becomes sole owner of the property.

12. _____ A type of tenancy that requires unity of time, title, interest, and possession.

13. _____ A type of ownership interest that consists of a separate fee interest in airspace and everything contained within the unit, plus an undivided interest in all common or public areas of the development.

14. _____ A planning and zoning term describing land not subject to conventional zoning requirements.

15. _____ An interest in real property that is held by someone who is not the owner.

16. _____ An encumbrance that creates a legal obligation to pay, a money encumbrance.

17. _____ Limitations placed on the use of property which may be placed by a private owner, a developer, or the government.

18. _____ The right to enter or use someone else's land for a specified purpose.

19. _____ An easement that is connected to a particular property and is transferred along with that property.

20. _____ In an easement, the land one person owns that is being used by someone else.

21. _____ An easement where there is only a servient tenement.

22. _____ Placing a permanent improvement that extends over the lot line into adjacent property owned by another.

23. _____ The authority of the state to enact laws within constitutional limits to promote the order, safety, health, morals, and general welfare of our society.

24. _____ The regulation of structures and uses of property within selected districts.

25. _____ Zoning that does not meet the current requirements but may be allowed by obtaining a special permit.

26. _____ Occurs when a city or county allows a structural design or land use that is expressly prohibited by the current zoning laws.

27. _____ A guaranty by the seller regarding the property being transferred.

28. _____ The person conveying the property.

29. _____ A legal process in which property reverts to the state because the owner dies intestate, or with no will or legal heirs.

30. _____ The power of the government to take over private property for the public good after paying just compensation to the owner.

31. _____ The process by which the government acquires private property for public use.

32. _____ A legally enforceable agreement made by competent parties, to perform or not perform a certain act.

33. _____ To approve after the fact.

34. _____ An offer by one party and acceptance by the other party.

35. _____ An act meant to deceive in order to get someone to part with something of value.

36. _____ Use of force to obtain agreement to a contract.

37. _____ A contract in which agreement is shown by act and conduct rather than words.

38. _____ A contract where a party promises to perform without expectation of performance by the other party.

39. _____ A contract where all parties have completely performed their part of the agreement.

40. _____ A contract that is valid and enforceable on its face, but may be rejected by one or more of the parties.

## *Multiple Choice Questions*

**Instructions:**   Circle your response and go to Appendix B to read the complete explanation for each question.

1. An owner who can dispose of his estate by will owns which type of estate?
    a.  Perpetual estate
    b.  Reversion estate
    c.  Life estate
    d.  Intestate estate

2. If an owner violates any condition on a fee simple qualified estate:
    a.  the owner will be arrested.
    b.  the owner will be fined.
    c.  the owner will lose title.
    d.  nothing will happen.

3. Lowell deeds his property to his first wife, Verna, with the condition that after his second wife, Elizabeth, dies, the property title will pass to his daughter, Laura.  What type of estate does Verna possess?
    a.  Fee simple qualified
    b.  Life estate
    c.  Less-than-freehold estate
    d.  Estate at will

4. Which type of estate does a tenant possess?
    a.  Freehold
    b.  Fee simple
    c.  Less-than-freehold
    d.  Life

5. Who has exclusive possession and use of the rented property?
    a.  Lessor
    b.  Lessee
    c.  Leasehold
    d.  Leased Fee

6. A property manager lives on the property free of charge. Which type of leasehold is this?

    a. Estate for years

    b. Estate at sufferance

    c. Estate from period to period

    d. Estate at will

7. A retail tenant has to pay rent plus all property expenses, such as maintenance, insurance, and property taxes. Which type of lease does he have?

    a. Triple net

    b. Absolute net

    c. Net-net-net

    d. Any of the above

8. Kim rents a small retail space for $900 per month plus 8% of any profits over $2,500. Kim made $3,217 dollars this month. What was her rent?

    a. $  957.36

    b. $1,157.44

    c. $1,100.00

    d. $  971.46

9. Which type of concurrent ownership includes the right of one tenant to will his interest?

    a. Ownership in severalty

    b. Joint tenancy

    c. Tenancy in common

    d. Common interest developments

10. Bill, Bob, and Beau take joint tenancy of a vacation house. Bill sells his share to Blake after 3 years. Which of the following is true?

    a. Bill, Bob, and Blake are joint tenants.

    b. Bob, Beau, and Blake are joint tenants.

    c. Bob and Beau are joint tenants with Blake as a tenant in common.

    d. Bob, Beau, and Blake are tenants in common.

11. Janice owned a flower store for four years before she married Ron.  After she married, she purchased another store with proceeds from her original store.  The flower stores:

    a.  are both considered separate property.

    b.  are both considered community property.

    c.  The original flower store is separate property, and the new one is community property.

    d.  The original flower store is community property, and the new one is separate property.

12. When Frank purchased real estate, he received an undivided interest in a parcel of land as a tenant in common with all the other owners.  He and the other owners have the nonexclusive right to the use and occupancy of the property.  What type of ownership is this?

    a.  Common interest development

    b.  Condominium

    c.  Undivided interest

    d.  Tenancy in common

13. An interest in real property that is held by someone who is **not** the owner is known as an:

    a.  encumbrance.

    b.  encroachment.

    c.  escheat.

    d.  estate at sufferance.

14. A mortgage is an example of a(n):

    a.  encumbrance.

    b.  specific lien.

    c.  voluntary lien.

    d.  All of the above

15. An easement, a building restriction, an encroachment, and a lease are all examples of:

    a.  money encumbrance.

    b.  non-money encumbrance.

    c.  lis pendens.

    d.  mechanic's lien.

16. CC&Rs is an acronym for:
    a. considerations, conditions, and restrictions.
    b. covenants, conditions, and reconveyances.
    c. covenants, considerations, and reconveyances.
    d. covenants, conditions, and restrictions.

17. Eva deeds her house to Melissa with the condition that title will **not** pass to Melissa until she is legally married. This is an example of a:
    a. covenant.
    b. condition subsequent.
    c. condition precedent.
    d. restriction.

18. Because of how the street access is set up, Charlie's driveway must cross over Leigh's property. Which of the following describes this scenario?
    a. Leigh has a negative appurtenant.
    b. Charlie is the dominant tenement.
    c. Leigh is the dominant tenement.
    d. Charlie is the servient tenement.

19. A cable company has an easement permitting them to install wiring for digital cable and broadband internet services. What kind of easement is this?
    a. A negative easement
    b. An easement in gross
    c. A prescriptive easement
    d. An avigation easement

20. The authority of the state to enact laws within constitutional limits to promote the order, safety, health, morals, and general welfare of our society is called:
    a. novation.
    b. police power.
    c. eminent domain.
    d. lawful object.

21. Brandi has a convenience store in a district that was rezoned residential. If she cannot get a special use permit, she has a:
    a. non-conforming use.
    b. variance.
    c. conditional use.
    d. encumbrance.

22. If a city requires that all the buildings in its downtown retail district be a Spanish-style stucco that is uniform in color, this would be an example of:
    a. incentive zoning.
    b. aesthetic zoning.
    c. visual zoning.
    d. reverse condemnation.

23. Which type of deed has no warranty whatsoever?
    a. Quitclaim deed
    b. Warranty deed
    c. Grant deed
    d. Deed of reconveyance

24. Which of the following is the act of taking private property for public use?
    a. Police power
    b. Eminent domain
    c. Escheat
    d. Condemnation

25. Which of the following is **not** a basic element of any contract?
    a. Legally competent parties
    b. Mutual consent between the parties
    c. Statute of limitations
    d. Sufficient consideration

26. Generally, the phrase "legally competent" excludes which of the following?
    a. Minors
    b. Individuals not of sound mind
    c. Intoxicated individuals
    d. All of the above

27. Meagan gives Adrianna the authority to act on her behalf.  Adriana is the:
    a. power of attorney.
    b. attorney-in-fact.
    c. principal.
    d. incumbent.

28. If one party unknowingly provides wrong information when entering into a contract, he or she has committed:
    a. fraud.
    b. innocent misrepresentation.
    c. mistake.
    d. duress.

29. What occurs when all parties to a contract agree to cancel the agreement?
    a. Unilateral rescission
    b. Breach
    c. Specific performance
    d. Mutual rescission

30. When using a pre-printed form for a contract, which of the following is **not** generally true?
    a. Specific information takes precedence over general information.
    b. Typed clauses and insertions take precedence over the pre-printed material
    c. Handwritten clauses and insertions take precedence over the typed and pre-printed material
    d. Pre-printed material takes precedence over handwritten and typed insertions.

# *Value and Economic Principles*

## Introduction

What is value? Most people have a general understanding of value and could explain it adequately, but the idea of value is a multifaceted and vague concept.

Four elements combine to create value, but many other dynamics influence value on a local, regional, and national level. There are also different types of value, which each have their own particular meaning and particular context. Being familiar with these factors and different types of value, as well as when a certain type is appropriate for an assignment, is a major responsibility of an appraiser.

Value and economic principles are interrelated. In order to perform the function of estimating value accurately, the appraiser also needs to have an understanding of the basic foundational economic principles applicable in the valuation of real estate.

### Learning Objectives

After reading this chapter you will be able to:

- describe the four elements that create value.

- identify the factors that influence value.

- summarize the different types of value.

- discuss the principles of valuation.

# What is Value?

The concept of value affects all areas of the real estate industry. Property value considerations are at the core of real estate activity and are of critical importance. A synonym of "value" is the word "worth." When appraisers indicate the value of property, they are usually indicating an estimate of its monetary worth. **Value** has been defined as the monetary worth of a property, good, or service to buyers and sellers at a given time. Similarly, USPAP defines value as the monetary relationship between properties and those who buy, sell, or use those properties. It is important to note that people create value. Value is not built into an item. An item is valuable because people perceive it has worth.

Though the term value is often used imprecisely in everyday conversation, it has a very specific meaning in appraisal. Appraisers estimate the value of a property. More precisely, the majority of appraisal assignments entail estimating the "market value" of a property. The "price" of buying a property or the "cost" of building a property is often considered an indicator of value. However, there can be large differences between the price, the cost, and the market value of a property. Be careful not to confuse value with the related concepts of price and cost.

## Price

**Price** is the amount a particular purchaser agrees to pay and a particular seller agrees to accept under the circumstances surrounding their transaction. The Uniform Standards of Professional Appraisal Practice (USPAP) define "price" as "the amount asked, offered, or paid for a property." USPAP goes on to say, "Once stated, price is a fact..." It also says, "...price may or may not have any relation to the value that might be ascribed to that property by others."

**Figure 4.1** Price may not have any relation to the property value.

When thinking of the concept of price, realize it applies to "exchange." In other words, a seller is willing to exchange his property for money (or its equivalent). On the other hand, the buyer is willing to exchange his money (or its equivalent) for property.

## Cost

Cost is a third related concept. As used by appraisers, cost applies to production. **Cost** is the total dollar expenditure to develop an improvement and applies to either reproduction of an identical improvement or replacement with a functional equivalent. In other words, cost is the amount of money it takes to build a structure.

**Figure 4.2** Cost is the amount of money to build a structure.

**Value** — The worth of a property, good, or service to buyers and sellers at a given time.

**Price** — The amount asked, offered, or paid for a property.

**Cost** — The amount of money it takes to build a structure.

# Four Elements That Create Value

For real property to have value, four elements of value must be present: (1) the property must be in demand, (2) it must have usefulness or utility, (3) there must be a degree of scarcity, and (4) it must be possible to transfer it legally in title or use.

## Demand

**Demand** is desire or ability to purchase a commodity. For real property to have value, it must be in demand. People have to want to own or use the property for some reason.

**Figure 4.3** People have to want to own or use property to create a demand.

However, wanting a property is not enough by itself. The market participants must have purchasing power. This creates what is known as **effective demand**, which is desire coupled with the ability to satisfy the desire. Desire that is not backed by purchasing power creates a demand that is impotent and makes no impact in the financial marketplace.

## Utility

**Utility** is the ability or power of an item to perform a service or meet a need. For real property to have value, it must have a distinct usefulness — there has to be a distinct utility for the land to contribute to value. The utility of property can be affected by many factors including the location of the property, the physical attributes of the property, and government regulations such as zoning and environmental restrictions. These are only a few of the factors that can affect the utility or usefulness of a property.

**Figure 4.4** Property needs to perform a service to create value.

Added amenities may increase the utility or desirability of a property, so they often result in a higher value. The amenities may be off-site improvements that impact the value of the subject property, such as schools, parks, pools, lakes, theaters, stores, transportation facilities, or amusement parks. Alternatively, the amenities may be within the subject's property lines such as a swimming pool, a view, or a covered patio.

## Scarcity

The term **scarcity** refers not just to a shortage of an item, but a shortage of an item relative to the demand for that item. Some items fill significant needs — air for instance. It is so essential that life could not survive without it, so there is definitely a huge demand for air! Air, however, does not have value measurable in terms of money because it is so overwhelmingly abundant. In order to have monetary value, an item has to be scarce.

Land itself is finite in supply — there is only a certain amount. However, although the supply of land does not change, the supply of a particular type of property changes as buildings are constructed or destroyed. In the realm of real estate, there must be a relative scarcity of property for its value to increase. As an example, a house in the desert is relatively inexpensive. This is partly because desert land is not scarce. There are many thousands of similar acres available, all in the same area. In comparison, coastal land is much scarcer and, consequently, a house built on that land is more valuable. When scarcity combines with the other three elements (demand, utility, and transferability), value is enhanced immensely.

## Transferability

**Transferability** refers to the ability to transfer ownership of an item from one person, or entity, to another. This includes both possession and control. Certain items have utility, are scarce, and there is demand, however there is no way to effectively transfer ownership. A stolen car, for example, has definite utility. The car may even be scarce, and there may be plenty of demand for it, however, the problem is transferability. There is no legal way to transfer ownership of the car, so its value is negatively affected.

It is important to note that, in real estate, transferability does not have anything to do with physical mobility. Instead, transferability refers to the rights associated with ownership. The use or ownership of land must have the capability to be legally transferred. For example, a property that does not have a marketable title cannot be transferred, which dramatically affects its value.

**MNEMONIC — "DUST"**

- Demand
- Utility
- Scarcity
- Transferability

# Factors Impacting Value

In addition to the four elements that create value, there are other factors that impact value, both positively and negatively. These factors are classified according to their source — physical and environmental, economic, governmental, and social. However, there are hundreds of possible influences on real estate value, and they do not always fit neatly within one particular category. Following is a partial list of factors that influence value. You will be able to add to this list as you gain experience and discover local factors that influence real estate value in your area.

# Physical Characteristics and Environmental Forces

Many physical characteristics of land and property have a definite influence on value. Physical characteristics and environmental forces include the property's location, the surrounding climate, its topography and soil composition, the size and shape of the property, and the ease of navigation. These physical characteristics or environmental forces can exert major effects on values. Some of the physical characteristics can be changed, some can be worked around, and others are unchangeable. The expense of alteration must always be taken into consideration.

## Location

People who sell real estate say there are three factors to consider: "location, location, and location." Unlike other types of assets, land cannot be moved, so its location has an impact on its value. In fact, location may be the most important factor influencing value, particularly because it has such an effect on the usefulness of the property. For example, commercial properties that are located on a corner lot benefit from more exposure, while the value of residential corner lots may be negatively affected due to the lack of privacy.

As was discussed earlier, certain locations are scarcer and may be more valuable. For example, a house located right by the beach will be worth more than that same house would be if it were located in the desert.

**Figure 4.5** A house located near the ocean will be worth more
than the same house placed in the desert.

In addition, width of streets, traffic congestion, and condition of pavement affect the value of properties fronting on those streets. The term **front foot** defines the width of a property along a street or other boundary, and is most widely used as a measurement for properties located on beaches and lakeshores.

Another locational attribute that may affect a property is its exposure. The south and west sides of business streets are usually preferred by shopkeepers because customers will seek the shady side of the street, and window displays will not be damaged by the sun. The north and east sides are less desirable. Even if the lot is in a good location, a building's **orientation** on the lot in relation to exposure to the sun, prevailing wind, traffic, and accessibility from the street can dramatically affect value as well.

**Figure 4.6** Location of property to streets as well as sun exposure is important.

## Climate

Climate is a fairly obvious factor and plays an enormous role in the overall value of a property. Climatic conditions including snowfall, rainfall, humidity, temperature, topography, soil conditions, and prevailing winds are items of consideration that can promote, or hinder areas.

Anyone who has lived in harsh and frigid climates has noticed there are certain benefits to a more temperate climate. In fact, in the most extreme climates, population is generally sparse. Demand is much greater in areas with better climates. These conditions spell out benefits, and these benefits are measurable in the marketplace.

**Figure 4.7** Property in temperate climate generally has more value than property in harsh temperatures.

Climate must also be matched to the intended use of the property. If land is to be used as a ski resort, temperature and precipitation must be ideal to maximize the number of days there will be snow. Then, the value of such a property will also be impacted by other factors, such as accessibility and topography.

## Topography and Soil

Topography affects both the desirability of the land and its development. The nature and desirability of areas around the country are impacted by features such as rivers, lakes, streams, oceans, mountains, valleys, forests, meadows, prairies, and deserts. In developing a property, construction costs will be affected by the terrain and soil conditions. Limited irregularity in the contour is best for residential property. In many areas, all of the land is flat. Other areas are mountainous, hilly, or somewhere in between.

The characteristics of the soil at a given site can also have a direct impact on value, depending on the intended use of the land. Unproductive soil will have a negative impact on the value of farmland, but the same characteristic will have no impact on industrial land.

Land is not completely usable if it does not have full drainage capacity. Whether intended for residential, industrial, or commercial use, it is essential that there is no standing water on the land. If the appraiser inspects a property and no standing water is present on the land, he or she could detect evidence of a drainage problem by looking for water lines on any structures on the land. Correcting the problem can be expensive, and an appraiser would have to consult with the appropriate experts to determine the cost to cure such a problem.

**Figure 4.8** Land is not completely usable if there is a drainage problem.

On the other hand, land without access to water is probably not worth much in any marketplace. Water sustains life. Humans need it to inhabit land. Animals must have it to survive. Crops cannot be grown without water. Industrial and manufacturing processes cannot take place without the use of water.

Terrain and soil can limit an appraiser during the appraisal process. When appraising a single-family residence, the appraiser may find that the subject property is situated on approximately an acre of land, 100% useable. While the appraiser is searching for comparable sales on approximately the same size lot, he or she visits one of the comparable sales, and discovers that the lot is indeed approximately an acre, but only about 30% of it is usable. The remaining 70% is rocky slope. These two parcels are not comparable; and if used, would require a significant adjustment.

## Size and Shape

The size of the land must be accepted as is, unless an adjacent parcel could be acquired. The use of a property may be determined by the width and depth of the land. Some parcels of land are simply too small to be put to the desired use and must be put to a lesser use, generating a lesser value. If adjacent parcels can be obtained, the process of **assemblage** may occur. By putting several smaller, less valuable parcels together under one ownership interest the value of the combined parcels may increase.

The shape of the parcel also has significant influence on its usefulness, and therefore its value. Irregular-shaped lots are more difficult and expensive to develop. An acre of land that is 10 feet wide running parallel to a highway is certainly less valuable than another acre that is square in shape, and suitable for the construction of a single-family residence.

**Figure. 4.9** A lot's size determines the value of the property. Parcels by transportation systems also affect the value of the property.

## Transportation

Environmental forces can be man-made. The availability and ease of transportation is an important factor that affects real estate value. It is typically classified as an environmental force, but it is a good example of a factor that interweaves all four categories: physical, economic, social, and governmental.

Airports, freeways, railroads, and waterways used for navigation all have influences over surrounding areas and as such affect values. Similarly, if a parcel is conveniently accessible by road, it generally will have greater value than if it is in a remote location accessible only by a dirt road. The impact that accessibility has on the property value will depend on the property's intended use.

# Economic Influences

Real estate values, price levels, and sales activity are directly influenced by the economic activity and economic well-being of both the country as a whole and the local real estate market. Some economic forces that influence value are the availability of money and credit, interest rates, industrial and commercial trends, employment trends, wage levels, price levels, regional and community economic base, new development, and rental and price patterns. Appraisers should be aware of the economic forces influencing value.

## Availability of Financing

The kind of financing available impacts property values. If there is a full array of financing for the properties in the area, this gives the buyers purchasing power. If financing is restricted for some reason, it is more difficult for buyers to purchase the property.

Remember that purchasing power is one of the elements essential to actual demand. Without the ability to purchase, houses do not get sold. Very few buyers purchase with all cash. Financing is extremely important in supporting the value of real property.

### *Interest Rate*

Related to financing is the prevailing interest rate. If a loan program is available, but the interest rate is prohibitive, the effect is the same as if financing was not obtainable. The interest rate determines the quality of the financing and the purchasing power of the buyers in the marketplace.

Interest rates, of course, are largely a function of government policy, inflation rate, and supply of funds in relation to demand. Local factors such as risk, however, can affect local interest rates. If an area were viewed by the lender to present a higher risk factor due to social or economic characteristics, interest rates could increase.

# Inflation

Inflation in the economy or just in the regional or local real estate market can cause an apparent increase in value. **Unearned increment** is the term used in real estate appraisal to indicate an increase in value that was not the result of anything the owner did. Both inflation and appreciation would be categorized this way, and it can be difficult to distinguish between the two.

# Employment and Wage Levels

Sources of employment are an obvious, but important, factor affecting the economic health of an area. Jobs may be offered from private enterprise, government sources, or military installations. The availability of good, high-paying jobs in an area can have a positive effect on the property values in the area. Wage levels provided by the employment in the area should be sufficient to support a family and buy a house.

Another important factor to keep in mind is whether employment in the area is dependant upon a single industry or even a single company. If this is the case, the risk of eventual economic obsolescence is higher than if the majority of employment were spread over several industries.

# Business Climate

The presence of shopping areas, offices and medical suites as well as financial, wholesale, industrial, and other consumer-friendly businesses is important to establishing value.

The presence of a college or university can have a significant impact in a local community. A major state university could have 25,000 students. The number of employees to operate such a university also will be in the thousands, creating further impact. The area surrounding the college will contain many quality rental units in constant demand, and numerous successful businesses providing a variety of needed products and services. The economic influence in the local area is significant, and will be reflected in the data from the local marketplace.

Most major urban centers have blighted area or areas. These are generally a section of the inner city, where the majority of buildings are run down. Occurrences of this depress property values in the blighted areas as well as properties on the outskirts. It creates a cycle where the decrepit atmosphere repels business and industry; in turn, the lack of this incoming business and industry further hastens the decline of the area. Only a large-scale revitalization of the areas can reverse the process.

## Natural Resources

Natural resources in the area can make an impact on value. Although this is a physical characteristic, natural resources typically have an economic impact. They can make all the difference in the economic viability of an area. In fact, they can be the primary source of wealth for the area, with industry and employment centering on them. Natural resources that attract dominant industries will be readily apparent to the appraiser.

**Figure 4.10**  Natural resources that attract dominant industries
are apparent to the appraiser.

# Political or Government Regulations

Governmental, political, and legal activity significantly affects the value of real estate. On the national level, some political forces that can affect value are tax policy, government loan-guarantee programs, and environmental regulations. At the state and local level, zoning and health regulations, building codes, health codes, rent controls, redevelopment districts, first-time homebuyer assistance programs, and public services such as police and fire protection are among the things significantly impacting real estate values. Appraisers must take special care to identify, examine, and analyze the potential influences govern-mental activity has on property values.

## Taxes

Federal, state, and local taxes can impact real estate values. High income taxes result in less money available for real estate purchases. Capital gains taxes and allowable depreciation schedules particularly impact real estate investors. If city taxes and other local fees are prohibitively high, developers and businesses may go elsewhere. Other cities, where fees are not as high, may offer a greater opportunity for development and profit.

## Federal Financing

FHA and VA loans are federal programs permitting a very low down payment or no down payment. This facilitates purchasing power and increases the number of potential buyers for housing. This makes home ownership a more attainable goal for more buyers. When these programs are not available in an area, conventional financing is the alternative. Since conventional financing requires a much higher down payment, this would eliminate some otherwise qualified buyers from the marketplace and decrease the effective demand.

## Environmental Restrictions

Much attention is given to protecting the environment today. Government organizations like the Environmental Protection Agency (EPA) as well as private groups like the Sierra Club and Greenpeace have combined to create a strong voice of concern about the environment.

In many regions of the country, habitats are protected for endangered species, restricting the development of lands for commercial purposes. Other protective decrees prevent all development of land. In areas where a housing shortage exists, environmental restrictions further limit supply. This condition raises the values of existing housing and makes the building of new housing even more expensive, if permitted at all. Whether one agrees or disagrees with each environmental decision on a case-by-case basis, this still has an economic effect on a given area.

## Building Restrictions and Zoning

The Planning Commission and the City Council can slow growth and determine the direction of growth by imposing certain zoning regulations. By consulting the **master plan** of any city or county, zoning and zoning changes for all parcels can be observed, and growth patterns and trends can be determined. Building restrictions and zoning ordinances also affect utility, which is the ability to use the property for the purpose intended.

**Building codes** pertain to the structures that will be placed on land; their main purpose is to provide minimum standards to protect the environment, the lives of occupants, and the general public. The local building code will deal with the issues of fire safety, building materials, heating, plumbing, gas and electrical systems, and energy efficiency. Building codes should be effective in promoting the public welfare in the ways intended. This enhances the desirability of the community by providing buildings that are safe and compatible with environmental needs. This, in turn, enhances value of individual properties and the community in general. However, a building department that is unreasonable can be a detriment to the normal growth and development of a community.

A city or county government may impose a moratorium on development, water accessibility, utilities, or anything deemed necessary at a given time. The purpose of a moratorium is to place a temporary restriction on development in a particular area. This is done by not allowing certain utilities to be installed, not allowing new water hookups, or not issuing building permits. Without the necessary element, development cannot occur in that area. Growth is stopped temporarily, and if demand for housing continues in the area, the value of the limited supply will increase.

## Public Services

Public services like police and fire protection, schools, hospitals, and city parks, pools and other recreational facilities can add appeal and value to a community. To most families, quality schools are probably the most important government-provided service, and families may go to great lengths to live in a specific school district.

**Figure 4.11** Quality schools are important to many families and this public service increases property value.

## Social Ideals and Standards

In each local real estate market, the number of people and their characteristics, lifestyles, standards, and preferences will influence the real estate values in that market.

## Population Trends

Birthrates, mortality rates, and migration to and from an area are all social influences on value. When there is an increase in the population in an area, there is a corresponding increase in the needs of that population. It naturally follows that the more people there are in an area, the more need for housing. The balance of supply and demand has a great impact on value.

**Figure 4.12** Population trends affect the balance of supply and demand.

This information can be determined for any given time frame: past, present and future. Present time frame will be most useful for knowing present value, but future trends are important to understand as well.

## Family Characteristics

Over the last several decades, changes in marriage rates, divorce rates, typical family size, and average household age have all impacted the demand for real estate of different types. Not only does family size have an impact on the necessary house size, what is important to the people who comprise a particular marketplace can have an effect on property values. Young and growing families may seek good schools, where older couples whose children have grown-up and moved out may seek smaller homes that are easy to maintain.

## Other Social Factors

Other societal changes can also impact real estate values. For example, as technology has become more advanced, more people have started working from home, so space and appropriate wiring for home office needs have become important. Other people have created media rooms where they can enjoy all the entertainment that technology offers.

**Figure 4.13**  Many people work at home and need a home office.

Tastes change dramatically over time as well.  Avocado green appliances and acoustic ceilings are out, stainless steel and crown molding are in.  These trends are constantly changing, and a "dated" look will affect a home's value.

A **stigma** is a lingering effect in the minds of people regarding the desirability or usefulness of a property.  The property is regarded as tainted in some way; and if the property is regarded as tainted in a given marketplace, it is tainted in that marketplace.  A home where a notorious murder occurred most likely will carry a stigma with it, at least for a generation and possibly longer, depending on the population turnover in that neighborhood.

# Types of Value

In a dictionary, you can find numerous definitions of value that each have to do with a specific context.  In real estate appraisal, value is the monetary worth of a property in a given marketplace at a given time.  It is not what an owner would like to think he or she can obtain.  It is what owners actually can obtain based on objectively reading the marketplace.

Appraisers will encounter several types of value and it is important to understand that different definitions of value produce different estimates of value.

## Market Value or Value in Exchange

The overwhelming majority of appraisals performed are concerned with estimating the market value of a property.  The concept of market value is extremely important in appraising real property.  Loans are granted and capital is invested based on a professional opinion of market value.  Real estate taxes, litigation, and legislation also reflect a concern for market value.

Both the Federal National Mortgage Association (Fannie Mae) and the Federal Home Loan Mortgage Corporation (Freddie Mac) use the following definition of **market value**:

> The most probable price which a property should bring in a competitive and open market under all conditions requisite to a fair sale, the buyer and seller, each acting prudently, knowledgeably and assuming the price is not affected by undue stimulus.

Implicit in this definition are the consummation of a sale as of a specified date and the passing of title from seller to buyer under conditions whereby:

(1) buyer and seller are typically motivated.

(2) both parties are well informed or well advised, each acting in what he considers his own best interest.

(3) a reasonable time is allowed for exposure in the open market.

(4) payment is made in terms of cash in U.S. dollars or in terms of comparable financial arrangements.

(5) the price represents the normal consideration for the property sold unaffected by special or creative financing or sales concessions granted by anyone associated with the sale.

The Uniform Standards of Professional Appraisal Practice (USPAP) defines market value as:

> ...a type of value, stated as an opinion, that presumes the transfer of property (i.e. a right of ownership or a bundle of such rights), as of a certain date, under specific conditions set forth in the definition of the term identified by the appraiser as applicable in an appraisal.

USPAP goes on further to say:

> "Appraisers are cautioned to identify the exact definition of market value, and its authority, applicable in each appraisal completed for the purpose of market value."

The definition of market value being used in an appraisal assignment must be clearly understood and communicated. Recognize that definitions of market value may vary slightly from jurisdiction to jurisdiction, as well as from client to client.

Understanding market value eliminates the consideration of any comparable sales in an appraisal that do not meet these qualifications. A foreclosure sale, for example, would mean the seller is under duress and does not have the luxury of a reasonable time for exposure in the marketplace. Such a sale would not be an arm's-length transaction and would not meet the definition of market value. An **arm's-length transaction** refers to a transaction where all parties involved are knowledgeable, acting in their own self-interest and are under no undue influence or pressure from other parties.

## Investment Value

**Investment value** is the value of a particular property to a particular investor. This value may be different from market value, reflecting the investor's unique needs and intended use of the property.

> For example, Bill is an investor who has purchased three of the four storefronts in a strip mall. He leases the storefronts to tenants, and he has determined that it would be more beneficial to own four contiguous storefronts than three out of the four would, so he wants to acquire the fourth property. If an individual buyer wanted to purchase the fourth storefront, that buyer would probably not be willing to pay as much for it as Bill would. The property would not be as valuable to someone who did not own the adjacent properties. This example illustrates that investment value is specific to a particular investor and that investment value can be higher than market value.

## Use Value

In some instances, the realities of the marketplace require other kinds of value. Use value (or value in use) is one of these. **Use value** is the value a property has under a given use.

> For example, vacant farmland is often suitable for development into commercial uses. Sometimes, owners and other interested parties want to know the worth of that property as both farmland and as if developed into another use. Though this property may be significantly more valuable if developed commercially, it still has value as farmland.

## Assessed Value

**Assessed value** is the value of a property as it appears in the tax assessor's office. A percentage is applied to this value to determine the amount of property tax the owner will pay. Different jurisdictions have different methods and formulas for determining assessed value. These are guided by law. Some jurisdictions apply mass appraisal formulas to numerous properties. In other areas, the purchase price of the property at the time of acquisition determines assessed value.

From time to time, assessed value will be adjusted. This is also dictated by law and policy within the local jurisdiction. In most areas, assessed value has no relationship to market value, which fluctuates freely with the market. Assessed value will be determined as of a particular time, and probably will adjust more slowly. Only appraisers employed by the tax assessor's office will work to determine assessed value.

## Replacement Value

Also called insured value, **replacement value** is of importance to insurance companies and property owners alike. If improvements have been lost to fire, flood, wind or other natural disasters, the amount of money required to replace them needs to be determined. Finding this value requires expert knowledge of the cost approach to appraising, and the appraiser should be familiar with all methods of estimating building costs and pricing building components.

**Figure 4.14** Home improvements lost to fire, flood, wind or other natural disasters need to be appraised for replacement value.

## Liquidation Value

The value that can be received from the marketplace when the property has to be sold immediately is called **liquidation value**. It precludes the element of a reasonable time of exposure in the marketplace that is included in the definition of market value. Circumstances arise when an owner must sell immediately. With no time to list and sell through normal channels, the property owner may call a company or investor who will perform quickly with cash, but will require a substantial discount on the price.

Liquidation value can be determined by first estimating market value. Then, by observing distressed sales in the marketplace, the appraiser calculates how much below market value these prices are and applies that discount to the subject's market value. This valuation is not common in the residential appraiser's daily practice but a client may occasionally need it.

## Going Concern Value

**Going concern value** is the value of an entire business operation. As such, it applies only to a business that is currently operating. It is based on capitalizing the net income produced by that business. Like any other income-producing entity, a business has value because it has the capacity to produce. If the business were to cease operation, it would still have value because of the capital assets it owns, but it would not have going concern value.

In a situation where a business has ceased operations, the capital assets could be sold or liquidated, usually at a fraction of their value to a going concern. A business as a going concern has more value, not only because the value of the capitalized income is greater than the liquidation value, but also because a prospective owner can look to the future and anticipate continued years of operation. The appraisal of businesses as a going concern is a specialized area of appraisal, and experience must be gained to perform competently.

## Salvage Value

The expected price of improvement items removed with the intent of using those items elsewhere is called salvage value. Often older properties have unique building components that are highly prized by collectors or are desired for use in other structures. Those building components, such as windows, fireplace mantels, stairways, banisters, unique plumbing and lighting fixtures, and building materials are often "salvaged" from an older structure for use elsewhere.

**Figure 4.15** Older properties have building components highly prized by collectors which can be placed in other structures. Many times these components have salvage value.

## Subjective Value

Sometimes known as sentimental value, it is quite different from market value. **Subjective value** — as the name implies — is not based on objective market data. It is based on the emotional and personal reasons of the one forming the opinion. Subjective value is more easily justifiable on properties that have their value centered in the enjoyment of their amenities, or upon an emotional tie, rather than on income. Consider the following example:

> Grandparents own a property with a large yard where they entertain their grandchildren. They are enjoying this phase of their lives. Market value for their property is $300,000. Someone comes along and offers them $350,000. They turn down the offer. Why? Because to them, at this time and for their purposes, there is more value in keeping the property than in receiving $350,000 for it. So to them, the property is worth more than $350,000. That is a subjective valuation, formed in the minds and hearts of the owners. It does not equate with the marketplace, but it is, nonetheless, very real to them.

## Other Types of Value

We can see that there are many types of value, each involving unique circumstances and requiring specific definitions. Other types of value that are used in appraisal include mortgage loan value, book value, capitalized value, easement value, security value, listing value, tax value, potential value, extrinsic value, contract value, corner value, front-foot value, square-foot value, advertising value, intrinsic value, cash value, face value, interim value, nuisance value, depreciated value, fair value, etc., etc.  This indicates how complex the value concept is, and how specific the appraiser must be in understanding exactly what type of value is sought.

# Principles of Valuation

The following principles are interrelated.  Their relative importance will vary depending upon other factors affecting the property being appraised.

Appraisers must have a good working knowledge of the principles of valuation.  In the field, many special conditions and unusual circumstances can be found — situations that may not have been previously encountered.  The appraiser cannot be expected to know in advance every nuance that can arise.  However, equipped with a working knowledge of the principles of valuation, the appraiser can recognize when a special situation makes an impact on value, and then determine how to reconcile such information into the final value estimate.  A working knowledge of the principles of valuation is indispensable to becoming a competent appraiser.

## Principle of Change

Cities and neighborhoods are always changing, and individual homes within those neighborhoods reflect that change.  An appraiser must be aware of trends that affect the value of real estate.  Economic, environmental, governmental and social forces are always dynamic, causing changing values in real property.

Change may occur rapidly or proceed very slowly over time.  Societal, economic, physical, and governmental forces act to bring about change.  Rapid changes may be caused by natural disasters, plant closings, new construction, or governmental action.  Slower change may be the gradual change in land use over years from primarily residential to commercial in nature.  This kind of change may be almost imperceptible from one year to the next.

Some changes are internal to a property while others are external. Physical, functional, or locational factors may combine to bring about change to a property as well.  Room additions, remodeling and the addition of upgrades are examples of positive changes internal to a property.  Rezoning of an area by the local governing agency, the building of a new regional mall nearby, or the closing of a nearby military base are examples of external changes.

**Figure 4.16** Remodeling or upgrading a room adds value to a property.

All these changes affect property values. Though not all changes are detrimental to a property, they are inevitable. It is the appraiser's responsibility to research and identify these changes, and consider these changes when formulating their opinions and conclusions.

## Principle of Supply and Demand

Like all other marketable commodities, real estate is affected by supply and demand. The law of **supply and demand** is almost universally recognized as being the first step in how market prices are determined. In order to understand the principle of supply and demand, both concepts need to be understood.

In referring to real estate, **supply** refers to the total amount of a given type of property for sale or lease, at various prices, at any given point in time. Land itself is finite in supply — there is only a certain amount. However, although the supply of land does not change, the supply of a particular type of property changes as buildings are constructed or destroyed. As market conditions change or as properties become more or less available for various reasons, supply fluctuates.

**Demand** refers to the desire and ability to acquire goods and services through purchase or lease. When speaking of real estate, this is refined to include the total amount of a type of real estate that is desired for acquisition, through purchase or lease, at various prices. The price range is an important factor since demand must be accompanied by purchasing power. If a beautiful, 10 million-dollar home is constructed in a middle-class neighborhood, everyone will like it, but if no one can afford to buy it, there is no real demand.

Increasing supply or decreasing demand will reduce the price in the market. Reducing supply or increasing demand will raise the price in the market. When appraising real property, the appraiser cannot avoid the influence of the principle of supply and demand.

# Principle of Substitution

The principle of substitution is the foundation for all of the appraisal process. **Substitution** is a principle of value which holds that the maximum value of a property is set by the cost of acquiring an equally desirable and valuable substitute property (assuming no cost delay in making the substitution). Simply put, an owner cannot expect to sell his property for more than someone would ordinarily pay for a similar property under similar conditions. Given the choice of two like properties with similar utility and amenities, a buyer will naturally gravitate to the less expensive one. Similarly, a landlord cannot expect to rent property for more than someone would pay to rent a similar place.

In this regard, the principle of substitution is the basis for all three approaches to value and is found most prominently in the sales comparison analysis when using comparables sales. Comparable properties are chosen on the basis of their overall similarity to the subject. For purposes of analysis, they are considered to be substitutes for the property being appraised. In the cost approach, appraisers use the principle of substitution for reproduction estimates of like properties as well as finding comparable land. Finally, in the income capitalization approach, substitution is utilized when determining capitalization rates and gross rent multipliers.

# Principle of Competition

**Competition** is another of the economic principles affecting valuation. Buyers compete with each other to purchase properties. Sellers compete with each other to attract buyers to their properties.

When two or more prospective buyers are competing to obtain a particular property, the one giving the most attractive offer to a seller is the one most likely to prevail. In this case, buyers are in competition with one another to obtain a property.

In order to attract prospective buyers, a seller must price his or her property competitively with other comparable offerings. The seller must balance the desire to attract buyers with the desire to obtain the most favorable sales agreement possible. In this case, the seller is in competition with other sellers offering similar properties.

This also holds true for landlords and prospective tenants. In order to lease their properties, landlords have to offer properties and rates that are competitive with similar lease offerings. Prospective tenants, similar to buyers, must compete with other prospective tenants in order to obtain the property they desire.

In the same way, properties also compete with one another. Amenities, physical characteristics, and location serve to make a property more, or less, desirable. Property owners will often upgrade properties in order to attract more prospective buyers or tenants.

Competition is fundamental to the dynamics of supply and demand in a free enterprise, open market economy. Competition amongst properties leads to a continual shift in availability of different kinds of properties.

## Principle of Opportunity Cost

The principle of **opportunity cost** recognizes another type of competition — one that occurs between industries. Investors have many options in choosing where to put their investment dollars. For any investor, real estate is one of the many investment alternatives available, but it is not the only investment alternative. Whenever one investment is chosen, other options are not chosen. **Opportunity cost** is the profit lost on an investment you were unable to make because the money was already invested in something else.

> For example, if $10,000 is invested in a real estate investment, that $10,000 is not available to be invested in the stock market. If the investor receives a return of 6% on the real estate investment, but could have received a return of 9% by investing in the stock market, the opportunity cost is the 3% (9% - 6%) "lost."

Opportunity costs are often used in real estate appraisal analysis when estimating rates of return that are necessary to attract investment. Appraisers consider alternative investments in selecting a rate of return for a property being appraised. This affects the final estimate of value for that property.

## Principle of Conformity

The principle of **conformity** states that the more the form, manner, and character of structures are in harmony with one another, the more valuable is each of those structures. A home's maximum value is realized when surrounding land uses are compatible and nearby homes are similar in design and size. This similarity is called conformity, and it upholds neighborhood values. Where there are mixed types of homes, unstable real estate values may occur.

# Principle of Progression

The principle of **progression** states that the value of an inferior property is enhanced by its association with better properties of the same type. A lesser-valued property will be worth more because of the presence of greater-valued properties nearby.

> For example, Joe purchased a 20-year old condominium in excellent condition and in a very good neighborhood. Not long after his purchase, developers put in a brand new high-end high-rise condominium complex adjacent to his property. As a result, the value of his property rose dramatically and immediately. In addition, having a brand-new modern-styled structure in the area encouraged the various local neighborhood associations to revitalize their strip mall edifices and public streets, contributing to an overall better looking neighborhood. As a result, property values in the entire area rose.

# Principle of Regression

The opposite of progression, the principle of **regression** states that the value of a superior property is adversely affected by its association with an inferior property of the same type. A higher-valued property will be worth less because of the presence of lower-valued properties nearby.

While constructing a new housing complex in an aging neighborhood elevates the surrounding property values, the surrounding, older properties can prevent the new complex from realizing its highest potential value.

# Principle of Balance

The principle of balance states that real estate value is created and sustained when contrasting, opposing, or interacting elements are in a state of equilibrium. A careful mix of varying land use creates value. Over-improvement or under-improvement will cause imbalance.

An example of balance could be the construction of a strip commercial center located near a primarily residential neighborhood. Though these two uses are dissimilar, they are compatible since residents of the homes surrounding the strip center frequent the stores located in that center. By extension, the people who work in that center live close by in the surrounding residential neighborhood.

## Principle of Four-Stage Lifecycle

All neighborhoods change. They start out as young, dynamic areas, and eventually disintegrate in the process of passing years. Property goes through four distinct changes called a **neighborhood lifecycle**:

- Growth (development)
- Stability
- Decline
- Revitalization

Development is initially the stage when the subdivision is being built. The infrastructure is established, trees are planted and the houses are constructed. Values are established and may increase.

Stability is usually an extended period of time when the amenities are enjoyed and used by families. During this time, we could expect that the values gradually will be on the rise.

Old age and decline eventually come. The properties are not as desirable as they once were. The neighborhood is not as appealing. There may be other, newer subdivisions nearby that are preferred in the marketplace. Construction styles may have changed, and property values may suffer from functional obsolescence. Social and economic factors may have combined to cause a loss in value.

Growth and decline is normal in all areas, and many times it can be reversed just as it reaches the last stages. For example, when a lovely neighborhood grows to be old and worn out, young families may choose to move in and completely restore the process of change by starting the life cycle of the neighborhood all over again with revitalization.

## Principle of Anticipation

The principle of **anticipation** expresses that value is created by the expectation of future benefits. Probable future benefits to be derived from a property will increase its value. An appraiser estimates the present worth of future benefits when he or she assigns a value based on anticipated returns.

> For example, the purchaser of a home has the perception he or she will be able to enjoy the use of that home in the future. They are anticipating the future benefits they are purchasing. Similarly, the buyer of a commercial property might be anticipating the future income, as well as possible tax benefits, associated with property ownership.

Often, nearby off-site improvements will have an effect on value. Schools, freeways, roads, parks, utilities, airports, and commercial developments are just of few of the many off-site improvements that may affect the value of a particular property. In many cases, the off-site improvements are only in the planning stages at the time of the appraisal, but anticipation is already having an effect upon the value for the subject property. USPAP requires the appraiser to "analyze the effect on value, if any, of anticipated public or private improvements, located on or off the site, to the extent that market actions reflect such anticipated improvements as of the effective appraisal date."

The principle of anticipation applies not only to positive future benefits but to anticipated negative future influences as well.

> For example, a property might be located in a small town where the major employer indicated their operation would permanently close in the near future. In response to this news, property values would decrease due to anticipation. Similarly, a home in a presently quiet location could lose value if it is located next to the vacant field where the new extension of the interstate freeway is to be built.

It is important that appraisers stay fully informed of local community affairs as well as local economic trends in order to accurately analyze the effect of anticipation in the subject property's market.

## Principle of Contribution

The principle of **contribution** is the concept that the worth of a particular component is calculated in terms of its contribution to the value of the whole property, or its worth is calculated as the amount that its absence would detract from the value of the whole.

This principle is based on the premise that the value of a component part, whether it is added to land or building, is only equal to what it adds to the overall value of the property regardless of the actual cost of the improvement.

> For example, this happens with swimming pools in most instances. Although a home is worth more if it has a pool, the actual cost of adding a pool is higher than the expected increase in value. A new family room, however, generally increases the value of the house by more than the cost to build. The principle of contribution must be kept in mind by home-owners who want to remodel in some way. Before making any changes, the homeowner should try to determine if the changes will contribute enough to the property's value to justify the costs.

## Principle of Increasing and Decreasing Returns

The principle of increasing and decreasing returns is the idea that successive increments of one or more agents of production added to fixed amounts of other agents will enhance income, in dollars, benefits, or amenities, at an increasing rate until a maximum return is reached. Then, income will decrease until the increment to value becomes increasingly less than the value of the added agent or agents.

The **four agents of production** are land, labor, capital, and management. Each of these may be increased in varying amounts to increase the value and/or income attributable to a property. There is a point, however, where additional investments no longer add value proportional with the amount invested.

Increasing returns applies when additional investment in a property adds a reasonable return on that investment. At a certain point, maximum value will be reached. At this point, decreasing returns apply; continued investment will yield less-and-less return.

Imagine an older office building in an aging commercial district. In order to perpetually maintain the value of the building, certain upgrades must be considered, things like repainting, re-roofing, upgrading of fixtures; eventually, the entire edifice may have to be remodeled to conform to whichever style is popular at that time. Eventually, though, no matter how much money the owners sink into the office building, it will have outlived its usefulness and further investment will not provide enough return to be worth the investment. It will have evolved from an investment that provides increasing returns to one that provided decreasing returns. At that point, demolition and reconstruction is oftentimes the most economically feasible option.

## Principle of Surplus Productivity

As mentioned earlier, there are four agents of production: land, labor, capital, and management. Under traditional economic theory, land earns rents, labor earns wages, capital earns interest, and management earns profits.

Labor, capital, and management are all expenses of ownership. Once these ownership expenses have been paid, any remaining surplus is attributable to land and is the investor's return on the use of the land (otherwise known as land rent). Land rent is the basis for residual land valuation techniques discussed later.

# Summary

In order for an appraiser to value things like land and attachments, and even different property interests properly, he or she will need to have a complete understanding of value. Understanding **value** includes determining which definition of value is appropriate for each assignment. Typically, appraisers will be estimating **market value,** but there will be occasions when an appraiser must determine one of a number of other varieties of value.

Appraisers must also be familiar with the various **forces that create and influence value.** Remember that **demand, utility, scarcity, and transferability** must be present in order for something to have any value. When value does exist for an item, there are **physical, economic, political, and social forces** that impact and shape value further.

There are also myriad principles of valuation that, depending on how they are applied and analyzed, will affect the appraiser's overall analysis. The root of all appraisal is the **principle of substitution** and it can be found to varying degrees in all three approaches to value. Other value principles, however, will factor into the appraisal process. As these factors interact, property values will increase or decrease in response.

With practice, the picture of what value is and which components combine to create and shape it will become clearer.

# Review Exercises

## Matching Exercise

**Example:** Look up the meaning of the terms in the Glossary, then write the letter of the matching term on the blank line before its definition. Answers are in Appendix B.

### Terms

A. anticipation

B. arm's-length transaction

C. assemblage

D. balance

E. building code

F. conformity

G. contribution

H. cost

I. demand

J. effective demand

K. four agents of production

L. front foot

M. neighborhood lifecycle

N. opportunity cost

O. price

P. progression

Q. regression

R. scarcity

S. stigma

T. substitution

U. supply

V. transferability

W. unearned increment

X. utility

Y. value

### Definitions

1. _____ The ability or power of an item to perform a service or meet a need.

2. _____ The ability to transfer ownership of an item from one person, or entity, to another.

3. _____ A shortage of an item relative to the demand for that item.

4. _____ Desire coupled with the ability to satisfy the desire.

5. _____ The process of obtaining and combining parcels to create a larger, more valuable parcel.

6. _____ The width of a property along a street or other boundary.

7. _____ An increase in value that is not the result of anything the owner did.

8. _____A lingering effect in the minds of people regarding the desirability or usefulness of a property.

9. _____The price an object or service would bring in a fair, open market.

10. _____The amount of money it takes to build a structure.

11. _____A transaction where all parties involved are knowledgeable, acting in their own self-interest and are under no undue influence or pressure from other parties.

12. _____A principle that affirms that the maximum value of a property tends to be set by the cost of acquiring an equally desirable and valuable alternate property.

13. _____The total amount of a given type of property for sale or lease, at various prices, at any given point in time.

14. _____The highest-valued alternative investment that was not chosen.

15. _____The concept that the form, manner, and character of structures are in harmony with one another.

16. _____The principle that states that the value of a superior property is adversely affected by its association with an inferior property of the same type.

17. _____The worth of a particular component is calculated in terms of its contribution to the value of the whole property, or as the amount that its absence would detract from the value of the whole.

18. _____Land, labor, capital, and management

19. _____Growth, Stability, Decline, and Revitalization

20. _____The principle which expresses that value is created by the expectation of future benefits.

## Multiple Choice Questions

**Instructions:** Circle your response and go to Appendix B to check your answers and to read the complete explanation for each question.

1. What are the four elements that create value?
   a. Transferability, utility, scarcity, and discount
   b. Demand, utility, substitution, and transferability
   c. Demand, uniformity, scarcity, and transferability
   d. Transferability, demand, scarcity, and utility

2. What is the difference between demand and effective demand?

    a. Demand is the desire or ability to purchase a commodity; effective demand is the desire and ability.

    b. Demand is the desire and ability to purchase a commodity; effective demand is the desire or ability.

    c. There can be no demand without effective demand.

    d. There is no difference.

3. A lot that previously supported a gas station is contaminated because of its prior use. Which of the four elements that create value does this property most likely lack?

    a. Demand

    b. Utility

    c. Scarcity

    d. Transferability

4. A major corporation purchases several waterfront commercial lots with the plan of demolishing the current structures and erecting a large retail complex. This is known as:

    a. an arm's-length transaction.

    b. anticipation.

    c. assemblage.

    d. conformity.

5. A lakefront property in Seattle, Washington is currently on the market for $850,000. It has 2,500 square feet and the lot is 50 feet deep. What is the cost per front foot?

    a. $1,700

    b. $17,000

    c. $340

    d. $3,400

6. Which exposure orientation would a street front retailer prefer?

    a. South and east

    b. North and east

    c. North and west

    d. South and west

7. Corey purchases a home in Phoenix, Arizona in the first phase of development. By the time the home is prepared for occupation, Corey's property value has risen by 35%. This is an example of:

    a. progression.

    b. regression.

    c. unearned increment.

    d. opportunity cost.

8. Abigail is a real estate agent who has been trying to sell the old McPherson place on Brewster Lane for several years. Even though it is on the market under value, the property will not sell because the local townspeople are convinced it is haunted. What term describes this property?

    a. Stigma

    b. Utility

    c. Effective demand

    d. Scarcity

9. Joan sold her house to her son for $250,000. Similar properties in the area are selling for $325,000. $250,000 is representative of this property's:

    a. value.

    b. price.

    c. cost.

    d. going concern value.

10. In real estate, the term "worth" is synonymous with which of the following terms?

    a. Value

    b. Price

    c. Cost

    d. All of the above

11. If a 3 bedroom/2 bath house cost $200,000 to build last year and recently sold for $250,000, what is its value?

    a. $200,000

    b. $250,000

    c. $300,000

    d. Depends on what the property would bring in the current fair and open market.

12. Which of the following is an example of an arm's-length transaction?
    a. Parent sells family home to child for $25.00.
    b. Wealthy eccentric must have neighboring lot and overpays.
    c. Seller does not notify buyer of known property stigma.
    d. None of the above.

13. In a typical appraisal assignment, which type of value is of greatest importance to an appraiser?
    a. Value in exchange
    b. Appraisal value
    c. Value in use
    d. Subjective value

14. Which principle of valuation is the underlying principle of all approaches to value?
    a. Substitution
    b. Supply and demand
    c. Competition
    d. Contribution

15. Which one of the following statements is most correct:
    a. When supply is high and demand is high, then value tends to be high.
    b. When supply is low and demand is high, then value tends to be high.
    c. When supply and demand are in equilibrium, then value tends to be high.
    d. When supply is high and demand low, then value tends to be high.

16. Josh is presented with Investment A and Investment B, both very attractive. Josh can only afford to invest in one and chooses Investment B. One year later, he learns that Investment A yielded 80% more profit than the investment he chose. Which principle is applied in this situation?
    a. Substitution
    b. Opportunity cost
    c. Unearned increment
    d. Regression

17. Leonard purchased adjacent lots in a suburban area where the typical house is a 3 bedroom/2 bath under 2000 square feet.  Leonard intends to combine the lots and build a 7 bedroom/6 bath Spanish style mansion.  Which principle of valuation is Leonard disregarding?

    a.  Principle of progression

    b.  Principle of regression

    c.  Principle of conformity

    d.  All of the above

18. Chet bought a cabin in the mountains for $45,000.  He repaired the furnace, redecorated the interior, and repainted the exterior.  All of this work totaled just over $7,000.  When he tried to resell it, the best offer he got for his cabin was $48,500.  Which principle of valuation does this scenario exemplify?

    a.  Opportunity cost

    b.  Competition

    c.  Regression

    d.  Contribution

19. Which of the following is one of the four agents of production?

    a.  Management

    b.  Demand

    c.  Supply

    d.  Value

20. What are the four stages of the neighborhood lifecycle?

    a.  Growth, stability, demand, and revitalization

    b.  Regression, growth, stability, and decline

    c.  Decline, revitalization, growth, and stability

    d.  Scarcity, decline, revitalization, and growth

# Real Estate Markets and Analysis

# Introduction

In the last chapter, we discussed value, the factors that create value, the forces that influence value, and numerous economic principles that affect value. However, before appraisers can determine the value of a particular property, they must also understand real estate's role in the economy, how real estate purchases are financed, and the characteristics that make the real estate market unique.

## Learning Objectives

After reading this chapter, you will be able to:

- describe the role of money and finance and their influence on the real estate market.
- identify the different types of real estate markets.
- discuss the characteristics of a real estate market.
- identify the different aspects that make up a market study.

# Role of Money and Capital Markets

Purchasing power is influenced by the availability of money. Imagine buying a house and being required to pay the total price in cash. With the average price of a single-family home being so high, buyers almost invariably have to borrow funds in order to purchase real estate. In most instances, buyers place a down payment on a property and finance the balance of the purchase price. As a result, the availability of funds to purchase real estate has a direct impact upon the demand for real property.

The availability of funds for financing real estate, and thus the ability of buyers to buy real estate, is heavily tied to government policy, monetary policy, lender requirements, and the overall economy. For example, the availability of funds used for loans to purchase real estate also affects the interest rate charged for those loans. The greater the availability of capital to finance real estate, the lower the interest rate. Conversely, if capital is scarce, the interest rates will be higher. Since financing has such a dramatic impact upon real estate markets, appraisers need to be aware of factors influencing this aspect of real estate transactions.

# The Federal Reserve System

The **Federal Reserve System** has the greatest effect upon the availability of money in the economy. Regulating the money supply is one of the most significant roles of the Federal Reserve. The supply of money in an economy greatly affects the availability of credit in that economy. Since the real estate market relies so heavily upon credit, the actions of the Federal Reserve have a significant effect upon real estate markets.

**Figure 5.1** The Federal Reserve regulates the money supply.

The Federal Reserve is the central bank of the United States and is an independent banking system designed to manage money and credit and to promote orderly growth in the economy. While it operates within the general structure of the government, it operates independently from the government.

The Federal Reserve has the authority to fix the amount of reserves a member bank must keep on hand. The **reserves** are the total percentage of deposits banks are required to keep on hand and not lend. Once a depositor places funds into an account in a bank, that bank can lend out a portion of that money to its borrowers. The amount the banks may lend out is a percentage of the total deposit. By changing the amount banks are required to keep on hand, the availability of credit changes.

The Federal Reserve also makes loans to its member banks. In order to increase its availability of funds, member banks borrow from the Federal Reserve at the **discount rate**. When this rate is high, banks are reluctant to borrow and credit is generally restricted. On the other hand, when this rate is low, banks are willing to borrow and more credit is available.

The Federal Open Market Committee (FOMC) is another way the Federal Reserve regulates credit. The FOMC buys and sells **government-backed securities** on the open market. When the FOMC purchases these securities, the supply of money in the economy is increased thus increasing available credit in the economy. When the Federal Reserve sells securities, the amount of money in the economy is reduced. This causes a slowing of economic growth. Through the FOMC, the Federal Reserve influences the rate at which the economy grows.

By utilizing these three tools, the Federal Reserve manages the money supply in the United States' economy. Appraisers need to be aware of the actions of the Federal Reserve in order to identify trends.

## Sources of Capital

Numerous sources of capital are available to purchase real estate. Sources of capital for purchasing real estate are divided into two categories: (1) equity investors, and (2) debt investors.

**Figure 5.2** Real estate investors are either equity investors or debt investors.

## Equity Investors

Typically, equity investors are active in the operation of the investment, have an ownership interest in the property, and assume a relatively higher risk. Trusts, partnerships, joint ventures, syndications, pension funds, and life insurance companies are sources for equity financing.

### *Trusts*

A **trust** is a legal arrangement in which an individual (the **trustor**) gives fiduciary control of property to a person or institution (the **trustee**) for the benefit of beneficiaries. **Fiduciary** means that those controlling the trust act for the benefit of others and have a standard of care that is higher than what is typically found throughout the rest of society. Trusts can be temporary, conditional, or permanent in nature. In a trust, title to and control of property is placed in the hands of a party called the trustee. The trustee acts to benefit, and protect the interests of the person(s) called the **beneficiary**. Individual investors, as well as groups of investors employ trusts as an investment strategy in order to reap the benefits while avoiding the liabilities of ownership.

Relatively small groups of investors pool their assets in order to acquire larger properties and have successfully used Real Estate Investment Trusts (REITs). REITs give their investors freedom from personal liability while offering shares that are readily transferable. The trustee oversees management of the real estate.

## *Partnerships*

Partnerships are common ways for individuals to pool their funds with others to acquire properties. Partnerships are arrangements where two or more partners jointly own an asset and share in the profits or losses. General and limited partnerships are the two types of typical partnerships.

In a general partnership, all partners have a proportionate share in the gains and losses associated with the property. However, the individual partners also have full responsibility for all liabilities of the partnership. The fact that general partners have full responsibility is one of the disadvantages to this kind of arrangement.

A limited partnership is an arrangement consisting of general and limited partners. The general partners have an active role in that they manage investment and assume full liability. The limited partners have a passive role and their liability is limited only to the amount of capital invested.

## *Joint Ventures*

Joint ventures are a contractual agreement joining two or more entities on a temporary basis for a specific project. These kinds of arrangements generally take the form of a partnership and are frequently used in large projects. These kinds of developments usually involve one entity providing management expertise and a financial institution that provides a bulk of the capital needed.

## *Syndications*

Syndications are used to raise real estate equity capital. A syndication is a public or private partnership that pools funds to purchase and develop projects. Private syndications are small and relatively free of government regulation. Public syndications tend to be large and are subject to federal rules and regulations. Syndications are often set up and promoted by a general partner who advertises the investment opportunity and assumes full financial responsibility. Other investors buy shares in the syndication and are limited partners. Syndication agreements are written so as to offer an unequal distribution of tax benefits as an enticement to investors.

## *Life Insurance Companies*

Through their sale of policies, life insurance companies accumulate large amounts of capital. They actively look for investments where they may place these funds and often invest in real estate both as equity investors and as mortgage lenders. Financial managers within these companies look for investment opportunities offering growth in the value of their investment as well as protection against inflation.

## *Pension Funds*

Private and government pension funds are major equity investors in real estate. Employers and employees contribute funds to pension funds with the anticipation of paying retirement income to the employee upon retirement. Pension funds are usually under the control of a trustee obligated to invest the funds prudently for the benefit of the employees. In order to ensure the growth of these funds, the trustee actively seeks investments offering growth potential and safety. The amount of money controlled by pension funds is extremely large (over $1 trillion) which consequently has a significant effect upon real estate markets.

## Debt Investors

Debt investors have a relatively passive role in the operation and management of the real estate. They usually do not participate in the management nor the gains or losses associated with buying and selling real estate. These sources of capital seek conservative investments, with relatively little risk, that produce income and repayment of principal with a high degree of certainty. These sources invest in debt and expect a priority claim on the property used to secure the debt. Though these organizations are thought of as lenders, they are investors since they are investing their funds into loans with the expectation of earning a return on (interest) and a return of (principal) their investment. Banks, savings and loans, commercial banks, credit unions, thrifts, and life insurance companies are examples of debt investors. Since appraisers receive so much of their business from these capital sources, they should be familiar with how they operate.

### *Savings & Loans*

Savings & loan associations, also known as thrifts or S&Ls, are either federal or state-chartered financial institutions that take deposits from individuals with which they fund loans and pay dividends to investors. Originally, they only offered savings accounts and mortgages. They have been the traditional source of capital for home loans. Thrifts are required by law to make a certain percentage of their loans as home mortgages.

### *Banks*

Since deregulation in the 1980s, the distinction between S&Ls and commercial banks has blurred. Commercial banks have traditionally been the largest source of loans to small business and have historically specialized in short-term loans. Today they offer a variety of long-term real estate loans. Among other things, they offer mortgages and consumer loans, credit cards, and deposit products including savings accounts and certificates of deposit (CDs). They also offer checking accounts for individuals and businesses. Because of deregulation, banks now offer such products as insurance, mutual funds, and Individual Retirement Accounts (IRAs). Many banks also offer trust services, asset management, and estate planning as well.

### Credit Unions

Credit unions are nonprofit, cooperative financial organizations of individuals having a common bond. They are formed by large organizations and companies for the benefit of their members or employees. They accept deposits from members, pay interest in the form of dividends on deposits, and use their funds mainly for consumer installment loans. Credit unions often offer higher interest rates on deposits and have a tendency to offer lower rates on the loans they make. When a person makes a deposit to a credit union, he or she becomes a member of that credit union because his or her deposit is considered partial ownership in that credit union.

### Mortgage Companies

Mortgage companies, also known as mortgage bankers, are prime sources for real estate mortgage loans. Unlike banks, S&Ls, and credit unions, mortgage companies do not obtain funds from deposits. Mortgage bankers fund loans with their own money, or with a warehouse line of credit with a large commercial bank, and then sell the loans they originate to investors, other lenders, and the major secondary market agencies. Mortgage companies not only originate the loans, they often service the loan as well (i.e., collect the monthly payments).

### Private Investors

In addition, real estate loans are made by private individuals. When interest rates are high or credit difficult to obtain, sellers may personally offer to finance a part of the sale as a way to facilitate the transaction. In these cases, the financing is tied to a particular property and the sale price is usually higher because of the private financing. When it is offered, it is often for a shorter term than other kinds of real estate financing. It often has a balloon payment which requires the buyer to refinance the loan.

In most instances though, private investors actively seek to make real estate loans. Usually working through mortgage brokers, private investors make loans that more traditional lenders refuse to lend on such as damaged homes, atypical construction, or unique properties. Often financing from private investors is above the market rate for conventional financing and usually comes with shorter loan terms.

### *Mortgage Brokers*

While technically not a source of financing capital, mortgage brokers bring together borrowers (mortgagors) and lenders (mortgagees). Mortgage brokers usually do not have the money themselves to fund the loans. Mortgage brokers serve as facilitators in that they find the borrower(s), process the application, and submit the loan package to a wholesale lender who ultimately makes the loan. Brokers have a great amount of flexibility because they can use many different lenders thereby finding the loan that best suits the needs of the borrower. Brokers are paid a commission by the wholesale lender based upon the amount of the loan.

## The Mortgage Markets

Both equity investors and debt investors can provide the capital necessary to purchase real estate. Collectively, debt investors or lenders who make loans directly to borrowers are referred to as the **primary mortgage market**. However, as the demand for financing grew, this market was not enough.

Historically, savings and loans, banks, and other lending institutions have accumulated funds by offering to pay interest on deposits to that institution. The institution would in turn lend out most of those deposits at a higher interest rate than that being paid to the depositors. The difference became income to that institution.

**Figure 5.3**  A bank can increase its profits by lending out deposit money at a higher interest rate than is paid to the depositors. The difference between these rates becomes income to the bank.

However, once the deposits had been lent to borrowers, there were no funds for any additional loans. The only way a bank or S&L association could make new loans was to attract new deposits, or make loans from the funds collected from payments as the prior loans were being paid off.

In addition, this system led to a problem with cash flow. Real estate has a relatively high purchase price and in order to afford to buy it, purchasers have to be able to obtain loans that have a relatively long term. On the other hand, most deposits to lending institutions are held in accounts for a relatively short period.

In situations when large amounts were withdrawn, the liquidity of the institution was threatened. These kinds of situations sometimes led to **panics** — where all depositors of an institution would try to withdraw their funds at the same time. Since most of the deposits had been lent out, there was usually not enough cash on hand to give back to depositors. In these cases, the bank had to borrow funds in order to meet its obligations. Sometimes the bank could not borrow the necessary funds, and it had to default. Situations like this made bankers hesitant to make long-term loans. These conditions tended to make real estate loans costly, which meant that fewer people could buy homes.

The whole economy suffers when capital is scarce and interest rates are too high to be affordable. One way the government has found to stimulate a sluggish or depressed economy is to encourage both home building and sales. In order to encourage home building and sales, and to also counter the other problems mentioned above, government and private organizations have developed a number of institutions that are collectively known as the secondary mortgage market or the secondary market.

The **secondary mortgage market** is where existing loans are bought and sold. This market allows lenders to sell groups of real estate loans to investors at competitive rates. By selling their real estate loans, the lenders have the funds to lend; they are more liquid and in a position to quickly adjust to market conditions. Most importantly, they will be able to continue making loans where they otherwise would not be able. The lenders are also more inclined to make long-term loans if they are not required to hold on to them.

The **Federal National Mortgage Association** (FNMA), the **Federal Home Loan Mortgage Corporation** (FHLMC), the **Government National Mortgage Association** (GNMA), and the Federal Agricultural Mortgage Corporation (FAMC), are among the major organizations operating in the secondary market. These organizations are commonly referred to by their nicknames — Fannie Mae, Freddie Mac, Ginnie Mae and Farmer Mac respectively.

## Federal National Mortgage Association (FNMA)

The federal government established Fannie Mae, as it is known, in 1938. Its purpose was to expand the flow of mortgage money by creating a secondary market. FNMA accomplished this by buying FHA insured mortgages. In 1968, Fannie Mae became a stockholder-owned company and expanded its operations to include other mortgages in addition to FHA loans. Fannie Mae does not lend money directly to borrowers. FNMA buys loans meeting its standards from lenders, which enables those lenders to continue making more loans. Upon purchasing a loan, Fannie Mae might keep that loan in its portfolio as an investment or it may be packaged as a debt security and sold to other investors as a **mortgage-backed security** (MBS).

## Federal Home Loan Mortgage Corporation (FHLMC)

Freddie Mac is a stockholder-owned corporation chartered by the United States Congress in 1970. Though Freddie Mac has the same charter, congressional mandate and regulatory structure, it pursues a different business strategy than Fannie Mae. It purchases residential mortgages and mortgage-related securities from approved banks and lenders. Freddie Mac packages these mortgages into securities that they sell to investors. Freddie Mac guarantees those securities to the investors.

Freddie Mac was created primarily for thrifts to provide a secondary market for conventional mortgages. Unlike Fannie Mae, Freddie Mac holds very little of the loans they purchase in portfolio. Most often, they sell the mortgages they acquire to investors.

## Government National Mortgage Association (GNMA)

Ginnie Mae is a government organization regulated by the Department of Housing and Urban Development (HUD). In 1968, Fannie Mae was split into two separate entities: (1) Fannie Mae and (2) Ginnie Mae. Fannie Mae became a federally chartered, privately owned corporation and Ginnie Mae became a wholly owned government organization that gets financial support from the U.S. Treasury.

Ginnie Mae exists to ensure liquidity for U.S. government-insured mortgages including those insured by the Veterans Administration (VA), Federal Housing Administration (FHA), and the Rural Housing Administration (RHA). Ginnie Mae purchases loans on the secondary market and then issues federally insured mortgage-backed securities. Additionally, Ginnie Mae services a portfolio of loans owned by the U.S. government and is the only issuer of mortgage-backed securities guaranteed by the U.S. government.

Ginnie Mae securities have the full faith and credit of the U.S. government, making these securities an extremely safe investment. The mortgages purchased by Ginnie Mae are typically to low-to-moderate income or first-time homebuyers.

## Federal Agricultural Mortgage Corporation

The Federal Agricultural Mortgage Corporation, also known as Farmer Mac, is a federally chartered, stockholder-owned organization created by the U.S. Congress in 1988 to attract capital for financing agricultural and rural properties. It is primarily designed to benefit farmers and ranchers by maintaining a dependable and competitive supply of mortgage credit.

Like the other secondary-market participants, Farmer Mac purchases qualified loans from lenders thereby replenishing their source of capital to make new loans. It sells securities to investors backed by the mortgages it purchases. Farmer Mac also guarantees timely payment of principal and interest on securities backed by guaranteed portions of farm ownership and farm-operating loans as well as rural business and community-development loans. Though much smaller that Fannie Mae, Freddie Mac, and Ginnie Mae, it provides a much-needed secondary market for loans on rural properties, farms and ranches.

# Competing Investments

Like any other investment, the desirability of real estate depends upon the individual needs of an investor. Investors buy real estate for a variety of investment purposes including income, appreciation, and as a tax shelter.

While real estate may compare favorably in some of these aspects to other investments, it does not compare favorably in others. Risk to the investor is an element that needs consideration also. Investors demand returns in proportion to the risk associated with the investment. Risk and yield usually go hand-in-hand. Low risk investments typically provide a lower yield to the investor than higher risk investments.

In making their investment decisions, individual investors consider the pros and cons of owning real estate as opposed to other competing investments. In doing so, investors examine the costs of buying (or selling) the asset and the historical performance of that investment. Investors also identify whether the investment will provide income, increase in value, or both. At any time, real estate may be seen as superior or inferior to other investments. Other investment opportunities that compete for real estate investment dollars include stocks, bonds, mutual funds, certificates of deposit, and US Treasury Bills.

## Stocks

**Stocks** are shares of ownership in a company or corporation. The benefits may include cash or stock dividends declared by the company. A **cash dividend** is a cash payment to a corporation's stockholders, usually based on profitability. A **stock dividend** is a dividend paid out in stock, rather than cash. Additionally stocks may increase or decrease in value. Stocks are very liquid and are traded in various stock exchanges such as the New York Stock Exchange or NASDAQ. Stocks can be subject to significant changes in value over a short period. There is no guarantee that dividends will be paid to stock investors therefore this investment may be inappropriate to the investor seeking income on a regular basis.

**Figure 5.4** People purchase stocks to receive benefits such as cash or stock dividends.

## Bonds

**Bonds** are essentially written evidence of loans made to corporations and government entities. These entities sell bonds to raise funds for operations and development. Bonds generally come with a fixed interest rate and a term exceeding one year. They earn interest at the stated rate for the term of the bond.

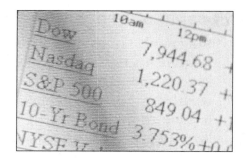

**Figure 5.5** Bonds are generally a safer investment (fixed interest rate and a term exceeding one year) than stock.

Corporate bonds are generally a safer investment than stocks since bondholders have prior claims to corporate assets above those of stockholders. Government-issued bonds are overall considered to be very safe investments since they have the backing of the government entity issuing the bond. Government-issued bonds also offer tax advantages over corporate issued bonds.

## Mutual Funds

**Mutual funds** are investment vehicles operated by investment companies. They raise money by selling shares of the fund to the public, much like any other type of company can sell stock in itself to the public. Mutual funds then take the money from the sale of their shares (along with any money made from previous investments) and use it to purchase various investment vehicles, such as stocks, bonds, and money-market instruments. Each mutual fund has a stated set of objectives and will invest according to those objectives.

**Figure 5.6** Mutual funds are another investment vehicle.

In exchange for the money they give to the fund when purchasing shares, shareholders receive shares in the fund and, in effect, invest in each of its underlying securities. For most mutual funds, shareholders are free to sell their shares at any time. The price of a share in a mutual fund will fluctuate daily, depending upon the performance of the securities held by the fund. Benefits of mutual funds include diversification and professional money management.

## Certificates of Deposit

Commonly called CDs, **certificates of deposit** are financial instruments representing time deposits with banks and other lending institutions. They are for fixed terms of one month, three months, six months, one year, up to seven years. The CD is a contract between a lending institution and depositor where the institution agrees to pay an agreed-upon interest rate and the depositor agrees to maintain the funds on deposit for the specified length of time. If the depositor withdraws the funds before the agreed-upon time, there is typically a substantial interest penalty to the depositor. The CD is backed by the credit of the issuing lending institution and is usually insured by the Federal Deposit Insurance Corporation (FDIC), making these kinds of deposits very secure. Many CDs are negotiable and tradable.

## U.S. Treasury Bills

**Treasury bills**, commonly called T-Bills, are short-term debts incurred by the U.S. government. They usually have a term of three months, six months, or one year. The government issues T-Bills in denominations of $10,000, $15,000, $100,000, and $1 million. These instruments do not have a specified interest rate but are sold to the investor at a discount. Upon maturity, the face value of the T-Bill is paid to the investor. The yield to the investor is greater when the discount is larger. U.S. Treasury Bills have the full faith and credit of the U.S. government and are considered a very safe investment.

**Figure 5.7** U.S. Treasury bills are backed by the U.S. government, and are considered a safe investment.

# Mortgage Terms and Concepts

As we have just discussed, a loan is an investment from a lender's point of view. At its most basic level, a loan is simply renting money. For a fee, the lender lends money to the borrower. By the end of the term of the loan, the borrower is expected to return the money that was borrowed. The fee for renting money is called **interest** and the amount borrowed is called the **principal**.

The interest charged on a loan is proportional to the risk involved with that loan. A riskier loan translates into a higher-interest rate. A safer loan generally means a lower interest rate will be charged. Numerous items are considered when determining the risk involved with a loan. The borrower's credit history, the value of the real estate, the amount of the loan, the relationship between the size of the loan in comparison to the value of the property, the cost of funds in the secondary market, the type of loan, etc., are all considered by the lender when setting interest rates.

In the past, real estate loans were for relatively short terms, usually ranging from 3-7 years. These early loans usually consisted of periodic payments of interest only with the full amount of the principal being due at the end of the loan. These kinds of loans are called balloon mortgages since the last payment is significantly larger than the periodic interest payment. Most of the time, borrowers did not have the funds to pay off the loan when it was due so they were forced to get another new loan to pay off the previous loan. During times of economic distress, such as during the Great Depression of the 1930s, lenders often could not grant new loans and many property owners lost their properties through foreclosure.

With the advent of government-backed financing, long-term financing for residential real estate became available. Additionally, loans were structured so that monthly payments included interest as well as repayment of the principal.

# Promissory Notes and Security Instruments

When a loan is made, the borrower signs a **promissory note**, or note, which states that a certain amount of money has been borrowed. The note, then, is the promise to repay the loan and evidence of the debt.

However, when money is loaned for financing real property, the borrower's promise to repay the loan is not enough by itself. Some kind of collateral, or security, is usually required. The lender wants some concrete assurance of getting the money back in addition to the borrower's written promise to pay.

The property being bought or borrowed against is used as the security for the debt. In other words, the lender feels more secure about making the loan if assured of the property ownership in case of default, or nonpayment, of the loan. Then the lender can sell it to get the loan money back.

The claim a creditor has in the property of a debtor is called a security interest. A **security instrument** is a document used to secure the loan. It describes the rights and duties of the lender and the borrower and establishes the creditor's priority claim to the property named. If the borrower defaults on the loan, the lender can sell the property and use the proceeds from the sale of that property to pay off the debt.

A promissory note may stand-alone as an unsecured loan or note, or may be secured by either a trust deed or mortgage. If there are conflicts in the terms of the note and trust deed or mortgage, generally the terms of the note will control or determine the issue.

## Types of Security Instruments

The security instruments used to secure the interest for the lender are trust deeds and mortgages. In some states, deeds of trust are the principal instruments to secure loans on real property. In other states, mortgages provide security for real property loans. As you will learn, trust deeds and mortgages differ in the number of parties involved, statute of limitations, and transfer of title. In fact, the only thing trust deeds and mortgages have in common is that the property is used as security for the debt. You will often hear the term mortgage used loosely, as in mortgage company, mortgage broker, and mortgage payment — but the term "mortgage" used here usually refers to a deed of trust.

### Trust Deed

The **trust deed** (or deed of trust) is a commonly used security instrument in real estate finance. There are three parties to a trust deed: the borrower (**trustor**), lender (**beneficiary**) and a neutral third party called a **trustee**. A trust deed is a security instrument that conveys title of real property from the trustor to the trustee. The trustee holds the deed of trust as security for payment of a debt on behalf of the beneficiary.

Under the trust deed, the trustor (borrower) has equitable title, and the trustee has bare or naked legal title to the property. **Equitable title** is the interest held by the trustor (borrower) under a trust deed and gives the borrower the equitable right to obtain absolute ownership to the property. **Bare legal title** is conveyed using a trust deed; however, it does not actually convey possession. Possession and equitable title remain with the borrower.

The trustee acts as an agent for the beneficiary and has two obligations. The first is to foreclose on the property if there is a default on the loan and the second is to reconvey the title to the borrower when the debt is repaid in full. When the debt is repaid in full, the beneficiary signs a Request for Full Reconveyance and sends it to the trustee requesting the trustee to reconvey title to the borrower. The trustee signs and records a Deed of Reconveyance to show the debt has been repaid and to clear the lien from the property.

### *Mortgage*

Another security instrument is a promissory note and mortgage. The promissory note shows the obligation of the debt and the **mortgage** is a lien against the described property until the debt is repaid.

**Figure 5.8** A mortgage is a lien against a property until the debt is paid.

There are two parties in a mortgage: a **mortgagor** (borrower) and a **mortgagee** (lender). The mortgagor receives loan funds from a mortgagee and signs a promissory note and mortgage. Once signed by the borrower, the lender holds both the note and mortgage until the loan is paid. Unlike a trust deed, under a mortgage both title and possession remain with the borrower.

## Repayment Plans

The promissory note terms create the basis for the repayment plan. The terms of the note include interest, repayment plan, and default. There are several types of repayment plans, each with a different kind of obligation made clear by the terms of the note. Some repayment plans are fully amortized payments, partially amortized with a balloon payment, interest-only payments, and single payment of principal and interest.

## Amortized (Installment) Payments

With amortized or installment payments, the loan is repaid in equal payments until the loan has been repaid in full. **Amortization** is described as the liquidation of a financial obligation. This type of loan is called "fully amortized" because the loan and interest are fully paid when the last payment is made.

The payment amount is determined by calculating the principal plus interest for the term of the loan and dividing the total by the number of payments during the term of the loan. The borrower makes regular, periodic payments (typically monthly) to include both interest and principal which pays off the debt completely by the end of the term.

When the borrower makes lower payments than what should be made on a fully amortized loan, negative amortization occurs. **Negative amortization** is the increase in debt that occurs when the monthly payment is not enough to cover the interest due. The difference between what should be paid and what is actually paid is added to the principal balance of the loan causing the principal to increase.

### *Fixed-Rate Fully Amortized Note*

A fully amortized fixed-rate note describes a loan with an interest rate that is fixed and payments that are level for the life of the loan. This type of note is the most common type with institutional lenders. It is characterized by regular, periodic payments of fixed amounts, to include both interest and principal, which pay off the debt completely by the end of the term.

> **Two Distinct Features of Fixed-Rate Fully Amortized Loans:**
> - Interest rate remains fixed for the life of the loan
> - Payments remain level for the life of the loan and are structured to repay the loan at the end of the loan term

During the early amortization period, a large percentage of the monthly payment is used for paying the interest. As the loan is paid down, more of the monthly payment is applied to the principal. A typical 30-year fixed-rate mortgage takes 22.5 years of level payments to pay half of the original loan amount. The longer the term of the loan, the lower the monthly payment; however, the total financing costs over the life of the loan will be higher.

Although fixed-rate mortgages are available for 40 years, 30 years, 20 years, 15 years and even 10 years, the most common fixed-rate loans are 15- and 30-year mortgages. There are also bi-weekly mortgages, which shorten the loan by calling for half the monthly payment every two weeks. Since there are 52 weeks in a year, the borrower makes 26 payments, or 13 months worth, every year.

## *Adjustable-Rate-Mortgage (ARM)*

Lenders have created alternative payment plans, such as the Adjustable-Rate-Mortgage (ARM), which allow borrowers to qualify for larger loans and at the same time help maintain the lender's investment return. An ARM has an interest rate that is tied to a movable economic index. The interest rate in the note varies upward or downward over the term of the loan, depending on the agreed-upon index. To protect the borrower from wild swings in interest rates there is usually a limit on how much the interest rate can change on an annual basis, as well as a lifetime cap, or limit, on changes in interest rate.

A lender may offer several choices of interest rates, terms, payments, or adjustment periods to a borrower with an ARM. The initial interest rate, or qualifying rate, is determined by the current rate of the chosen index. Then, a margin, which might be anywhere from one-to-three percentage points, is added to the initial interest rate to determine the actual beginning rate the borrower will pay. The margin is maintained for the life of the loan and does not change. The interest rate may change, however, as the chosen index changes, depending on the economic conditions that lead it.

The borrower's payment will stay the same for a specified period, which might be six months or a year, depending on the agreement with the lender. At the agreed-upon time, the lender re-evaluates the loan to determine if the index has changed, either upward or downward, and calculates a new payment based on the changed interest rate plus the same margin. That will then be the borrower's payment until the next six months or year pass and the loan will be reviewed again. The annual maximum increase is usually one-to-two percent while the lifetime cap is usually not allowed to go beyond five or six points above the starting rate.

Generally, adjustable-rate financing benefits the bankers because it allows for an inflow of extra cash during times of higher interest rates. In other words, the borrower's payments will increase because the interest rate will go up, therefore more money will flow into the financial institution.

## *Hybrid Loans*

Sometimes borrowers desire the lower initial interest rate associated with variable interest rate mortgages but also would like the security associated with a fixed-rate loan. To meet this demand, lenders have begun offering **hybrid loans** — loans that offer features from various loan types. Some hybrid loans initially start out with a variable interest rate but convert to a fixed rate after a certain period of time. As with the traditional ARM, there is some uncertainty associated with these loans because the future performance of the index to which these loans are tied is unknown.

Sometimes, loans are amortized as if they were 30-year loans; however, the loan has only a 5- or 7-year term. These are called "30, due in 5" or "30, due in 7" loans.

Some hybrid loans, such as a step-up mortgage, have a very low initial interest rate for the first year, with a set increase in the interest rate (and a corresponding increase in the monthly payment) to set interest rates on the second and third years. These kinds of loans eventually stay fixed at one interest rate.

## Partially Amortized (Installment) Payments

This type of repayment schedule is used to create lower payments. The partially amortized installment note calls for regular, level payments on the principal and interest during the term of the loan, but since the loan does not fully amortize over the original term, there is still a remaining principal loan balance. The last payment on this type of loan is called a balloon payment. A **balloon payment** is the single, large payment that pays the remaining balance due. It is much larger than the previous payments because it includes all of the remaining principal and interest. This type of repayment schedule may have extra risks because the borrower may not be able to pay the balloon payment and may need to refinance the property, possibly at a higher rate.

## Interest Only Payments

An interest-only loan offers consumers greater purchasing power and increased cash flow. It is currently a very popular alternative to traditional fixed-rate loans. The interest-only loan is also called a straight loan or term loan. It calls for regular interest payments during the term of the note. The interest rate is generally higher on a straight note and the principal does not decrease. A large payment is made at the end of the term to repay the principal and any remaining interest.

This type of loan works well for people who only want to stay in a home for a few years. For example, if the borrower plans to live in the house for only three-to-five years, an interest-only loan may be the right choice. With a conventional 30-year mortgage, most of the payment is applied directly to the interest of the loan with very little applied to the principal. With an interest-only loan the borrower will have a lower payment and have almost the same principal balance at the end of that time as if a conventional loan had been selected.

## Single Payment of Principal and Interest

Some loans have no regular payments of interest and/or principal. Instead, the borrower must pay off the loan all at once, at a specified future date. This payment includes the entire principal amount and the accrued interest.

**Figure 5.9** Some loans must be paid off all at once (a single payment that includes the entire principal amount and accrued interest) on a specified due date.

## Other Loan Options

Sometimes lenders cannot lend the amount of money desired by a borrower due to underwriting criteria set by the lender or by secondary market underwriting criteria. In order to assist these kinds of borrowers, creative means have been found to facilitate the transaction while still meeting underwriting criteria. For example, extending the term of the loan lowers the borrower's monthly payment. Moving a $250,000 loan from 15 years to 30 years will lower the monthly payment by over $600 per month.

At other times, high interest rates may keep a borrower from qualifying for a loan. If the interest rate can be lowered, more buyers may be able to get financing needed in order to buy property. For example, sellers can buydown a loan in order to help a buyer afford the loan. In these cases, the seller pays points. **Points** are prepaid interest paid to the lender. Each point equals 1% of the loan amount. The lender will then offer a loan at a lower interest rate to the buyer. For example, reducing a 6% interest rate to 5% on a 30-year loan for $300,000 will reduce the monthly payment by nearly $200. Appraisers should be aware of these situations since most of the time the purchase price is adjusted to reflect the seller's additional costs.

# Conventional and Government Backed Loans

All loans are classified according to their loan terms (e.g., fixed-rate loans or adjustable-rate loans). Additionally, they can be classified by whether or not they have government backing (conventional loans or government loans) and whether or not they meet certain guidelines (conforming loans or non-conforming loans).

Some lenders specialize in only conventional, conforming loans, whereas, full service lenders offer a wide selection of loan programs including conventional, government-sponsored FHA and VA loans, and non-conforming loans.

## Conventional Loans

A **conventional loan** is any loan made by lenders without any governmental guarantees. The basic protection for a lender making conventional loans is the borrower's **equity** in the property. A low down payment will mean greater risk for the lender and a higher interest charged to the borrower.

Conventional lenders usually require **private mortgage insurance** (PMI) on low down payment loans for protection in the event that the homeowner fails to make his or her payments. Private mortgage insurance protects the lender against financial loss if a homeowner stops making mortgage payments. Lenders usually require this when the loan exceeds 80% of the value of the property. Usually borrowers pay for PMI as part of the monthly payment. A few companies provide this insurance. Conventional loans may be conforming or non-conforming.

### *Conforming Loans*

**Conforming loans** have terms and conditions that follow the guidelines set forth by the Federal National Mortgage Association (Fannie Mae) and the Federal Home Loan Mortgage Corporation (Freddie Mac). These loans are called "A" paper loans, or prime loans, and can be made to purchase or refinance homes (1-4 residential units).

Fannie Mae and Freddie Mac guidelines establish the maximum loan amount, borrower credit and income requirements, down payment, and suitable properties. Fannie Mae and Freddie Mac announce new loan limits every year. This limit is reviewed annually and, if needed, modified to reflect changes in the national average price for single-family homes.

## *Non-Conforming Loans*

**Non-conforming loan**s are offered if the size of the loan or the borrower's creditworthiness does not meet conventional lending standards. These include jumbo loans and sub-prime loans.

### Jumbo Loans

Loans that are above the maximum loan limit set by Fannie Mae and Freddie Mac are called jumbo loans.  Because jumbo loans are not funded by these government-sponsored entities, they usually carry a higher interest rate and some additional underwriting requirements.

### Sub-Prime Loans

Loans that do not meet the borrower credit requirements of Fannie Mae and Freddie Mac are called sub-prime loans or "B" and "C" paper loans as opposed to "A" paper conforming loans.  Sub-prime loans are offered to borrowers that may have recently filed for bankruptcy or foreclosure, or have had late payments on their credit reports.  Their purpose is to offer temporary financing to these applicants until they can qualify for conforming "A" financing.  Due to the higher risk associated with lending to borrowers that have a poor credit history, sub-prime loans typically require a larger down payment and a higher interest rate.

Prior to 1990, it was very difficult for anyone to obtain a mortgage if he or she did not qualify for a conventional FHA or VA loan.  Many borrowers with bad credit are good people who honestly intended to pay their bills on time.  Catastrophic events such as the loss of a job or a family illness can lead to missed or late payments or even foreclosure and bankruptcy.  Sub-prime loans were developed to help higher risk borrowers obtain a mortgage.

## Government Loans

The federal government, as well as various state and local governments, has adopted policies and instituted programs that encourage home ownership and positively influence the availability of real estate financing.

At the federal level, two agencies help make it possible for people to buy homes they would never be able to purchase without government involvement.  These federal agencies are the Federal Housing Administration (FHA) and the Veterans Administration (VA).  Loan programs guaranteed or insured by these two organizations have helped millions of people buy homes.

## *Federal Housing Administration (FHA)*

The **Federal Housing Administration** (FHA) program, a part of HUD (U.S. Department of Housing and Urban Development) since 1934, has caused the greatest change in home mortgage lending in the history of real estate finance. The FHA was established to improve the construction and financing of housing. The main purpose of the FHA program has been to promote home ownership. Secondary results include setting minimum property requirements and systemizing appraisals. Appraisers are reprimanded if they do not use FHA appraisal guidelines when preparing appraisals for FHA loans. Additionally, an appraiser who intentionally misrepresents the value on FHA loan appraisals, which subsequently cause a loss, could be fined and face legal action. There are limits to the size of FHA loans; however, they provide a good source of financing for affordable housing nationwide. FHA loans offer low down payment loans to borrowers and have had a dramatic effect in encouraging home ownership in this country.

The FHA does not make loans; rather, it insures lenders against loss. Authorized lending institutions such as banks, savings banks, and independent mortgage companies make loans. As long as FHA guidelines are used in funding the loan, the FHA, upon default by the borrower, insures the lender against loss. If the borrower does default, the lender may foreclose and the FHA will pay cash up to the established limit of the insurance.

The lender is protected, in case of foreclosure, by charging the borrower a fee for an insurance policy called **Mutual Mortgage Insurance** (MMI). The insurance requirement is how the FHA finances its program. The premium may be financed as part of the loan or paid in cash at the close of escrow.

The FHA guidelines encourage home ownership by allowing 100% of the down payment to be a gift from family or friends and by allowing closing costs to be financed to reduce the up-front cost of buying a home. The down payment on FHA loans varies with the amount of the loan.

Interest rates are determined by mutual agreement between the borrower and the lender, not set by the Federal Reserve Board. Sometimes a borrower will pay points to the lender to increase the lender's yield and compensate the lender for the difference between FHA interest rates (which tend to be low) and conventional interest rates. The FHA requires monthly payments and does not allow a borrower to make semi-monthly or semi-annual payments.

The FHA maximum loan amounts vary from one county to another. It is important that the total loan amount, including financed closing costs, not exceed the maximum limit set by the FHA for the county in which the property is located. There are no income limits on FHA loans and an FHA loan is based on the selling price when it is lower than the appraisal.

The FHA will make a variety of types of loans. For example, borrowers can get qualified for an FHA loan before a builder starts construction, enabling both borrower and builder to count on the completion of the transaction.

## *VA Loan*

The federal **Department of Veterans Affairs** (DVA) offers loan programs to individuals qualified by military service or other entitlements. The VA does not make loans, but guarantees loans made by an approved institutional lender, much like the FHA. Both programs were created to assist people in buying homes when conventional loan programs did not fit their needs. There are two main differences between the two government programs:

- only an eligible veteran may obtain a VA loan.
- the VA does not require a down payment up to a certain loan amount, which means qualified veterans could get 100% financing.

As with FHA loans, there are no alienation or prepayment penalty clauses allowed in VA loans.

**Figure 5.10** Individuals qualified by military service are entitled to loan programs offered by the Department of Veterans Affairs.

A lender, such as a mortgage company, S&L, or bank, makes VA loans. The DVA's guaranty on the loan protects the lender against loss if the payments are not made and is intended to encourage lenders to offer veterans loans with more favorable terms. The amount of guaranty on the loan depends on the loan amount and whether the veteran used some entitlement previously.

### Other Government Insured Programs

State and local programs that assist first-time homeowners also have a significant impact. These programs utilize various techniques such as low-interest loans made directly by government, assistance with down payments, government assistance with monthly mortgage payments, little or no down payment requirements, interest-rate buydowns, incentives for rehabilitation of existing housing, etc.

### Low income and First Time Homebuyer Programs

State and local governments often try to encourage homeownership in their jurisdictions. In many instances, they will fund programs that encourage homeownership for first-time buyers and low-income individuals and families. There are literally hundreds of programs nationwide and they may vary dramatically from program to program. Sometimes the program will offer below-market loans, while other times, they assist with monthly payments. Sometimes they will pay the down payment on a purchase or they will buy down an interest rate. Some programs offer a variety of different options. Appraisers should recognize that these programs are available and are often used to purchase properties.

## Underwriting Criteria

In determining whether or not to make a loan, lenders consider many criteria. They attempt to control the probability of default and the losses associated with those defaults. They also ensure that legal requirements for the property used as collateral are satisfied and they also meet the underwriting requirements, guidelines and criteria set by government regulators, the secondary market, and security ratings services.

Underwriters look at the borrower's income since that is usually what the borrower relies upon to make their monthly loan payments. They consider consumer debt such as car payments, and credit card debt. The lenders need to know how much of a borrower's income is available to pay off debt of various forms.

They also look at the borrower's credit history as reported by the three major credit reporting bureaus: TRW, Equifax, and Trans Union. In the past few years, lenders have relied more and more heavily upon what is known as credit scoring. Fair Isaac & Company (**FICO**) has developed a credit-scoring model that serves to evaluate risk to lenders. This credit score is based upon criteria such as payment history, outstanding debt of all kinds, credit history, new accounts, kinds of credit, etc.

The credit-scoring model assigns a number ranging from 400 to about 900. The higher the score, the greater the likelihood the borrower is a good credit risk. Generally, FICO scores that are less than 620 are assigned to borrowers at the greatest risk of defaulting — borrowers having the worst credit. Borrowers with FICO scores ranging from 620 to 660 are middle of the road and this is where a majority of borrowers fall. Borrowers with FICO scores greater than 660 are considered the best credit risk. Fair Isaac's scoring system has been very successful and is used in approximately 75% of loan applications.

Underwriters working for lenders also look at the collateral for the loan. Usually lenders do not wish to make loans that are greater than the value of the collateral. If a borrower owes more money on a mortgage than what the home is worth, they are much more inclined to default on that mortgage. With this in mind, lenders often require borrowers to have equity in their homes. Loan-to-value ratios are important in this aspect. Lenders look at how large the loan is in relation to the overall value of the property. Lenders feel safest making loans that are 80% or less than the value of the property. The remaining 20% is the amount of the borrower's equity in that property. It has been statistically shown if the borrower has an equity position that is 20% or greater in a property, they are significantly less inclined to default on a mortgage on that property. Appraisers estimate the value of the property used as collateral for the loan.

If the loan is greater than 80% of the property's value, the lender typically requires private mortgage insurance (PMI). PMI pays the lender for any losses if the loan goes into default. It is insurance for the lender; however, the borrower pays for it by paying the premium for PMI in his or her monthly payment.

# The Real Estate Market

A market may be defined as "trade in a specified commodity." It also refers to the "group of people associated with such trade." Buyers and sellers are brought together in markets through the pricing for commodities.

Markets exist for virtually every known commodity. There are markets for stocks, and markets for bonds. There are money markets and markets for commodities such as steel, coal, diamonds, wheat, and aluminum. Likewise, there is a market for real estate. Appraisers must base their estimates of value using indicators they observe in a given market.

# Characteristics of the Real Estate Market

The real estate market has characteristics that set it apart from other markets. Most commodities are bought and sold in markets that are efficient and organized. An efficient market is one in which goods and services are easily produced and readily transferable, there are a large number of buyers and sellers, and market prices adjust rapidly to reflect new information. An organized market is one in which participants operate under recognized rules for the purpose of buying and selling a particular commodity. The nature of real estate, on the other hand, causes it to operate in a relatively inefficient and disorganized market.

These inefficiencies are due, in a large part, to the nature of real estate. Though new technologies attempt to streamline some of the processes associated with buying, selling, and financing real estate, the complex nature of the real estate market tends to minimize their impact. Some of the root causes of these inefficiencies include the following:

- Real estate as a product is unique and immobile.
- The real estate market is local and segmented.
- There are relatively few buyers and sellers, and one cannot transfer property to the other quickly or easily.
- Information is not readily available, and there is no one source to buy or sell real estate.
- The supply of land is limited, and suppliers cannot produce (i.e., construct) new properties quickly.

Recognizing the challenges associated with the real estate market highlights the need for competent and ethical appraisers.

## Unique

In efficient markets, products tend to be uniform and virtually identical to one another. One product may be readily substituted for another. For example, an ounce of gold purchased in New York City is identical to an ounce of gold bought in Los Angeles. Likewise, a new car purchased in Texas is virtually identical to the same make and model car that is sold in Minnesota.

On the other hand, each piece of real estate is unique. No two properties are identical. This causes the real estate market to be disorganized. Even if the improvements on two different pieces of land are identical, each property is the only one in its particular location and this makes it unique. Since each property is unique, it is not readily substituted for another property.

## Immobile

Real estate markets are relatively inefficient because real estate is immobile. In efficient markets, goods are easily moved, quickly supplied, and readily consumed by buyers. As demands change, commodities move to where they are needed. They move to areas where that commodity is in short supply or they can be stored until needed. This is not true for real estate. Land cannot move elsewhere. It is impossible to relocate land to a location where it would be more desirable.

**Figure 5.11** Real estate is immobile. It cannot be moved to a location where it would be more desirable.

## Individual Markets

In real estate, there is no single "market"; there are many individual markets. There are individual markets for virtually every kind of real property, including markets for residential property and markets for commercial property. There are markets for industrial and agricultural properties. There are even markets for land that may never be developed.

One of the major tasks appraisers perform is identifying the market in which a property operates. Markets can be limited to a specific neighborhood within a city. Other times a market for a particular kind of property may range over numerous states. Markets may even be international in scope. While individual real estate transactions are local in nature, it is important to recognize that forces influencing real estate markets operate at the county, state, regional, national, and in some instances, international level. These market forces include such things as population level, demographics, location characteristics, topography, economic, financial, as well as property specific physical characteristics.

Additionally, there are submarkets within individual real estate markets. The process of identifying and analyzing submarkets within larger markets is called **market segmentation**.

For example, there is an overall market for single-family dwellings within a city. Within that larger market, there are submarkets for higher priced, luxury homes, moderately priced homes and entry-level homes. Each of those submarkets are further differentiated according to location within the city and physical characteristics such as age, style, bedroom and bath count, gross living area, lot size, etc. Legal considerations such as type of ownership (fee simple, condominium, PUD) also further differentiate the market. When determining which market a property operates in, criteria such as these are considered.

Five broad categories of **real estate markets** include residential, commercial, industrial, agricultural, and special purpose.

These categories are the starting point to identify the market for the property being appraised. An appraiser will identify which of the broad categories describes the market for the subject property.

## *Residential*

Residential properties are designed for people. They include houses, condominiums, apartments, lofts, and co-op buildings. They may be either attached or detached and can be single story, multi-story, mid-rise, or high-rise. They may be further categorized as being low-priced, medium-priced and high-priced. They can be built using standard construction materials and techniques, or be factory-built. They may be located in a tract of similar homes or situated in a rural location far from any other residences.

**Figure 5.12**  Residential property

## *Commercial*

Commercial properties are designed for a business purpose. Typically, they generate rental income if non-owner occupied. Commercial properties include office buildings, retail buildings, hotels, etc. Commercial properties may have only one tenant or multiple tenants.

**Figure 5.13**  Commercial property

## *Industrial*

Industrial properties are typically used to assemble, process, or manufacture products. They are also used for industrial services such as storage, warehousing, and recycling facilities. Industrial properties include factories, warehouses, industrial plants, and mining facilities.

**Figure 5.14** Industrial property

## *Agricultural*

As the name implies, agricultural properties are those devoted to an agricultural purpose, such as farming, pasturing, timberland, orchards, groves, and ranches. Dairy farms, feedlots, and facilities for raising cows, chickens, hogs, or any other livestock are included in this list.

**Figure 5.15** Agricultural property

### *Special Purpose*

Special purpose properties include the remaining properties not included in the above lists. Special properties include, but are not limited to, government facilities, parks, open space, houses of worship, cemeteries, landfills, museums, colleges and universities, convention centers, theatres, recreational and historic properties.

**Figure 5.16** University property

## Few Buyers and Sellers

Efficient markets have a large number of buyers and sellers creating a free market. Typically, none of the participants in the market has a large enough share to have a direct measurable influence on the prices within the market. In any given real estate market, few people are active in the process of buying and selling of real estate at any particular time. In addition, relatively few sales of real estate in a market can have a significant influence on prices within that market.

## Illiquidity and Regulations

It is also important to recognize that real estate is illiquid (not liquid). In other words, real estate assets cannot be quickly sold for full market value. While it is true that in some instances real estate is sold very quickly, there are typically unusual circumstances at work. For example, the quick sale may be due to the seller discounting the purchase price, or it may be caused by low supply coupled with high demand in a particular market. However, the reality is that most markets do not allow for the quick sale of real estate at market value.

Other commodities, such as stocks and bonds tend to be liquid assets. When these types of assets are sold, owners usually receive the cash proceeds within a day or two. In the real estate market, it may take weeks, even months, before a buyer is found and even more time for the transaction to be finalized.

Real estate prices are high in comparison to other commodities. Since very few people have the funds to purchase real estate with cash, financing is necessary. The financing process increases the complexity involved in transferring real estate and substantially increases the time involved.

The real estate market is also highly regulated. In most markets, there are relatively few government restrictions influencing value; the market is self-regulating. While government oversight is becoming more widespread all the time, many commodities are still bought and sold with relatively little government regulation. However, in real estate the processes involved in transferring ownership are heavily regulated. Also, government regulations and zoning restrict the uses of property.

## Availability of Information

Buyers and sellers in organized markets are knowledgeable because information on bids, offers, and sales is readily available. Buyers and sellers of most commodities may become knowledgeable with relative ease.

However, buyers and sellers of real estate are often inexperienced. Additionally, information is often difficult to access, since real estate transactions are confidential. Most of the time, buyers and sellers must rely upon those having this specific knowledge to assist them in achieving their goals. This lack of knowledge on the part of buyers and sellers is one of the main reasons participants in the real estate marketplace use services provided by real estate brokers and appraisers.

## No Organized Market Mechanism

Market participants are brought together by an organized market mechanism in efficient markets. Sellers enter the market relatively easily in response to demand. For example, the stock market is a highly organized market where buyers and sellers are able to interact very quickly. Though efforts are continually being made to streamline the process, buying and selling real estate is slow and cumbersome relative to other markets.

## Changes in Supply and Demand

In organized markets, the price to purchase a particular commodity is relatively uniform, stable, and low. Competition has a limiting effect on the market and keeps supply and demand in balance so prices remain relatively stable.

If there is increased demand, producers of the commodity will see an opportunity to profit and will increase their production relatively quickly to fill the need. More suppliers will enter the market vying for those profits. In turn, the influx of these additional suppliers will act to keep prices down as supply rises to meet the demand.

The opposite holds true for decreasing demands. If there are too many producers for a given commodity, suppliers will stop producing that commodity since there is less profit incentive.

This is usually not the case with real estate. Land itself is limited in supply, and once an area has been built up, it can be very difficult to change the supply of a particular type of property. Zoning changes or other modifications may be necessary. Even in an area that has vacant land, production cannot quickly change to match a change in demand for a particular type of property. In the housing market, it can take years to increase the existing housing supply. Because the supply of real estate does not increase quickly or easily, the real estate market is much more susceptible to changes in demand.

# Market Analysis

A market analysis is a key step in every appraisal assignment. The goal of the **market analysis** is to identify, research, and analyze the particular market in which the appraised property operates. Appraisers rely upon their market analysis to identify the scope of work necessary to produce a reliable estimate of value. When identifying the subject property's market, an appraiser needs to address the following questions:

- What is the location of the property being appraised?

- Which kinds of properties are comparable to the subject property?

- What is the location, and geographic distance from the subject, of possible comparable properties that would compete with the subject?

- Are the comparable sales used in the analysis of reasonable substitutes within the market for the subject property?

By categorizing the subject's market, the appraiser can identify where to look for comparable data used in performing the appraisal.

Real estate market analysis reflects the most current market conditions and analyzes development, leasing, sales, and absorption trends that have occurred over the past 10 years. In addition, appraisers interview local development and real estate professionals in order to understand the nuances of the subject market and to identify any structural or regulatory barriers that may be inhibiting local development activity.

The general purpose of a market analysis is to identify future opportunities for growth and development within the region, with a specific emphasis on the subject market. With a few exceptions, it is generally believed that recent development trends will be a reasonable predictor of future development over the next three-to-five years. Beyond five years, it is very difficult to predict with any certainty how a community might grow. One can only make reasonable assumptions about regional economic trends, land and building absorption rates, and regulatory constraints, and provide a range of possible outcomes.

## Demographic Data

Through **demography**, or the study of population statistics, appraisers can reveal a clearer picture of a market's participants. An age, income, and family size, among other statistical factors, can give the appraiser valuable information about who is buying, and who is renting, which help the appraiser to anticipate the future of a market as well. For example, if population trends have been increasing for a certain market for the past eight years, an appraiser might conclude that the need for housing will continue to increase.

## Absorption Analysis

The purpose of an absorption analysis is to predict the absorption rate of a certain type of property in a given market. An **absorption rate** signifies the rate at which a type of property is either bought or leased, i.e. *absorbed* by the market. This is useful because it indicates how fast a property will sell or rent considering the availability of competing properties, the projected supply and space surplus, as well as the needs of that particular market.

> For example, Bob is building a new 16-unit apartment complex. He hired an appraiser to do an absorption analysis, and the appraiser estimated the absorption rate at four units per month. This means that it will take four months to rent the entire building.

An absorption analysis will also reveal the price point for marketing a property to the public so that the units sell or rent at the highest price in the shortest period.

## Forecasts

Demographic data and absorption analysis are usually parts of a larger study known as a feasibility analysis. A **feasibility analysis** is a study of the cost-benefit relationship of an economic endeavor. In performing a feasibility study, the appraiser forecasts the likely success of a project and considers the demographics and absorption rates of a market. In addition, the appraiser examines the costs associated with the project and the likely return the investors can expect.

# Summary

Numerous sources of **capital** are available to purchase real estate. Sources of capital for purchasing real estate are divided into two categories: **equity investors** and **debt investors**. Typically, equity investors are active in the operation of the investment, have an ownership interest in the property, and assume a relatively higher risk. Debt investors, like banks, S&Ls, and other lending institutions, are considered passive, and invest their funds into loans with the expectation of return on top of their initial investment.

In the past, real estate financing had been expensive for the borrower and high-risk for the lender. The advent of the **secondary mortgage market** was a critical step that helped to create liquidity in the funds available and enabled debt investors to continue lending money.

People purchase real estate for a variety of reasons, and both equity and debt investors are no exception to this. When investors purchase real estate, they consider tax benefits, income, and appreciation, among other things. The perceived desirability of competing investments like stocks, bonds, mutual funds, CDs, and T-bills also affect an investor's decision to purchase real estate.

The money borrowed from a debt investor is called the **principal**, and the fee paid to borrow that money is called **interest**. As long-term financing for real estate has become more and more common, the variety of loan choices has increased. Payments may be **fully or partially amortized**, and the interest rate may be **fixed** or **variable**.

For most loans, the lender's protection is the borrower's equity in the property. These are conventional loans, and they may be conforming or non-conforming, depending on whether or not they follow Fannie Mae and Freddie Mac guidelines.

In addition, the U.S. government has encouraged home buying by participating in the real estate market. Two federal agencies, the **Federal Housing Administration** (FHA) and the **Veterans Administration** (VA), help make it possible for people to buy homes they would never be able to purchase without government involvement.

The **real estate market** is unique compared to other markets like the **stock exchange**. This is due to numerous factors. No two properties are alike, and land cannot be moved from one place to another. The real estate market's **segmentation** also contributes to its inefficiency, which ultimately has a great influence on price fluctuation. There are relatively few buyers and sellers, and a seller cannot quickly or easily transfer property to a buyer. In addition, while other organized market participants are generally well informed and knowledgeable about that market, most that buy and sell real estate are inexperienced. This is why there is such a need for brokers and appraisers. Additionally, government regulations and a limited supply of product also make the real estate market unusual.

The real estate market is divided into five unique markets. These are the residential, the commercial, the industrial, the agricultural, and the special purpose markets. Part of the appraisal process is identifying and analyzing the market for subject property.

Appraisers use many different dynamics in a **market analysis**. The appraiser studies **demographics**, or demography, to obtain statistical data for the market's population. Another important aspect of any real estate market analysis is the **absorption analysis**. By performing an absorption analysis, the appraiser determines how quickly a given property type should sell or rent. By forecasting project costs and profits in a **feasibility study** in conjunction with the above analyses, it can be determined if a certain housing project or commercial center is a worthwhile venture in a specific market.

# Review Exercises

## Matching Exercise

**Instructions:**  Look up the meaning of the terms in the Glossary, then write the letter of the matching term on the blank line before its definition.  Answers are in Appendix B.

### Terms

A.  absorption rate

B.  amortization

C.  bare legal title

D.  beneficiary

E.  bonds

F.  cash dividend

G.  Certificates of Deposit (CDs)

H.  conforming loan

I.  conventional loan

J.  demography

K.  equitable title

L.  feasibility analysis

M.  Federal Home Loan Mortgage Corporation

N.  Federal National Mortgage Association

O.  fiduciary

P.  interest

Q.  market analysis

R.  market segmentation

S.  mutual funds

T.  negative amortization

U.  note

V.  panics

W.  points

X.  primary mortgage market

Y.  principal

Z.  reserves

AA.  secondary mortgage market

BB.  security instrument

CC.  security interest

DD.  stock dividend

EE.  stocks

FF.  treasury bills (t-bills)

GG.  trustee

HH.  trustor

### Definitions

1.  _____The percentage of deposits that banks are required to keep on hand and not lend.

2.  _____A standard of care that is higher than what is typically found throughout the rest of society.

3.  _____The individual who gives fiduciary control of property to a person or institution.

4. _____ The person who receives fiduciary control of property.

5. _____ The group of debt investors or lenders who make loans directly to borrowers.

6. _____ The market where existing loans are bought and sold.

7. _____ Also known as Fannie Mae, this organization was created to expand the flow of mortgage money by creating a secondary market.

8. _____ Also known as Freddie Mac, this organization was created primarily for thrifts to provide a secondary market for conventional mortgages. Unlike Fannie Mae, Freddie Mac holds very little of the loans they purchase in portfolio.

9. _____ A cash payment to a corporation's stockholders, usually based on profitability.

10. _____ Investment vehicles operated by investment companies.

11. _____ Written evidence of a loan made to a corporation or government entity. They generally come with a fixed interest rate and a term exceeding one year.

12. _____ The amount of money borrowed.

13. _____ The fee for borrowing money.

14. _____ A signed document that states that a certain amount of money has been borrowed.

15. _____ The claim a creditor has in the property of a debtor.

16. _____ The type of title that is conveyed using a trust deed but does not actually convey possession.

17. _____ The liquidation of a financial obligation.

18. _____ The result of making lower payments than what should be made on a fully amortized loan.

19. _____ Prepaid interest paid to the lender.

20. _____ Any loan made by lenders without any governmental guarantees.

21. _____ A loan whose terms and conditions follow the guidelines set forth by the Federal National Mortgage Association and the Federal Home Loan Mortgage Corporation.

22. _____ The process of identifying and analyzing submarkets within larger markets.

23. _____ An analysis of the cost-benefit relationship of an economic endeavor.

24. _____The rate at which a type of property is either leased or bought by the market.

25. _____The study of population statistics.

## *Multiple Choice Questions*

**Instructions:** Circle your response and go to Appendix B to read the complete explanation for each question.

1. The central bank of the United States is known as:
   a. the Federal Bank of America.
   b. the United States Reserve.
   c. the Federal Reserve.
   d. the National Reserve.

2. In a trust, the _____ gives control to the _____ on behalf of the _____.
   a. trustor, mortgagee, fiduciary
   b. trustee, trustor, beneficiary
   c. trustor, trustee, beneficiary
   d. fiduciary, beneficiary, trustee

3. Regarding partnerships, which of the following is true?
   a. Partnerships are an arrangement where two or more partners share profits and losses.
   b. There are general partnerships and limited partnerships.
   c. A limited partner's liability is limited to only the amount of capital he or she invested.
   d. All of the above

4. Which of the following is true regarding the difference between debt investors and equity investors?
   a. Equity investors are passive and debt investors are active.
   b. Equity investors are active and debt investors are passive.
   c. Debt investors invest in higher risk investments than equity investors.
   d. There is no difference.

5. Which of the following is **not** considered a debt investor?
   a. A mortgage broker
   b. A credit union
   c. A thrift
   d. All of the above are debt investors.

6. Low risk investments typically provide:
    a. a lower yield to the investor than higher-risk investments.
    b. a higher yield to the investor than higher-risk investments.
    c. the same yield to the investor as higher-risk investments.
    d. None of the above. Risk and yield are unrelated.

7. Of the competing investments discussed in this chapter, which are considered safe?
    a. T-bills
    b. CDs
    c. Government-issued bonds
    d. All of the above

8. Joan borrows $20,000 for an auto loan with a term of six years at 9%. When she pays off the loan in full, her total cost will be $25,956.72. The difference of $5,956.72 is known as:
    a. the principle.
    b. the interest.
    c. the principal.
    d. the equity.

9. When using a trust deed, a neutral third party holds the deed as security:
    a. on behalf of the borrower.
    b. until the beneficiary pays off his or her debt.
    c. while the trustor repays the trustee.
    d. and has bare title.

10. A major difference between a mortgage and a trust deed is:
    a. a trust deed has one more involved party.
    b. the borrower retains both title and possession in a mortgage.
    c. Both a. and b.
    d. Neither a. nor b.

11. Meredith has a fully amortized mortgage and owes the bank $1,500 in monthly payments. She has only been paying $1,450, however. The monthly difference of $50 a month:
    a. causes negative amortization.
    b. is added to the loan balance.
    c. increases the principal.
    d. All of the above

12. When a repayment schedule has a final payment that is significantly larger than the other payments, this final payment is known as a(n):

    a. amortization.

    b. interest-only payment.

    c. balloon payment.

    d. graduated payment.

13. Jane wants to purchase a house for $335,000 using a conventional loan. What is her minimum down payment requirement if she does **not** want to carry PMI?

    a. $33,500

    b. $61,500

    c. $67,000

    d. $83,750

14. Prime loans are also known as:

    a. "A" paper.

    b. "B" paper.

    c. non-conforming.

    d. hybrid.

15. Appraisers are reprimanded if they fail to use specialized guidelines when preparing an appraisal for:

    a. friends and family.

    b. GNMA.

    c. FHA-backed loans.

    d. the Department of Veterans Affairs.

16. Which of the following organizations does **not** operate within the secondary mortgage market?

    a. FHA

    b. FNMA

    c. FHLMC

    d. Farmer Mac

17. Which of the following is responsible for the real estate market's inefficiency?

    a. Each property's uniqueness

    b. Real estate's illiquidity

    c. The limited supply

    d. All of the above

18. Which of the following is **not** one the five broad categories of real estate markets?

    a. Residual

    b. Industrial

    c. Special Purpose

    d. Agricultural

19. If a property is "illiquid," it means that:

    a. the property has improper drainage.

    b. the property cannot be sold quickly for full value.

    c. the property has poor plumbing.

    d. the property is in a flood zone.

20. A new subdivision's first phase took a full year to sell and it contained 60 units. The next two phases contain 30 units each, and the appraiser concludes that the absorption rate will decrease by one third per year. How many more years will it take to sell the remaining units?

    a. 1 year

    b. 2 years

    c. 3 years

    d. 3 ½ years

# *Ethical Appraisal Practice*

# Introduction

As we discussed in the last chapter, real estate is a major purchase, and most people need financing to make that purchase possible. The appraisal profession exists primarily to protect lenders and to bring an impartial eye to the valuation of real estate.

In order to ensure that appraisers meet this responsibility, each state has a board that licenses and regulates appraisers, as we discussed in Chapter 1. Nationwide, the *Uniform Standards of Professional Appraisal Practice* (USPAP) are the recognized standards that appraisers must follow. This chapter introduces USPAP and discusses some of the ethical challenges that appraisers face.

## Learning Objectives

After reading this chapter, you will be able to:

- identify the different sections of USPAP.

- recognize the topics covered in each of the five Rules.

- identify the appraisal discipline to which each Standard applies.

- identify common violations of USPAP and ways to avoid them.

# Overview

The *Uniform Standards of Professional Appraisal Practice* (USPAP) are the generally recognized and accepted standards of appraisal practice in the United States. They are the standards for ethics and competency in professional appraisal practice. USPAP (pronounced USE-pap) permeates what real estate appraisers do, and the professional appraiser must have a thorough knowledge of USPAP. USPAP requirements are referred to throughout this textbook.

USPAP has legal authority as it is adopted, cited, or implemented by government agencies through regulation or administrative action. USPAP also may become enforceable through private enterprise when following USPAP is a part of the client's contract with the appraiser. At this point, all licensed and certified appraisers in each state are expected to follow USPAP.

The Appraisal Standards Board (ASB) modifies USPAP on a regular basis to address ever-changing needs. Individuals are required to take a 15-hour USPAP course before they can obtain a real estate appraisal license. In addition, licensed and certified real estate appraisers are required to take a 7-hour USPAP course every two years. Since professional appraisers must take a USPAP course, only a short overview is given here.

# Structure

The USPAP document, as it is currently structured, contains the DEFINITIONS, PREAMBLE, Rules, Standards, Standards Rules, <u>Comments</u>, and Statements on Appraisal Standards. For convenience, the USPAP document also includes the Advisory Opinions (AOs), but these are not technically part of USPAP.

## Introductory Sections

For this overview, we will refer to the DEFINITIONS, PREAMBLE, and Rules together as the "introductory sections". These three sections precede the Standards because the information is both relevant and required for understanding and following the Standards.

The DEFINITIONS section is the first section of USPAP. The definitions that appear in the USPAP document are specific to USPAP. You will see words with which you are familiar, but the definitions found in this section may or may not correspond to definitions of the same word in other sources. Keeping the definitions straight will aid in understanding USPAP. In fact, confusion as to what USPAP requires often centers around a misunderstanding of the definitions.

For example, the terms "appraisal" and "appraisal report" are often used synonymously. According to USPAP, an appraisal is an "act or process" of developing an opinion of value. An appraisal report is "any communication, written or oral, of an appraisal, appraisal review, or appraisal consulting service that is transmitted to the client upon completion of the assignment." Therefore, an appraisal is considered a mental process according to USPAP. One cannot mail an appraisal to a client. One would mail an appraisal report to a client.

The second part, the **PREAMBLE**, is a one-page mission statement that explains the goals of the USPAP document and describes its overall structure.

The third part consists of five **Rules**. These rules address how an appraiser must conduct himself while performing appraisal practice and also cover record keeping, jurisdictional issues, and others. These rules are extremely important to the practicing appraiser, and we will discuss them in detail once you have an understanding of the ten Standards.

## Standards

There are ten **Standards** within USPAP, and each Standard includes a series of Standards Rules. The **Standards Rules** specify what the appraiser must do.

The ten Standards cover the various appraisal disciplines and types of assignments. The type of assignment you are completing will determine which standard(s) you need to follow. When USPAP was developed, it was designed to encompass all appraisal disciplines, but in this text, we will focus on the sections of USPAP concerning real estate appraisal (Standards 1 & 2), since these are the ones that a beginning real estate appraiser will need to apply.

Dispersed throughout the DEFINITIONS, Rules, and Standards Rules in USPAP are Comments. **Comments** are extensions to these components of USPAP, providing interpretation, and establishing context and conditions for application. They are an integral part of USPAP and have the same weight as the component they address.

## Statements on Appraisal Standards

The purpose of the **Statements on Appraisal Standards** is to clarify, interpret, explain, or elaborate on a Rule or Standard. Statements have the full weight of a Standards Rule.

## Other Communications

In addition to developing, publishing, interpreting, and amending USPAP, the Appraisal Standards Board (ASB) issues what are called "Other Communications." Advisory Opinions, among other published materials, are considered to be "other communications". The ASB issues Advisory Opinions to illustrate the applicability of Standards in specific situations and to offer advice for the resolution of appraisal issues and problems. Although Advisory Opinions are for guidance only and are not considered an integral part of USPAP, the published volumes of USPAP contain Advisory Opinions for convenience of reference.

# Content

Now that you know a little about the structure of USPAP, we can examine each piece in more detail.

## Standards

The Standards are the meat of USPAP. They are essentially systematic instructions as to what to do when you are appraising something, and they give the requirements for reporting this appraisal to the client.

As written, USPAP encompasses real property appraisal (STANDARDS 1 and 2), appraisal review (STANDARD 3), appraisal consulting (STANDARDS 4 and 5), mass appraisal (STANDARD 6), personal property appraisal (STANDARDS 7 and 8), and business appraisal (STANDARDS 9 and 10).

### Real Property Appraisal, STANDARDS 1 and 2

As mentioned before, STANDARDS 1 and 2 are the ones that are most applicable for the beginning real estate appraiser.

#### STANDARD 1: Real Property Appraisal, Development

STANDARD 1 covers the requirements for developing a real estate appraisal. It identifies what an appraiser needs to consider when formulating his or her opinions and conclusions. This Standard also requires the appraiser not to "commit a substantial error of omission or commission", nor to "render appraisal services in a careless or negligent manner." This covers the first part of the appraisal process.

Example: Jane followed all of the steps in STANDARD 1 and found out the market value of the condo she was appraising. Her supervisor says, "Great! You developed your appraisal well; now communicate it to the client." Knowing USPAP, Jane goes to STANDARD 2 and finds that she has options as to how to report her appraisal to the client.

## *STANDARD 2: Real Property Appraisal, Reporting*

STANDARD 2 covers the requirements for reporting a real estate appraisal. When reporting a real estate appraisal, the appraiser must, among other things, "clearly and accurately set forth the appraisal in a manner that will not be misleading", and the report must "contain sufficient information to enable the intended users of the appraisal to understand the report properly".

A signed certification is required for all reports, and it is important to note that anyone who signs the certification takes full responsibility for the report.

**Figure 6.1** Standards 1 and 2 are the most important for beginning appraisers like Jane.

## *Report Options*

In addition to the rules that govern report clarity and content, STANDARD 2 also provides three reporting options: Self-Contained, Summary, and Restricted Use. The difference between the three types of reports is the level of detail, with the Self-Contained being the most detailed and the Restricted Use being the least detailed.

None of the reporting options is superior to another; they all must produce credible and reliable results. The reporting option chosen to communicate an appraisal depends on who the client is, the intended use, etc.

> Example: After following the steps outlined in STANDARD 1, Jane knows that the property is worth $250,000. After explaining the three reporting options to the client, they agreed to go with the Summary Appraisal Report. The information that must be included in a Summary Appraisal Report is outlined in STANDARD 2. Jane knows that she will be doing many summary appraisals in the future, so she has memorized the major things that have to be in every appraisal, such as the intended use, effective date, and date of the report.

**Figure 6.2** An appraiser must choose which of the three report
types best meets the client's needs.

It is also permissible to communicate a report orally. If that is done, the oral report must at least meet the requirements for a summary report.

The **Summary Appraisal Report** option is the most common as it fulfills the minimum requirements for lenders to process their loans. If the client does not specifically state the desired report format, the report should at least meet the requirements of a Summary Appraisal Report. The Uniform Residential Appraisal Report (URAR) is an example of a summary report and is probably the most widely used form.

The **Self-Contained Appraisal Report** option contains the most detailed information. An appraiser preparing this type of report would include significant details instead of just summarizing information.

> For example, when completing a Summary Report, an appraiser might simply check a box to state that the property values in the neighborhood are increasing. In a Self-Contained report, the appraiser would state the details that led to that conclusion.

The **Restricted Use Appraisal Report** option is unique, because with this option the client is the only one allowed to use the report. This option would not be used for the common lender appraisal. The information would be too limited for the lender to use in securing a loan. Remember, this option contains the fewest details.

## Appraisal Review, STANDARD 3

STANDARD 3 is the first standard to contain both the development and reporting requirements. It lists the steps an appraiser must follow to judge another appraiser's analysis, research, and conclusion.

STANDARD 3 gives the review appraiser the option to develop his or her own value opinion based on the information available when the original appraisal was completed.  If the review appraiser does so, the assignment becomes two-fold: a new appraisal as well as a review assignment.

## Appraisal Consulting, STANDARDS 4 and 5

**Appraisal consulting** is defined as the act or process of developing an analysis, recommendation, or opinion to solve a problem, where an opinion of value is a component of the analysis leading to the assignment results.  The main type of appraisal consulting assignment is a feasibility analysis.  A **feasibility analysis** is a study of the cost-benefit relationship of an economic endeavor.

> Example:  Jane is contacted by a developer who would like to know whether he should build homes or apartments.  Jane determines this is appraisal consulting because she is trying to solve a problem (whether to build single-family or multi-family dwellings).  However, she realizes that in order for it to be appraisal consulting, in addition to solving a problem, an opinion of value must be part of her assignment. She goes forth with the assignment and includes two opinions of value: one for the potential homes and another for the apartments.

## Mass Appraisal, STANDARD 6

A **mass appraisal** is appraising more than one property using standard computerized techniques (statistical analysis, regression, automated valuation models, etc.).  This standard contains technical terminology specific to this type of appraising which the beginning appraiser will not use.

**Figure 6.3**  Mass appraisals are primarily used for ad valorem tax appraisals.

Mass appraisal is used primarily for *ad valorem* tax appraisals. *Ad valorem* is a Latin phrase that means "according to value". Property taxes are an example of an *ad valorem* tax since the amount of tax paid is based on the value of the property being taxed.

## Personal Property, STANDARDS 7 and 8

**Personal property** includes all tangible assets that are not real property, such as jewelry, autos, boats, etc. A real estate appraisal license does not permit an appraiser to appraise this type of property. The appraiser must be fully competent in the type of property he or she is appraising (see the COMPETENCY RULE).

**Figure 6.4** Personal property.

## Business Appraisal, STANDARDS 9 and 10

These standards cover the appraisal of business entities including intangible assets, like logos or copyrights. The rules are similar to those for real property appraisal.

## Rules

In addition to the Standards, USPAP contains five rules: the ETHICS RULE, the COMPETENCY RULE, the SCOPE OF WORK RULE, the JURISDICTIONAL EXCEPTION RULE, and the SUPPLEMENTAL STANDARDS RULE. Regardless of the type of assignment, an appraiser must follow these five rules at all times.

# ETHICS RULE

The ETHICS RULE identifies the requirements for "integrity, impartiality, objectivity, independent judgment, and ethical conduct". The ETHICS RULE is divided into four sections: <u>Conduct</u>, <u>Management</u>, <u>Confidentiality</u>, and <u>Record Keeping</u>.

## *Conduct*

As its name implies, the <u>Conduct</u> section of the ETHICS RULE identifies issues regarding conduct. This section states that appraisers must be impartial and unbiased, and that they may not act as advocates. Acting as an advocate means you represent someone or have a bias towards a party or issue. This is forbidden under the <u>Conduct</u> section.

Many appraisers are also real estate salespeople, real estate brokers, lawyers, etc., and are required to be advocates as part of their non-appraisal duties. Advocacy is acceptable within those roles.

> Example: Appraiser Jane is also a licensed real estate broker. In her role as a broker, she is helping a client sell his home, and she is trying to get him the best possible price. In this situation, Jane is an advocate for her client. This would not be a violation of USPAP since Jane is acting as a broker, not an appraiser.

> In contrast, Jane is not an advocate for anyone when she is acting as an appraiser. Her role as an appraiser is to collect and analyze data to determine property value.

## *Management*

The <u>Management</u> section discusses the disclosure of certain fees and commissions, identifies prohibited compensation arrangements, and discusses certain prohibited advertising and solicitation issues. For example, paying a finders fee would qualify as something to disclose, and generally any undisclosed fees in connection with an assignment are a violation. This section also prohibits accepting an assignment where the fee is contingent on a predetermined or future result.

> Example: Appraiser John is contacted by Ray of ABC Loan Corporation. Ray engages John in an appraisal assignment for a property for which his company is lending $200,000. Ray tells John that he will pay John for his services as soon as the loan closes. This arrangement is not acceptable because John will have an incentive to make the loan close by providing Ray with the required property value.

### *Confidentiality*

The Confidentiality section of the ETHICS RULE states that the appraiser must protect the confidential nature of the appraiser-client relationship and is obligated to obey all confidentiality and privacy laws. The Confidentiality section also identifies to whom confidential information may be disclosed. USPAP defines confidential information as either information that is classified as confidential or private by law or regulation, or information that is identified by the client as confidential and is not available from any other source.

**Figure 6.5** Information that is identified as confidential by the client must be classified as such.

### *Record Keeping*

The Record Keeping section of the ETHICS RULE identifies the record-keeping requirements appraisers must follow. An appraiser must keep his workfiles for at least five years or two years after final disposition of any judicial proceeding involving the file. The appraiser's **workfile** for a particular assignment consists of all the documentation necessary to support the analyses, opinions, and conclusions conveyed in the appraisal report.

> Example: Appraiser John works for QC Appraisals and the firm has contracted with a third party to retain all of their files. After two years, he moves on to another company but is concerned about complying with the Record Keeping section of the ETHICS RULE. He refers to USPAP. He realizes that he must continue to retain his workfiles but finds out that USPAP does not require him to have custody of the files. He makes arrangements with QC Appraisals to access his files in the future.

## COMPETENCY RULE

While the ETHICS RULE covers ethical behavior on the part of appraisers, the COMPETENCY RULE and the three remaining Rules cover performance standards imposed upon appraisers.

The COMPETENCY RULE identifies requirements for experience and knowledge both when completing an appraisal and prior to accepting an appraisal assignment. When an appraiser is offered an assignment he or she is not competent to handle, this rule outlines the steps an appraiser should follow, which include speaking with experienced professionals to gain education, subcontracting experienced professionals to handle the aspects of the assignment that the appraiser is not competent in, or simply declining the assignment.

> Example: A client asks John to appraise a single-family residence (SFR) in a town where he has never previously appraised property. Following the COMPTETENCY RULE, John discloses his lack of geographical knowledge to the client and explains the steps he will take in order to gain competency. The client agrees to these terms. Appraiser John then speaks to several real estate brokers in the area in order to get a better understanding of that town's market.

## SCOPE OF WORK RULE

The SCOPE OF WORK RULE requires the appraiser to do all the analysis necessary to complete the appraisal assignment and provide reliable and credible results.

The SCOPE OF WORK RULE is also concerned with providing credible results. According to USPAP, the SCOPE OF WORK RULE requires the appraiser to:

1. identify the problem to be solved,
2. determine and perform the scope of work necessary to develop credible assignment results, and
3. disclose the scope of work in the report.

Each of these steps has its own section in the SCOPE OF WORK RULE. The sections are titled <u>Problem Identification</u>, <u>Scope of Work Acceptability</u>, and <u>Disclosure Obligations</u>.

The SCOPE OF WORK RULE gives the appraiser a lot of flexibility in determining the scope of work. However, this means that responsibility rests with the appraiser to do so correctly.

**Figure 6.5A** There are certain procedures to the SCOPE OF WORK RULE to complete appraisal assignments.

## JURISDICTIONAL EXCEPTION RULE

The JURISDICTIONAL EXCEPTION RULE recognizes that in some instances, portions of USPAP may be contrary to law or public policy. This rule serves as a severance clause; it voids any part of USPAP that contradicts local laws or public policy, while still preserving the remainder of USPAP. This means that the remainder of USPAP must still be followed even if one or more parts of USPAP are not valid in a particular jurisdiction.

If this is an issue in a particular assignment, the appraiser must disclose which part(s) of USPAP he did not follow and which legal authority justified that action. The appraiser must still follow all of USPAP's remaining requirements.

## SUPPLEMENTAL STANDARDS RULE

The SUPPLEMENTAL STANDARDS RULE provides the means for certain agencies to add to the requirements of USPAP. It allows for government agencies, government sponsored enterprises, or other entities that establish public policy to require more in an appraisal.

> Example: Appraiser John is contacted by the Federal National Mortgage Association (Fannie Mae) to do a real property appraisal. He follows the Rules and makes sure he meets all requirements of STANDARD 1 and reports his findings according to STANDARD 2.
>
> Fannie Mae returns his appraisal report stating that he did not meet their requirement of including photos of the subject property. John's rebuttal was that he did not violate USPAP because he followed the Rules and STANDARDS 1 and 2. He also claimed that STANDARD 2 did not require him to include photos. Unfortunately, John was in violation of USPAP, particularly the SUPPLEMENTAL STANDARDS RULE because Fannie Mae is a government agency that is able to add additional requirements like the inclusion of photographs.

# Practical Application

Not only is following USPAP a legal requirement, conscientious compliance with USPAP will help the appraiser avoid becoming involved in mortgage fraud or giving in to lender pressure.

**Fraud** is intentional deceit, the act of misleading someone in order to induce him or her to part with something of value. Historically, real estate fraud has been a white-collar crime that has gone largely unpunished. However, in recent years, the law has begun treating real estate fraud with more severity.

Appraisers most often are caught up in fraud when mortgages are involved, because **mortgage fraud** requires the help of an appraiser. The appraiser is usually not paid an additional fee and may not even be aware of the fraudulent situation.

Mortgage fraud is committed by individuals as well as organized crime rings. They operate by submitting exaggerated appraisals to lenders for inflated loan amounts. HUD has unknowingly granted many loans based on these fraudulent appraisals. These deceptive practices are accomplished by using:

- falsified credit applications.
- credit reports that are cleansed, altered and/or forged.
- altered or forged Verifications of Employment.
- altered and forged Certificates of Deposit.
- appraisals that are inflated by the appraiser, lender, or borrower.

The following excerpts from newspaper articles illustrate the problem of fraud:

---

RIVERSIDE, CA

Riverside Press Enterprise, 7/14/00

"Seven Southern California residents were charged Thursday with operating a mortgage-fraud ring in the Inland Empire that resulted in losses of more than $10 million and involved more than 100 homes. The U.S. attorney's office in Los Angeles said the defendants set up an imaginary credit union and used phony names, bank statements, appraisals, employment records, and other information to obtain home loans for amounts far greater than the homes were actually worth."

---

SCHENECTADY, NY

Albany Times Union, 3/15/01

"A couple was renting an apartment when their landlord offered to sell the building to them. The husband and wife are both mentally retarded and unable to read or write. The wife also suffers from cerebral palsy and uses a wheelchair. Their sole income is public assistance. They signed papers and bought their house for $65,000. They subsequently lost their Medicaid because they had obtained an asset, and had to default on their loan.

According to an independent appraisal done afterwards, the property was valued at $19,000. It had been on the market for 7 years and was listed 4 years prior for $46,000. Another lawsuit claims the same landlord sold another property for $60,000, which was later appraised for $24,500.

The lawsuits allege that the landlord conspired with an appraisal agency and a local mortgage broker to inflate the value of the properties and then teamed up with a lender to offer loans on the inflated real estate. The lender sold the loan almost immediately. The attorney said 'the bigger the appraisal, the bigger the mortgage; the bigger the mortgage, the bigger the fee for 'flipping' the loan and assigning it to another lender.'"

**Figure 6.6** With more frequency, appraisers are lured
into committing mortgage fraud.

## Common Fraud Schemes

The following three examples are some of the most common fraud
schemes being implemented these days.

### Flipping

**Flipping** occurs when a person buys a property at one price and
quickly sells it to another at an inflated price.  The second sale may
occur on the same day (double escrow), or take place a few days later.

Often the second buyer is an accomplice of the seller and is in on the
fraud.  The sale appears to be an arm's-length transaction, but the
inflated sales price is designed to defraud the lender.

Many times the flipper (the first buyer) provides comparable sales for
the appraisal.  Many of the comparables are also fraudulent and may be
properties that were also flipped.  Appraisers who are hired for these
deals are usually from another area and do not completely confirm the
sales, as we will discuss later in this chapter.  Occasionally the appraiser is in on the scam, but usually the appraiser receives the regular fee
and inadvertently helps in the transaction by providing an appraisal
that is over value, either by not following the rules of appraisal or by
inattention to detail.

### Packed Sales

A **packed sale** charges excessive points, fees, and interest rates to
unsuspecting buyers.  Elders, minorities, and subprime borrowers
are common targets.  This fraud may be accomplished without an
appraiser.

## Bogus Sales

A **bogus sale** occurs when a lender asks an appraiser to inflate his or her estimate of value for a property to a certain degree, providing justification for a higher selling price.

These sales often occur between a bogus seller and another person or group conspiring with the seller. In effect, the seller is selling the property to himself or his fellow conspirators. The increased selling price is equal to the amount that would be paid by a buyer for a down payment. The lender can then offer the buyer a zero down payment, 100% financing deal, and ultimately collect more interest from the buyer. Of course, none of this is possible without an appraisal to justify the higher price.

## Lender Pressure

Pressure from lenders is an on-going problem in real estate appraisal. **Lender pressure** involves the lender directly or indirectly pressuring the appraiser to hit a certain number.

Sometimes the pressure is obvious. For example, it is not unusual for a lender to fax over an appraisal request that specifically states the desired value along with a comment like, "If the value isn't there, stop and notify us." Accepting this assignment could be a violation of USPAP, since the lender is basically making payment for the assignment contingent upon hitting a pre-determined value.

The pressure does not end there, however. Picture a conscientious appraiser who accepts an assignment from a lender who "suggests" that in order for the loan to fund, the appraisal needs to reach a minimum of $335,000. The appraiser scrupulously completes the assignment and arrives at a value of $305,000. Then the appraiser receives a call strongly questioning his conclusions. The appraiser stands by his work, but realizes that it is unlikely that the lender will use him for future jobs. Appraisers feel the pressure when they begin to lose jobs because of their unwillingness to give the lenders the value they want.

In these cases, the lender is not out to explicitly defraud a buyer or seller. In fact, some lenders may actually believe they are assisting the borrowers. Most homeowners will not complain either. Homeowners love to be told that the value of their property has increased. However, inflated appraisals can lead to situations where property owners and investors discover that they are "upside-down" on their loan, that is they owe more than their property is actually worth. In fact, this practice has a ripple effect that inflates property values across the board in a neighborhood. Another appraiser could use an inflated refinance appraisal as a comparable for a sale the following day, which would inflate the sale price of the transaction.

In theory, the practice goes against the lender's best interests. If a borrower defaults, lenders need to be able to recoup their losses, so they need to have an accurate estimate of the property value before they make a loan. However, with the practice of selling loans on the secondary mortgage market, the risk is transferred to secondary market institutions like Freddie Mac. For today's lender, it boils down to this equation: the greater quantity of loans at the highest possible loan value equals a higher profit for the mortgage lender.

**Figure 6.7** Appraisers may feel as if their hands were tied because of lender pressure to meet predetermined values.

## Fraud Prevention

USPAP contains several sections that can help you avoid potentially fraudulent situations. In particular, the **COMPETENCY RULE** states that an appraiser should not perform an appraisal outside of his or her market or geographic area without taking the steps necessary to learn the important nuances of the different market. **Standards Rules 1-4** and **1-5** prevent an appraiser from using a flip sale as a true comparable sale and **Standards Rule 1-2** requires the appraiser to look out for and eliminate bogus sales, whether they are the subject or the comparables.

The US Department of Housing and Urban Development (HUD) also has some important guidelines in its valuation directive. HUD's valuation directive states:

"The appraiser must verify all market and comparable information used in the appraisal process and is accountable for any information presented as 'fact' used to develop the subject property's value estimate. Verification ensures that the information is accurate and meaningful and provides the appraiser with a firm understanding of market motivations and trends. The goal of the verification process is to ensure that only information that accurately reflects current market conditions and trends is presented and that meaningful conclusions can be reached from this information.

During the verification process, it is necessary for the appraiser to gain an understanding of the motivations surrounding the sale in order to:

- determine if the sale is arm's length and not distressed.

- understand current market conditions that influence value...."

Verification involves much more than checking with two sources and providing a document number. Verification involves interviewing someone directly involved in the transaction to determine the buyer and seller's motivations, the conditions of the sale, whether there was consideration given outside of escrow, and whether the transaction was truly at arm's length.

The **HUD valuation directive** is used by lawyers in civil and criminal cases to prove the appraiser failed to exercise due diligence. (This is true even if the transaction is not for an FHA loan.) Properly verifying the sale is a time-consuming step, but it is a critical part of good appraisal practice.

## Common Violations

The most common violations according to California's Office of Real Estate Appraisers are:

- failure to state which reporting option was used.

- failure to address scope of work.

- failure to analyze current agreement of sales or sales history.

- failure to identify client, intended use, and intended users of a report.

- failure to incorporate license number with signature on appraisal reports.

- failure to comply with the COMPETENCY RULE.

- inaccurate or insufficient property descriptions.

### Problems with the Cost Approach
- No support for cost per square foot
- Minimal support for depreciation estimates

### Problems with the Sales Comparison Approach
- Using generic discussion and minimal support for adjustments
- Inconsistency of adjustments among comparable sales
- Using out-of-neighborhood comparable sales when sales are available within
- Failure to use MLS as a data source

### Problems with the Income Capitalization Approach
- Generic discussion of rental comparables, no discussion of relative comparability
- Lack of due diligence in extracting GRM (Gross Rent Multiplier), and misuse of actual vs. projected rents

# Case Study

Steve is a Certified Residential Appraiser who appraises single-family residences and small income properties. Most of his work is done around his city. A year ago, he wanted to diversify his business and began soliciting work from attorneys who practice estate planning. One attorney asked Steve to perform a series of estate appraisals in Riverside, a city 40 miles away. The properties to be appraised were six duplexes and two triplexes that were all approximately 30 years old.

Steve was informed that the properties were going to be sold, and that the attorney wanted a high value for his clients. Steve stated the values could not be changed, but he would keep the request in mind, as there is considerable room in the typical range of value for a high "point estimate" of value. He agreed to perform the appraisals.

The attorney informed Steve that the property owner would meet him at the sites and would also bring some recent comparable sales, because Steve did not have any sources of comps in Riverside. Steve also requested rental data for the units. The owner agreed to bring the information, but pointed out that the rents were below market because many rents had not been raised to current market rates.

The property owner furnished Steve with information on nine comparable sales, including the sales price and the recorder's document numbers. The sales prices ranged from $280,000 to $320,000 for the duplexes, and $295,000 to $330,000 for the triplexes. No rental data was supplied for the comparables.

Steve performed the appraisals primarily using the sales comparison approach. However, he did not research the sales histories of the comparables because the data was too hard to obtain. Steve did not belong to the local Multiple Listing Service (MLS) and did not know any local real estate agents. He considered the cost approach, but did not use it because the few land comparables were all over 30 years old. He also considered using the income approach, but stated in the report that he could not find many comparable rents, and those he did find were about the same as the subject. He concluded that the whole area seemed to be renting below market, and that the income approach was not a reliable indicator of value.

He valued the duplexes at an average of $310,000 and the triplexes at an average of $325,000. Steve received a good fee for the appraisals and did not give the assignment another thought for over a year. Then, to his dismay, a group of Federal Fraud Investigators who had a Certified General Appraiser on their team contacted him to talk about his appraisals.

The investigators discovered that, although the comparable sales had document numbers, they were the result of flips. The buyers purchased the properties for around $160,000 and then "sold" them to an accomplice for the higher figures, through either a double escrow or an escrow a short time later. The fraud occurred when FHA loans were secured based on Steve's appraisals. After the money was taken from the FHA loans, the buyers left town and the properties went into default.

Steve was eventually charged with real estate fraud and providing fraudulent appraisals. His defense was that he did not know anything about any fraud and was only doing his job as an appraiser. Unfortunately, for Steve, this defense was not adequate. Although he was not knowingly involved in the fraud, he was culpable because of his failure to exercise reasonable care and because he did not follow USPAP or verify the sales as required in the HUD valuation directive.

Reasonable care requires the appraiser to meet the steps in STANDARD 1 of USPAP, which dictates how the appraisal is performed and determines the completeness of the research performed. Failure to verify and investigate data breaches the duty of care when facts are present that would alert a reasonable person to possible misrepresentations.

An appraiser cannot satisfy the duty of reasonable care by blindly relying on representations made by others. The appraiser must perform his own research and adequately verify information about comparable sales. In Steve's case, there was adequate information that he could have easily discovered, which makes his neglect even more difficult to justify.

To protect yourself from becoming involved in, or suspected of fraud, consider the following suggestions:

- Do not give in to lender pressures. Do your appraisals in a professional manner. Forget the idea that one has to "hit the number" if sales and other data do not support the conclusion of value.

- Verify everything. According to The Appraisal Foundation, "...to ensure the reliability of value conclusions derived by applying the sales comparison approach, the appraiser must verify the market data obtained and fully understand the behavioral characteristics of the buyers and sellers involved in property transactions." In addition, Standards Rule 1-4 of USPAP states "In developing a real property appraisal, an appraiser must collect, verify, and analyze all information applicable to the appraisal problem, given the scope of work identified in accordance with SR 1-2(f)."

# Summary

USPAP will permeate the appraiser's professional life, as it is comprised of the minimum standards that licensed appraisers are required to follow. USPAP is not limited to real property either, but covers all aspects of professional appraising, including personal property and business assets.

As a whole, USPAP helps to ensure ethical and accurate appraisals and provides the appraiser with guidance in developing and reporting each appraisal assignment. Following USPAP conscientiously and consistently will keep the appraiser from inadvertently becoming involved in real estate fraud.

# Review Exercises

## *Matching Exercise*

**Instructions:** Look up the meaning of the terms in the Glossary, then write the letter of the matching term on the blank line before its definition. Answers are in Appendix B.

### Terms

A. appraisal consulting

B. bogus sale

C. Comments

D. COMPETENCY RULE

E. ETHICS RULE

F. flipping

G. lender pressure

H. packed sale

I. personal property

J. PREAMBLE

K. Restricted Use Appraisal Report

L. Self-Contained Appraisal Report

M. Statements on Appraisal Standards

N. Summary Appraisal Report

O. USPAP

### Definitions

1. _____ The recognized and accepted standards of appraisal practice in the United States.

2. _____ Extensions of the USPAP that provide interpretation and establish context and conditions for application.

3. _____ They clarify, interpret, explain, or elaborate on a Rule or Standard.

4. _____ The report option that contains the most detailed information.

5. _____ The report option that prohibits any other user than the client.

6. _____ The act or process of developing an analysis, recommendation, or opinion to solve a problem, where an opinion of value is a component of the analysis leading to the assignment results.

7. _____ All tangible assets that are not real property.

8. _____ Buying a property at one price and quickly selling it to another at an inflated price.

9. _____ Charging excessive points, fees, and interest rates to unsuspecting buyers.

10. _____ States that an appraiser should not perform an appraisal outside of his or her market without taking the steps necessary to learn the important nuances of the different market.

## *Multiple Choice Questions*

**Instructions:** Circle your response and go to Appendix B to read the complete explanation for each question.

1. USPAP contains many sections.  Which of the following is **not** technically considered part of the USPAP document?
    a.  DEFINITIONS
    b.  Advisory Opinions
    c.  Statements on Appraisal Standards
    d.  Comments

2. Why is it necessary for the PREAMBLE, DEFINITIONS, and Rules sections to precede the Standards?
    a.  Because they are required for understanding the Standards
    b.  Because they define a Standard
    c.  Because they explain the difference between Standards and Standards Rules
    d.  None of the above

3. Regarding the Standards, which of the following statements is most correct?
    a.  USPAP covers real estate appraisal only.
    b.  Some standards deal with aspects of appraisal that are not real estate related.
    c.  Most beginning appraisers need only concern themselves with STANDARDS 1-5.
    d.  The comments found within the Standards are less than the Standards themselves.

4. Which of the following illustrates the applicability of Standards in specific situations and offers advice from the ASB for the resolution of appraisal issues and problems?

    a. Comments

    b. Statements on Appraisal Standards

    c. Advisory Opinions

    d. Rules

5. Every appraisal discipline encompassed within the USPAP has two Standards associated with it **except** two. Which two appraisal disciplines are these?

    a. Appraisal Review and Appraisal Consulting

    b. Mass Appraisal and Appraisal Review

    c. Business Appraisal and Personal Property Appraisal

    d. Real Property Appraisal and Personal Property Appraisal

6. Which of the following is a requirement of STANDARD 2: Real Property Appraisal, Reporting?

    a. An appraiser must not commit a substantial error of omission or commission.

    b. An appraiser must not render appraisal services in a careless or negligent manner.

    c. An appraiser must clearly and accurately set forth the appraisal in a manner that will not be misleading.

    d. An appraiser must be impartial and unbiased, and may not act as an advocate.

7. Which of the following is **not** a report option recognized by the USPAP?

    a. Limited-Use Appraisal Report

    b. Self-Contained Appraisal Report

    c. Restricted-Use Appraisal Report

    d. Summary Appraisal Report

8. When an appraiser is contracted to develop an opinion regarding another real estate appraiser's work as well as develop his or her own value opinion of the subject property, this assignment is:

    a. a review appraisal.

    b. an appraisal consulting assignment.

    c. a mass appraisal.

    d. a review appraisal and a real estate appraisal.

9. Bill is hired to appraise a residence and all of its contents, including appliances and furniture. Which of the following is true?
    a. This appraisal assignment includes personal property.
    b. Bill should contact an experienced appraiser if Bill has never appraised furniture and appliances before.
    c. This assignment is considered a mass appraisal because it encompasses several different disciplines.
    d. Both a. and b.

10. A lender hired Nora to appraise Jim's retail store because Jim is using the store as collateral for taking out a loan to purchase a warehouse. This is an example of a:
    a. business appraisal.
    b. personal property appraisal.
    c. real property appraisal.
    d. none of the above

11. The ETHICS RULE is divided into four subsections. These sections are called:
    a. Conduct, Management, Confidentiality, and Competency.
    b. Conduct, Management, Competency, and Record Keeping.
    c. Confidentiality, Management, Competency, and Record Keeping.
    d. Conduct, Management, Confidentiality, and Record Keeping.

12. According to the Conduct section of the ETHICS RULE, when is advocacy acceptable?
    a. When acting as an appraiser
    b. When working in non-appraisal related professions
    c. When buying or selling property for a client
    d. Both b. and c.

13. Kelly accepts an assignment that stipulates she will be paid if the appraised value comes in above $300,000. This assignment is:
    a. permitted within the context of USPAP.
    b. prohibited by the Management Section of the ETHICS RULE.
    c. permitted if the fees are disclosed properly.
    d. prohibited by the JURISDICTIONAL EXCEPTION RULE.

14. Ezekiel completed an appraisal for Popular Bank on December 13th of 2005. According to the record keeping section, when is the soonest he will be able to dispose of the files?

    a. 12/13/2010
    b. 12/13/2007
    c. 12/13/2012
    d. 12/13/2010 assuming there are no judicial proceedings involving this appraisal.

15. Which of the following is **not** a scheme that may entangle an appraiser in mortgage fraud?

    a. Lender pressure
    b. Flipping
    c. Packaged sale
    d. Bogus sale

# Chapter 7

# The Appraisal Process

## Introduction

Professional appraisers have developed an orderly, systematic method to arrive at an estimate of value. This method is known as the **appraisal process** or the **valuation process**.

The appraisal process can be described in a variety of ways. In this book, there are five main steps that will be discussed.

1. Define the problem.
2. Determine the scope of work.
3. Collect, verify and analyze all relevant information.
4. Reconcile the information analyzed.
5. Report the assignment results.

This chapter compares a competitive market analysis with an appraisal report and introduces the appraisal process. In the rest of the textbook, each step of the appraisal process will be explored in detail.

## Learning Objectives

After reading this chapter, you will be able to:

- identify the steps in the appraisal process.

- identify key differences between a competitive market analysis and an appraisal report.

- recognize the key parts of defining the problem.

- recognize the types of data appraisers collect and analyze.

- identify the approaches to value.

- recognize the definition of reconciliation and its role in the appraisal process.

# Competitive Market Analysis vs. Appraisal Report

Appraisers are not the only professionals who value property. Valuation services are services that pertain to some aspect of property value whether those services are performed by an appraiser or by someone else.

Typically, a homeowner's first experience with any type of valuation service occurs when he or she sees a competitive market analysis (CMA). A **competitive market analysis** is a comparison analysis that real estate brokers use to help determine an appropriate listing price for the seller's house. A CMA may also be referred to as a **broker price opinion (BPO)**. CMAs are sometimes described as "informal appraisals".

Although they appear similar on the surface, there are many differences between a competitive market analysis and an appraisal report. The central difference is that appraisers must follow a more stringent process in preparing an appraisal report than real estate brokers do when preparing a competitive market analysis. Brokers collect and analyze data, apply a version of the sales comparison approach, and report the results to their client. However, they do not follow any of the other steps in the process.

The goal of a competitive market analysis is to determine an appropriate listing price for a property. An appraiser's goal is to find the value of the property. While a CMA can also serve as "ballpark" estimate of value, an appraisal gives a carefully researched and documented opinion of value.

**Figure 7.1** Appraisals differ significantly from CMAs in that appraisers carefully research and document their opinion of value.

An even bigger difference can be seen when looking at the parties who create these two different reports. For a real estate agent, creating a CMA is only a small part of the job. For an appraiser, creating an appraisal report *is* the job. Also, since the real estate agent's pay is tied to the price of the house, it could be argued that it is in the agent's best interest to come up with a high number. Appraisers are expected to give an unbiased and impartial analysis. In addition, USPAP's Competency Rule requires appraisers, before accepting an assignment, to disclose any lack of knowledge and/or experience that would keep them from competently completing the appraisal assignment.

## Competitive Market Analysis

To create a CMA, the broker finds recently sold houses that are similar to the seller's house in location, style, and amenities. These similar sales are called **comparable sales** or more simply **comps**. If there are any significant differences between the seller's house and the comps, the broker adjusts the selling prices of those properties to derive a market value range and an appropriate list price for the house. The CMA includes a summary of the features of the seller's house, photos of the house, and photos of the comparable houses.

A CMA usually includes data on current listings, recently sold houses, and listings that expired recently. This helps the seller to see what other people are asking and what other people have received. They can also see which homes were left unsold because the asking price was too high.

Once the seller and the broker have determined together an appropriate listing price for a property, the broker markets the property for the seller to find a buyer. Potential buyers look at the property, and eventually one buyer presents an offer that is accepted by the seller. Overjoyed, the buyer goes to a lender to obtain financing for the purchase. This is where the appraisal comes in.

# Appraisal Report

An appraiser gives his or her opinion of value in an appraisal report. The appraisal report will state or summarize the information that the appraiser has researched and analyzed. The appraiser's **workfile** for a particular assignment consists of all the documentation necessary to support the analyses, opinions, and conclusions conveyed in the appraisal report.

Lenders use an appraisal to determine how much a house is worth. Based on that amount, they then determine how much they are willing to loan. This protects the lender in case of default by the borrower. If a house is priced significantly higher than its appraised value, it can be very difficult to get a loan, since lenders do not want to lend on a house that is priced higher than it is worth. A buyer should think twice before purchasing a home if its price is higher than its appraised value. The buyer may not be able to resell it without losing money.

Each appraiser follows specific steps to create an appraisal report. The basic steps of the appraisal process include the following:

1. **Define the problem.** This includes identifying the client and other intended users, the intended use of the appraiser's opinions and conclusions, the type and definition of the value sought, and the effective date of the appraiser's opinions and conclusions. The appraiser must also identify the property, relevant characteristics of the property, and any special or unusual conditions involved in the assignment.

2. **Determine the scope of work.** The **scope of work** in an assignment is essentially the amount of work that is done. Scope of work applies to the type and extent of research done and the type and extent of analysis applied. While defining the problem, the appraiser gathers the information needed to determine the scope of work.

3. **Collect, verify, and analyze all relevant information.** This includes collecting, verifying, and analyzing both general and specific data. For example, appraisers gather general information about any social, economic, physical, or governmental forces that may impact the value sought. They also collect specific data about the subject property and the comparables.

    This step also includes applying the relevant approach(es) to value. There are three approaches to finding value:

    The **Sales Comparison Approach** is the most straightforward of the three approaches, and it is typically the most accurate approach when appraising a residential property. Using the sales comparison approach, the appraiser compares the subject property with other, similar homes that have recently sold.

By adjusting for any differences in size, amenities, etc., the appraiser is able to determine the value of the subject property.

The **Cost Approach** values a property by determining what it would cost to replace the improvements, subtracting any deterioration or depreciation from that, and then adding the value of the site.  **Improvements** are buildings or other structures that are permanently attached to the land.  A **site** is land that has been prepared for use with grading, utilities, and access.

The third approach, the **Income Approach**, is most accurate for valuing income-producing properties.   Using the income approach, an appraiser estimates what an investor would pay for a property based on the income it produces.

Not every approach will apply to every assignment, so the appraiser must determine which approach(es) apply.  Once the appraiser has determined this, he or she must analyze the data using the appropriate approach(es).

4. **Reconcile the information analyzed.**   Since the three approaches will not give the same exact value, the appraiser must reconcile the quantity of data available, the quality of the data analyzed, and the suitability of the approaches used to determine the most accurate final value estimate.

5. **Report the assignment results.**   Once the appraiser has determined the final value estimate, he or she is ready to report to the client.

This structured, detailed, and systematic process is what sets appraisal apart from other valuation services.

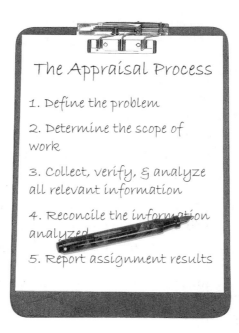

**Figure 7.2** The appraisal process is made up of five basic steps.

# Define the Problem

Defining the appraisal problem is the first step in the appraisal process. Appraisers need to identify the essential elements of the problem to be solved.

There are a variety of elements appraisers need to identify as part of defining the problem. This step includes identifying what property they are appraising, for whom they are appraising the property, and why they are appraising the property. They also need to identify relevant physical, legal, and economic characteristics of the property being appraised, the effective date of the appraisal, and any conditions or assumptions that need to be considered in the assignment.

In other words, to define the problem, appraisers need to identify:

- the client and other intended user(s).
- the intended use of the appraisal.
- the type of value to be estimated.
- the date of the value estimate.
- the subject property and its relevant characteristics.
- any unusual assignment conditions.

## Identify the Client and Intended Users

One of the first things an appraiser needs to do when beginning an appraisal assignment is to identify the client. The **client** is the party, or parties, that hire the appraiser for a specific assignment.

> For example, in a typical appraisal assignment, appraisers are hired by the lender, not the buyer or seller, so the lender is the client.

Identification of a client in an assignment is necessary since the appraiser must know to whom he or she has a responsibility. In the course of completing an assignment, appraisers will often obtain information that is confidential in nature. Appraisers need to protect the legitimate interests of their clients in regard to the use of otherwise confidential information.

Often clients order an appraisal with the intention that other parties will rely upon the report generated by the appraiser. Parties intending to use an appraisal are called **intended users** by USPAP. Appraisers need to identify all intended users of their appraisal reports in order to make sure their reports are meaningful to those parties.

For example, a mortgage broker may order an appraisal with the intention of giving that appraisal, along with other documentation, to a wholesale lender. The wholesale lender will use the appraisal to help determine whether or not they will make a loan on the property. The mortgage broker is the client, and the wholesale lender is an intended user.

## Identify the Intended Use

Along with identifying the client and the intended users, the appraiser must identify the intended use of the appraisal. This lets the appraiser know why he or she is being hired to appraise the property.

Appraisals are requested for many different reasons. They are often performed in order to obtain financing for a real estate purchase. Appraisals are also done in order to settle estates and for use in lawsuits. They may be requested for property tax purposes, condemnation purposes, or for a variety of other reasons.

Appraisers need to identify the intended use of an appraisal in order to know the amount of detail needed in the appraisal report and what types of information should be gathered.

## Identify the Type of Value to Be Estimated

Appraisers need to know which type of value they are being asked to analyze in an appraisal assignment. The type of value provides the context upon which a value estimate is based. To simply state that a property is worth $250,000 is relatively meaningless. That could be market value, insurable value, investment value or possibly even "sentimental" value. As explored in Chapter 4, there are many types of value that may be identified in an appraisal assignment and appraisers need to be aware of the kind of value they are to estimate.

Within each type of value there are also differing definitions.

For example, most of the time, appraisers are requested to estimate the market value of a property. Market value usually centers on the concept of *most probable price*. Sometimes however, the definition of market value may be based upon the concept of *highest* price. This slight change in wording in the definition could have a significant effect upon the final value estimate.

Different kinds of value or different definitions of value produce different value estimates. In order to produce a value estimate meaningful to the client, appraisers need to identify the exact type and definition of value they are using in the appraisal assignment.

# Identify the Date of the Value Estimate

Appraisers need to know the effective date of the appraisal. The effective date of an appraisal can be a present, past, or future date. Think of an appraisal as being a snapshot in time, like a photograph. If you were to view a snapshot of yourself at age 10, that picture would appear much different than at age 20, 30 or 40. Estimating the value of a property as of April 14, 1975 would produce a very different value for that property than if the value were based upon current market expectations.

In most instances, the effective date of an appraisal is the date it is inspected by the appraiser. In this situation, the effective date for the value is the present. In some instances however, the effective date of value is at some point in the past, or may even be at some point in the future.

Retrospective appraisals look at the value of a property at a point of time in the past.

> For example, when appraising properties for estate and probate purposes, appraisers are typically requested to appraise a property as of the date of death of the property owner. It is not unusual for an appraiser to be contacted by an estate attorney six months or even a year after the owner died. In instances such as this, the appraiser would not be analyzing the market as it currently is, but as it was at some point in the past.

A retrospective appraisal could also be used to find the value of a house that has since burned down.

A prospective appraisal looks at the value of a property at a future point of time. Appraisers are sometimes asked to perform a prospective appraisal.

> For example, properties that are fully rented are usually more valuable than properties that are vacant. New, high-rise office buildings typically have few tenants upon completion of construction. It may take years to fill up that building with tenants. Clients may wish to identify what that high-rise office building may be worth once it has become filled with tenants at some point in the future.

**Figure 7.3**  Appraisals are snapshots in time.  Retrospective appraisals examine a past value and prospective appraisals examine a property's future value.

Other times, an appraiser might be asked to determine if houses should be built for sale in a particular area.  Part of the appraiser's work would be to value the houses as if they were finished.  This is a common request from lenders who are providing construction loans.

## Identify the Subject Property

The property being appraised is called the **subject property.** Appraisers obviously need to know what property they are appraising, but identifying the property that is the subject of an assignment is not always as easy as one may think.  Simply knowing the address of the subject property may not be enough to identify the subject property. Sometimes the property to be appraised is vacant land and has no address.  In other instances, the subject of an assignment has only one address but includes multiple distinct parcels of land.  Sometimes the owners do not have legal descriptions to their properties but they know that it is the "third property from the corner on the north side of the street".

Some appraisers have mistakenly appraised the wrong subject property because it was incorrectly identified to them.  While the appraiser needs to include enough information in the appraisal report to identify the subject, clients may not always be clear in communicating this information to the appraiser.  The appraiser needs to be careful to avoid confusion in this area.

## Identify Any Special Assignment Conditions

In some instances, there are certain conditions and assumptions that need to be identified in an assignment.  These conditions and assumptions significantly affect how appraisers perform their work.  A **hypothetical condition** is defined in USPAP as "that which is contrary to what exists but is supposed for the purpose of analysis".  An

**extraordinary assumption** is defined as "an assumption, directly related to a specific assignment, which, if found to be false, could alter the appraiser's opinions or conclusions." These two types of limiting conditions may occur together or separately.

> For example, Appraiser John was asked to appraise a property that is currently under construction. In this assignment, he is appraising the property as if it were complete even though it is not. In fact, the building only exists on blueprints. For all intents and purposes, he is appraising an imaginary structure. This is an example of a hypothetical condition. This kind of analysis is usually required to assist a lender in deciding whether or not to make a construction loan.

In other cases, appraisers need to make assumptions where they do not know all the facts.

> For example, Appraiser Jane was asked to appraise a property that is located near another property that has hazardous waste contamination. There is no information available indicating whether or not the subject property is also contaminated. If there is no evidence to the contrary, she may base her appraisal on the fact that the subject is not adversely affected. This is an example of an extraordinary assumption.

Hypothetical conditions and extraordinary assumptions are covered in more detail in the 15-hour USPAP course that is required for individuals who want to become licensed appraisers.

# Determine the Scope of Work

It is necessary to identify these elements in order to determine the scope of work in the assignment. The scope of work in an assignment is essentially the amount of work that is done. Scope of work applies to the type and extent of research done and the type and extent of analysis applied.

> For example, more in-depth research, verification, and analysis are usually required of appraisers appraising homes for litigation purposes than is required of those appraising the same kind of property for loan purposes.

This is because the needs of clients in these instances are different. The scope of work varies from property to property and from assignment to assignment in the following ways:

- the degree to which property is inspected or identified.

- the extent of research into physical or economic factors that could affect the property.

- the extent of data research.
- the type and extent of analysis applied to arrive at opinions or conclusions.

Some appraisals merely require a drive-by visual confirmation that the subject exists. Others require an in-depth, painstaking analysis of the property's operating statement as well as comparable properties' operating statements.

**Figure 7.4** Depending on the scope of work, an appraisal may require only a drive-by property verification or it may require a detailed interior inspection.

## Collect, Verify, and Analyze All Relevant Information

Once the appraiser has defined the appraisal problem and determined the scope of work, he or she needs to collect and analyze data applicable to that assignment. In the process of determining the scope of work, the appraiser will be able to identify the amount and kind of data needed in the appraisal assignment.

The amount and kind of data needed to appraise a property varies by assignment and property type. The amount and kind of data an appraiser would gather to appraise a high-rise office building would be drastically different from the data required to estimate the value of a single-family home. In Chapters 8–13, we will discuss collecting and analyzing the data needed when applying each of the different approaches.

## Collecting Data

Data is collected and gathered from many sources. When collecting data for an appraisal assignment, appraisers start from a broad, market-wide base and gradually focus more and more on the subject.

They gather general data regarding items affecting the subject's market. This includes general economic, demographic, environmental, and sociological information affecting markets and trends in specific real estate markets. Next, they collect information on local area and neighborhood employment, income levels, trends, access, and convenience of location. Finally, they gather specific data for both the subject and comparable properties.

Appraisers analyze all these levels of data because most factors that influence a property's value occur outside of the subject property itself.

> For example, if Sally's house is exactly the same as Joe's, Joe's house may still be worth more if it is located in a different neighborhood.

## General Data Sources

A substantial amount of data is collected and published by federal, state, and local government agencies.

National data can be obtained from government publications, newspapers, and magazines. Federal government agencies such as the U.S. Census Bureau and the U.S. Department of Commerce provide a wealth of demographic and employment information.

Regional data (metropolitan areas such as San Francisco Bay, Houston-Sugar Land-Baytown, or the Florida Gold Coast) can be gathered from monthly bank summaries, regional planning commissions, and government agencies. State offices such as transportation agencies, departments of housing and community development, and departments of commerce and economic development may provide information regarding future development, employment trends, income levels, etc.

## Local Data Sources

Community data (town or city) can be obtained from the Chamber of Commerce, City Planning Commission, city government agencies, banks, and real estate boards.

Neighborhood data can be obtained from personal inspections, real estate agents, or area builders.  The appraiser notices the age and appearance of the neighborhood; any negative influences such as physical or social hazards (rundown buildings, evidence of criminal activity); evidence of future development; and proximity to schools, businesses, recreation, and transportation.

Local agencies such as building departments, zoning departments, planning and land use departments, health departments, property tax assessor's offices, county recorder's offices, chambers of commerce, etc., provide a wealth of data regarding local economies and trends, as well as information on both the subject property and comparable sales. Among other things, these local agencies provide information regarding such items as building permits, property zoning information, property tax information, environmental issues, sewage disposal information, and recording information.  Information obtained from these sources is often free.  However, appraisers may need to travel to the offices to obtain needed information.

## Specific Data Sources

Appraisers must also gather data about the specific property being appraised.  In addition, specific data must be collected and analyzed for sales and listing prices of comparable properties in the area.

When determining the value of a particular house, appraisers consider the general condition and age of the house, the size of the building and the surrounding land, the location of the house (including its view or any other remarkable features), the features of the home (e.g. number of bedrooms and bathrooms), any major improvements or additions to the property, and any features that are especially sought after (like a fireplace or a skylight).

Appraisers gather the same kinds of information on the comparable sales or rental comps used in an assignment by either a personal inspection or a drive-by inspection from the street.

Appraisers can verify the legal description of the subject property and comparable properties from county records.  They can also double-check the age of the buildings and other information regarding improvements at the tax assessor's office or city building department.

**Figure 7.5** Useful data sources include the Internet, newspapers, and other publications.

Sales information is usually obtained from data sources such a local multiple listing service (MLS), real estate agents and brokers, property buyers and sellers, county assessor's offices, title companies, on-site sales offices, private data providers offering both online and published sales data, and the appraiser's own database.

| **Review — Information Gathered for Appraisals** | | |
|---|---|---|
| **General Data** | **Local Data** | **Specific Data** |
| Country | Community | Improvements (buildings) |
| State | Neighborhood | Lot |
| Region | | Location |

## Verifying Data

Once all the data has been obtained by the appraiser, it is checked for both accuracy and reliability. Some data sources are updated rarely and may be out of date. Sometimes information obtained from one data provider conflicts with data obtained from another source. Appraisers need to make a determination regarding which data sources are the most reliable and which should be given more credence.

An appraiser may also find that, in the course of uncovering one piece of information relevant to an assignment, other items are uncovered that may require additional research.

For example, upon verifying building permits for a property, an appraiser may find a permit for environmental remediation. This permit would indicate that property probably had some kind of adverse environmental influence. Additional research by the appraiser would then be needed to identify the problem, the work performed, and its possible effect on value.

The scope of work may need to be increased when additional information is uncovered in the course of an assignment.

# Analyzing Data

With all of the pertinent facts at hand, the appraiser needs to analyze how the information applies to the value of the subject property. There are three commonly accepted methods used to value real estate. They are the sales comparison approach, the cost approach, and the income approach. Each of these approaches to value has strengths and weaknesses in any given assignment.

Often one or two of these approaches are not performed in an assignment since they may not be applicable to that particular assignment. Even if all three approaches to value are applicable in an assignment, there is usually one that has the greatest significance in the valuation problem.

The "how to" details for each of these approaches will be covered later in this textbook. Here, we will cover a basic definition of the approaches.

## Sales Comparison Approach

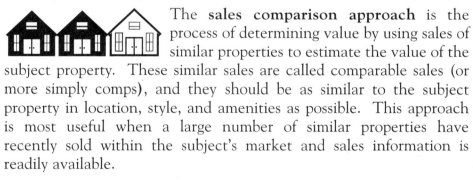 The **sales comparison approach** is the process of determining value by using sales of similar properties to estimate the value of the subject property. These similar sales are called comparable sales (or more simply comps), and they should be as similar to the subject property in location, style, and amenities as possible. This approach is most useful when a large number of similar properties have recently sold within the subject's market and sales information is readily available.

The sales comparison approach uses the comparable property's sales price as an indicator of its market value. For the sales price to be an accurate indicator, the sale must have been an arm's-length transaction. An **arm's-length transaction** is one in which neither the buyer nor the seller is acting under duress, the property is on the market for a reasonable length of time, and the buyer and the seller both have reasonable knowledge of the property's assets and defects. If there is any indication that the sale was not an arm's-length transaction, it should not be used as a comp.

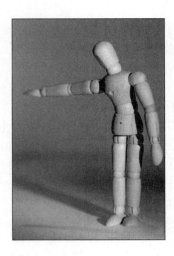

**Figure 7.6** An arm's-length transaction is one in which neither the buyer
nor the seller is acting under duress, the property is on the market for
a reasonable length of time, and the buyer and the seller both have
reasonable knowledge of the property's assets and defects.

Sometimes it is easiest to understand arm's-length transactions by
looking at what they are not. A sale is not an arm's-length transaction
if it has been forced for any reason or if there is some other motivation
that would affect the selling price. Foreclosures, tax sales, and estate
liquidations are all forced sales. Transactions that are motivated by
the need to purchase adjoining property or the need to sell property
before the owner is transferred would not be arm's-length transactions.
In addition, if the buyer and seller are related individuals or corporations, the appraiser must assume that the relationship affected
the terms of the sale and prevented it from being an arm's-length
transaction.

Once the appraiser has found similar properties that sold under normal
circumstances, the next step is to collect data on the comparable
properties. Typical areas of comparison include: property rights being
conveyed, financing terms, neighborhood location, square footage,
number of bedrooms and bathrooms, age, and architectural style.

**Figure 7.7** Adjustments are made to comparable sales to account
for any significant differences.

The appraiser gathers information on both the subject property and
the comps and notes the differences. Then, the appraiser analyzes
each comparable property in turn. He or she starts with the sales price

of the comparable property and adjusts it for any differences to arrive at the market value for the subject property. The more similar a particular comp is to the subject, the stronger it is as an indicator of value for that subject property.

## Cost Approach

As its name implies, the **cost approach** is the process of determining value by adding up the costs involved. This process is based upon the premise that the value of a property is equal to the cost of the land plus the cost of actually building the improvements. When using this approach on buildings that are not brand new, the appraiser also has to subtract the amount of depreciation that has occurred. **Depreciation** is a loss in value from any cause.

The starting point of this approach is to identify the value of the land component of a property. Typically, recent comparable sales of vacant land are found and are used as indicators for the value of the subject's site. This portion of the cost approach is similar to the sales comparison analysis in that the comparable land sales are adjusted to reflect the differences between those properties and the subject property. Differences such as size, zoning, location, access to utilities, and view are items attributable to a site that appraisers would consider in the adjustment process.

Once the site value has been estimated, the cost to replace or reproduce the existing improvements is estimated. This information can be obtained from a variety of sources. Depreciation is then deducted from the cost estimated for the subject's improvements. The depreciated cost of the improvements is added to the land value to get the value estimate for the property.

**Figure 7.8** When using the cost approach, the value of a new building is equal to its construction cost.

The cost approach is used most often for appraising new buildings and special-purpose or unique structures. This is because depreciation on a new building is relatively easy to determine, so the cost approach is at its most accurate. Also, it is difficult to find comparable sales for buildings that are unique or one-of-a-kind, such as a church, fire station, or hospital, so the cost approach is used with these types of buildings.

Occasionally, the cost approach is the only one an appraiser can use even with residential property. If there have been no recent sales (such as during a recession or when interest rates are very high), there will be no comparables for the sales comparison approach. If the subject is not an income-producing property, the income approach cannot be used. So, the cost approach is a reliable way for an appraiser to determine the value of a property when other options are not available.

There are situations where the cost approach is not reliable, however. The cost approach is impractical with older buildings because of the difficulty in estimating depreciation. Also, because the cost approach calculates value by adding the value of the land to the depreciated value of the improvements, this approach may not apply to properties with special ownership interests.

For example, condominium owners own their particular unit and have the right to use common areas. The land is not sold with the condo, so condominiums cannot be valued using the cost approach.

## Income Approach

 The **income approach** is the process of determining value based on the amount of income that the property is expected to produce. The income approach to value is based upon the premise that the more income a property generates for its owner, the more valuable it is. This approach recognizes that there is a direct relationship between the value of a property and the income it is expected to produce.

This method is used to estimate the value of income-producing property, like apartment and office buildings. Single-family residences usually do not generate income (unless the property is being rented), and most single-family residential properties are not purchased for their income-producing potential. Even though an appraiser may use the income approach to value when appraising a single-family residence, it would typically be given little weight in the final estimate of value. It would be necessary, however, for the appraiser to mention this in the appraisal report.

The income approach to value uses mathematical techniques to identify the present value of future benefits from ownership of a property. There are two simple calculations that are the basis of this approach. They are:

$$\text{Gross Income} \times \text{Gross Income Multiplier} = \text{Value}$$

and

$$\text{Net Operating Income} \div \text{Capitalization Rate} = \text{Value}$$

The first calculation is called a gross income multiplier calculation. **Gross income** is total annual income received before any expenses are deducted. Sale prices of comparable properties are divided by the gross income they generate to provide a multiplier. The multiplier indicated by the comparable sales is multiplied by the subject property's gross income to provide a value estimate.

Using the second calculation typically involves more detailed and in-depth analysis on the part of the appraiser. Net operating income (NOI) is used instead of gross income. **Net operating income** is gross income minus operating expenses. The net income a property is forecasted to generate over time is divided by a capitalization rate to produce a value estimate. A **capitalization rate** (cap rate) is the appraiser's estimate of the rate of return a property will produce on the owner's investment. The cap rate is used to determine the present value of the property's future earnings. Choosing a capitalization rate is the hardest part for appraisers using the income approach.

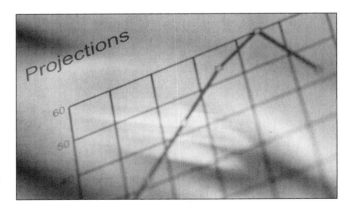

**Figure 7.9** The income approach relies on the anticipation of future income.

To use this approach, an appraiser needs to collect data that will enable him or her to estimate the subject's potential gross income, the loss in potential gross income due to expected vacancy and collection losses, anticipated operating expenses, the pattern of a property's anticipated income, the anticipated resale value of a property at some point in the future, and competitive investments available to potential investors in real estate.

# Reconcile the Information Analyzed

The next step in the valuation process is reconciliation of the various approaches to value into a final value estimate. **Reconciliation** is the process of analyzing the values obtained using the different approaches in order to determine the final estimate for the property in question. During the reconciliation process, the appraiser reviews his or her work and considers: 1) the scope of work, 2) the quantity and quality of the data collected in each approach, 3) the inherent strengths and weaknesses of each approach, and 4) the relevance of each approach to the subject property and market behavior.

Many times an appraiser will use all three methods to arrive at the market value of a property. In most appraisals, all three approaches will have something to add. Each method is used independently to reach an estimated value.

Among the various approaches to value employed in an assignment, the reconciliation process is used to identify which one provides the strongest and most reliable indication of value. In some instances, one or two of the approaches may not provide strong or reliable indicators of value.

> For example, since most single-family residential properties are not purchased for their income-producing potential, an appraiser estimating the market value of a single-family residence would typically give little weight to the income approach in the final estimate of value. In this case, the sales comparison approach would be given the most consideration in determining the final estimate of value.

Reconciliation can also be used within a particular approach. When reconciling within the various approaches, the appraiser makes a determination which data provides the strongest and most reliable indication of value. The data providing the strongest and most reliable indication of value would therefore be given most consideration in a particular approach.

> For example, an appraiser using the sales comparison approach may find that, of the comparables used, Comparable Sale #1 is overall most similar to the subject property. Therefore, that sale would be given the most weight in determining the value of the subject property using this particular approach.

The reconciliation process depends upon the nature of the subject property, the approaches to value that were used in the assignment, and the reliability of the value estimates indicated by the various approaches to value.

Sometimes the appraiser gets to this final step and finds it difficult to state the value. This happens when the appraiser is missing a vital piece of information, and — deep down — knows it. When this happens, it is time to stop the procedure, and go back to the point where the information is missing. This may require the appraiser to make more inquiries or another trip to the field.

**Figure 7.10**  Part of the reconciliation process is determining if the three approaches are applicable to the subject.

## Report the Assignment Results

Once the appraiser has completed formulating his or her opinions and conclusions, the final task is to communicate those assignment results to the client. This is accomplished by presenting either a written or oral report.

The appraisal report is the expression of the appraiser's service to the client. It usually includes the data considered and analyzed, the methods and approaches used, and the reasoning that led the final value estimate of the property. Proper reporting allows the reader to understand the appraisal problem and the scope of work performed. This includes the data considered in formulating the opinion of value and the reasoning employed by the appraiser in estimating the final estimate of value for the subject.

The detail and style of report is determined when the appraiser and client first meet to discuss the client's needs and decide on the scope of work. While most clients require written reports, there are some instances, such as courtroom testimony, where an oral report is requested.

Depending upon the needs of the client, the intended use of the appraisal, and the kind of property being appraised, appraisal reports may go into significant detail and include hundreds of pages of documentation and analysis. In other instances, the appraiser may only need to summarize his or her opinions and conclusions on a preprinted form. There are even situations where the needs of the client and the requirements of the assignment are such that the report must only contain certain minimal information.

## Summary

Professional appraisers have developed an orderly systematic method called the **appraisal process** that they follow to arrive at an **estimate of value**. This orderly, systematic process is one of the reasons that an appraisal is different from other types of valuation services like a **competitive market analysis**.

The first step of the appraisal process is to **define the problem**. To do so, the appraiser determines the client, the intended use, and the type of value to be estimated, the date of the value estimate, the subject property, and any special assignment conditions.

The next step in the appraisal process is to **determine the scope of work**. The scope of work varies from property to property and from assignment to assignment.

The third step in the process is to **collect, verify, and analyze the data.** Significant quantities of data must be collected from different sources, whether it is general data, local data, or specific data. The data must be properly analyzed in order for the appraiser to come to an accurate value conclusion. The appraiser analyzes the data using the three **approaches to value**. The appraiser can use any combination of three different approaches to value the subject, depending on which approaches are applicable to the assignment.

If more than one approach was used, step four is for the appraiser to **reconcile** the different values produced by each approach. When only one approach is used, the appraiser still needs to verify and review the appropriateness, the accuracy, and the quantity of evidence, as well as ascertain that the problem originally defined has been solved and that the predetermined scope of work has been met.

Finally, after a supportable conclusion has been reached, step five is to convey the appraiser's findings to the client, usually by way of a **written appraisal report.**

# Review Exercises

## *Matching Exercise*

**Instructions:** Look up the meaning of the terms in the Glossary, then write the letter of the matching term on the blank line before its definition. Answers are in Appendix B.

### Terms

A. appraisal process

B. arm's-length transaction

C. broker price opinion (BPO)

D. capitalization rate

E. client

F. comparable sales (comps)

G. competitive market analysis (CMA)

H. cost approach

I. depreciation

J. extraordinary assumption

K. gross rent

L. hypothetical condition

M. improvements

N. income approach

O. intended users

P. net operating income (NOI)

Q. prospective appraisal

R. reconciliation

S. retrospective appraisal

T. sales comparison approach

U. scope of work

V. site

W. subject property

X. valuation process

Y. workfile

### Definitions

1. _____ An orderly, systematic method to arrive at an estimate of value.

2. _____ Another term for the appraisal process.

3. _____ Consists of all the documentation necessary to support the analyses, opinions, and conclusions conveyed in the appraisal report.

4. _____ Land that has been prepared for use with grading, utilities, and access.

5. _____ Buildings or other structures that are permanently attached to the land.

6. _____ The type and extent of research done and the type and extent of analysis applied in an appraisal assignment.

7. _____ The party, or parties, that hire the appraiser for a specific assignment.

8. _____ The property being appraised.

9. _____ Appraisals that look at the value of a property at a future point of time.

10. _____ That which is contrary to what exists but is supposed for the purpose of analysis.

11. _____ An assumption, directly related to a specific assignment, which, if found to be false, could alter the appraiser's opinions or conclusions.

12. _____ The process of determining value by using sales of similar properties to estimate the value of the subject property.

13. _____ Similar properties used in the sales comparison approach to estimate the value of the subject property.

14. _____ A transaction where neither the buyer nor the seller is acting under duress, the property is on the market for a reasonable length of time, and the buyer and the seller both have reasonable knowledge of the property's assets and defects.

15. _____ The process of determining value by adding up the costs involved.

16. _____ A loss in value from any cause.

17. _____ Gross income minus operating expenses.

18. _____ The process of analyzing the values obtained using the different approaches in order to determine the final estimate for the property in question.

## *Multiple Choice Questions*

**Instructions:** Circle your response and go to Appendix B to read the complete explanation for each question.

1. Regarding valuations services, CMAs, and BPOs, which of the following statements are true?
    a. Valuation services are performed by appraisers and brokers perform CMAs.
    b. CMAs are different from BPOs in that only brokers can perform BPOs.
    c. CMAs, BPOs, and appraisals are all types of valuation services.
    d. CMAs, BPOs, appraisals, and valuation services are all one in the same.

2. When using CMAs, if there are significant differences between the seller's house and the comps, a broker will:

    a. adjust the selling prices of the comparable properties.

    b. adjust the selling price of the subject property.

    c. do both of the above.

    d. do neither of the above.

3. Which practice commonly used by appraisers is similar to a Broker's Price Opinion?

    a. Cost Approach

    b. Defining the problem

    c. Competitive Market Analysis

    d. Sales Comparison Approach

4. If a house is priced _____ than the appraised value, lenders may _____.

    a. lower, not fund the loan

    b. higher, not fund the loan

    c. same as, not fund the loan

    d. lower, require mortgage insurance

5. Identifying the client, the definition of value, and the effective date are all included in which step of the appraisal process?

    a. Identify the assignment

    b. Determine the scope of work

    c. Define the problem

    d. Reconciliation

6. Social forces are an example of:

    a. general data.

    b. economic influence.

    c. specific data.

    d. physical influence.

7. Parties intending to use an appraisal report are known as:

    a. clients.

    b. intentional users.

    c. customers.

    d. intended users.

8. Cory was commissioned to appraise a house in a tax dispute on July 11, 2006. The dispute was over how much property tax the owner should have paid in November, 1999. The completed report was submitted to the tax authority on August 1, 2006 and used in a court proceeding on August 16, 2006. Which of the following is the effective date of the appraisal?

    a. July 11, 2006

    b. November, 1999

    c. August 1, 2006

    d. August 16, 2006

9. If Bill hires Frank to appraise the value of vacant land as if it were fully developed with an apartment building, this would be considered a(n):

    a. effective appraisal.

    b. retrospective appraisal.

    c. prospective appraisal.

    d. objective appraisal.

10. Jaime, an insurance appraiser is hired to appraise a residence that recently burned down. When Jaime appraises the home as if it were still in existence, she is using:

    a. a hypothetical condition.

    b. a retrospective appraisal.

    c. a limiting condition.

    d. all of the above.

11. When verifying data, should an appraiser encounter conflicting information, he or she must:

    a. determine which source is more reliable and give it more credence.

    b. ignore both pieces of data.

    c. count both pieces of information without explanation.

    d. count both pieces of information with brief explanation.

12. Which of the following is important when choosing comps for sales comparison analysis?

    a. All comparable sales should be arm's-length transactions.

    b. All comparable sales should be similar in location to the subject.

    c. All comparable sales should be similar in style to the subject.

    d. All of the above are true statements.

13. Which of the following is **not** a typical application for the cost approach?
    a.  Post office, library, hospital
    b.  40-year old tract home
    c.  Brand new office complex
    d.  Frank Lloyd Wright-inspired mansion

14. Which of the following is the formula used when calculating the income approach?
    a.  Gross income multiplied by net income multiplier equals value.
    b.  Net operating income multiplied by cap rate equals value.
    c.  Net operating income divided by cap rate equals value.
    d.  Net income multiplied by net income multiplier equals value.

15. When should an appraiser use reconciliation in the appraisal process?
    a.  In every instance
    b.  Only when two or more approaches to value are used
    c.  Only when there is conflicting information
    d.  When he or she is having difficulty expressing a property value

# Chapter
# 8

# Highest and Best Use and Site Valuation

## Introduction

In the appraisal process, the first step of data collection and analysis is to determine the highest and best use of the subject property. Closely related to this step is determining the value of the land or site separately from the value of any improvements. In this chapter, both of these different, but interrelated, ideas will be discussed.

Appraisers often need to determine the value of a site. There are many different reasons for this. Sometimes the subject property is a vacant lot. At other times, the subject property has improvements, but the appraiser needs to determine the land value separately in order to apply the cost approach or the income approach's building residual technique. Site value may also be needed in appraisals done for taxation purposes or condemnation proceedings.

This chapter focuses on site value, and the most important factor that influences site value. The highest and best use of a particular site has a direct effect on its value and on the property's overall value.

Not every aspect of site value is covered in this chapter. The methods used to estimate the value of the land component of a property are discussed in Chapter 12. This chapter covers in detail the different contributing factors that influence land value. These factors include the aforementioned highest and best use, physical aspects such as size, shape, soil and topography, as well as off-site factors like utilities and access.

Keep in mind that the information discussed here is applicable in assignments where vacant land is being appraised, as well as in situations where the land has been developed and built upon, but the value of the land needs to be identified separately.

## Learning Objectives

After reading this chapter you will be able to:

- recognize the tests of highest and best use.
- describe the highest and best use considerations of which appraisers need to be aware.
- identify the definition of a site.
- discuss the different types of lots.
- recognize factors that typically influence lot value.

# Highest and Best Use

The concept of highest and best use is one of the most important and least understood principles in real estate. The highest and best use of a property, more than anything else, is what determines its value. **Highest and best use** is defined as the use, from among reasonably probable and adequately supported alternative uses, that meets these four tests. To be the highest and best use, the use must be:

- physically possible.
- legally permitted.
- economically feasible.
- maximally productive.

When appraising a property, an appraiser first has to determine highest and best use. He or she does this with a site analysis and by applying the four tests. Appraisers cannot value land if they do not understand how the land is best used. They apply the four tests in two situations:

- vacant land (or improved property as if it were vacant).
- improved property.

The same process of analysis applies to each of these situations.  The following examples demonstrate how important it is for the appraiser to analyze highest and best use in order to determine the property's value, whether the property is vacant or improved.

**Example 1:**

In one community, many vacant lots flanked a major east-west thorough-fare.  These were large parcels—5, 10, even 20 acre lots.  Gradually, as the local and regional economies picked up, the lots sold and major corporations began building corporate headquarters and large office complexes on these lots.  The last vacant lot in this area produced lettuce up until last year.  It is now being developed into a similar office complex.

Due to the growing economy and changing demands, these lots have the capacity to produce income.  It is no longer prudent to leave them vacant.  Moreover, it is not in the highest and best use of the land to grow lettuce.  Growing lettuce produced some income, but a more profitable use is now possible.  Building corporate headquarters and office complexes represents that highest and best use.  When the economy is growing and demand is present, the use of land will transition to produce a greater net income.

**Example 2:**

A similar situation occurred in a community located in Southern California.  Beachfront land had been leased to a mobile-home park for a period of 50 years.  When the lease expired, the owners of the land thought that, with a booming economy and the desirable location of the land, perhaps there would be a higher and better use.  They did their research and went through all of the legal processes with the city council and public participation.  They are now developing plans for a hotel resort community that will include major hotels, condominiums and a park.  Leasing to a mobile-home park produced decent income, but if the current plans are approved, the new use of the land will produce more.

**Example 3:**

As stated earlier, land value is strongly influenced by its highest and best use and therefore its value needs to be estimated under this use.  To illustrate this point, assume a site is currently improved with only a single-family dwelling; however, the zoning allows ten apartment units.  The value of this land would, in most instances, be less if it were valued as a single-family lot than if it was valued as an apartment site.  A typical buyer or seller would consider its potential as an apartment site when making their buying or selling decisions.

**Example 4:**

Improvements are valued according to how they contribute to (or detract from) the value of the land. If a property is not already at its highest and best use, a building may need to be renovated. In other situations, a building may need to be torn down to make way for a replacement that would make the property more valuable.

Consider an older, run-down, single-family house in an area zoned for commercial use. If there is a greater demand for residential property than for commercial, it most likely will benefit the owner to remodel the house and make it a rental. In fact, if residential demand is great enough, the highest and best use might be to expand the rental into a duplex to create more income. Then, as commercial demand increases, converting the house into office space may produce the best revenue opportunity. However eventually, if demand for conventional retail buildings becomes high enough, demolition and reconstruction become the most prudent alternative.

Sometimes highest and best use is easy to determine. Other times, it is not so clear. Through the four tests, a property's highest and best use is determined. Much of the highest and best use analysis is a study of cost/benefit relationships. Each of the tests will yield or eliminate alternative uses that may be possible but not plausible because of the costs associated with transforming the property.

**Figure 8.1** A property's value may benefit from renovation, remodeling, or even demolition of the improvements.

## Physically Possible

Every site has physical characteristics that determine its highest and best use. Some properties have value-enhancing views and frontages like beach or lake properties. Other properties are limited by poor access, steep topography, or unstable soil. The site may have poor drainage and require an expensive type of septic system. It may be in the path of urban growth or in the middle of nowhere.

Sometimes you have to balance the positive and negative attributes. For example, an ocean front property may have geologic problems that require special foundation work, but the value of the ocean frontage may be worth the expense.

**Figure 8.2** The first test for highest and best use is to verify if the use is physically possible.

## Legally Permitted

Current zoning and other land use regulations normally define **legally permitted** uses. As discussed in Chapter 3, zoning is the legal way a municipality or local government regulates the use of privately owned real property. These restrictions govern property use (commercial or residential applications), height restrictions for buildings, signage height and size restrictions, and parcel and lot sizes. They also regulate setbacks for fences and buildings from property lines, as well as the number of units that are allowed to be built for building within an area.

There are many different types of zoning laws and classifications. A **zoning law** is used to execute master plans and control the mix of properties in a particular area. Most local governments include organizations that are responsible for planning and zoning. Generally, the Planning Commission develops a general plan and the City Council/ Board of Supervisors adopts and implements the general plan.

Zoning is not the only legal barrier an appraiser needs to consider. There are also easements and CC&Rs that may limit the property's legal uses. For example, the developer may have included a condition that prohibits the sale of alcohol on the land. This would certainly preclude a liquor store or bar as the highest and best use of the subject property.

Often, if zoning prevents a certain use, the owner can petition for a zoning change. However, this is costly, so the appraiser must analyze and determine the cost versus the benefit of implementing these changes.

**Figure 8.3**   Local zoning laws will determine if a current or proposed use is legally permissible.

## Non-Conforming Uses and Use Permits

**Legally non-conforming uses** are those that become **grandfathered** in when new zoning regulations are adopted. Legally nonconforming uses can change the highest and best use and often produce a higher value than what the current zoning ordinance will allow.

> For example, James opens a convenience store in an area zoned for mixed residential and commercial use. A few years later, the city council rezones the neighborhood to allow only single-family homes. The store is now a non-conforming use. However, James is allowed to continue operating his business as a legally non-conforming use.

Most zoning ordinances allow non-conforming uses to continue until they fall out of use for a period (usually one year) or are destroyed by fire, disaster, or neglect.

Typically, the local zoning authority is allowed to issue **conditional use permits** or **variances**. These permit certain uses that are not otherwise allowed in a certain zoning district, but which are beneficial to the community. A city may grant conditional use permits to daycare centers, parking lots, and churches in residential zones.

Amy wants to have a pool installed in her backyard. However, her city has a zoning ordinance that requires swimming pools in R1 residential zones to be set back at least 25 feet from the property lines. The dimensions of Amy's property do not provide adequate space to place a pool 25 feet from the rear property line. Amy can apply for a variance permitting her to install the pool only 20 feet from the property line.

## Interim Use

**Interim use** is a short-term and temporary use of a property until it is ready for its expected highest and best use.

For example, if a ten-acre lettuce field gets rezoned R-1, the highest and best use would be single-family homes. However, there may already be hundreds of lots on the market and little or no demand for them. Until the market can support more single-family homes, its interim use will remain a lettuce field.

# Economically Feasible

**Economic feasibility** is based on supply and demand. This often requires extensive market research and the accurate prediction of trends. This entails finding out who the competition and the potential buyers, tenants, and customers are.

Franchise operations such as McDonald's and Starbucks have made a science out of location studies. They analyze traffic patterns and study community age and income profiles. In this way, they have been able to successfully predict financial feasibility and effectively operate many different locations within a concentrated area.

**Figure 8.4** The test of economic feasibility is highly dependent on current supply and demand trends.

## Maximally Productive

The **maximally productive use** is the one that produces the greatest return on investment.  For income property, figuring out the highest rate of return might involve studying several alternatives and design configurations.

> For example, it has been determined that the highest and best use for a site is an apartment complex.  Determining its maximum production would include distinguishing the appropriate mix of one, two, and three bedroom apartments the property can sustain; whether or not to have laundry facilities or hookups built into each apartment; garages or centralized parking, etc.

**Figure 8.5** A residence located in a commercial district most likely will not be maximally profitable.

Even when building or remodeling a house, there are ways to determine what will produce the highest value.  If the owner decides to build a four-car garage in a neighborhood typically consisting of two-car garages, it may be considered an over-improvement, even if it serves his personal interests.  If he under-improves, like eliminating a garage in favor of a large garden, he may not be creating the highest value either.

> ### Review — The four tests of highest and best use
> **P** hysically possible
>
> **L** egally permitted
>
> **E** conomically feasible
>
> **M** aximally productive

## Application of the Tests

The convention is that these criteria usually be considered sequentially, as a "process of elimination".  A use may be economically feasible but this is irrelevant if it is physically impossible or legally prohibited. Only when there is a possibility that one of the prior, unacceptable conditions can be changed is it appropriate to proceed with the analysis. For example, if current zoning does not permit a potential highest and best use, but there is a possibility that the zoning can be changed, the proposed use can be considered in that case.

The appraiser applies the four tests in order.

1. Physically possible

2. Legally permitted

3. Economically feasible

4. Maximally productive

Essentially, physically possible and legally permitted aspects are considered together, but for the sake of semantics, physically possible considerations edge out legally permitted ones as the primary consideration in the sequence. This is because if a potential use were contrary to the laws of nature, considering the other three criteria would be futile. Legally permitted uses are checked next. Many zoning laws will limit the property's uses to a few or even one use, thus eliminating multiple options. Remaining possibilities are then analyzed for economic feasibility and finally maximum production.

> For example, Joe is appraising a vacant lot located in a commercial district. He immediately supposes that some variety of commercial use would most likely meet the highest and best use for this property. However, upon investigation, he discovers that it is zoned non-commercial, which leaves only agricultural, residential, and industrial possibilities. Because of the nature of the soil on the lot, an agricultural use is not physically viable, not without expensive soil cleaning or importation, the cost for which far exceeds the benefit. Appraiser Joe also determines that any type of residential use would not be economically feasible because there would be significant loss in demand due to its commercial surroundings. After analyzing the surrounding area, he deduces that local businesses have a need for a storage and distribution facility and concludes that a warehouse would yield the best production of the remaining industrial options for the site, as there is virtually no competition for this type of use.

## Non-Economic Highest and Best Use

Analyzing the property on as many levels as possible will lead to the most thorough and sound result possible. There is one other highest and best use consideration an appraiser may need to consider. There is a controversy within the appraisal profession and conservation movement regarding something termed **non-economic highest and**

**best use**.  According to this belief, sometimes the highest and best use does not necessarily produce the most income, but instead takes into account the contribution of a specific use to the community and community developmental goals.  These uses include parks, greenbelts, open spaces, wetlands, wildlife habitats, and other types of natural lands.

**Figure 8.6**  Land that is at a non-economic highest
and best use is for community enjoyment.

While the support for this type of highest and best use is on the rise, there exist no widely accepted methods of estimating non-economic value.  Current appraisal practice requires that properties are appraised based on their conventional economic use (residential, commercial, industrial, etc.) regardless of their conservation potential.

## Inspecting a Site

When the appraiser shows up at the subject property, it must first be determined if it is a tract or a site.  A **tract** is a piece of land in an unimproved state, i.e. it does not have utilities, sewer lines, etc.  It is not ready to build on.  Once a tract has been prepared for construction, it becomes a **site**.

**Figure 8.7** Once a tract has been prepared to be built upon it becomes a site.

The appraiser must be able to describe the site in the report based on its physical characteristics and any neighborhood characteristics that affect the site.  It is also important for the appraiser to be able to distinguish between favorable and unfavorable characteristics and to determine their affect on the value of the property.

## Size

The size of a site is a key factor in determining its value because the size influences how the site may be used.  For example, zoning laws may require that a property meet certain size requirements before development of the land can commence.

Appraisers can often find the size of the appraisal site in official legal documents.  Acres or square feet make up the measurements for size in appraisal.

However, legal documents do not report the usable area of the site, which is more important than gross area.  **Usable area** is the portion of the site that is suitable for building.  Some areas of the site may not be usable because the soil or topography cannot support buildings.  Usable areas can be limited also by zoning regulations such as setback requirements.

If the size of a particular piece of land limits its utility, the limitation can be overcome in various ways.

## Assemblage and Plottage

Land is often worth more as one entirely incorporated and unified unit than it is as a number of divided individual parcels. **Assemblage** is the process of combining two or more small sites to form a larger one. This usually happens with income or commercial properties in order to create a larger building, with higher income, on the larger site.

> For example, imagine a major farming enterprise. To obtain more efficient production, they would seek to control as many adjacent acres as possible. As they acquire more lots to add to their farmland, the total of the entire body as a single site exceeds the value of the individual lots that comprise it.

**Plottage** refers to the value that is added as the result of this process. It is a term that is often used interchangeably with assemblage. For clarification between the two, examine the following.

> Each of the separately owned business in one block of a major metropolitan area is viable and generates average to good income. When the lots are appraised as if vacant and divided, they are valued at approximately $400,000 total. A developer wanting to build a large luxury hotel with conference rooms and other business related facilities hires an appraiser to perform a feasibility study for such a venture. In the study, the appraiser finds that lots similar to the size of the combined individual parcels range in value from $500,000 and upwards. If the developer does indeed buy out the current proprietors and assembles the lots, the plottage would be $100,000 minimum.

Assemblage does not always result in higher land values. Sometimes, the assembled lot will result in a lower value than the combined values of the separate lots.

## Excess Land

**Excess land** is surplus land beyond that which is needed to support the property's highest and best use. Excess land can be dividable or undividable. With residential properties, taking a large parcel and subdividing it into smaller, more marketable parcels is a common example of changing the size of a site in order to increase its overall value. However, if the land cannot be divided, the excess land often has a separate highest and best use.

> For example, if a four-acre lot is zoned single family residential and is undividable, then it can only support one house, with maybe a back house, and will have over three acres of excess. If the owner cannot petition to make it a divisible parcel, which would entail rezoning, this excess might be best used as a grove or in some other agricultural means.

# Shape

After estimating the size of the parcel of land, the **shape** of it comes into play. The appraiser should note its shape in a geometric form if possible. The shape of a site can affect both its usable area and its overall utility. Lots are described based on their shape and placement.

A **cul-de-sac** is sometimes known as a dead-end street. It is a street that has only one way in and out, but the lot may be oddly pie-shaped if it is on the turn-around section of the street. They are desirable for residential use because of the privacy and quiet. The lack of access makes them less desirable for industrial or commercial purposes.

A **corner lot** is found at the intersection of two streets. It may be desirable for a gas station or convenience store because of its accessibility and visibility, but may also be noisy and expensive to maintain because of the increased frontage. Usually, a corner lot is less desirable for residential use due to lack of privacy, noise, and potential pollution from multiple sides.

A **key lot**, so named because it resembles a key fitting into a lock, is surrounded by the back yards of other lots. It is the least desirable because of the lack of privacy and visibility.

A **T-intersection lot** is one that is fronted head-on by a street. The noise and glare from headlights detract from this type of lot for residences, but these same influences may make it desirable for commercial use.

An **interior lot** is one that is surrounded by other lots, with frontage on the street. It is the most common type of lot and may be desirable or not, depending on other factors.

A **flag lot** looks like a flag on a pole. The lot is usually behind another lot fronting a main street. The pole represents the access to the lot. This type of lot has access and visibility problems.

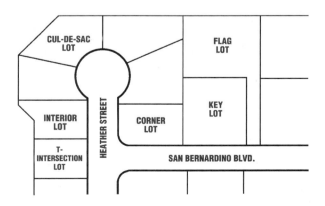

**Figure 8.8** Diagram of lot types.

## Soil and Topography

The ability of the soil to support the weight of the building is largely determined by the composition of the soil. There is a great deal of variation in soil composition in different parts of the country, and the appraiser must be familiar with the local conditions. Soil formation is a product of time, climate, and the characteristics of the native plants and animals.

The **topography** of a parcel of land refers to its contours and features. Terms like flat, hilly, rolling, and sloping (moderately or severely) all describe the site's topography. Topography also includes items like creek beds or swamps that may be on the parcel of land.

The site's topography can affect its value. A site may decrease in value if the irregular topography decreases the usable area or makes it difficult for construction. However, sometimes irregularities can actually increase property value. For example, a home built on hilly land may have a good view of the surrounding area that can significantly increase the value of the home.

## Drainage and Flood Hazards

The site's soil and its topography affect the site's drainage. **Drainage** refers to natural processes or artificial pipes and drains that remove water and moisture from land. Drainage helps to keep water from building up on a parcel of land and flooding a home.

The appraiser should be aware of hazardous drainage conditions not only for the inspected parcel but also for other neighboring land that may drain onto the inspected parcel. The **Federal Emergency Management Agency (FEMA)** is a government agency that is involved with all the different aspects of emergency management from preparation to recovery and prevention. As a part of its work, FEMA identifies flood-prone areas called **Special Flood Hazard Areas**. If the subject property is within a flood hazard zone, it needs to be noted in the appraisal report.

## Grading

Before structures of any variety are placed on a lot, the land must be prepared. This includes grading, building retaining walls and foundations, as well as landscaping for aesthetic appearance.

**Grade** is the slope of the surface of the ground expressed as a percentage. An example would be a 2% grade, where the slope climbs 2 feet for every 100 feet of horizontal distance. Sometimes the level or elevation of the ground has to be changed or altered using bladed machines that literally scrape the earth in a process known as **grading**.

Grading is important so that water runs away from the foundation and the structure itself. If the pitch or slope of the soil is toward the house, basements or crawlspaces may flood during storms, and damage to the foundation may occur over time.

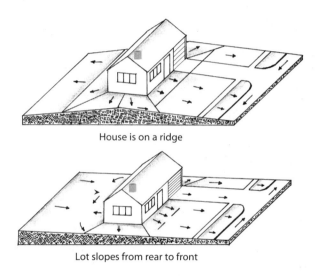

House is on a ridge

Lot slopes from rear to front

**Figure 8.9** Diagram of typical grading methods.

## Retaining Walls

**Retaining walls** hold back earth. They are usually found where elevation changes on a property and soil must be held back from falling down.

Retaining walls come in many material types and have some type of reinforcement. There are numerous guidelines for their construction. They also should have drainage by means of spaces or holes in the face of the wall or drain tiles at its base.

## Landscaping

**Landscaping** is the use of vegetation around a house to prevent erosion and improve its aesthetic appearance. Different types of landscaping are appropriate for different climate zones. For example, desert climates use a form of landscaping known as **zeroscaping**, where little or no water is needed. Another type is called **xeriscaping**, where water efficiency is achieved by using plants appropriate for the natural environment.

Appropriate landscaping has the ability to increase the value of the home so the appraiser should pay attention to it. Conversely, poorly landscaped properties can lose value because of the lack of curb appeal, the visual appeal of a property when viewed from the street. In more severe cases, poor landscaping can actually cause structural, roof, and cosmetic damage to homes. This happens when the grade slopes towards a home and water penetrates the home as a result.

## View

The **view** of the surrounding area can be one of the most favorable physical characteristics for a property. Views that usually increase value include views of lakes, the ocean, mountains, and greenbelts. However, the view can have a negative influence — for example, looking a trash dump is not considered favorable. Either way, the appraiser should note in the report if there is a view that could affect the property value.

**Figure 8.10** A property's view can have a positive influence on value.

# Off-Site Factors

The immobility of real estate means that the value of a given parcel of land is strongly affected by factors outside its boundaries. These **off-site factors** include the uses that are made of neighboring parcels; the availability and quality of off-site improvements or infrastructure (e.g., water, sewer, utility, and transportation systems); and the quality of public services, including schools, police protection, and fire protection. All of these off-site factors originate outside of a particular parcel of real estate.

## Utilities

Utilities originate off-site, so they are classified as an off-site factor. However, the appraiser should note the utilities available at the site or to the home when he or she is inspecting the site. The utilities in question include municipal water service or wells, electrical service, and/or solar panels. Utilities also refer to storm sewer or septic systems, solid waste disposal systems like trash removal, and natural gas or bottled propane. Amenities such as telephone and cable television service are included in this category as well.

**Figure 8.11** Utilities are an important value component.

These utilities can be above ground or below ground. If the visual inspection does not reveal which ones are present, the appraiser should interview the property owner to find out which ones may be present. The appraiser can also contact the city or municipality in which the property exists to confirm which utility services are used. Once the presence of utilities is verified, the appraiser should check to see what capacities are available for these utilities.

## Access

Another key off-site factor is **access**. Accessible land is more valuable than inaccessible land. The appraiser must note the **ingress** (access to the site or property) and **egress** (exit from the site or property) and how they contribute to the property's use. This is important because accessibility directly relates to a site's use potential or value if developed.

Traffic volume of the surrounding area can also affect the access to a parcel. The **traffic volume** is the number of cars and pedestrians that travel by a location in a given span of time. Generally, high traffic volume benefits a retail location and negatively affects a residential location.

**Traffic flow** can also be a factor in an appraisal. Not only does it produce noise and air pollution, in some areas traffic tends to bog down, causing a hazard for residents of surrounding areas. Poor flow or movement of traffic can adversely affect the value of a home.

## Summary

**Highest and best use** is a foundational concept that appraisers apply every time they value a property. Regardless of its current use, a site is usually valued at its highest and best use, which is defined as that use which is **physically possible**, **legally permitted**, **economically feasible**, and **maximally productive**.

When analyzing a property's highest and best use, appraisers consider **vacant land** or **improved property as if it were vacant**, and **property as improved**. Valuing a site separately from its improvements is also necessary when finding the land value component for the cost approach, and is an important factor in other uses as well.

There are many different physical characteristics and features of a site that appraisers need to consider in order to determine the highest and best use and value of a site. Similarly, appraisers gather legal and financial information to analyze as well. Determining highest and best use is a process of weighing alternative uses.

# Review Exercises

## *Matching Exercise*

**Instructions:**   Look up the meaning of the terms in the Glossary, then write the letter of the matching term on the blank line before its definition.   Answers are in Appendix B.

### Terms

A.  assemblage

B.  cul-de-sac

C.  drainage

D.  egress

E.  excess land

F.  Federal Emergency Management Agency (FEMA)

G.  grading

H.  highest and best use

I.  ingress

J.  interim use

K.  legally nonconforming use

L.  plottage

M.  off-site factors

N.  site

O.  special flood hazard areas

P.  topography

Q.  tract

R.  usable area

S.  variance

T.  zoning law

### Definitions

1. _____ The use, from among reasonably probable and adequately supported alternative uses, that is physically possible, legally permitted, economically feasible, and maximally productive.

2. _____ A parcel of land ready for construction.

3. _____ A piece of land in an unimproved state, i.e. it does not have utilities, sewer lines, etc., and is not ready to build on.

4. _____ The portion of the site that is suitable for building.

5. _____ A dead-end street.

6. _____ The process of combining two or more small sites into a larger one.

7. _____ The increment of change between a parcel's value as divided, compared to its value as one unified unit.

8. _____ The contours and features of a parcel of land.

9. _____ The natural processes or artificial pipes and drains that remove water and moisture from land.

10. _____ A government agency that is involved with all the different aspects of emergency management from preparation to recovery and prevention.

11. _____ Changing the elevation of the ground using bladed machines.

12. _____ Implemented to execute master plans and control the mix of properties in a particular area.

13. _____ A use that becomes grandfathered in when new zoning regulations are adopted.

14. _____ Surplus land beyond that which is needed to support the property's highest and best use.

15. _____ A short-term and temporary use of a property until it is ready for a more productive highest and best use.

## Multiple Choice Questions

**Instructions:** Circle your response and go to Appendix B to read the complete explanation for each question.

1. What is the primary factor that determines a property's value?
   a. Its highest and best use
   b. The cost of its improvements
   c. Its proximity to the beach
   d. Its zoning

2. A property is at its highest and best use when it is:
   a. at its most legally permitted state.
   b. most profitable while being possible both physically and legally.
   c. physically feasible.
   d. vacant.

3. Which of the following tests of highest and best use would a business operating in a residential neighborhood most likely violate?
    a. Economically feasible
    b. Physically possible
    c. Legally permitted
    d. Maximally productive

4. Converting a gas station into an orange grove is **not**:
    a. economically feasible.
    b. physically possible.
    c. legally permitted.
    d. maximally productive.

5. The most common type of lot is a:
    a. cul-de-sac.
    b. corner lot.
    c. interior lot.
    d. flag lot.

6. Jeremy drives to the subject property and discovers that it is vacant except that there are major utility hook-ups installed. On his report, Jeremy would identify the subject as a:
    a. parcel.
    b. tract.
    c. site.
    d. lot.

7. Roy purchases two adjoining lots. His appraisal estimates that the value of the lots combined into a single lot will almost double the total value of lots if kept separate. This added value is known as:
    a. yield.
    b. assemblage.
    c. plottage.
    d. none of the above.

8. Which of the following is **not** classified as an off-site improvement?
   a. Retaining wall
   b. Access
   c. Zoning
   d. Utilities

9. Heavy traffic in front of a property may adversely affect:
   a. noise and air pollution.
   b. ingress.
   c. egress.
   d. all of the above.

10. A church in the middle of an area zoned for single-family residences is an example of:
   a. a legally nonconforming use.
   b. a variance.
   c. an interim use.
   d. non-economic highest and best use.

# Chapter 9

# *Property Inspection and Description*

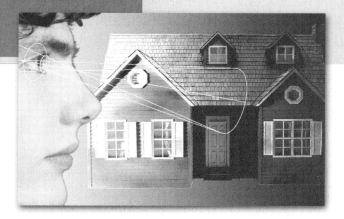

## Introduction

One of the most important parts of the data collection process is the inspection of the subject property by the real estate appraiser. Depending on the intended use of the appraisal, the on-site inspection may involve driving by the property or actually entering the house, measuring it, and photographing it.

In the last chapter, we covered key features and characteristics of the site itself. This chapter covers the key features and characteristics of the improvements, i.e. buildings, located on the site. Most appraisers start their career appraising single-family residences, so inspecting and describing a home is the focus of this chapter. Although the process is similar, an appraiser inspects and describes different characteristics when appraising other types of buildings.

### Learning Objectives

After reading this chapter, you will be able to:

- identify property characteristics that may influence value.
- recognize architectural styles and types of houses.
- identify construction terminology.

# Inspecting the Improvements

To illustrate what an appraiser's property inspection is, first we will explain what it is not. An appraiser's inspection of a house is significantly different from one done by a home inspector. (Although their roles are not the same, an appraiser should be familiar with much of the home inspection terminology.) For example, while appraisers perform unbiased valuation services for their client, a home inspector is working in the interest of the homebuyer. A home inspector never assigns value; he or she merely examines the home for defects or signs of possible defects. Home inspectors perform a much more thorough inspection and are held to different standards.

When an appraiser is appraising a property for an FHA-backed loan, the FHA (Federal Housing Authority) requires that any defects the appraiser uncovers through customary inspection be disclosed to the client. General ethics also dictate this practice. However, appraisers are not responsible for issues or adverse conditions undetectable by the standard visual walk-through.

An appraiser's building inspection usually has two main parts: the **exterior inspection** and **interior inspection**. In a typical appraisal, the appraiser measures, sketches, and photographs both the exterior and interior of the home. Appraisers also look at the mechanical systems and equipment within the home, as well as the car storage available, and any other site improvements that may affect the home's value.

When appraising a new home or appraising a home from the plans, an elevation sheet for the home can aid the appraiser. The **elevation sheet** is a labeled diagram or cutaway of the home detailing its features and building components, both interior and exterior.

Throughout the inspection, the appraiser judges the condition and quality of the building. Terms such as "good" or "average" are used to describe features that are adequate and equal in quality and utility to that same feature in similar homes. "Fair" or "poor" are used to describe features that are less than adequate and below average for that neighborhood. In order to judge effectively the condition and quality of the building and its features, an appraiser must have at least a general knowledge about the different aspects of house construction and the advantages and disadvantages of each.

# Exterior Inspection

Two sections make up the exterior of a home: the superstructure and the substructure. The **superstructure** refers to all the above grade improvements. **Above grade** refers to anything above ground level. These include the wood framing, the materials used to finish both the interior and exterior walls, as well as the various coatings, doors, and windows. The **substructure** refers to all the **below grade** improvements. The main underground component is the foundation; however, if there is a basement, it is also part of the substructure.

When an appraiser arrives at a site, one of the first things he or she notices is the type of home and its architectural influence or style. The appraiser will take note of the exterior characteristics of the home, and use a tape measure to get the accurate dimensions of the home. Then, the appraiser sketches the dimensions on graph paper, a laptop computer, or a handheld computer.

## Housing Types

There are five basic types of houses in the United States: one-story, one and a-half story, two-story, split-level, and raised ranch style.

### *One-Story*

The one-story or ranch style design is typically the easiest type of house to maintain and is the most common type of single-family manufactured home in the United States. The one-story design often appeals to older people and people with disabilities because of the lack of stairs. Its simplified design sometimes translates into lower costs. However, a one-story home is often more expensive per square foot than a two-story home of the same size, in part because the one-story home has a larger roof area.

### One-and-a-Half Story

Technically a one-story house with an expansive attic, the one-and-a half-story home allows an occupant the benefits of living in a ranch style house. Sometimes the attic/second floor is without insulation, furnishings, etc., but often it is finished like the rest of the home to provide extra livable space.

### *Two-Story*

This **floor plan** offers the most living space within a set perimeter. Two-story houses also can cost less to heat, cool, and build because the plumbing and other interior fixtures are aligned. Other advantages include separation of living areas on the first floor from sleeping quarters on the second, contributing to quieter, private areas.

### Split-Level or Tri-Level

A split-level or tri-level house has similar benefits to those of a two-story home. The split-level usually has the garage and major appliances like air-conditioning unit, washer and dryer on the ground floor. The second level is typically offset one-half floor above the garage area and contains the living areas. The sleeping quarters are one-half floor above the living area and directly above the garage area. This floor plan offers more design possibilities than either the single or the two-story plan.

### Two-Story Split Foyer or Raised Ranch Style

This type of home is a one-story ranch style home on a raised foundation and is called the split-foyer, raised-ranch, or split-entry house. It allows for more livable square footage because the basement is partially above ground and usually finished with extra bedrooms and/or a bonus room.

### Factory-Built Houses

**Factory-built housing** allows for flexibility in design and function and is not always distinguishable from site-built homes. Because factory-built houses are built inside a factory instead of on-site, construction can continue year round. That combined with less waste, vandalism, and weather damage helps keep them economical to produce as well.

There are different types of factory-built houses, including manufactured, modular, panelized, and precut homes. **Manufactured houses** come out of the factory the most complete, usually in two halves. They only need to be hooked up to utilities and anchored to the foundation. **Modular housing** is similar but comes in smaller room sections that are assembled on-site. **Panelized homes** arrive to the site in even smaller units, usually as completed walls with all the wiring and plumbing intact. Once the foundation is poured, the walls are enclosed and the two-piece roof is attached. Finally, the **precut home** is like a house in a box. All the materials are delivered unassembled, but precut to fit exactly in place. It saves the time and cost of measuring and cutting on-site.

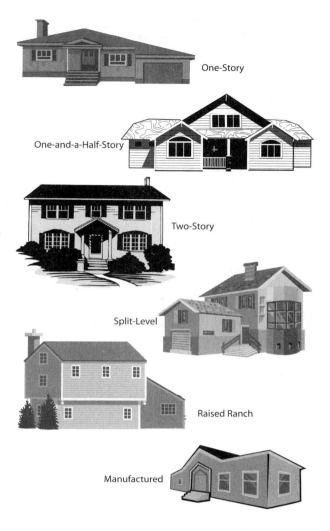

One-Story

One-and-a-Half-Story

Two-Story

Split-Level

Raised Ranch

Manufactured

**Figure 9.1** Different housing types.

## Architectural Style

Architects have adapted styles to fit more modern building techniques and materials available to construct them. This also has allowed the architecture to fit current tastes and living needs for the occupants of homes.

Appraisers should also have a basic understanding of the different **architectural styles** of the homes in their area. This gives appraisers a perspective on which homes are appropriate comparables for the property they are appraising. The appraiser may find that the architectural style of the home affects its value in some cases.

### Spanish or Mediterranean

A common style of home in many southwestern areas is the **Spanish style** or **Mediterranean style**. This style utilizes white or light-colored stucco on the exterior and an orange or brown clay tiled roof. In most cases, the Spanish style home is one story, but it can be two stories.

The two-story type may be known as a Santa Barbara or Monterrey style. Additionally, the Spanish style of home usually employs a court-yard and wrought iron trim and fencing.

### Ranch

Typically, a **ranch style** home is a one-story home with wood, masonry, or possibly stucco for the exterior. These homes are built on a very shallow crawlspace or directly onto a concrete slab as are the attached garages they feature.

### Townhouse or Row House

This type of home has one obvious feature. It is connected to or shares a common wall with a neighboring home. There are many different styles of townhouses.

### Cape Cod

This home may be one, two, or even more stories. The roof is a steeply pitched wood shingle roof and the exterior is a wood siding with wood shutters around the dormer windows. There are usually numerous multi-paned windows placed with relation to the front door. Many times, there is a shed addition as well.

### English Tudor

These are large, two-story homes with an exterior identified by brick, stone, and/or stucco with exposed wood timbers throughout. Additionally, this type of home usually has diamond-paned windows. Inside, English Tudor homes have intricate wood paneling or moldings.

### Contemporary

These homes can be one or more stories with stucco, masonry, or even wood exteriors. The roof is flat or very low-pitched. There is an open space floor plan utilized inside but very little decoration on the outside.

### Colonial

These are large homes with two or more stories. They feature wood exteriors with tall wood columns that are typically painted white. On occasion, this type of home may have a brick exterior.

### Victorian

These homes are more than one story and have wooden exteriors set off by elaborate decoration. They feature a wide porch that can some-times cover the entire front of the house. These homes used to be white, pastel, or even deep colors. The modern version usually employs siding and trim in contrasting colors.

Chapter 9 Property Inspection and Description **249**

## French Provincial

These large homes use white or other brick and stucco on the exterior. They also have a distinctive hip roof and are two stories. Sometimes these homes also feature dormers as well.

## Dutch Colonial

These homes are either one-and-a-half or two-and-a-half stories with dormers. Their very distinctive gambrel roof usually identifies them.

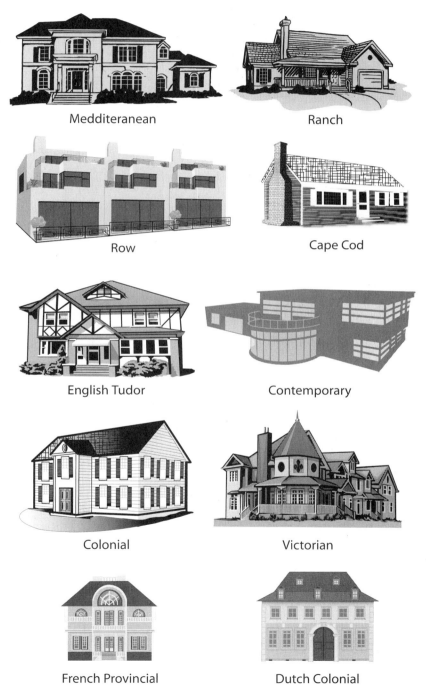

**Figure 9.2** There are several styles of architecture seen across America.

# Roofing

One area of architectural style is the **roof**. The style and condition of a roof can affect the value of a home, and a roof in poor condition can significantly detract from the value of the home.

There are many types of roofing available but eight main styles of which to be aware. These roof styles are:

- **Gable**
- **Gable with Dormers**
- **Hip**
- **Saltbox**
- **Pyramid**
- **Flat**
- **Gambrel**
- **Mansard**

Gable    Hip    Cone

Gable with Dormers    Mansard    Dome

Dust Pan    Pyramid    Flat

Salt-Box    Pagoda    Shed

A-Frame    Gambrel    False Thatched

**Figure 9.3** Different roof styles.

## Roof Coverings

There are a number of different materials used for roof coverings, but they all must share some common characteristics. They must be able to shed water and protect the interior of the home from the weather. Materials used for roofing must be durable, aesthetically pleasing, easy to apply, reasonably priced, and not too heavy. The appraiser should be familiar with all the different types of roofing materials used in his or her market area.

| **Common Roofing Materials** | |
| --- | --- |
| • Built-up roofing | • Asphalt composition shingles |
| • Slate | • Metal roofing and shingles |
| • Tile | • Wood shingles and shakes |

## Roof Framing

Normally the roof system uses joists and rafters spaced from 12 inches to 24 inches apart on centers. Joists usually span one-half the width of the structure. **Load-bearing walls** support the joists in the middle. (Local building codes deal with the acceptable span lengths for structural safety.)

### Rafters and Joists

The **rafters** and **joists** support the weight of the sheathing, roofing material, and roof mounted equipment. They also bear weight from weather such as wind, rain, or snow. Rafters may carry the ceiling loads below when Cathedral ceilings are present. Rafters and joists also create attic and ventilation space.

Rafters tend to push the walls apart, and the joists (wooden framing members that run perpendicular to rafters and have the ceiling nailed to them) contain this outward pressure and provide triangular rigidity to the roof system. Purlins, which are beams that run from the rafter to the joist and intersect the rafter at a 90-degree angle, reinforce the roof deck.

## Roof Ventilation

Adequate **ventilation** is essential to prolong the life of the roof covering as well as the building materials used in the roof structure. In addition to obtaining maximum life for the roof, proper ventilation can dramatically reduce the heating and cooling costs for the house. **Soffit vents** and attic fans aid ventilation of the roof.

## Cladding

**Cladding** in general can refer to any external, weatherproof protective skin or device for the exterior surfaces of the home. One of the most important functions of the cladding system is to prevent racking or twisting of the house frame. Underneath the cladding are vapor barriers. Cladding includes the surface coatings, siding, doors, windows, trim, shutters, entryways, flashings, and caulking.

### Surface Coatings

The outermost layer of house is a layer of paint or similar coating and is only a few thousandths of an inch thick. If properly applied and replenished, paint will protect tens of thousands of dollars worth of siding. Although there are several different chemical systems used in common home coatings, they are all applied as a liquid and, when dry, form tough plastic-like layers of protection on the surfaces to which they are applied.

| Coating Types | |
|---|---|
| • Enamel | • Lacquer |
| • Latex | • Shellac |
| • Epoxy | • Stain |

### Siding

**Siding** is used to protect the interior and framing from temperature and weather. Another critical function of the siding system is the management of condensation that forms between the inner and outer walls.

| Types of Siding | |
|---|---|
| • Wood | • Vinyl |
| • Masonry | • EIFS (Exterior Insulating and Finishing System) |
| • Stucco | |
| • Steel/Aluminum | |

## *Doors and Windows*

**Doors** and **windows** are openings created in the wall structure to allow for the passage of people and light. They must be sealed, caulked, and flashed to perform their intended function without leaking. It is also important to note that the opening for a door or window interrupts the structural integrity of the wall system. In order to restore the strength of the wall system, headers of the proper dimensions are installed.

Modern doors and windows come as pre-packaged units with all the necessary framing and hardware. The door and window units fit into the rough-cut openings and fasten into place. This method assures that doors and windows will function smoothly and lock properly.

### Doors

Doors usually come as packaged units that need to fit squarely in their frames, open, and close smoothly without binding. They come in solid, hollow, or paneled varieties. Typically, exterior doors are solid and interior doors are hollow.

| **Basic Types of Doors** | |
|---|---|
| • Wood | • Vinyl |
| • Metal | • Hardboard |
| • Glass | |

Doors can be hung in different ways. Traditional doors are hung with hinges on one side. French doors are double doors hinged at either side. Others run in tracks and are sliding doors. Others yet are suspended overhead on tracks, like pocket doors. Doors have different surfaces as well. They may be flush or level, glazed, paneled, or even louvered.

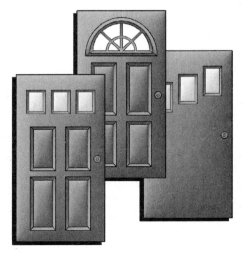

**Figure 9.4** Examples of different door styles.

In addition to knowing about doors, the appraiser should be familiar with the parts that surround a door. The **doorframe** is a general name that includes all the parts that surround a door. The **sill** is a strip of beveled wood or metal that is attached to the finished floor under an outside door. Its purpose is to keep water from entering the house. Interior doors have a **threshold** or **saddle** instead of a sill. The **casing** is the decorative wood finish trim that surrounds doors and windows. On exterior doors, some sort of **weather stripping** attaches to the jambs, header, and sill to prevent air from leaking into or out of the house. The weather stripping can take the form of metal flashing, a rubber or plastic gasket, or foam strips.

## Windows

Windows allow light and air into a home and improve airflow and circulation. They also function to keep weather out.

A description of windows usually starts with the types of the frames and sashes that hold the panes in place. **Window frames** and **sashes** are usually made of wood, metal, vinyl, or fiberglass.

Most **windowpanes** are conventional glass but some may be laminated glass, tempered glass, or even wired-glass. Acrylic coatings are used in many skylights, and polycarbonates are used to strengthen windows for security purposes. Windows also come in single-glazed, dual-glazed, or even triple-glazed varieties.

### *Window Types*

- Single-hung — the bottom portion moves
- Double-hung — both top and bottom parts are able to move
- Casement — the windows swing in or out
- Jalousie — glass slats are used and they open in or out
- Hopper — the window is hinged at the bottom and opens in or out
- Awning — the window is hinged at the top and opens out
- Fixed — windows do not open or move at all, like in glass block
- Bay — a window or series of windows protrudes from the exterior of a building leaving a recess within

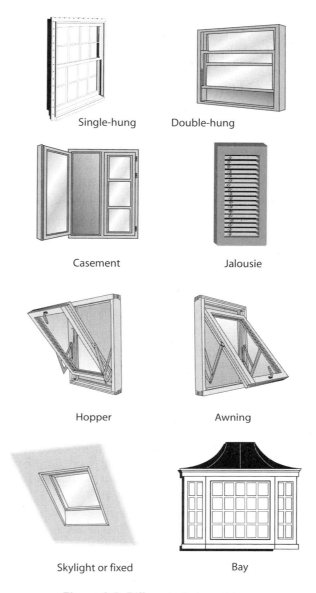

**Figure 9.5**  Different window styles.

## Skylights

**Skylights** typically do not open, but do serve to let light into a home. Skylights are estimated to let five times more light into a home than the same size window.  They can also serve to make a space look much larger than it is and add value to the home.

## *Flashing*

**Flashing** defines the material used to prevent the intrusion of water at the place where dissimilar materials or surface planes intersect. Typically, flashing is installed at any roof penetration where leaks may occur such as chimneys or vents, and any exterior wall openings such as windows or doors.  Flashings seal the edges of membranes or where membranes overlap.  They direct water away from the structure and its components.

Flashing is by nature corrosion resistant and can be made from copper, stainless steel, galvanized steel, and various plastics.

## Trim

**Trim** refers to the finishing materials in a building, such as moldings applied around openings (window and door trim) or at the floor and ceiling of rooms (baseboard, cornice, and other moldings). Trim around windows is also known as casing. Trim is usually a different color or material than the adjacent wall. It is located either on the outside or inside of the building and covers the space between the window frame or doorjamb and the wall.

Although largely cosmetic in nature, trim serves the purpose of protecting other more vital structural parts. All exposed trim needs proper painting, caulking, and freedom from rot. Rotten trim will usually be hiding rotten wood behind it.

## Wood Framing

Most homes employ wood alone or wood and other materials for their frame and structural support.

The two main classifications of wood are softwood and hardwood. **Hardwood** comes from deciduous trees that lose their leaves in the fall like oak, maple, and cherry. **Softwood** comes from evergreens like pine and fir. As the names suggest, hardwood is stronger and more durable than softwood. It is also considerably more difficult to work with and therefore not as desirable for home construction.

The most prevalent form of damage to wood is **dry rot,** which, paradoxically, is caused by water exposure. Wood should have no more than 19% moisture. When the moisture content gets too high through exposure to water sources, it can lead to **fungal growth** and wood-destroying **insect infestation**.

### Framing Types

There are three basic types of wood frames used in residential construction: platform frame, balloon frame, and post and beam frame construction.

**Platform frame construction** is the most prevalent for one and two story residences. In this type, only one floor is built at a time and each floor serves as a platform for the next to be built.

**Balloon frame construction** varies in that the studs run from the floor of the first level to the ceiling of the second story uninterrupted. In this method, ledger boards or ribbon boards are set into the interior edge of the studs where the second floor joists rest on them. Balloon frame construction is most common when the exterior of the structure will be brick, stucco, or a stone veneer.

**Post and beam frame construction** employs posts placed all over the home that are the base for beams. Ceiling planks rest on the beams for support. In some cases, the exposure of the posts and beams is part of interior decoration.

## Foundations

The **foundation** or substructure of a home has two purposes: (1) it supports the entire building, and (2) it transfers the weight of the building to the ground. Typically, foundations are made of poured concrete, cinder or concrete blocks, or wood. Local climate and soil conditions affect the choice of materials used, as do the size and weight of the structure and the location of the water table.

**Figure 9.6** A foundation supports the structure and transfers weight to the ground.

Foundation problems can be the cause of a multitude of other factors including plumbing leaks, squeaky and un-level floors, sticking doors, and cracked walls.

## Slab-on-Grade

Depending on the climate, soil conditions, and architectural requirements, the builder may use a **slab-on-grade** foundation, where the structure sits directly on the ground. In this case, the foundation and footings are one integral unit. A properly designed slab supports the weight of the entire structure and is unaffected by soil movement.

A **monolithic slab** is poured in one piece. It requires a wide base and steel reinforcement. The slab floor alone will not support interior load-bearing walls so an interior footing is trenched in before the slab is poured. A **floating slab** is composed of one section for the floor and another for the foundation wall, each poured separately. An expansion joint separates the two parts. A **screeded slab** is a wooden floor built on a concrete slab with no crawlspace underneath. The space under the wood flooring is usually used as a return for the heating and cooling system.

Steel bars or mesh reinforce poured concrete slabs. In some cases, a technique called post-tensioning is used. In a **post-tensioned slab**, cables laid in the wet concrete and put under tension after the concrete has cured give it added strength. This technique increases the strength of the finished foundation.

## Cinder or Concrete Block Foundations

**Concrete masonry units** (CMUs) are a very common material for foundation wall construction. Commonly called concrete or cinder block, this material is strong and durable if proper techniques are employed during its construction. To increase the strength and resistance to cracking, reinforcing steel should always be used in conjunction with masonry or poured concrete.

The foundation itself rests on a footing that should be at least one foot below the finished grade or the frost line, whichever is deeper. The thickness of a foundation wall is determined by the depth of its construction. The deeper the wall, the thicker it must be to offset the soil pressure (which increases with depth). For example, a concrete foundation wall needs to be 8 inches thick for depths up to 5 feet, but a similar wall must be 12 inches thick for a 7-foot depth. Similar increases hold true for poured concrete.

## Wood Foundations

In areas that are free from wood-destroying pests such as termites, wood can be an excellent foundation material. Wood is very simple to use, is a great insulator, and allows for flexibility of design. The depth of the foundation wall will determine the size of the studs to be used and their spacing.

## *Pier and Beam Foundations*

**Pier and beam construction** uses a system of piers and girders in conjunction with the foundation walls to support the structure. Girders are needed when the span is too great for the use of floor joists. Girders are secured to the foundation wall by two methods: using pockets or placing the girder on top of the wall.  The girders themselves may be formed from a solid piece of wood or built up from laminated planks.

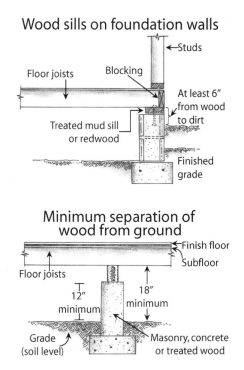

**Figure 9.7** The two types of pier and beam foundations.

### *Piers*

**Piers** are vertical columns that support a foundation.  In areas with stable soil conditions, piers are used economically to support the foundation system.  In some cases, piers can be used to bypass weak soil and reach a firmer bearing area.  Typically, the pier will rest on a footing and may have the lower end "belled" out to increase the bearing area.

### *Piles*

In cases where the underlying soil is not capable of supporting the structure, piles may be employed.  **Piles** are vertical foundation members that transfer the load to the ground and may be made of wood, steel, concrete, or a combination of these materials.  Piles are driven into the ground until either bedrock or friction will allow no further driving.  The ends are cut level and the foundation system is attached to the piles.

## *Basements and Crawlspaces*

Buildings with raised foundations will have either a basement or a crawlspace. A **basement** is the lowest story of a building and is partially or entirely below ground. A **crawlspace** is a low space beneath a floor of a building to give workers access to wiring and plumbing.

Often a drainage system is located below basements or crawlspaces and begins with a drain and a sump. A **sump** is a container that collects water until a certain level is reached. At that point, the water is pumped by a sump pump to the storm sewer or away from the structure to head off flooding. Sump pumps are essential in keeping a basement or crawlspace dry and preventing moisture and mildew problems. They also help to keep these areas from flooding altogether.

### Basements

In colder parts of the country where the frost line may be 5 or 6 feet deep, many homes are built with basements. **Basements** are the stories of a building that are below grade or below ground level that can be finished spaces or unfinished spaces. Good building practice and codes require the footing for the foundation to be below the area where the ground freezes. The reason for requiring footings to be placed below the **frost line** is to minimize the movement associated with the cyclical freezing and thawing of the soil during the winter.

Basements can add value to a home and should be noted by the appraiser. In some cases, the basement is a finished space with livable area. **Finished areas** are the enclosed areas in a home that are suitable for year-round use. These areas have flooring, insulation, etc. that is similar to the rest of the house. **Unfinished areas** are the areas of a home that do not meet these criteria. Sometimes, a finished basement can be what is known as a walk-out finished basement. In this case, the basement is not completely underground. At least one side is exposed and a door connects the livable space to the grade level outside.

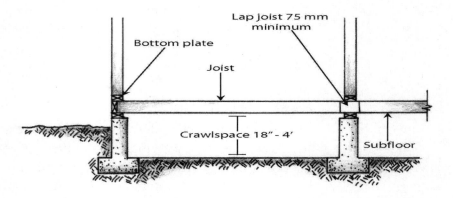

**Figure 9.8** Crawlspaces range from 18 inches to 4 feet in height.

**Crawlspaces**

In more moderate climates, homes built with pier and beam construction will have a crawlspace that may be 18 inches to 4 feet tall beneath
the floor.  The crawlspace is not large enough to be a finished or
livable space.  It serves the same purpose as the basement in that it
connects the foundation of the home to footings and piles that are
pounded into the earth below the frost line.

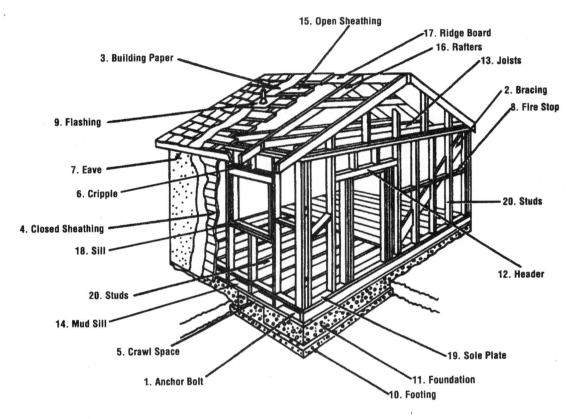

15. Open Sheathing
17. Ridge Board
16. Rafters
3. Building Paper
13. Joists
2. Bracing
8. Fire Stop
9. Flashing
7. Eave
6. Cripple
20. Studs
4. Closed Sheathing
18. Sill
12. Header
20. Studs
14. Mud Sill
5. Crawl Space
19. Sole Plate
1. Anchor Bolt
11. Foundation
10. Footing

**Figure 9.9** The exterior parts of a building.

# Interior Inspection

Once the basic examination of the outside is complete, the appraiser
can then move to the inside of the home.  At this point, the appraiser
has already drawn a sketch of the exterior of the house.  The appraiser now uses that perimeter sketch and fills in the room layout and
other interior details.

Size for the interior of the home is reported in terms of **gross living
area** (GLA), which is the total amount of finished, above ground
habitable space.  In most cases, attics, crawlspaces, and basements are
unfinished and do not count in the GLA measurement.  The **gross
building area** (GBA) is the total amount of all enclosed floor areas and
does include basements and attics.  The American National Standards
Institute (ANSI) has developed a standard method for calculating

floor areas in single-family dwellings, "Square Footage – Method for Calculating," ANSI Z765-2003. In some states, the state appraisal regulatory agency has adopted this standard method as a supplemental standard that appraisers must follow. Copies may be purchased from the NAHB Research Center, a subsidiary of the National Association of Home Builders (NAHB).

The appraiser also takes note of the construction features present in the interior of the home. Most appraisal reports contain a checklist that reminds the appraiser to check all the important features and provides a space for noting the condition of features present.

In many cases, the current owner can provide additional information about the condition or quality of improvements. If the homeowner is present during the appraiser's on-site inspection, he or she is usually happy to talk about the remodeling of the kitchen, when the interior of the home was last painted, and what major repairs have been completed recently.

## Floors

**Floors** exist in homes to provide walking spaces and to support furniture. They need to be level, well supported, smooth, and easy to navigate so they do not trip occupants. Floors should also be very durable as they are the most used components of the home interior. Floors get support from floor joists, which span the floors perpendicularly to the floor sills.

Floors can be made of numerous materials including concrete, wood strips or planks, carpet, resilient tile, and ceramic or quarry tile (stone and marble). Flooring in good condition and of certain materials, like finished wood or marble, can add to the value of the home.

## Walls and Ceilings

Interior walls and ceilings serve a similar function. They are primarily decorative. They conceal the electrical, mechanical, and plumbing systems and serve to strengthen the vapor barrier. They also improve overall rigidity and help to prevent racking and twisting of the structure.

### Interior Walls

Interior walls are a decorative finish that can be made of numerous different materials like plaster or drywall, wood planks or panels, fiber cement panels, masonry or concrete.

**Plaster** and **drywall** are the two most common types of interior walls. They are durable materials, considered inexpensive, easy to paint, cover, or wallpaper. Additionally, they are easy to fix when damaged, resistant to rodents and insects, good for blocking sound, and resistant to fire.

### Ceilings

Ceilings are made from the same basic types of material as walls. Materials used in ceilings include plaster, drywall, wood, paneling, or even acoustic tiling. Metal ceilings appear in some homes as well.

There are also different styles of ceilings. **Textured ceilings** are quick to apply to a drywall backing and are relatively inexpensive. However, because they tend to collect dirt and grease, they should not be used in kitchens or bathrooms. Dropped or **suspended ceilings** consist of **t-bars**, a framework of steel or metal channels suspended by wires, into which pre-cut acoustic tiles are placed.

## Stairs

Many modern homes are now multiple stories as well. Once inside, staircases make it possible to go up to another floor or down into a basement.

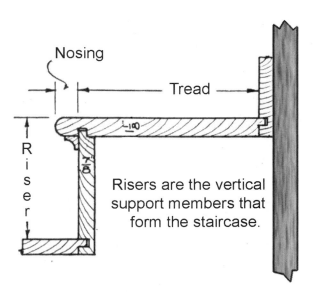

**Figure 9.10** The components of stairs.

Stairs in homes are usually made from wood but can also be concrete, brick, or even metal. The major components of stairs are the tread, the nosing, and the riser.

## Attics

The **attic** is the area of the home bounded by the underside of the roof and the upper side of the ceiling of the top floor. It may be large enough to stand up in or just barely large enough to be considered an attic. A hatchway built into the ceiling at an upstairs hallway or closet usually accesses the attic. Newer homes usually require a ladder to access the attic, but in older models, there may be a folding stairway to provide access.

### *Insulation*

Insulation is found in the walls and the attic. The concept of home insulation is a modern phenomenon arising from the increase in energy costs. As heat loss became both a comfort and economic issue, products and systems evolved to deal with it.

The natural dead-air space between walls and between the ceiling and the roof is not an effective insulator. The convection currents that form between the warm inner wall and the cooler outer wall transfer the heat away from the living spaces. The fitting of insulation in the wall cavity creates millions of tiny barriers to impede the convection flow. Installation in the attic helps to prevent heat loss from the living space down below.

**R-value** is the resistance to heat loss. The higher the R-value, the greater its insulating ability. The same R-value is required for insulation against both hot and cold temperatures.

Domestic insulation is available in many forms. Some of the most common forms encountered include batts (blankets), sheets, blocks, blowable particles, and liquids that turn to foam.

# Mechanical Systems and Equipment

There are four main systems: heating, cooling, plumbing, and electrical. Homes vary in their type and quality of systems. Similarly, although almost every home has plumbing and electricity, there can be wide variations in the quality of plumbing fixtures and electrical capacity.

## Heating System

One of the most common **heating system**s in homes is the gas furnace. In this system, natural gas is piped-in as the fuel source and burned to heat air. A furnace or ducting system with return and supply registers distributes the air through the home. The heated air is forced through the home with the use of blowers or fans, so this system is often referred to as a forced-air system.

Other heating systems include oil-fired systems that are similar to gas-fired systems in that the heated air is forced through the home. Electrical heating systems use electricity to heat the air and hydronic heat systems use water to carry heat through the home instead of air. The most primitive of heating systems are the wood burning ones, where a centralized stove or fireplace is used to burn wood or pellets to give off heat.

### *Fireplaces*

Once used as the sole source of heat for the home, fireplaces are now used as a focal point for winter comfort. Although they can be thought of as part of the heating system, fireplaces are quite inefficient as a heat source, and are usually included in homes as a valuable amenity. They are well-liked for the cozy atmosphere they provide.

### *Wood Stoves*

Wood stoves are often called space heaters for their ability to heat an area, but not really an entire home. **Space heaters** do not have ducting or piping connected to them which makes it hard to heat other rooms. Most wood stoves now are for pleasure and look like fireplaces with glass doors.

**Figure 9.11**  Appraisers may encounter a wood stove like this in older rural homes.

## Central Cooling System

Air conditioning is a **central cooling system** that is now a standard feature of many new homes. It can immensely improve the livability of the home during hot and humid summer months. The air conditioning takes warm air and moves it outside. The air conditioning system also removes humidity from the air, and by allowing windows to remain closed, outside noises are reduced, making the home quieter.

**Thermostats** are used to turn the cooling system on and off at the appropriate times to keep the room temperatures comfortable. They are put in rooms with representative temperatures for the entire home. Many thermostats control both the heating and air-conditioning. This is important to avoid having both systems running simultaneously.

## Plumbing System

Residential plumbing consists of two separate systems: These are the aseptic system and septic system.

### Aseptic System

The **aseptic system** is the clean water system and carries potable water. **Potable water** is water that does not have enough impurities to cause health problems. It meets the requirements set forth by local health departments for human consumption and use.

The aseptic system consists of lines originating at the supply or source of the water, such as a municipal water main or a domestic well, and includes all the associated valves and taps in the home, like faucets and showers. In addition to the piping, the potable system includes the water heater and any kind of water softening device.

### Septic System

The **septic system** includes all the piping, traps, drains, vents, and pumps that discharge waste from the home. The pipes carry water, solid wastes, and methane gas (a by-product of decomposition). The septic system needs to be large enough to help avoid health risks and to reduce odor.

In some cases, there are two systems for waste removal: one to handle sewage and the other to carry off storm water. When there are two systems employed, they must be kept separate.

In other cases, homes have a septic tank to rid the home of wastes instead of connecting to a municipal system. A **septic tank** is a watertight vessel designed to accommodate liquid and solid waste. It is located on the property and buried beneath the ground. A typical system includes a tank and a drain field. The effluent accumulates in the tank and then disperses through the drain field using a system of perforated pipes. The tank separates the solids from the liquids, allows for partial breakdown of the organic material, and lets the clarified liquid discharge to the drain field.

### *Plumbing Fixtures*

Fixtures like bathtubs, showers, toilets, faucets and sinks can be made of many different materials and may add value to the home. Brass, copper, stainless steel, fiberglass, and cast iron are some of the materials used for fixtures.

## Electrical System

Electrical power arrives at the home in two ways. In older communities, the power will come from an overhead transmission line or power pole. In newer communities, the power comes from subterranean lines that run to the home. In some homes, solar panels on the roof capture solar energy to provide the majority of power for a home.

The **main electrical panel** is the entrance and main distribution for electrical energy in the home. It also contains the main disconnect and the individual circuit breakers. The main disconnect allows for all the electricity in the home to be shut off with one switch. Circuit breakers provide a method to turn off different areas of the **electrical system** for servicing.

The appraiser should be able to tell the **voltage** for the home in the main panel and determine if it is sufficient for the appliances used in the home. In the old days, a home was wired for 110-volt capacity. Today, that would be insufficient for all the modern appliances, entertainment systems, and computers. The appraiser should be able to see a 220-volt or 240-volt wiring set-up (as noted by three-wire service entrance) for newer homes. Additionally, the appraiser should be able to see between 15 and 20 circuits for all the appliances powered in the modern home.

### *Energy-Efficient Items*

The appraiser should also make note of items that increase the **energy efficiency** of the home. These features can decrease the energy needed to heat and cool a home, and increase its value.

Some common energy-efficient items in a home are double, triple, or low energy glazed windows, which decrease the amount of heat loss in cold months and the cool air escaping during warm months. A home is also more energy-efficient when it is properly caulked and weather-stripped, which prevents heating and cooling loss. The efficiency of water heaters rises when they are properly insulated or jacketed to prevent them from losing heat. The appraiser should also note any built-in energy-efficient appliances in the home.

**Figure 9.12** Because of advances in technology, residential solar panels are becoming more prevalent.

The use of **solar energy** can also make a home much more energy efficient. **Solar panels** gather the sun's heat for use in a solar water heater, solar heating system and even as a source of electricity in the residence. Another means to increase energy efficiency is to use a heat pump or geothermal heat pump heating and cooling system to exchange hot and cool air with the soil in the ground.

## Counters and Cabinets

The appraiser should also note the quality, condition, and type of material used for the counters and cabinets located throughout the home.

**Counters** come in a number of materials like particleboard or plywood and have a variety of materials like wood, slate, granite, marble, stainless steel, and tile covering them. The choice of materials and colors is often dramatically affected by the prevailing styles. This is a reason why remodeling a kitchen can be an important way to "modernize" a home and increase its value. Whichever covering is used for the countertop, it should be waterproof, abrasion-resistant, durable, scorch-proof, and non-porous.

**Cabinets** provide storage in rooms like the kitchen and bathrooms. They are usually made from solid wood, particleboard, or even different types of metal. Plastic laminate covers the particleboard type of cabinet for protection. Quality cabinet materials and an abundance of cabinet space is another factor that can add to the value of the home.

# Car Storage

Once the appraiser has examined the exterior and interior of the home, he or she should also make note of any space designed for car storage. Usually, there are four places to park a car at the home site. Homes usually have an attached garage, detached garage or a carport. Other homes have only an uncovered driveway or on-street parking.

## Garages

The appraiser should note whether the **garage** is attached to or detached from the home, its size, and the number of cars it accommodates. The appraiser usually includes the garage in his or her sketch of the home.

## Carports

Like garages, carports cover the car. Unlike garages, carports do not enclose it. **Carport**s have no walls or doors with which to control access.

## Driveways

Most homes with a garage have a **driveway;** but sometimes, older homes have no garage and no carport. Instead, they possess only a driveway, and that is the private parking for the home.

The appraiser should also note the driveway surface and its condition. Driveways are made of solid materials like concrete or asphalt or pieced materials like stones, pavers, bricks, or gravel. They should be free of cracks and trip hazards where subsurface upward heaving has caused the concrete to crack or become uneven. Driveways should be sloped to drain water away from the home and garage.

## On-Street Parking

In some cases, there is no garage, carport, or a driveway where a car might be parked. The owner of the home must resort to parking the car on a public street in front of the home. Obviously, the appraiser should note this on a report if encountered.

# Site Improvements

In the last chapter we discussed the physical characteristics of the site, and we have covered the characteristics of the building in this chapter. In addition, the appraiser should note other improvements made to the site. These improvements include things around the perimeter of a building like patios, pools, fences, lighting, ponds, out buildings and even sports courts.

The appraiser also has to give **contributory value** to site improvements after identifying them. Sometimes the contributory value of site improvements does not equal the cost of building them. For example, swimming pools contribute to the overall value of a home, but their contributory value is less than the expense of building the pool itself. As with other property features, the appraiser determines the value of site improvements by considering market data.

## Fences

Fences add to the security of a property and can add to its value. They are usually made of masonry (brick or block) or various types of wood.

## Patios

Patios are surfaced exterior areas used for outdoor enjoyment of the home. Barbeques and patio furniture are often located out on these areas. Their construction type varies, as some are concrete, brick, stone, asphalt, or wood. No matter the type, they are usually at ground level. If the patio is more than two feet off the ground, it should have a guardrail.

## Swimming Pool

**Swimming pools** are becoming more and more prevalent in residential areas. They may be above ground or level with the backyard. The most common materials used in pool construction are concrete, fiberglass, and vinyl.

**Figure 9.13** Improvements such as pools, patios, fireplaces, and fences are desirable.

## Spa

A **spa** or **hot tub** is a small pool filled with circulating hot water for therapeutic soaking. It can be freestanding, attached to a pool, above ground or set into the ground. Although similar in construction to a swimming pool, a spa or hot tub is much smaller. The distinction between spa and hot tub is largely semantic, but the term "hot tub" usually refers to a round structure made from woods like cedar, redwood, cypress, oak, or teakwood.

## Sauna

A **sauna** is a Scandinavian invention consisting of a small, wood-lined room or house with the provision to be heated to 150°F or more. Like spas, saunas are considered therapeutic. The dry heat in a sauna increases perspiration, which causes "toxins" to be removed from the body, cleansing the skin pores. The heat also increases circulation and relaxes muscles.

# Summary

Depending on the scope of work involved with the assignment, the appraiser's inspection sometimes is a simple **drive-by visual verification**. Usually an appraiser will actually make an **on-site inspection** of the subject property, as well as the comps.

Appraisers are not responsible for any **defects** or **adverse conditions** that could not be identified in the course of his or her customary inspection. Appraisers inspect properties to **determine value**, not to discover defects. However, if a defect or adverse condition is known, the appraiser must factor this information into the **value conclusion**.

Appraisers inspect the **exterior and interior of the home**. They identify features that are or are not included, and they note the quality of the features that are present. In addition, they note **car storage** options and any other **site improvement**s that may affect the value of the subject property. For this reason, a sound understanding of **building types**, **architectural styles**, **construction components**, and **construction terminology** is of benefit to the appraiser.

# Review Exercises

## Matching Exercise

**Instructions:** Look up the meaning of the terms in the Glossary, then write the letter of the matching term on the blank line before its definition. Answers are in Appendix B.

### Terms

A. balloon frame construction

B. cladding

C. flashing

D. floating slab

E. gross building area (GBA)

F. gross living area (GLA)

G. monolithic slab

H. piers

I. piles

J. platform frame construction

K. post and beam frame construction

L. post-tensioned slab

M. R-value

N. screeded slab

O. sump

### Definitions

1. _____ Any external protective skin or device for the exterior surfaces of the home.

2. _____ The material used to prevent the intrusion of water at the place where dissimilar materials or surface planes intersect.

3. _____ A construction method where the studs run from the floor of the first level to the ceiling of the second story uninterrupted.

4. _____ A foundation that contains a one-piece slab that requires a wide base and steel reinforcement.

5. _____ A foundation where a wooden floor is built directly onto the concrete slab.

6. _____ Vertical columns that support a foundation.

7. _____ A container that collects water until a certain level is reached at which point the water is pumped to the storm sewer or away from the structure to head off flooding.

8. _____ The total amount of finished, above ground, habitable space.

9. _____ The total amount of all enclosed floor areas including basements and attics.

10. _____ Insulation thickness.

## Multiple Choice Questions

**Instructions:** Circle your response and go to Appendix B to read the complete explanation for each question.

1. A two-story house has economic benefit because:
   a. it contains the most living space in relation to the lot size.
   b. plumbing and other fixtures can be aligned.
   c. of both a and b.
   d. of neither a nor b.

2. A home that has a stucco exterior, an orange clay tiled roof, a courtyard, and wrought iron trim and fencing is described as:
   a. Spanish.
   b. Contemporary.
   c. Cape Cod.
   d. Victorian.

3. Which of the factory-built homes comes out of the factory in the smallest components?
   a. Modular houses
   b. Panel houses
   c. Precut houses
   d. Manufactured houses

4. Subject inspection is divided into which two parts?
   a. Drive by and walk through
   b. Interior and exterior
   c. Construction and amenities
   d. Subject and neighborhood

5. Kelly has just completed her inspection of the subject property. Her measurements identified the total area of 1,524 square feet. The attic measured 298 square feet and the combined area of the 2 ½ baths measures 132 square feet. The kitchen and dining area measured 102 square feet and the backyard measured 121 square feet. What is the gross living area for this property?

    a. 1,524 sq. ft.

    b. 871 sq. ft.

    c. 1,105 sq. ft.

    d. 1,094 sq. ft.

6. Which part of a structure is the support for the entire building?

    a. Crawlspace

    b. Flooring

    c. Foundation

    d. Superstructure

7. Foundation problems can cause which of the following factors?

    a. Un-level floors

    b. Plumbing problems

    c. Sticking doors

    d. All of the above

8. Why are some homes built with a basement?

    a. Because their foundations must be below the frost line

    b. To add value to the home

    c. Builder's preference

    d. None of the above

9. Which of the following is **not** a type of commonly used foundation?

    a. Monolithic slab

    b. Floating slab

    c. Post-tension slab

    d. Raging slab

10. The three basic types of wood framing are:

    a. platform, balloon, and post-tension.

    b. platform, floating, and post and beam.

    c. balloon, post and beam, and platform.

    d. screeded, balloon, and post and beam.

# Chapter 10

# *Sales Comparison Approach*

## Introduction

The sales comparison approach is the most commonly used approach among residential appraisers. The sales comparison approach even appears in a limited form when using the cost and income approaches to value. This approach is deeply rooted in the principle of substitution and is widely regarded as the simplest of the three major approaches to value.

In the real estate market, no two properties are ever exactly alike (if only because no two properties may be in the same location), so exact comparability is impossible to obtain. However, by using market analysis, it is possible for the appraiser to identify any aspect of a real estate transaction or any characteristic of the property that may affect the property's sales price. From this, appraisers are able to identify economic comparability, which is essential to proper estimation of market value.

In this chapter, you will thoroughly explore the ins and outs of this process, including data collection and analysis. You will also be introduced to the comparison grid or matrix, and learn how adjustments are determined and applied. Finally, this chapter will cover the topic of reconciling the adjusted prices of the comparable properties to determine the value of the subject property.

## Learning Objectives

After reading this chapter, you will be able to:

- discuss the limitations and applications of the sales comparison approach.

- identify the multitude of data sources for this approach.

- discuss the types of adjustments made to the comparable properties.

- identify the sequence of adjustments.

- describe the methods by which adjustment values are typically derived.

- recognize Fannie Mae's adjustment guidelines.

- discuss the comparable reconciliation process and identify why the practice of bracketing is applicable.

# Overview of the Sales Comparison Approach

The **sales comparison approach** is also known as the market data approach, or simply the market approach. This valuation approach relies heavily upon the principle of substitution discussed in Chapter 4. The principle of substitution states that the maximum value of a property is set by the cost of acquiring an equally desirable and valuable substitute property.

The principle of substitution is frequently the basis of consumers' buying decisions. For example, when buying a gallon of milk, consumers decide whether to buy Brand A or Brand B. If they perceive little or no difference between the two competing brands, consumers overwhelmingly choose to purchase the least expensive brand. Consumers employ this same process when purchasing real estate. A typical buyer will pay no more for a property than what he or she could pay to obtain a reasonable substitute for that property. Quite often, buyers make their purchasing decisions based upon the sales prices of other similar properties.

Based on the principle of substitution, the appraiser can assume that similar properties will have similar market value, since property values are based upon the perceptions of buyers and sellers and result from the negotiations between these parties. In the sales comparison approach, the market value of the subject property is estimated by comparing it to other similar properties that have recently been sold, been listed for sale, or for which offers have been made.

The appraiser obtains an indication of the subject property's value by adjusting the prices of the comparable properties to account for their differences from the subject property. Real estate appraisers compare the legal, economic, locational, and physical characteristics of the property they are appraising to those corresponding characteristics of similar sales, listings, or pending sales. Then, the appraiser adjusts up or down the sales price of each of the comparable properties to account for differences between the subject property and the comparable properties. These **adjustments** are values expressed in percentage or dollar amounts that the appraiser adds to or subtracts from the sales prices of the comparable properties. The formula looks like this:

Comparable Property Sales Price ± Adjustments = Adjusted Value

The adjusted prices are then reconciled into an estimate of value for the subject property.

Here is a brief illustration of the basic adjustment process, which we will examine in further detail later in this chapter.

*Comparable House A* sold for $355,000 with a garage.

*Subject House B* has no sales price and is virtually identical to *House A* except it has no garage.

Your job as an appraiser is to determine a value for *Subject House B*. If a garage is valued at $5,000 in this neighborhood, and the two houses are identical in every way except *Comparable House A* has a garage,

then, subtract the value of the garage from *Comparable House A* to determine an appropriate value for Subject *House B*.

$355,000 - $5,000 = $350,000
Comparable Property Sales Price ± Adjustments = Adjusted Value

**Figure 10.1** The basic adjustment process.

# Applications of this Approach

The sales comparison approach is most useful when appraising:

- property types that are bought and sold on a regular basis.

- single-family residences.

- condominiums.

- small multi-residential properties.

- vacant land.

The sales comparison approach is applicable when appraising all kinds of real property interests. It is most reliable in situations where there are a sufficient number of arm's-length sales transactions to indicate patterns within that market.

Although it is not usually the primary method employed, sales comparison analysis is often useful when appraising many kinds of commercial property. If sufficient sales data is available, appraisers use this approach as a check on the reasonableness of the value estimates obtained from the income and cost approaches to value.

# Limitations of this Approach

The sales comparison approach has limited usefulness when appraising:

- property types that are bought and sold infrequently.

- properties in a market with few arm's-length transactions.

- property in a rapidly changing market.

- special-use properties.

- unique properties.

Lack of market data can limit the usefulness and reliability of the sales comparison approach. Some types of properties are sold infrequently, so there is not enough market data to apply this approach. In situations where there are few comparable sales that are close substitutes for the subject property, the lack of data limits the reliability of this approach. In fact, the sales comparison approach usually is not applicable when appraising special-use properties or unique properties, such as churches or historic landmarks.

**Figure 10.2** The comparison approach is not usually applicable for highly unique properties such as churches and government buildings.

Another limitation is that the sales comparison approach to value is based on the assumption that a property's sales price is equal to its value. While this assumption is valid in most cases, in some instances a sales price is not indicative of what a property is actually worth. The appraiser's job is to find sales that are truly reflective of the market. This means that the appraiser must carefully research the conditions of each sale before using it as a comparable. Sales that do not meet the conditions of an arm's-length transaction are not good indicators of market value.

The reliability of the sales comparison approach is also limited by its heavy reliance on historical data. When a property sells, the purchase price is agreed upon sometimes months prior to the actual close of escrow. Consequently, that sales price is indicative of market perceptions as of the date an offer to purchase was accepted; not necessarily of market conditions as of the date it closes escrow. It also follows that a comparable sale's purchase price is indicative of market reactions at some point in the past and may not be reflective of the present market. If the appraiser is attempting to estimate the current value of a property, current market data, such as active listings and pending sales, also need to be considered in the analysis.

**Uniform Residential Appraisal Report**    File #

| There are | comparable properties currently offered for sale in the subject neighborhood ranging in price from $ | | | to $ | | |
|---|---|---|---|---|---|---|

| There are | comparable sales in the subject neighborhood within the past twelve months ranging in sale price from $ | | | to $ | | |
|---|---|---|---|---|---|---|

| FEATURE | SUBJECT | COMPARABLE SALE # 1 | | COMPARABLE SALE # 2 | | COMPARABLE SALE # 3 | |
|---|---|---|---|---|---|---|---|
| Address | | | | | | | |
| Proximity to Subject | | | | | | | |
| Sale Price | $ | | $ | | $ | | $ |
| Sale Price/Gross Liv. Area | $   sq. ft. | $   sq. ft. | | $   sq. ft. | | $   sq. ft. | |
| Data Source(s) | | | | | | | |
| Verification Source(s) | | | | | | | |
| VALUE ADJUSTMENTS | DESCRIPTION | DESCRIPTION | +(-) $ Adjustment | DESCRIPTION | +(-) $ Adjustment | DESCRIPTION | +(-) $ Adjustment |
| Sale or Financing Concessions | | | | | | | |
| Date of Sale/Time | | | | | | | |
| Location | | | | | | | |
| Leasehold/Fee Simple | | | | | | | |
| Site | | | | | | | |
| View | | | | | | | |
| Design (Style) | | | | | | | |
| Quality of Construction | | | | | | | |
| Actual Age | | | | | | | |
| Condition | | | | | | | |
| Above Grade | Total Bdrms. Baths | Total Bdrms. Baths | | Total Bdrms. Baths | | Total Bdrms. Baths | |
| Room Count | | | | | | | |
| Gross Living Area | sq. ft. | sq. ft. | | sq. ft. | | sq. ft. | |
| Basement & Finished Rooms Below Grade | | | | | | | |
| Functional Utility | | | | | | | |
| Heating/Cooling | | | | | | | |
| Energy Efficient Items | | | | | | | |
| Garage/Carport | | | | | | | |
| Porch/Patio/Deck | | | | | | | |
| | | | | | | | |
| | | | | | | | |
| Net Adjustment (Total) | | ☐ + ☐ - | $ | ☐ + ☐ - | $ | ☐ + ☐ - | $ |
| Adjusted Sale Price of Comparables | | Net Adj. % Gross Adj. % | $ | Net Adj. % Gross Adj. % | $ | Net Adj. % Gross Adj. % | $ |

I ☐ did ☐ did not research the sale or transfer history of the subject property and comparable sales. If not, explain

My research ☐ did ☐ did not reveal any prior sales or transfers of the subject property for the three years prior to the effective date of this appraisal.

Data source(s)

My research ☐ did ☐ did not reveal any prior sales or transfers of the comparable sales for the year prior to the date of sale of the comparable sale.

Data source(s)

Report the results of the research and analysis of the prior sale or transfer history of the subject property and comparable sales (report additional prior sales on page 3).

| ITEM | SUBJECT | COMPARABLE SALE # 1 | COMPARABLE SALE # 2 | COMPARABLE SALE # 3 |
|---|---|---|---|---|
| Date of Prior Sale/Transfer | | | | |
| Price of Prior Sale/Transfer | | | | |
| Data Source(s) | | | | |
| Effective Date of Data Source(s) | | | | |

Analysis of prior sale or transfer history of the subject property and comparable sales

Summary of Sales Comparison Approach

Indicated Value by Sales Comparison Approach $

**Figure 10.3**   The sales comparison approach section of Fannie Mae Form 1004.

# Sales Comparison Analysis Procedure

The sales comparison analysis procedure is a part of the appraisal process, and if applicable, it is only one of many steps. When using the sales comparison approach, Uniform Standards of Professional Appraisal Practices (USPAP) requires the appraiser to "collect, verify, and analyze all information applicable to the appraisal problem."

There is a systematic process an appraiser should follow when performing the sales comparison analysis.  This process includes:

- performing market research to collect information regarding comparable sales, listings, and offers to purchase properties that would be considered as substitutes in the market for the subject property.

- selecting the most appropriate comparable properties.

- verifying the comparable sales information found to ensure that it is accurate and reflective of open market activities.

- applying appropriate adjustments to the comparable properties chosen for the analysis.

- reconciling the various adjusted indicators of value into a value estimate.

The remainder of this chapter expands upon the above steps.

> ### Review — Steps for the Sales Comparison Approach
> - Collecting market data
> - Selecting market data
> - Verifying market data
> - Applying adjustments
> - Reconciling adjusted comparable property values

## Collecting Market Data

After the appraiser has identified the appraisal problem, determined the scope of work, and decided that the sales comparison analysis needs to be performed, the appraiser then collects data applicable to the assignment.  The quality of the analysis performed in an appraisal assignment is directly related to the quality of the data relied upon in an assignment.

The **data sources** appraisers use may vary from area to area and from property type to property type.  For example, the data sources an appraiser would rely upon when appraising a large commercial facility typically would not be the same as those relied upon by an appraiser performing single-family residential appraisals.  Likewise, the various real estate data services in existence do not provide information for all geographic areas or for all property types.  Often, a data source heavily relied upon in one area is not even available in another area.

Since no single data source is absolutely complete or accurate, appraisers need to rely upon multiple data sources. Local practices often dictate which data sources an appraiser will use for a particular assignment. Consulting multiple data sources will help the appraiser to minimize discrepancies, inaccurate details, and incomplete records. If discrepancies are found between differing data sources or if data is incomplete, the appraiser needs to do additional research to determine why the discrepancy exists or where to find the missing information. Only if the data used is the most complete and accurate to be found will the appraiser be able to provide the best analysis of the assignment.

## Multiple Listing Service

Commonly referred to by the acronym "MLS", the **multiple listing service** is an invaluable source of data. This service is provided by local real estate boards for its members and is designed as a tool for marketing real estate. Real estate brokers input individual records, called **listings**, into the MLS system to notify other brokers of properties for sale. Real estate brokers and sales associates use information in the MLS for purposes of buying and selling real estate.

While not specifically designed as a data source for appraisers, MLS systems provide a wealth of information. Information such as the seller's asking price and the property's total days on market is almost always included in MLS listings. This information is often difficult, if not impossible, to obtain elsewhere. Usually, MLS systems also provide comments specific to a property describing items of interest to buyers (and appraisers) of real estate. MLS systems often provide neighborhood-specific statistical data such as average sales prices and median days on market before a property sells. One of the most important pieces of information found in an MLS listing is the phone number(s) of the real estate brokers directly involved in the transaction.

There are different types of MLS systems. In many instances, there are separate residential and commercial MLS systems available. Older MLS systems and smaller real estate boards in some areas publish books of MLS listing information. Modern MLS systems are typically Internet-based and they provide extensive search capabilities. Sometimes individual listings provide interior and rear view photos showing items not visible to an appraiser performing a drive-by inspection from the street. Some computer-based MLS systems even provide virtual tours of a property showing 360° views from various locations both inside and outside a property. These items enable appraisers to compare comparable sales and listings with the subject property more accurately.

Although MLS systems are a good source of data, appraisers need to remember that property listings found on MLS systems are designed to sell properties and not specifically to assist appraisers. Since listing records are generated by individuals desiring to sell properties, there is a tendency toward overstating positive attributes and understating negative factors of a property. For example, in some listings, houses suffering from deferred maintenance are labeled as "handyman's delights" and properties with small rooms are labeled as being "cozy". Separating hype from factual information in MLS listings is another of the tasks appraisers perform.

## Public Record Information

In most states, information recorded at county recorder's offices, as well as some property tax assessor's information, is considered to be public. As such, the public can often obtain data from these sources, usually for free. Some counties provide this information online through the Internet while others require a trip to county offices.

**Figure 10.4**   Recent technology has simplified gathering public record information.

Public records, like those in the County Recorder's Office, show evidence of the conveyance of title or transfer of an interest in real property. Data obtained from these sources, however, varies in accuracy, quality, and completeness from county to county and state to state. In many instances, especially in areas of low population or rural location, this information is not computerized, so the appraiser is required to manually search through cumbersome card catalogues and property lists. Sometimes, sales information does not appear on these public record systems until months after the actual sale occurred.

Public records are also significant for determining a property's sales price based on the documentary transfer tax stamps affixed to the deed. The deed lists the transfer tax amount, so if the appraiser knows the local millage rate, he can determine the property's sales price. A **millage rate**, which can vary from district to district and county to county, expresses the property tax rate in terms of tenths of a cent per dollar of property value. A **mill** equals one-thousandth of a dollar and is numerically expressed as $0.001. Ten mills equal one cent, one-hundred mills equal ten cents, and one-thousand mills equal one dollar. Tax assessors use mills to determine the tax amount, and appraisers who know the formula can use it to work backwards and calculate the sales price.

The assessor first determines how much of the property's value is assessed for taxation, known as the assessed value. If there are any exemptions, like a homeowner's exemption, it is deducted from the assessed value. The millage rate is then applied to the assessed value (minus any exemption) to determine the transfer taxes for that property.

> For example, the tax rate is 32 mills in District A and is applied to the assessed value of a home, which is 40% of the purchase price of $350,000. To calculate the tax amount, first determine the assessed value by multiplying the property value by the assessment percentage ($350,000 × 40% = $140,000). Then apply the millage rate to the assessed value to determine the dollar amount of the property taxes ($140,000 × $0.032 = $4,480).

This knowledge serves the appraiser in reverse order. To illustrate, imagine this scenario:

> The appraiser finds a recorded deed for a potential comparable. From the tax stamp information, he sees that the property tax amount was $1,500, assessed at 30% of market value with a millage rate of 40. First, the appraiser must divide the tax bill by the millage rate to determine the assessed value ($1,500 ÷ $0.04 = $37,500). Then, knowing that the assessed value is 30% of the sales price, he would divide the assessed value by the assessment percentage ($37,500 ÷ 30% = $125,000) and determine what this property sold for.

This information is useful, but appraisers should never assume a sales price based solely upon the amount of transfer tax cited in a recorded deed. The amount of these taxes may be deliberately and illegally overstated or understated for tax or investment purposes. For example, sometimes the transfer tax is deliberately overstated in a deed for purposes of committing mortgage fraud.

## Data Services

Today, there are numerous companies engaged in the business of selling data to real estate appraisers, called **data services**. Almost all of these data services obtain their data from information disseminated by local county recorders and assessors. Some of the services provide information that has been submitted by real estate appraisers and lenders. A good number of these online data sources provide unlimited access to their database for a flat monthly fee. Others may charge per record, and, in some instances, the data is free. Some of these systems are geared toward providing data to residential real estate appraisers whereas others specialize in providing data for commercial appraisers. Sometimes, private online data sources provide their data in conjunction with local MLS services. Additionally some data providers may also publish books containing sales data on a monthly or quarterly basis. Some of these services provide data that is updated monthly on CDs sent to appraisers and others provide data online over the Internet.

**Figure 10.5** Data service subscriptions supply data in periodic books, on CDs, or through the Internet.

While many of these services have good search capabilities, appraisers need to remember they often provide only raw data such as addresses, sales prices, sale dates, bedroom and bath counts, and improvement size. In most cases, they do not provide information concerning quality, condition, income and expense information, buyer and seller motivation, or special amenities associated with a property. Appraisers who rely solely upon information obtained from these sources may misstate some critical aspect of the property.

## On-Site Sales Offices

There is often no online or public record information available for a property in a new development. In many instances, newly constructed properties do not appear on these data sources until months after they are completed and sold. In such instances, often the only reliable source of sales and information within that development is the on-site sales office. **On-site sales offices** are often very good sources of data, since the person providing the information is involved in all the transactions within that tract. Additionally, the sales agreements for both the subject and comparable sales are often available for inspection by the appraiser.

## Parties to the Transaction

**Parties to the transaction** are the people directly involved — the buyer, the seller, the buyer's broker, and the seller's broker. It may sound overly simple, but often knocking on a door is a good way to obtain information on a property. In many cases, owners are more than willing to talk to appraisers regarding the property they just purchased. Though more cumbersome than other methods, this way of gathering data has been around as long as there have been appraisers, and it still works.

> For example, suppose that an appraiser becomes aware of a sale that was not recorded. The appraiser goes to that property, and the occupant reveals an unrecorded deed indicating the occupant as the owner, a purchase agreement, and the price that was paid. This information could not have been obtained from any of the information brokers.

Although the information an appraiser learns from people in the field can be invaluable, it must be verified and corroborated. If the appraiser is talking to buyers or sellers, they may have a vested interest to misrepresent the facts. They know exactly what happened in a transaction, but may not convey that information accurately to the appraiser.

**Figure 10.6** Parties to the transaction include the buyer, the seller, and both the buyer's and seller's agents.

## Appraiser Office Files

In most new home developments, sales brochures and price lists are available for free. Many appraisers collect these sales brochures and price lists from new developments within the areas they appraise. This information could prove useful if the appraiser were asked to perform work in that development at some later time.

Appraisers also rely on information obtained when performing previous appraisals. While this may be a very good source of information, appraisers have to be careful to maintain confidentiality. Sometimes, the appraiser is precluded from using information obtained in an earlier assignment since using it would violate confidentiality laws. Appraisers need to be aware of the Confidentiality section of the Ethics Rule of USPAP in order to comply with this requirement.

## Other Sources of Market Data

There are numerous other sources available to appraisers. Though these sources rarely provide all the information appraisers require to perform their services, they may provide a starting point for further investigation by an appraiser.

### *Newspapers*

Real estate classified ads, as well as the real estate and public notices sections of a newspaper, often provide data regarding properties for sale, the buyers, the sellers, and any brokers involved in transactions. Often, information found in newspapers fills gaps in the information obtained from other sources such as the MLS and public records. The classified ads in newspapers are also a good source for current rental data information. The real estate sections of local newspapers often provide local market trend information.

### *Internet Research*

The Internet is a useful resource when researching real estate. As time goes on, more and more properties are listed on national Internet databases. In addition to sales and listing data, market area trends, and in some cases, local zoning and assessors' information is available.

### *Title Companies*

For years, title companies have maintained **title plants**. These are libraries of real estate information used by the title companies for research related to the issuance of title insurance policies. In the last few years, many of the larger title companies have started to provide free online access to their databases to real estate brokers too as a tool to assist them in their marketing efforts. Sometimes appraisers can obtain free access to these databases by contacting a title representative from one of the major title insurance companies.

## Selecting the Comparables

After appraisers gather information, they must select the comparables that are the most appropriate. Buyers and sellers rely upon information gathered from the market in making their buying or selling decisions. In performing appraisals, appraisers should rely upon the same information.

The appraiser needs to identify which data is appropriate and applicable to the assignment at hand. For instance, sales from high-rise condominium developments are not usually good indicators of value for single-family detached homes. However, in some instances, sales of single-family detached condominiums are very strong indicators of value for detached, single-family homes in nearby planned unit developments.

The geographic area an appraiser would typically search for comparable sales data depends upon the nature of the real estate being appraised. If similar properties are commonly bought and sold within a neighborhood, such as single-family residences, an appraiser would typically limit the search for sales data to similar properties located within that area. On the other hand, the market for some kinds of properties may be national or even worldwide in scope. Appraisers valuing regional malls, golf courses, high-rise office buildings, and industrial properties would most likely have to consider properties located long distances from the subject property.

**Figure 10.7** When comparable properties are bought and sold with frequency, like single-family homes, appraisers can usually limit their comp search to the neighborhood.

Most clients require a minimum of three comparable sales to be included in their reports. While this is a minimum number of sales needed, this number certainly can be increased to include more than three sales. Often, active listings and pending sales are included in the sales comparison analysis. Even though these additional comparable properties may not be closed sales as of the date of the appraisal, they provide a glimpse of current market expectations and can lend support to the final estimate of value. The more comps an appraiser can analyze, the more sound and supportable his or her conclusions will be. Therefore, an appraiser should utilize as many comps as necessary to arrive at his or her conclusion.

## Elements of Comparison

When appraising single-family residential properties, the appraiser considers numerous elements of comparison. An **element of comparison** is any aspect of a real estate transaction or any characteristic of the property that may affect the property's sales price. Appraisers will need to consider different elements of comparison for different assignments. Selecting truly comparable sales minimizes the amount and size of adjustments. For a typical residential appraisal, the comparable properties should:

- have a sale date as close to the effective date of the appraisal as possible.
- be as similar in age as possible to the subject property.
- be as similar in location as possible to the subject property.
- be as similar, if not identical, in physical, legal, and economic characteristics to the subject property.

Items needing consideration include the property rights being appraised of the subject versus the property rights conveyed in the comparable sale transaction. Financing terms for the comparable sales, any conditions of sale and atypical seller motivations affecting the sales price of the comparable property, and the effective date of the appraisal in comparison to the date the comparable property sold are other items requiring contemplation. Additionally, the appraiser must examine locational, physical, and legal differences between the subject and the comparable property.

Appraisal report forms in general use, such as the Fannie Mae Forms 1004 and 2055, identify most of these elements in a grid format. However, the adjustment grids in these forms do not include all items that may need to be adjusted. Items such zoning, landscaping, auxiliary units, etc., are not specifically listed in the grids on these commonly used forms. If items such as these are applicable within a particular assignment, the appraiser is obligated to consider them in the adjustment process as well.

| FEATURE | SUBJECT | COMPARABLE SALE # 1 | | COMPARABLE SALE # 2 | | COMPARABLE SALE # 3 | |
|---|---|---|---|---|---|---|---|
| Address | | | | | | | |
| Proximity to Subject | | | | | | | |
| Sale Price | $ | | $ | | $ | | $ |
| Sale Price/Gross Liv. Area | $ sq. ft. | $ sq. ft. | | $ sq. ft. | | $ sq. ft. | |
| Data Source(s) | | | | | | | |
| Verification Source(s) | | | | | | | |
| VALUE ADJUSTMENTS | DESCRIPTION | DESCRIPTION | +(-) $ Adjustment | DESCRIPTION | +(-) $ Adjustment | DESCRIPTION | +(-) $ Adjustment |
| Sale or Financing Concessions | | | | | | | |
| Date of Sale/Time | | | | | | | |
| Location | | | | | | | |
| Leasehold/Fee Simple | | | | | | | |
| Site | | | | | | | |
| View | | | | | | | |
| Design (Style) | | | | | | | |
| Quality of Construction | | | | | | | |
| Actual Age | | | | | | | |
| Condition | | | | | | | |
| Above Grade Room Count | Total Bdrms. Baths | Total Bdrms. Baths | | Total Bdrms. Baths | | Total Bdrms. Baths | |
| Gross Living Area | sq. ft. | sq. ft. | | sq. ft. | | sq. ft. | |
| Basement & Finished Rooms Below Grade | | | | | | | |
| Functional Utility | | | | | | | |
| Heating/Cooling | | | | | | | |
| Energy Efficient Items | | | | | | | |
| Garage/Carport | | | | | | | |
| Porch/Patio/Deck | | | | | | | |
| | | | | | | | |
| | | | | | | | |
| Net Adjustment (Total) | | ☐ + ☐ - | $ | ☐ + ☐ - | $ | ☐ + ☐ - | $ |
| Adjusted Sale Price of Comparables | | Net Adj. % Gross Adj. % | $ | Net Adj. % Gross Adj. % | $ | Net Adj. % Gross Adj. % | $ |

**Figure 10.8** The adjustment grid, FNMA 1004.

While it is not possible in every instance to find sales or listings that are identical to the subject in all these areas, appraisers should strive to find sales, offers to purchase, and listings that are as similar to the subject property in all aspects as possible. Using comps that are as similar as possible to the property being appraised will enable the appraiser to produce the most credible, and the most reliable, estimate of value.

## *Property Rights Conveyed*

In a majority of appraisal assignments, appraisers are asked to appraise the fee simple interest in a property. In other instances, appraisers are requested to estimate leasehold or leased fee interests in a property. The owner of a leasehold interest in a property does not own the complete bundle of rights in that property. That owner only has a portion of the rights associated with that property, and therefore, the leasehold interest in a property is usually not equal to the fee simple interest in a property.

Though it is not always possible, appraisers should try to use comparable properties that include the same property rights as the subject property in their analyses since property rights tend to have a large influence on value. Once the property rights for the subject and the comparable sales are established, the appraiser can relate and, if necessary, adjust the market data for the comparable properties to the subject property.

## *Financing Terms and Cash Equivalency*

The **financing terms** used to purchase a property can affect the price a seller is willing to accept. In fact, differences in financing can cause the sales price of one property to be significantly higher than that of an almost identical property that sold in the same period.

Financing can vary in many ways. Sometimes, in order to facilitate a sales transaction, a seller will pay fees that a buyer would traditionally pay, such as discount points, loan origination fees, and closing costs. In those situations, the seller will usually add those additional fees to the sales contracts, seller financing, or a buyer assuming an existing loan with a favorable interest rate can all have significant effects upon sales prices.

Adjustments for financing are different from other adjustments in one very significant way. Other adjustments are based upon differences between the comparable sale and the subject. However, adjustments for financing are based upon the difference in financing for the comparable sale and financing typically found in the market. If typical financing was used, the sale is referred to as a **cash-equivalent sale**.

When adjusting for financing, appraisers typically adjust for cash equivalency. The **cash-equivalency technique** is a procedure whereby the sales prices of comparable properties selling with atypical financing are adjusted to reflect financing that is typical in a market. The calculations used to derive cash-equivalency adjustments will vary depending upon the kind of financing used to purchase the comparable property and the terms associated with that financing.

> For example, situations often arise where the seller of a property will pay discount points to a lender so that a buyer may get financing at a below-market rate. (Points refers to prepaid interest lenders accept in order to finance a loan at below-market interest rates.) In these situations, the seller usually incorporates the additional points into the sales price he or she is willing to accept. If using this sale as a comp, an appraiser would typically deduct from the sales price a dollar amount equal to the amount paid by the seller.

In some cases when atypical financing is used, the appraiser may not be able to adjust for its effect on the sales price, and he or she will have to use a different comp.

## Conditions of Sale

Unusual conditions of sale may affect the final purchase price of a comparable sale and cause the sales price to reflect the market improperly. If the buyer's motivation is atypical for the market, the sales price may be atypical as well. The appraiser looks for arm's-length transactions where all parties involved are knowledgeable, acting in their own self-interest, and under no undue influence or pressure from other parties. In situations where the buyer or seller is acting under duress, or in situations where a buyer or seller is not acting knowledgeably, properties may be bought and sold at prices that are not indicative of market value.

> For example, an extremely wealthy property owner desired to purchase his next-door neighbor's property. The adjacent property owner did not wish to sell; however, the wealthy neighbor wanted the adjacent property so much that he eventually offered an extremely high price — much higher than the actual worth of the property. The offering price was so high the adjacent property owner could not refuse. This selling price would not be a good indicator of market value.

Sometimes the conditions of a sale lead to a lower price. A seller who wants to sell quickly may discount the property's price, or family members may sell properties at a discount to other family members.

Obviously, it is best to use comparable sales that have no unusual conditions of sale. If the appraiser finds it necessary and unavoidable to use a sale of this type, the appraiser must exercise great care. The appraiser must make appropriate, market-based adjustments to compensate for these conditions and their effect on the sales price of the comparable property.

## Market Conditions and Time Considerations

An appraisal is a snapshot in time. Just as a photograph documents an instant in time, an appraisal documents a property and its value at a specific point in time.

In most instances, the date of value of an appraisal is the date an appraiser inspects the subject property. However, in some instances, appraisers perform appraisals with a retrospective date of value, that is, the appraiser estimates the value of a property at some point in the past. On other occasions, appraisers are asked to estimate the value of a property as of some point in the future, which is known as a prospective appraisal.

Market data that reflects the market conditions effective as of the date of value needs to be considered by appraisers. Relying upon market data effective as of summer 2004 is a poor indicator of value for a property valued as of June 1, 1997. Sales, offers to purchase, and listings in early 1997 would be the data an appraiser would need to rely upon in that assignment.

**Market conditions** and property values change over time. Some markets have relatively stable values for long periods of time. In other markets, property values may increase or decrease at an astonishingly fast pace. In situations where markets are changing, adjustments need to be applied in order to reflect the change in the market from the time a property sold to the time it was used as a value indicator.

While the term **time adjustment** is usually applied to adjustments made because of changing market conditions, these adjustments are not based merely on the passage of time. In a stable market, a relatively long period of time may have elapsed, but no adjustment would be needed. Likewise, in a quickly changing market, relatively significant adjustments may be necessary even though only a short period of time has elapsed between the sale of the comparable property and the date of the appraisal. The passage of time by itself is not sufficient reason to apply a time adjustment. Changes in market conditions that are spread over time are what really constitute time adjustments.

Many things bring about changes in market conditions. Any and all changes in interest rates, inflation, deflation, employment trends, building trends, and inward and outward population shifts produce changes in supply and demand. As supply and demand changes, property values change.

Time adjustments are based upon the change in market conditions between the date the comparable property sold and the date of the appraisal. Time adjustments are usually expressed as a percentage increase, or decrease over time. Typically, this percentage change is then converted to a dollar adjustment and is applied to the sales price of the comparable property.

Often the percentage of change is expressed as a yearly amount. Appraisers will usually convert this yearly percentage change to a monthly amount and multiply the monthly percentage change by the number of months that have elapsed between the sale of the comparable property and the date of the appraisal.

> For example, an appraiser identifies a comparable within the same planned development (PUD) as the subject. The comparable sold ten months ago for $550,000. Because each property has the same floor plan and is in the same PUD, only the time of sale must be adjusted.

From his research, the appraiser concludes that the property values in the local market have increased an average of 4% per year. To convert this to a monthly percentage, he divides the yearly percentage by twelve (the total number of months in a year) and then multiplies this by the number of months for which he must account.

$$0.04 \div 12 = 0.00333$$

$$0.00333 \times 10 = 0.0333 \text{ or } 3\tfrac{1}{3}\% \ (3.33\%)$$

The final step is to adjust the comparable's sales price up by the percentage.

$$\$550{,}000 \times 3.33\% = \$18{,}315$$

$$\$550{,}000 + \$18{,}315 = \$568{,}315, \text{ or } \$568{,}300 \text{ (rounded)}$$

## *Location*

The properties used as indicators of value for the subject should be influenced, if possible, by the same market forces as the subject. Since real estate is immobile, the market forces that influence a property are usually determined by the property's **location**. In any neighborhood, many forces combine to influence the market perception, and therefore the values, within that neighborhood. In most appraisal assignments, the appraiser identifies the boundaries of the neighborhood in which the subject property is located.

**Figure 10.9** Rivers and major thoroughfares create natural neighborhood boundaries.

A **neighborhood** may be defined by physical boundaries such as a freeway, a body of water, or the base of a mountain. In other cases, the neighborhood boundary may be established by a change in land uses, such as a transition from residential to commercial uses. Items that may not be evident when passing through an area may establish other neighborhood boundaries. ZIP code boundaries, school district boundaries, city limits, or improvement district boundaries are all examples of items that may define the boundaries of a neighborhood but are not readily evident.

If possible, appraisers should rely upon comparable properties located in the same neighborhood as the subject. Using comparable properties outside the subject's neighborhood requires the appraiser to perform additional analysis to account for locational differences between the subject and the comparable properties used.

A location adjustment is usually required when the subject property has locational influences that are significantly different from those influencing a comparable sale. Even though the subject and the comparable sales are located in the same neighborhood, sometimes variations within that neighborhood would affect value. In a desirable neighborhood, for example, there may be a residential property that backs to a major interstate freeway whereas another home in that same neighborhood may back to a private lake.

Commercial properties can be extremely susceptible to differences in location. For example, most gasoline service stations are located in corner locations because these are more advantageous. Studies have shown that customers most often will patronize a retail business with good vehicular access, be it a restaurant, gas station, or retail center, over one that has inferior access. In some instances, the side of the street a property is located on will have a significant effect on value.

A location that is detrimental for one land use is often beneficial for another land use. Single-family residential properties located on very busy thoroughfares tend to be less desirable than similar properties located on quiet streets. Busy street locations, on the other hand, are much more desirable for retail establishments than quiet street locations.

Sometimes, locational differences have nothing to do with physical differences and are based upon market perception. Location within, or outside of school district boundaries, ZIP codes, police and fire protection, or historical and improvement districts may also have a significant effect on value and are things an appraiser needs to consider in the adjustment process.

## *Physical Characteristics*

The **physical characteristics** of a subject property and a comparable may vary greatly. Differences in site area, view, amenities, quality, condition, design and appeal, age, and size of improvements are all items that have an influence on a property's value. For example, all other things being equal, a three-bedroom home is usually the best indicator of value for a three-bedroom home. Likewise, a property with a panoramic ocean view is usually the best indicator of value for another property with a panoramic ocean view. Other items such as functional utility (usability), amenities, room count, and architectural style are all things that appraisers need to consider when making adjustments for physical differences between the subject and a comparable property.

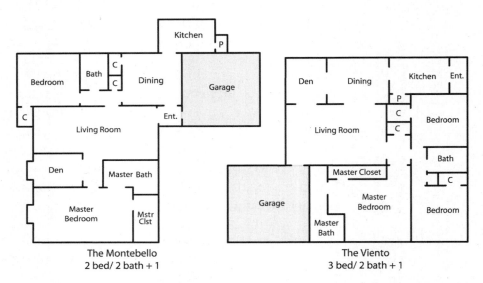

The Montebello
2 bed/ 2 bath + 1

The Viento
3 bed/ 2 bath + 1

**Figure 10.10** Different floorplans within the same subdivision make suitable comps even if there are different features. Typically, they will share more in common with each other than with a property in a different tract.

## *Other Characteristics*

Other physical, legal, and economic characteristics of the subject and comparable properties should be considered. For example, properties with similar zoning (legal) or similar income-producing capacity (economic) are usually better indicators of value than properties that differ in these characteristics.

### Non-Real Property

On occasion, personal property may be sold along with real property. For example, a seller may choose to sell appliances that are not built in the house. If the sales price of the comp includes such items, the appraiser may need to make an adjustment.

## Highest and Best Use

As we discussed in Chapter 8, the highest and best use of a property is the main factor that determines its value. For this reason, most appraisers will not use a comp if its highest and best use is different from that of the subject property. One of the simplest ways to check highest and best use is to see if there is a difference in zoning.

Differences in zoning may have a large influence on a property's value. An appraiser should attempt to use comparable sales that have the same zoning designation as the subject. In situations where comparable sales have different zoning than the subject property, an adjustment may be necessary. Typically, properties that have zoning which allows a more intensive use are more valuable than ones that have zoning which allows less intensive development. This is because the owner of the more intensively zoned property has more options for how he can use his property.

## Economic Characteristics

Most beginning appraisers start with residential property appraisals. However, the sales comparison approach can be used with income-producing properties as well. Ideally, if the subject property is producing income, the comps should produce similar amounts. If not, an adjustment may be necessary.

> For example, Appraiser Jane is using the sales comparison approach to value a convenience store that has annual revenue of $900,000. Two similar convenience stores sold recently: one has annual revenue of $820,000 and sold for $700,000; and the other has annual revenue of $600,000 and sold for $490,000. In this situation, the first comp is more similar to the subject in its capacity to produce income.

# Verifying Comparable Information

After identifying the best comparable properties, the next step is to verify the data. The verification process is extremely important since it is used to identify which possible comparable properties are, or are not, reflective of activity in the open market. **Verification** is an inquiry into the circumstances surrounding and affecting a sale. This includes the reason for the sale of the property and any items affecting its price. The appraiser must be careful to ensure that data used to formulate the appraiser's opinions and conclusions reflect arm's-length transactions within the market.

It is important to verify the information of the comparable properties to confirm that the physical, legal, and economic information about each comparable property found in other data sources is accurate and correct. Verification also identifies whether or not the comparable property is an open market and arm's-length transaction. In this part of the process, the appraiser identifies buyer and seller motivations and resolves any apparent conflicts and/or discrepancies found in the data sources. Additionally, the appraiser resolves any questions he or she may have regarding any gaps in the data or any other items that need further explanation.

The verification process may take a number of forms and may vary as to its depth depending upon the scope of work being performed in an assignment. Whenever possible, the appraiser should verify a sale by contacting a party directly involved in the transaction such as the buyer, the seller, the seller's agent or broker, or the buyer's agent or broker. The appraiser may also verify some of the market data information with such parties as tenants, property managers, developers, etc. Some appraisal assignments may require the appraiser to verify the sale with both the buyer (or buyer's agent) and the seller (or seller's agent).

Sometimes the verification process performed by appraisers is minimal and entails simply confirming the transaction through more than one data source. Appraisers performing only this level of verification are at much greater risk of improperly analyzing the comparable data. While this level of verification is a relatively common practice, it does not relieve the appraiser of liability associated with negligent appraisal practice.

In some instances, verification of the data may cause an appraiser to eliminate a sale as a value indicator in an assignment. This happens when information uncovered during the verification process shows that the reported transaction is not indicative of the market. It also may happen when information about a comparable property cannot be verified to the appraiser's satisfaction.

## Applying Adjustments

Once the appraiser has collected, analyzed, and verified market information, this information must be applied in the appraisal. At this point in the process, the appraiser has already narrowed down the number of sales, listings, and pending sales to those most similar to the subject. The next step is to **apply adjustments** to the comps.

Adjustments are applied to the sales prices of comparable properties in an effort to "equalize" the comparable sale, in an economic sense, to the subject property. When appropriate comps have been identified and verified, the appraiser can assume that the sales price of the comparable property is indicative of its value. Then, he or she adjusts that sales price for major differences between that comparable property and the subject property. As a result, the adjusted sales price of the comparable property is indicative of the value of the subject property.

The accuracy and the reliability of the sales comparison approach hinges upon the accuracy of the adjustments applied to the comparable properties. The importance of making proper adjustments to the comparable properties cannot be overemphasized. The adjustments applied to the comparable properties must be derived from the market and reflective of the actions of typical buyers and sellers in the real estate market within which the subject property operates. One of the pitfalls in performing the sales comparison analysis is the tendency for some appraisers to apply improper, unsupported, and even arbitrary adjustments to comparable properties. In more than a few instances, appraisers have significantly over-valued properties based on improper adjustments. USPAP is very clear when it states, "…an appraiser must be aware of, understand, and correctly employ those recognized methods and techniques that are necessary to produce a credible appraisal…"

As a beginning appraiser, you will:

1. identify differences between the comp and the subject property.

2. decide if the difference makes the comp more or less valuable.

3. determine the value of the difference.

4. make value adjustments in order.

## Identify Differences

When looking at the various elements of comparison, appraisers first have to identify if there is a difference for which adjustment is necessary. We discussed earlier the different elements of comparison that appraisers look at when selecting the most appropriate comparables. Now that comps have been chosen, the appraiser looks at the same elements of comparison and checks for any special sales and financing considerations and any differences between the comps and the subject property in time-related, locational, and physical characteristics.

In performing the sales comparison analysis, the subject and the comparable sales are usually entered onto an **adjustment grid**, or **matrix**. This grid lists important items affecting value such as site area, location, design and appeal, quality, condition, gross building area, basement area, room count, view, age, amenities, etc. Using this grid helps to ensure that the comparable sales are adjusted consistently. It also shows, in an easy-to-read format, how the subject compares to the comparable properties in various characteristics and the adjustments the appraiser makes.

# Decide if the Comp is More or Less Valuable

Once differences are identified, the appraiser's next step is to analyze each of the differences one-by-one and determine if a particular difference makes the comparable sale superior or inferior.

For example, the comparable property shown in the grid below is not in as good condition as the subject property and does not have as many bathrooms. However, it does have a larger garage and a pool, while the subject property does not.

|  | Subject Property | Comparable Sale | |
|---|---|---|---|
| Sales Price | ??? | $205,000 | |
| Condition | Good | Fair | Inferior |
| Bedrooms | 4 | 4 | Same |
| Bathrooms | 3 | 2 | Inferior |
| Garage | 2-car | 3-car | Superior |
| Pool | No | Yes | Superior |

We already know the sales price of the comparable property, and we are trying to determine the probable sales price of the subject property. Since the comp's condition and number of bathrooms are inferior to the subject, we know that the subject property would be worth more than the comp in these areas. However, the comp has a larger garage and a pool, so the subject would be worth less than the comp in those areas.

By comparing the two properties in this way, the appraiser knows if he has to make a positive or a negative adjustment to the comparable sales price, even before he determines the actual dollar value of the adjustment.

---

**Direction of Adjustments**

1. If the comparable property has a feature that is superior to the subject property or if the comparable property has a feature that is missing from the subject property, the comparable property is considered to be worth more than the subject in regard to that item. In that case, the sales price of the comparable would need to be adjusted down to account for the contributory value of that superior feature and its effect upon the sales price of that property.

2. If the comparable property has a feature that is inferior to the subject property or if the comparable property is lacking a feature that the subject property has, the comp is worth less than the subject in regard to that item. In that case, the sales price of the comparable property would be adjusted up to account for that difference.

**\*Adjustments are always made to the comps. The appraiser cannot adjust the value of the subject property because the value of the subject is unknown.**

---

To see how this works, let's make adjustments to the two properties in our example:

Through careful analysis, it is determined that a pool in this market-place is worth $10,000. The comparable property has a pool and the subject property does not, so the adjustment process requires that the appraiser subtract $10,000 from the sales price of the comparable. In essence the question being asked is, "What would the comparable have sold for if it were like the subject property and did not have a pool?"

The subject property has three bathrooms and the comparable sale has only two bathrooms. An extra bathroom in this marketplace is worth $5,000. In this case, add $5,000 to the sales price of the comparable, to answer the question, "What would the comparable have sold for if it had a third bathroom, just like the subject property?"

## Determine the Adjustment Value

When the appraiser has identified a particular characteristic where the subject property and the comparable property are different, it is the appraiser's job to identify the amount the market would pay for that difference. By tabulating the pluses and minuses of all of the adjustments made to the comparable sale, we arrive at the adjusted selling price. The following grid illustrates the concept:

| | Subject Property | | Comparable Sale | |
|---|---|---|---|---|
| Sales Price | ??? | | $205,000 | |
| Condition | Good | Fair | +$5,000 | |
| Bedrooms | 4 | 4 | | |
| Bathrooms | 3 | 2 | +$5,000 | |
| Garage | 2-car | 3-car | −$5,000 | |
| Pool | No | Yes | −$10,000 | |
| Adjusted Sales Price | | | $200,000 | |

In this example, some features are superior to those of the subject property. These require a negative adjustment. Other features are inferior. These require a positive adjustment. This enables the appraiser to zero in on an indicated value for the subject property.

Adjustments made to the prices of the comparable sales may be applied either in dollars or as a percentage. For example, an enclosed patio may add $15,000 in value (dollar adjustment) or a home located adjacent to a noisy freeway may be found to be worth 15% less (percentage adjustment) than other homes not similarly affected.

The manner in which the adjustment is extracted from the market determines which way the adjustment is applied. Some adjustments are applied to reflect specific property features or physical characteristics. Views, swimming pools, and additional garage parking spaces fit this category. Dollar values are used for these types of adjustments. Other adjustments are made to the sales prices of comparable properties to reflect items affecting the overall value of that property. Sales and financing concessions as well as property rights conveyed would be items fitting this description. Since these items affect the overall value, the sales price of the comp is adjusted by a percentage.

In some appraisal assignments, the appraiser makes adjustments to a particular **unit of comparison** rather than the property as a whole. For example, when appraising an apartment complex, or a large hotel, the appraiser may analyze comparable sales on the basis of price per unit. Theaters, sports facilities, and auditoriums may be analyzed in terms of price per seat. RV and mobile home parks and parking lots may be analyzed in terms of price per space. Some properties are analyzed on the basis of price per square foot, price per acre, or even price per cubic foot.

> For example, Alex is appraising a warehouse. He found a comparable that recently sold for $21 per cubic foot. Alex's market investigation reveals that a negative 4% adjustment for age should be made and a positive 7% adjustment for physical differences. Alex would first subtract 4% from the price per unit ($21 − 4% = $20.16), and then add 7% ($20.16 + 7% = $21.57) to find the adjusted value per unit, $21.57 per cubic foot.

Identifying how much to adjust for a particular item is the most difficult aspect of the sales comparison approach. Adjustments must be market derived, and in some situations, readily available market data is inconclusive. There are numerous methods for identifying how large an adjustment should be, and some methods work better than others. Appraisers need to be aware of all the following methods and exercise sound judgment in determining the applicability of any particular method to the appraisal problem at hand. The following section will explore the benefits and limitations of the most widely used methods.

## Paired Sales Analysis

The **paired sales analysis** is used to identify the amount of an adjustment when at least two sales are found that are virtually identical in all aspects except one. The one differing item between the sales logically accounts for the difference in price between the two properties.

To illustrate how the paired sale analysis works, assume two homes sold in a tract of homes all developed by the same developer. Both of the homes in this example have the exact same floor plan and both are in similar locations. The two homes are virtually identical in all regards except one has a remodeled kitchen and the other does not. The home with the upgraded kitchen sold for $425,000 and the one without sold at about the same time for $410,000. Both homes sold with similar financing in a market where values are stable.

In the above scenario, the difference in price is $15,000. The only significant difference between the two properties is the fact one has a remodeled kitchen and the other does not. In this example, it would be reasonable to assume that the kitchen has a contributory value of $15,000. Appraisers would then be able to state, with a high degree of certainty, that a similar kitchen in that same neighborhood would warrant a $15,000 adjustment upwards or downwards. The direction of the adjustment would be dependent upon whether the subject or the comparable sale was the property with the upgrade.

Suppose an appraiser needs to know the value of a pool in a particular marketplace. He or she searches for two sales that are similar in all characteristics, except for the pool:

| Sale 1 | 3 bedroom | 2 bath | 1600 sq. ft. | pool | $200,000 |
| --- | --- | --- | --- | --- | --- |
| Sale 2 | 3 bedroom | 2 bath | 1625 sq. ft. | no pool | $192,000 |

This paired sales analysis reveals that a pool in this marketplace is worth about $8,000. The two properties have the same number of bedrooms and bathrooms. They are close enough in size that no adjustment needs to be made (a 25 square-foot difference is not perceptible in the marketplace). Assuming that all other characteristics are similar, the only recognized difference is the pool.

Sale 1
$200,000

Sale 2
$192,000

**Figure 10.11** Paired sales analysis is used to identify the amount of an adjustment in a particular marketplace.

This marketplace appears to support the value for a pool at $8,000. Following the verification principle discussed at length earlier in this chapter, as well as to strengthen the position that a pool in this marketplace is worth $8,000, more evidence is needed. The diligent appraiser continues to search and finds another pair to analyze:

| Sale 1 | 4 bedroom | 2.5 bath | 2000 sq. ft. | pool | $232,000 |
| --- | --- | --- | --- | --- | --- |
| Sale 2 | 4 bedroom | 2.5 bath | 2000 sq. ft. | no pool | $223,500 |

This time the two properties are a match with the exact same square footage, room count, and floor plan. The only recognized difference is Sale 1 has a pool while Sale 2 does not. The difference in the selling prices is $8,500. Since the properties are a bit more expensive, the slightly higher pool value can be justified. However, the difference is not significant and still supports the opinion that a pool in this market-place is worth approximately $8,000. The more evidence he or she can extract from the marketplace, the stronger his or her opinion will be.

This method is accurate, but, unfortunately, it is often impractical. In most cases, there are not enough sufficiently similar sales available to identify the contributory value of a particular variable. Typically, very few sales are available that have only one significant difference between them, and most of the time, when sales like this do exist, the difference between the two is not the item the appraiser is trying to identify. When this method is used, frequently a series of adjustments is required in order to isolate the effect of a single characteristic. The problem arises in this scenario in knowing how much to adjust for the other items when attempting to isolate the effect of that single charac-teristic.

Even though the data available to perform the paired sale analysis may be limited, appraisers should not discard this method of extracting adjustments. In many cases this method will provide meaningful results in spite of the limited available data. In these cases, the apprais-er should check the reasonableness of the data by using some other available analytical methods.

## Case Study

The following example is meant to illustrate how paired sales analysis applies in a practical scenario.

> Appraiser Jane is commissioned to appraise a new house in an upscale development situated in the hills overlooking a valley and a freeway. She began her investigation by pulling comparable sales and setting up a workfile. She then went to the site to examine the circumstances.
>
> Upon doing the physical inspection, she discovered that the subject prop-erty was situated at the end of a short cul-de-sac. Looking from the rear of the property, the subject property definitely had an outstanding view of the valley and the freeway. Comparable 1 was situated on the same cul-de-sac but was on the opposite side of the street. Because of a hillside and the homes opposing it, its view was obstructed. Comparables 2 and 3 were situated in the same subdivision so as not to have any view at all. From her physical inspection thus far, she knew that the subject property did indeed have a superior view to the comparables but still did not know how much the view is worth or what the adjustment should be.
>
> These homes were about a year old and the subdivision was still under construction, so subsequently she went to the sales office to see if any recent sales could be paired up, isolating the view in order to determine what the view is worth. No such comparison could be made, but she was able to verify in the sales office that the owner of the subject property had

paid a $50,000 view premium for that particular lot. By then, though, the subdivision was a year older and there was still no concrete proof of what a view was worth in this subdivision.

The appraiser revisited the data pulled at the beginning of the assignment and noticed five sales of new homes in a less expensive neighboring community on the other side of the freeway, about five miles away, all on the same street. She observed that the five sales were described almost identically: approximately 2,200 square feet with all the same amenities, but there was a disparity in the prices. They ranged from $275,000 to $329,000; three of the sales clustered between $275,000 and $279,000; and the other sales were $325,000 and $329,000. They evidenced no descriptive difference in amenities, yet the price range was $50,000.

She decided to drive over and investigate. The top level of the street was about 15-to-20 feet higher in altitude than the lower level of the street, and the street was shaped like a horseshoe. House A sold for $325,000 and had an outstanding view from the rear yard, a view of the same valley and freeway but from the other side. Houses B, C and D on the opposite side of the street sold for $275,000, $277,000, and $279,000 respectively. They were very similar homes to House A, but they had no views because of the obstruction of the homes on the opposite side of the street. House E, situated on the corner of the upper level of the street, sold for $329,000, and had an outstanding view from the rear yard over the roof of the homes on the lower level of the street.

These five properties matched up perfectly as being practically identical, except for their views. The sales prices were approximately $50,000 apart, indicating that the view in this neighborhood was worth about $50,000. Because this is a lower-priced neighborhood than that of the subject property, it is logical to say that since the view was worth approximately $50,000 in this marketplace, it would be worth at least $50,000 in the more expensive marketplace.

## Sale-Resale Analysis

Sometimes a property is sold and is resold in a relatively short period of time. Assuming both sales are arm's-length, open market transactions, and assuming that there have been no significant changes to the property during the time between the two sales, the difference in price could be a basis for a time adjustment. This is called the **sale-resale analysis**.

To illustrate this method, assume a property was purchased for $375,000 on June 1, 2003 and resold on April 1, 2004 for $395,000. The increase in value over that time period was $20,000. This $20,000 increase was spaced over a 10-month period and was a 5.33% increase over the original sales price. The 5.33% increase equals a .53% increase in value per month.  Rounding this figure, it would be safe to say that property values in this property's market are increasing at approximately $1/2$% per month or approximately 6% per year.

In some instances, a property may be in a stable market where values are not changing to any significant degree.  If the improvements have been remodeled during the time between the two sales, the sale-resale analysis method could identify the contributory value of the remodeling.

However, like the paired-sale analysis, this method is not always practical.  Rarely do properties sell and resell with no other changes taking place.  In many instances, properties are purchased, remodeled, and resold in markets that are also increasing in value.  To identify how much of the increase in value between the two sales was attributable to the remodeling and how much was attributable to the increasing market may be difficult to determine.  Sale-resale analysis can prove to be a powerful analytical tool in the appraiser's overall set of analytical techniques.

**Figure 10.12**   If a property is sold and resold in a relatively short period of time, the difference in sale price can be used as the basis of the time adjustment.

In Chapter 6, we discussed a practice known as flipping.  Flipping is another possible threat to the quality of an appraiser's sale-resale analysis.  Flipping occurs when a person buys a property at one price and quickly sells it to another at an inflated price, usually within a short period of time.  The sale appears to be an arm's-length transaction, but the inflated sales price is designed to defraud the lender. With proper verification, the appraiser should be able to avoid flipped properties.

## Multiple Regression Analysis

**Multiple regression analysis** is an analytical technique using statistical methods to analyze comparable sales and estimate individual adjustments. The theory of multiple regression analysis has been around for a long time. However, it was of little value to most appraisers because even the simplest analysis required a large number of calculations.

With the advent of the personal computer and the development of software capable of quickly performing the numerous computations required, appraisers now can more easily use the technique. Appraisers use multiple regression analysis not just to identify the amount of an adjustment, but also to help estimate property values. The problem with using multiple regression is that most of the time all sales in an area are factored into the analysis, not just the sales that are comparable to the subject. Less than arm's-length transactions and even fraudulent sales often get included in these analytical models. Obviously, these non-market-based transactions can distort the results obtained from a multiple regression analysis.

Like the other methods, multiple regression analysis has benefits and limitations. Since it is a statistical method, multiple regression analysis works best where distinct, quantifiable data can be identified. Items such as age, building size, sales price, room count, site area, etc., are easily quantifiable. Other items having an effect on value such as quality, condition, view, design and appeal, and location are not easily quantifiable and therefore not readily applicable in a program that is based upon mathematical calculations.

In areas where properties have a high degree of homogeneity, where most homes are of approximately the same age, size, quality, condition, design and appeal, etc., a multiple regression analysis may produce credible results. In areas where all the properties are custom built, where no two properties are similar, and where there are amenities such as a view, multiple regression analysis does not usually produce meaningful results.

## Contingent Valuation Methodology

Also called the survey method, the **contingent valuation methodology**, if performed properly, can yield very good results. There are participants in any given market that are active in, and extremely knowledgeable about, that market. Sometimes, all the appraiser has to do to identify how much a particular feature affects the value of a property is to ask those who are knowledgeable about that market. If an appraiser surveys enough knowledgeable participants within a market in a systematic manner, the appraiser can generate data that is found nowhere else.

The major benefit to this method is that it can be used even when there is no sales data available, since this method does not rely on sales data to determine the adjustment value.

However, this method has limitations as well. Like any type of survey, a significant number of interviews needs to be performed in order to obtain accurate and quantifiable results. The appraiser needs to exercise care in crafting questions to be asked that are not leading and which do not introduce bias into the results, and in order to get meaningful results, the appraiser should ask all interviewees exactly the same questions.

## Make Adjustments in Order

Since appraisers use both dollar amount and percentage adjustments, the adjustments must be made in a specific sequence. This is true if percentage adjustments are made alone, or if they are made in combination with dollar adjustments. If the adjustments are made strictly on a dollar basis, the sequence in which adjustments are made is unimportant.

Adjustments that affect overall property value are made first, followed by those which only affect individual property features. Typically, the appraiser will make adjustments in the following order:

1. rights conveyed.
2. financing and sales concessions.
3. conditions of sale.
4. market conditions.
5. location adjustments.
6. physical characteristics.

## *Working with Dollar Adjustments*

Comparables with dollar adjustments only are relatively uncomplicated. This is because the sequence in which adjustments are made is unimportant.

For example, a comp sold for $335,000 but required several adjustments:

| Comparable | |
|---|---|
| Sales Price | $335,000 |
| Condition | – $   5,000 |
| 1/2 bath | + $   8,000 |
| Garage | – $ 12,000 |

Since this example only involves dollar adjustments, the appraiser can add up the adjustments in any order, and the adjusted price will always be $326,000.

The appraiser can even total the adjustments, and then combine the net adjustment amount with the sales price to get the adjusted price: − $5,000 + $8,000 − $12,000 = − $9,000 net adjustment; $335,000 − $9,000 = $326,000.

## *Working with Percentages Adjustments*

Since a percentage adjustment affects the overall property value, applying several percentage adjustments can cause the outcome to vary considerably. Unlike dollar adjustments, one can not simply add the percentages together and then apply the ultimate percentage to the comparable's price. When applying percentage adjustments, inter-mediate adjusted prices are calculated. Subsequent adjustments are applied to the previous intermediate price thereby calculating a new intermediate price. This results in a cumulative value estimate that could be significantly affected by the sequence in which adjustments are applied. An example should help to illustrate this.

A suitable comparable has been found and it sold for $310,000. However, three percentage adjustments are required to account for its differences to the subject.

The location of comparable is superior to the subject, which requires a 10% negative adjustment to make up for its superiority. The appraiser has also discovered that the financing used to purchase the property was not typically of that market, so sales price of the comp needs to be adjusted up by 2%. Finally, it sold 14 months ago, and due to changing market conditions, it will need to be adjusted up 5%.

Let's look at two different ways to determine the adjusted sales price:

First, following the logic of dollar adjustments, one could simply add the three percentages together to get a net percentage of -3%: 2%+5%-10% = -3%. If you subtract three percent from the sales price of the comparable, its adjusted value is $300,700.

| Combined | |
|---|---|
| Sales Price | $310,000 |
| Net % | × .97 |
| Adjusted Price | $300,700 |

However, we get a different result if we apply the adjustments in the correct sequence:

### Sequence

| | |
|---|---|
| Sales Price | $310,000 |
| Financing Terms | × 1.02 |
| | $316,200 |
| Market Conditions | × 1.05 |
| | $332,010 |
| Location | × .90 |
| Adjusted Price | $298,800 (rounded) |

As you can see, there is a difference of almost $2,000 when using step-by-step percentage adjustments, and with larger numbers the discrepancy becomes more glaring.

## *Working with Percentage and Dollar Adjustments*

When this scenario arises, it is crucial to follow the sequence of adjustments, for any improperly applied adjustment will affect the following adjustment(s).  Examine the following scenario.

Appraiser Jane is appraising a large, multi-million dollar home.  She found a comparable property that recently sold for $5,500,000.  However, there are several adjustments that she needs to make: a $20,000 adjustment for the presence of a pool, a 7% adjustment for market conditions, and a -10% adjustment for external obsolescence associated with proximity to a freeway.  In addition, Jane discovered during her research that the seller bought down the buyer's loan, which accounted for $111,000 of the sales price.

When applied properly, the sequence of adjustment reveals that the proper adjusted value of this particular comparable is $5,209,600 (rounded).

**Sequence 1**

| Sales Price | $5,500,000 |
|---|---|
| Financing | − $111,000 |
| | $5,389,000 |
| Market Conditions | × 1.07 |
| | $5,766,230 |
| Location | × .90 |
| | $5,189,607 |
| Physical Characteristics | + $20,000 |
| | $5,209,607 |

If the adjustments are applied in any other order, the appraiser's final result will be off from as little as $4,000 to as much as $12,500.

**Sequence 2**

| Sales Price | $5,500,000 |
|---|---|
| Physical Characteristics | + $20,000 |
| | $5,520,000 |
| Location | × .90 |
| | $4,968,000 |
| Financing Terms | − $111,000 |
| | $4,857,000 |
| Market Conditions | × 1.07 |
| | $5,196,990 |

## Reconciling

In the reconciliation of the sales comparison analysis, it is important for the appraiser to weigh all indicated values derived from the sales, pending sales, and listings that were considered. Careful thought as to the reliability of each indication of value must be considered.

When the adjustment process is completed, each comparable sale will produce an adjusted sales price that is an indicator of value for the subject property. Sometimes these adjusted sales prices may match one another, most often they do not. It is not proper appraisal practice simply to average the adjusted sales prices together. It is the appraiser's job at this point to identify which of the comparable sales is given most weight in this analysis and the reasoning why it is the one most heavily weighted. The appraiser must use sound reasoning and judgment, not mere mechanical calculation, to reconcile the individual value indicators into a value estimate.

Often, the comparable sale having the smallest amount of gross adjustments is the sale given most weight in the sales comparison analysis. This stands to reason since the property requiring the least amount of adjusting on a gross basis is likely the one that is overall most similar to the subject. Additionally, sales that require the largest amount of adjusting on a gross basis would tend to be the least similar sale to the subject and consequently the weakest indicator of value.

While the property having the least amount of adjusting on a gross basis is often the one given the most weight, this is not always the case. Sometimes the sale having the fewest number of adjustments, or the sale that is most recent in time to the date of the appraisal is weighted most heavily.

## Adjustment Guidelines

There comes a time when a comp ceases to be an appropriate comparable. This occurs when one has to make too many adjustments to the comparable, but what is too many? The **Federal National Mortgage Association** (Fannie Mae) has established **adjustment guidelines**.

Fannie Mae states that a single line item adjustment should not exceed 10% of the sales price of the comparable. For example, if a property sold for $200,000, no single adjustment should exceed $20,000. Keep in mind that this is not a steadfast rule; it is a guideline. The appraiser can still make the adjustment, even if it exceeds the 10% guideline for a single line item, as long as market data supports it.

Fannie Mae has also established guidelines for the total adjustment amounts. There are two types of totals – net and gross.

The net adjustment amount is determined by combining all the adjustments and adding or subtracting them as indicated. The appraiser divides this amount by the sales price to determine the percentage of net adjustments. FNMA's guideline is that the percentage of net adjustments should not exceed 15%.

However, the net adjustment guideline is not enough, since the net adjustment amount allows for offsetting adjustments. In theory, an appraiser could apply 100 different adjustments that balance each other out and result in a net adjustment amount of $0. Fannie Mae has also established a guideline for the acceptable percentage of gross adjustments in a single comparable sale. The amount of the gross adjustment is determined by adding all individual adjustments, without regard to whether they are positive or negative adjustments. Then, the appraiser divides that sum by the comparable property's sales price to determine the percentage of gross adjustment. Fannie Mae states that this percentage should not exceed 25% of the sales price of the comparable. The following grid demonstrates the concept.

| Sales Price | $100,000 |
| --- | --- |
| Condition Adjustment | +$5,000 |
| Bedroom Adjustment | – $3,000 |
| Bathroom Adjustment | – $2,000 |
| Pool Adjustment | – $7,500 |
| Location Adjustment | +$5,000 |
| Age Adjustment | +$3,000 |
| Gross Living Area Adjustment | +$2,000 |
| Net Adjustment | $2,500 |
| Percentage of Net Adjustments | 2.5% |
| Gross Adjustment | $27,500 |
| Percentage of Gross Adjustments | 27.5% |

In this case, the percentage of net adjustments is well within the guideline at only 2.5%. However, the gross percentage of adjustments is too high. This is a clear red flag, as there appears to be too many significant quality differences between the two properties for them to be comparable. Again, this is only a guideline that can be exceeded within reason, but in those occasional cases, the appraiser needs to include discussion about why such large adjustments were necessary.

## Bracketing

The appraiser should take one more step after he or she has determined which comps are the best, adjusted those comps, reconciled them, and determined a value for the subject property. At this point, he or she should double-check the appropriateness of the subject property's value by bracketing.

**Bracketing** is the idea that the sales prices of the comparables chosen for the appraisal will not all be higher than the value of the subject property, nor will they all be lower. They will bracket the value of the subject — that is, one or two of the sales will be higher, and one or two will be lower. When considering the marketplace, bracketing produces a much more solid conclusion.

> For example, a property appraised for $200,000, and all of the comparable sales sold for a price in the low $190,000s. How can the appraiser justify his opinion of value when all of the comparable properties are lower? If the appraiser cannot find an appropriate comp that sold for $200,000 or more, then the value he came up with may be questionable.

Similarly, if all of the comparables are higher in price than the value of the subject property, a question should arise as to whether or not appropriate comparables were used. If the subject property appraises for $200,000, and all of the comparable sales are between $210,000 and $215,000, there must be several significant differences that account for the difference in values. If they are truly similar, then why isn't the subject worth between $210,000 and $215,000? Moreover, if they are not that similar, the appraiser should look for more appropriate comparables.

# Summary

Deeply rooted in the **principle of substitution**, the **sales comparison approach** is a powerful tool in the marketplace for appraising land and residential properties (1 to 4 units). It is an accurate tool if the appraiser follows proper professional procedures to extract the relevant data from the marketplace and takes care to apply the information appropriately to the appraisal problem at hand. The appraiser must always objectively read the marketplace, not try to make the marketplace fit a predetermined notion. With practice and varied experience, the appraiser will become an expert at applying these techniques and using this methodology.

Though it is complicated and the most widely used approach to value, the Sales Comparison Approach does have its limitations. The fact that it relies so heavily on historical data is the primary drawback. Additionally, the need for multiple arm's-length transactions of similar property types can limit it for unique properties, but makes it a powerful tool when working in an active market.

This approach to value relies heavily on bona fide **market data** and proper **verification**. Thus, exacting measures must be taken by appraisers when collecting, analyzing, and verifying their information. Similar rigorousness should be implemented when applying and reconciling the data.

# Chapter 10 Review Exercises

## *Matching Exercise*

**Instructions:** Look up the meaning of the terms in the Glossary, then write the letter of the matching term on the blank line before its definition. Answers are in Appendix B.

### Terms

A. adjustment

B. bracketing

C. cash equivalency

D. matrix

E. mill

F. millage rate

G. Multiple Listing Service (MLS)

H. multiple regression analysis

I. neighborhood

J. paired sale analysis

K. parties to the transaction

L. sale-resale analysis

M. title plant

### Definitions

1. _____ A value expressed in dollar or percentage amount that is added or subtracted from the sales price of a comparable property.

2. _____ A service that is provided by local real estate boards for its member agents and brokers and is designed as a tool for marketing real estate.

3. _____ The property tax rate that is expressed in terms of tenths-of-a-cent per dollar of property value.

4. _____ A library of real estate information used by the title companies for research related to the issuance of title insurance policies.

5. _____ A buyer, seller, buyer's agent, or seller's agent involved in a transaction.

6. _____ A technique where an appraiser makes an adjustment for atypical financing to reflect typical market financing.

7. _____ Defined by physical boundaries such as a freeway, a body of water, or the base of a mountain; or intangible boundaries like a transition from residential to commercial uses.

8. _____ A grid that identifies important items affecting value such as site area and location.

9. _____ A method that uses at least two sales that are virtually identical in all aspects except one — the one differing item between the sales accounts for the difference in price between the two properties.

10. _____ An analytical technique that uses statistical methods to analyze comparable sales and estimate individual adjustments.

## Multiple Choice Questions

**Instructions:**   Circle your response and go to Appendix B to read the complete explanation for each question.

1. The overruling principle behind the sales comparison approach is:
    a. anticipation.
    b. substitution.
    c. multiplication.
    d. supplication.

2. When presented with two like commodities, the typical buyer will buy:
    a. the more expensive commodity.
    b. the least expensive commodity.
    c. both commodities.
    d. neither commodity.

3. Adjustments are applied to:
    a. the comparable properties.
    b. the subject property.
    c. the property being appraised.
    d. both the subject and comparable properties.

4. When is the comparison approach most applicable?
    a. When there is a sufficient number of comps
    b. When appraising property types that are bought and sold regularly
    c. When appraising vacant land
    d. All of the above

5. In which situation can the sales comparison approach be used?
   a. When appraising single-family residences, multi-residential properties, and vacant land only
   b. When appraising residential and income property
   c. Any property where sufficient comparable data is available
   d. When appraising special-purpose buildings, residential property, and qualified-income properties

6. Which of the following lists the steps for the sales comparison approach in order?
   a. Collect data, verify data, apply adjustments, reconcile values
   b. Collect data, analyze data, reconcile values, apply adjustments
   c. Analyze data, verify data, reconcile values, apply adjustments
   d. Analyze data, apply adjustments, verify data, reconcile values

7. Where should appraisers collect data?
   a. MLS only
   b. MLS and the newspaper
   c. Anywhere they can get information
   d. Multiple sources that provide accurate and reliable information

8. The service that appraisers and real estate agents use to research information on properties currently for sale is called the:
   a. County Recorder's Office.
   b. Multiple Regression Service.
   c. Title Plant Distributor.
   d. Multiple Listing Service.

9. The Johnsons live in a district where the tax rate is 26 mills based on 36 percent of the appraised value. The Johnsons receive a $2,000 homeowners' exemption as well. About how much tax is owed if their house appraises at $335,000?
   a. $3,100
   b. $3,320
   c. $3,515
   d. $1,585

10. A warehouse is subject to a property tax rate of $1.30 per $100 of assessed value. What is this property's millage rate?

    a. 26 mills

    b. 13 mills

    c. 1.3 mills

    d. .26 mills

11. Adriana is researching a property and while at the county recorder's office, she discovers that the property was assessed at 40% of the purchase price with a tax rate of 30 mills. The tax bill is $4,125 annually. Using this information, Adriana concludes that this property probably sold for:

    a. $343,750.

    b. $3,437,500.

    c. $34,375.

    d. $49,500.

12. As a market data resource, a party to a transaction is:

    a. a principal, like the buyer or the seller.

    b. a local real estate agent.

    c. other appraisers in the area.

    d. all of the above.

13. Sales information for a 30,000-square foot warehouse is a good indicator of value for:

    a. high-rise office space.

    b. single-family residences.

    c. warehouses of similar volume.

    d. none of the above.

14. Which of the following statements is not true in regards to comparables and geographic area?

    a. It may be necessary to consider comparables in other neighborhoods.

    b. Appraisers should limit the comparables to the neighborhood of the subject.

    c. Depending on the property type, an appraiser may need to look in different states for a comparable.

    d. The distance an appraiser will have to go for comparable information will vary from assignment to assignment.

15. How many comparables should an appraiser use on each assignment?
    a. Three closed sales
    b. Three closed sales and three pending sales
    c. Three sales of any kind
    d. As many as it takes to arrive at a credible analysis

16. While researching comparable properties, Frank finds an identical comp in the same tract of homes. He notes that as part of the sales agreement, the seller partially financed the sale. Frank should:
    a. use the comparable with no further action.
    b. not use the comparable because it has atypical financing.
    c. apply a cash equivalency formula to the comparable to adjust for the non-market financing.
    d. apply a cash equivalency formula to the subject to adjust for the non-market financing.

17. A comparable sold nine months ago for $268,000. The appraiser concludes that property values have increased by 5% per year. What should the adjustment be?
    a. $278,000
    b. $10,000
    c. $27,800
    d. $13,400

18. Locational adjustments may be based on:
    a. changes in zoning.
    b. proximity to negative influences like an airport.
    c. market perception.
    d. all of the above.

19. If the _____ property has a feature that the _____ property does not have, _____ the value of the feature _____ the comparable price.
    a. subject, comparable, add, to
    b. comparable, subject, add, to
    c. subject, comparable, subtract, from
    d. comparable, comparable, subtract, from

20. Adjustments are made on _____ basis.
    a. a dollar only
    b. a percentage only
    c. a fractional
    d. both dollar and percentage

21. The transaction price of a comparable property is $200,000. The appraiser determines that the comparable is 5% more desirable because of special financing; the conditions of the sale affected the subject negatively by 8%; the location of the comparable is 15% better but it is physically 5% worse than the subject; and since the comparable sold, the market has improved by 20%. What is the indicated value of the subject?
    a. $187,000
    b. $253,000
    c. $220,000
    d. $169,000

22. Which of the following lists the proper sequence of adjustments?
    a. Financing, seller motivation, location, time, and physical
    b. Financing, physical, seller motivation, location, and time
    c. Physical, seller motivation, location, time, and financing
    d. Financing, seller motivation, time, location, and physical

Use the following grid to answer 23-25:

| Characteristic | Subject | Sale 1 | Sale 2 | Sale 3 |
|---|---|---|---|---|
| Price | | $200,000 | $235,000 | $190,000 |
| Square Feet | 1,500 | 1,500 | 1,500 | 1,500 |
| Fireplace | One | One | One | One |
| Pool | Yes | No | Yes | No |
| Garage | 1-car | 2-car | 2-car | 1-car |

23. What is the adjustment value for a pool in this neighborhood?
    a.  $35,000
    b.  $45,000
    c.  $17,500
    d.  $10,000

24. What is the adjustment value for an extra garage space in this neighborhood?
    a.  $35,000
    b.  $45,000
    c.  $17,500
    d.  $10,000

25. According to the adjustments above, what is the indicated value of the subject property?
    a.  $245,000
    b.  $210,000
    c.  $225,000
    d.  $190,000

26. A flower shop was purchased in the Summer of 2004 for $500,000.  It sold in the Summer of 2006 for $450,000.  Using the sale-resale analysis, determine the annual rate at which this market is decreasing.
    a.  10%
    b.  1%
    c.  5%
    d.  9%

27. A comparable sold recently for $100,000 and has required a positive adjustment for locational differences of $12,000 and a negative adjustment for physical differences of $7,500.  Under normal practice should an appraiser use this comp?
    a.  Yes.
    b.  No, because it exceeds the federal guideline for single line item.
    c.  No because it exceeds the GNMA guideline for gross adjustments
    d.  No, because it exceeds the FNMA guideline for single line item.

28. Based on the following information, is this comp acceptable?

| Selling Price | $160,000 |
|---|---|
| Bedroom Adjustment | $ 8,000 |
| Fireplace Adjustment | –$ 3,000 |
| Garage Adjustment | $ 7,000 |
| Locational Adjustment | –$ 10,000 |
| Age Adjustment | $ 8,000 |

a. Yes

b. No, because it exceeds the federal guideline for single line item.

c. No because it exceeds the GNMA guideline for gross adjustments

d. No, because it exceeds the FNMA guideline for single line item.

29. Using the information from question 28, what is the adjusted value of the comparable?

a. $196,000

b. $170,000

c. $124,000

d. $150,000

30. After careful analysis, Brandi determines the adjusted values for the three best comparable properties are $400,000, $420,000, and $425,000. What is the indicated value of the subject?...

a. $415,000

b. $412,500

c. $422,500

d. It depends on which property or properties Brandi gives most weight in her analysis.

# Chapter

# 11

# Income Capitalization Approach

## Introduction

Properties are purchased for a variety of reasons. The anticipation of future benefits associated with owning a particular property is a principal reason. In other words, people acquire real estate based not only upon the property's expected use, but also on the anticipation of the benefits they will receive because of owning that property. For example, a family may acquire a single-family residential property primarily to live in it. Human beings need shelter from the elements and residential property meets this need. However, the family also considers secondary benefits such as income tax and investment benefits, location, prestige, and privacy.

Real estate investors most often purchase or develop properties with the expectation of deriving a flow of revenue. From that perspective, the income earning potential of a property is a major consideration for prospective buyers.

Owners of properties such as apartment complexes, shopping malls, hotels, and office buildings rent out units, storefronts, rooms, and offices respectively. The rent charged to these tenants is income to the property owners. It therefore makes sense that the more income a property generates for an owner, the more valuable that property should be. For example, a high-rise office building generating millions of dollars a year in income is more valuable than a small, multi-residential development only generating an income of a few thousand dollars annually.

## Learning Objective

After reading this chapter, you will be able to:

- identify potential gross income, effective gross income, and net operating income.

- categorize which expenses are operating expenses.

- identify the formula for gross rent multiplier.

- recognize direct capitalization methods.

- describe the six functions of a dollar.

# Overview of the Income Approach

In its simplest form, the income approach is based upon the premise that there is an identifiable relationship between the income a property can generate and the value of that property. All of the income approach techniques rely upon the expectation that a property will produce income.

The principle of anticipation states that value is created by the expectation of future benefits. The amount a buyer will typically pay for a property is directly proportional to the future income benefits the buyer expects to derive from that property. One of the major benefits of owning income-producing property is the right to receive all profits generated by that property while owned. Prospective purchasers and property investors typically identify how much income they would expect to receive from a property once they obtain ownership.

The appraiser's job when using the income approach is to estimate the value of the present worth of future benefits. Identifying this relationship between the income a property generates and value of that property is at the core of the income capitalization approach.

## Application of this Approach

The application of the income approach is straightforward. The income approach is most useful when appraising:

- properties whose ability to produce income is considered by potential buyers.

The income approach to value is solely dependant on a property's income, real or potential.  If a property's ability to produce income is an important factor to potential buyers, then this approach is the best indicator of value.  Even if the property is not currently producing income, this approach can convert its potential income into a current value.

## Limitations of this Approach

The income approach has limited usefulness when:

- current rental data and operating statements are not available.

The income approach will require current market data for rentals of like properties as well as careful analysis of the operating statements.  Sometimes these pieces of information are difficult to obtain and analyze.  In addition, determining the appropriate capitalization rate is very difficult, and at times, can become very complex.

This approach is not applicable if the subject and comparable properties are not purchased for that income-producing ability.

# Estimating Income

An appraiser examines an income property's income statement and analyzes the information to calculate the income properly.  Income is estimated both as **gross income**, total income before deducting expenses, and as **net operating income**, income received after expenses have been deducted.  This section covers potential gross income, effective gross income, and net operating income (NOI).

## Potential Gross Income

The simplest income to calculate is the **potential gross income**, which is the maximum income a property could generate.  The most obvious income a property produces is the rent paid by tenants of a property.

This may not be the only source of income a property produces. Sources of additional income include laundry and vending machines, parking fees, interest earned on security deposits, and possibly, income resulting from government programs.  Potential gross income encompasses all of these possible sources.  This is important because, in some instances, such as retail stores in shopping centers, rents are based upon a percentage of gross sales generated by the business leasing that store.

**Figure 11.1**  Potential gross income includes income from all possible sources.

As stated earlier, income properties are purchased in anticipation of the income they can generate for their owner(s).  Therefore, it is important to recognize that potential gross income is even more important in this analysis than actual gross income, since potential income is more reflective of the anticipated benefits.

When determining the subject property's potential gross income, the first step is to identify its current gross income.  Once the current gross income is established, that income level needs to be analyzed to determine if it will continue into the near future.

The appraiser must consider questions like:

- What is the likelihood this property will continue to generate that same amount of income into the near future?

- Can the income be increased?

- If so, by how much?

- If not, how come?

The appraiser should investigate if there are lease arrangements that limit the amount of rent a landlord can charge, or if there are there government restrictions such as rent control or low-income occupant limitations.

During this process, the appraiser will need to be aware of market trends.  Large employers that close their operations in an area can have a serious negative effect upon the local market for rental housing. Similarly, a large retailer that is opening a superstore in an area may obliterate the demand for commercial properties in the downtown business districts of some smaller towns.  Conversely, a new university campus under construction or a newly built sports facility can draw large numbers of people to an area, causing greater demand for rental properties. There are both positive and negative influences, which are either actual or merely perceived, that the appraiser must identify and analyze when projecting potential income for a property.

Additionally, the appraiser will need to compare the subject's income to other properties in the area. In competitive markets, rents tend to gravitate to similar levels. The next step therefore, is for the appraiser to identify properties that are similar to the subject property and perform a rental survey of those properties. A **rental survey** is an analysis of competitive rents. The purpose of this task is to identify the amount of income the subject property might generate. By identifying the current gross income and analyzing the current terms of the rental/lease agreements of the comparable properties, the appraiser can forecast a reasonable estimate of the subject's potential income.

When identifying appropriate rental comps, the appraiser should investigate properties that are overall as similar to the subject property as possible. The rental comps chosen should be as indicative of the subject's current market as possible. Just because a nearby property is similar to the subject in physical characteristics does not necessarily mean it is indicative of the subject's rental market. Small, multi-esidential income properties with long-term tenants often rent below market levels and may be unsuitable for use as rental comps. Items such as physical characteristics, location, amenities, and rental/ lease terms all deserve consideration. Similarly, rental incentives being offered to tenants or premiums being demanded by landlords also need analysis.

Differences between the subject property and the rental comps in terms of physical characteristics, amenities, and lease arrangements all need to be analyzed by the appraiser when forecasting the subject property's income. In a process similar to that used in the sales comparison approach, appraisers develop an estimate of the subject's projected income by adjusting the rents obtained from the rental comps to compensate for differences between the subject and the rental comps.

### Review — Steps to Determine Potential Gross Income

1. Identify the subject property's current gross income.
2. Identify properties that are comparable to the subject property and perform a rental survey of those properties.

## Effective Gross Income

Few properties realize their maximum income, so appraisers also estimate the property's effective gross income. The concept of effective gross income accounts for the discrepancy between potential and actual income. **Effective gross income** is the property's income after vacancy and collection losses are deducted from the estimate of projected potential gross income.

**Vacancy loss** is the amount of income lost due to vacant units in a property. Vacancy losses are deducted from potential gross income because income-producing properties are not 100% occupied all the time at market rent. In a typical income-producing property, tenants come and go and it often takes time to rent, or lease, the vacant property. For example, when renters move out of an apartment, there is a period between an occupant vacating a property and a new tenant moving in. Even in markets where there is high demand for rental properties, the landlord needs a few days after a tenant vacates a property in order to clean, repaint, or possibly remodel a unit to prepare it for the new occupant.

**Figure 11.2** Income properties are rarely at maximum occupancy. Effective gross income accounts for this discrepancy.

Effective gross income also accounts for instances where tenants do not pay their agreed-upon rents. When this happens, the owner would typically begin eviction proceedings. Sometimes it takes months to evict a tenant legally. In these situations, owners often incur costs ranging from hundreds to thousands of dollars. This kind of loss is called a **collection loss**.

Though good management may minimize vacancy and collection losses, no property is immune to suffering losses in income. Deducting vacancy and collection losses from the potential gross income accounts for the reasonable expectation that a property will not produce income at all times.

Usually, vacancy and collection losses are combined and are expressed as a percentage of potential gross income. When vacancy and collection loss is deducted from a property's potential gross income, the resultant amount is called the **effective gross income**.

# Net Operating Income

**Net operating income (NOI)** is the income remaining after the operating expenses are deducted from the effective gross income. NOI is probably the best value indicator for any income property since it most accurately reflects the income for a given property.

To calculate net operating income, an appraiser deducts operating expenses from effective gross income. **Operating expenses** are those expenses necessary to maintain the property and to help ensure the continued production of income. They include, but are not limited to, items such as property management, insurance, property taxes, utilities, and maintenance. Operating expenses will vary from property to property.

> **Calculating Net Operating Income**
>
>    Potential Gross Income
> −  Vacancy and Collection Losses
>    Effective Gross Income
>
> −  Operating Expenses
>    Net Operating Income

## Operating Expenses

Operating expenses are divided into three broad categories: fixed expenses, variable expenses, and replacement reserves.

**Fixed expenses** are ongoing expenses regardless of whether or not the property is occupied. Property taxes and insurance premiums and licenses typically fall into this category.

**Variable expenses** are operating expenses that will vary based upon numerous criteria such as the level of occupancy, the income a property generates, and the amount of services provided by the owner to the tenants. Variable charges vary from property type to property type but usually include the following:

---

### Variable Expenses

- Advertising
- Building maintenance
- Cleaning
- Decorating
- HVAC
- Landscape maintenance
- Marketing
- Parking area maintenance
- Payroll
- Pest control
- Property management
- Repairs
- Security
- Snow removal
- Trash removal
- Utilities

---

**Replacement reserves** are funds set aside by the property owner to pay for the replacement of certain building components and fixtures that periodically wear out in a property. They are items that are part of the real estate that wear out more rapidly than the building itself.

---

### Items Paid for with Replacement Reserves

- Appliances
- Exterior Painting
- Floor Coverings
- Kitchen, Bath, and Laundry Equipment
- Re-Roofing
- Resurface Driveway and Parking Area
- Window Coverings

---

Replacement reserves are set aside with the expectation that building components and fixtures will eventually need replacement. Sometimes, the costs of replacing building components can be very high.

For example, replacing all the roofs and repainting all the buildings in a 500-unit apartment complex may cost hundreds of thousands, if not millions, of dollars. Unless replacement reserves are set aside, the owners of these kinds of properties may find themselves in a position where they cannot afford the necessary replacements when needed.

Since property owners know they eventually will need to replace these items, setting aside replacement reserves ensures they will have the funds necessary to perform these replacements when needed.

**Figure 11.3** Unless replacements for reserves are set aside on a regular basis, apartment building owners may find it to costly to repair or replace fixtures and major components.

### *Excluded Expenses*

Accountants record property expenses in a different manner from that of appraisers. Expense and operating statements prepared by accountants for property owners and supplied to appraisers typically include all the expenditures an owner makes for a property, even those that are not operating expenses. Items such as financing expenses, income taxes, book depreciation charges, and capital improvements are all expenses that property owners incur. However, an appraiser rectifies the operating statement by omitting these expenses since they are not operating expenses and vary from owner to owner.

### Financing Expenses

The property may be owned free and clear, so there are not any financing expenses. If there are financing expenses, they will vary from owner to owner. One owner may take out a mortgage with a fixed interest rate while another owner may have a variable rate. In almost all cases, a property's value is independent of financing.

### Income Taxes

Federal and state income taxes vary in each situation. Property may be owned by a corporation or by an individual. Each form of ownership has different tax implications, but the property itself is not worth more or less because of an owner's tax situation. A buyer would not pay more for a property simply because the seller is in a low tax-bracket. Property values are independent of their owner's tax obligations; therefore, income taxes are not included in operating expenses.

## Book Depreciation

**Book depreciation** is an accounting process that recovers an investment over a set period. A formula strictly for income tax purposes, book depreciation is not typically reflective of actual market conditions. This expense will also vary from owner to owner, so it is not included in an appraiser's estimate of operating expenses.

## Capital Improvements

Appraisers do not include **capital improvements**, such as roof or window replacement, in operating expenses since they are not reflective of annual expenses. Though they may add value to a property, the fact that they are not recurring on an annual basis excludes them from operating expenses. Capital improvements are accounted for in replacement reserves, so counting them as an operating expense would cause these items to be counted twice.

## Insurance Expenses

Sometimes, operating expense charges are not segregated from other expenses. For example, an insurance bill may include coverage not just for the building, but also for business inventory, furniture, machinery, and equipment, or other personal property. In that instance, portions of the insurance bill that do not cover the real estate need to be deducted from the overall insurance charge.

---

### Review —Types of Income and Expenses

**Potential gross income** — the total estimate of all possible income sources for a property without any deductions

**Effective gross income** — income remaining after vacancy and collection losses are deducted from the potential gross income

**Operating expenses** — expenses that are necessary to maintain a property and that help it to continue the production of its effective gross income

**Net operating income** — income left after deducting operating expenses from effective gross income

# Converting Income to Value

There are numerous methods used to analyze the income a property produces to determine the value of that property. We will discuss the basic three: the gross income multiplier, direct capitalization, and discounted cash flow analysis (also called yield capitalization). The appraiser decides which, if any, of the above three methods to use based on the type of property being appraised and the data available.

## Gross Income Multiplier

One of the simplest ways to estimating a property's value based on its income is to use a **gross income multiplier (GIM)**. Following this method, the appraiser multiplies the subject property's projected gross income by a multiplier extracted from other similar properties. This is the equation:

Potential Gross Income × Gross Income Multiplier = Value

The gross income multiplier is obtained from recent comparable sales. It is calculated by dividing the sale price of the comparable sale by its gross income at the time of sale. Multiplying the subject property's potential gross income by this multiplier gives an indication of the value of the subject property.

Gross income multipliers may be applied to monthly or yearly income. Monthly income is used primarily when appraising small multi-family residential properties or in situations where there are virtually no seasonal variations in the projected income of either the subject property or the comparable sales used. In most other situations, an annual gross income estimate is used.

Use care when employing this technique. The comparable properties chosen must be similar to the subject in terms of physical, locational, and overall economic property characteristics. Properties that are similar to the subject in physical characteristics may have vastly different operating expenses, which would make these properties not comparable for income valuation purposes.

### Gross Rent Multiplier

The **gross rent multiplier (GRM)** is similar to the GIM method. The distinction between the two is that GIM accounts for all possible potential income, whereas GRM accounts only for the property's rental income. A benefit of GRM is that it is far quicker to calculate, but consequently, it is not as accurate or detailed as the GIM.

## *Illustration*

The subject property is a 10-unit apartment complex that has five 1-bedroom apartments and five 2-bedroom apartments. By looking at the property's actual gross income and performing a rental survey of similar properties, the appraiser determined that the 1-bedroom apartments can rent for $725 per month and the 2-bedroom apartments can rent for $850 per month. The following chart illustrates the subject's potential gross income forecast.

### Subject Property

| | |
|---|---|
| Five Units × $725 rent/month | = $3,625 |
| Five Units × $850 rent/month | = $4,250 |
| Total Forecasted Monthly Gross Income | = $7,875 |

Three recent apartment sales comparable to the subject were found. Unfortunately, no sales were found that have the same number of units as the subject. The comparable sales are described as follows:

### Comparable Sale #1

A twelve-unit apartment complex, it has nine 1-bedroom units that are rented for $725 per month and three 2-bedroom units that are rented for $850 per month. It recently sold for $1,115,000.

| | |
|---|---|
| Nine Units × $725 rent/month | = $6,525 |
| Three Units × $850 rent/month | = $2,550 |
| Total Gross Monthly Income | = $9,075 |

Divide the sale price of this property ($1,115,000) by its monthly income ($9,075) to get a GRM of 122.86 (rounded to 123).

### Comparable Sale #2

A nine-unit apartment complex, it has nine 1-bedroom units that are renting for $725 per month. It sold for $830,000.

| | |
|---|---|
| Nine Units × $725 rent/month | = $6,525 |
| Total Gross Monthly Income | = $6,525 |

Divide the sale price of this property ($830,000) by its monthly income ($6,525) to get a GRM of 127.20 (rounded to 127).

### Comparable Sale #3

A thirteen-unit apartment complex, it has ten 1-bedroom units that are rented for $725 per month and three 2-bedroom units that are rented for $850 per month. It sold recently for $1,220,000.

Ten Units × $725 rent/month             = $7,250
Three Units × $850 rent/month           = $2,550
Total Gross Monthly Income              = $9,800

Divide the sale price of this property ($1,220,000) by its monthly income ($9,800) to get a GRM of 124.5 (rounded to 125).

The three sale comparable properties produced gross income multipliers ranging from 123 to 127 (summarized on grid). Based upon this information, one could reasonably indicate the gross income multiplier for the subject at 125.

| Comparable | Income | Sales Price | GRM |
|---|---|---|---|
| Comp 1 | $9,075 | $1,115,000 | 123 |
| Comp 2 | $6,525 | $830,000 | 127 |
| Comp 3 | $9,800 | $1,220,000 | 125 |

As stated earlier, the subject's estimated income is $7,875. The indicated GRM is 125. Multiplying the forecasted income by the GRM produces an indication of the subject's value.

$7,875 × 125 = $984,375

Rounded down, the subject's value is $984,000.

## Limitations of this Method

The GIM technique is a simple tool to use. However, it has some significant drawbacks that cause it to be inapplicable. The main drawback is that this technique is based upon gross income, and it ignores the net income that a property generates. In many cases, buyers and sellers are more interested in net income than in gross income. The appraisal process is to be reflective of the attitudes of buyers and sellers in the market, so when this occurs, it is inappropriate to use a gross income multiplier analysis since it is not reflective of the actions of buyers and sellers in the market. Two properties may generate very similar levels of gross income; however, one may have significantly higher net income since it has lower operating expenses. All other things being equal, the property with the higher net income would tend to be in greater demand therefore more valuable. Using the GIM technique, this difference is ignored.

# Direct Capitalization

Any interest in real property may be estimated by the technique known as direct capitalization. Direct capitalization is the process of estimating the value of an income-producing property by forecasting the net operating income that the property is expected to generate during a specific period (usually one year) and dividing it by a capitalization rate. Like the gross income multiplier, direct capitalization relies upon the premise that there is a relationship between the income a property produces and the value of that property.

The **overall capitalization rate** (R) is a market-derived ratio reflecting the relationship between the net operating income a property generates and its value. Sometimes called the capitalization rate, or simply the cap rate, this method converts annual expected net operating income (NOI) generated by a property into a value estimate (V) for that property.

To determine the appropriate capitalization rate, the appraiser analyzes the relationship between the sales prices of competing properties in the subject's market and the yearly net operating incomes generated by those properties. Once determined, the capitalization rate is divided into the yearly net operating income for the subject property, resulting in a value estimate for the subject property. The following formulas are used in direct capitalization.

| Capitalization Formulas | |
| --- | --- |
| Determine a property's value: | NOI ÷ Cap Rate = Value |
| Determine the cap rate: | NOI ÷ Value = Cap Rate |
| Calculate a property's NOI: | Value × Cap Rate = NOI |

Example: An income-producing property has a yearly NOI of $80,000. The cap rate is estimated to be 11%. By using the following formula, the value of the property is determined.

|  NOI | ÷ | CAP Rate | = | Value |
| --- | --- | --- | --- | --- |
| $80,000 | ÷ | 11% | = | $727,272 |

## Estimating Capitalization Rates

As stated earlier, capitalization rates convert income into value. However, several methods may be used to derive capitalization rates. The quality and quantity of data available to the appraiser determines which technique is most appropriate. Before studying these methods, the beginning appraiser needs to understand what a high or low cap rate means.

## Capitalization Rate and Risk

When deciding whether to invest in a property, prospective buyers have two overriding concerns. First, they want the money they invest to return some profit. This profit, called interest, is a **return *on* investment.** Second, they want to be reasonably certain the funds they place in an investment will be returned to them at some point, which is the **return *of* investment.**

The return *on* investment and return *of* investment requirements have an inverse correlation to one another. If an investment is considered safe, it means that the return of investment is probable. The investor will probably get back the money he or she has invested. However, a safe investment, will have a relative low return on investment, i.e. a low interest rate. Riskier investments typically have higher rates of return in order to attract investors.

In real estate appraisal, cap rates reflect this difference. Low risk investments are ones with a low possibility of losing the money invested. So, a property with a low risk is generally worth more than one with a high risk where investment loss is more likely to occur.

> **Review — Rate and Risk**
>
> Low risk  =  Low capitalization rate  =  High value
>
> High risk  =  High capitalization rate  =  Low value

This chapter covers four techniques used to estimate the subject property's capitalization rate: comparable sales, band of investment, effective gross income analysis, and residual techniques.

### Using Comparable Sales

The comparable sales method to estimate capitalization rates is preferred when there is sufficient comparable data available to the appraiser. In order to use this method, the appraiser needs to research the comparable properties' sales price, income, expenses, financing arrangements, and market conditions at the time of sale. It is especially important for the appraiser to be sure that the net operating income for each of the comparable sales used is calculated in the exact same manner as it is for the subject. Failure to perform this task will result in incorrect estimates.

This approach is similar to the GIM approach. Once the comparable sales have been identified and the appropriate data about each sale researched, the appraiser can then divide each comparable sale's net operating income by its sales price resulting in a capitalization rate estimate for each property. The capitalization rate chosen by the appraiser from those indicated by the comparable sales would be the one indicated by the sale that is overall most similar to the subject property.

## Illustration

The operating statement for the subject property shows that its NOI is $575,000. After researching the market area, the appraiser came up with the following comparable information.

| Comparables | NOI | Sales Price | Cap Rate |
|---|---|---|---|
| Comp 1 | $450,000 | $5,000,000 | 9.% |
| Comp 2 | $357,750 | $3,578,000 | 10.% |
| Comp 3 | $1,506,800 | $25,113,000 | 6.% |
| Comp 4 | $600,000 | $6,316,000 | 9.5% |

After further analysis, the appraiser concludes that Comp 3 is not especially indicative of the market, even though on the surface it appeared to be wholly comparable to the subject. Looking at the remaining comps, the appraiser concludes that the cap rate most likely should be in between 9 – 9.5%. The appraiser ultimately selects 9.5% because Comp 4 was the most comparable to the subject. $575,000 ÷ 9.5% = $6,052,631. The subject has a value of $6,053,000(rounded).

## Operating Statement Ratios

At times, actual operating expense information for the comparable sales is unavailable; however, their gross income and sale price information is. In those situations, the appraiser must analyze the market to determine what the typical market operating expenses are. From this market estimate, an appraiser can estimate operating expenses for the chosen comparable property. Then, the appraiser subtracts the estimated operating expenses from each comp's effective gross income to determine the property's NOI.

The market estimate of operating expenses can be expressed as a ratio. The **operating expense ratio** is calculated by dividing the property's operating expenses by its effective gross income. A **net operating income ratio** is the ratio between the net operating income of a property and its effective gross income. Because these two ratios are complementary, adding them together will result in 1.0 or 100%. This relationship will be useful when you are able to calculate one and need the other. To do this, subtract the known ratio from 1.0 or 100%.

For example: A property has an effective gross income of $78,000 and operating expenses totaling $31,200. The NOI is $46,800 ($78,000 – $31,200). The following chart shows how the operating expense ratio and net operating income ratio are inverses of one another.

| | | | |
|---|---|---|---|
| Net operating income ratio | $46,800 ÷ $78,000 | = | 60%  (0.6) |
| Operating expense ratio | $31,200 ÷ $78,000 | = | 40%  (0.4) |
| | | | 100%  (1.0) |

### *Band of Investment Method*

The **band of investment method** determines the capitalization rate based on the fact that the funds used to purchase a property typically come from two primary sources: buyers and lenders. In a typical purchase transaction, a portion of the purchase price is paid directly from funds a borrower already has and the remainder of the purchase price is paid for by funds the buyer borrows from a lender. The amount a buyer invests into a property is called **equity capital** and the amount borrowed by the buyer to purchase a property is called **debt capital**. Almost all real estate investments have an equity component and a debt component. In the band of investment technique, capitalization rates for both the equity and debt positions in a property are determined and then combined into an overall rate for the property.

Assume a property is being purchased for $800,000. The buyer makes a 20% down payment ($160,000) and the balance of the purchase price ($640,000) is financed with a mortgage. The following diagram shows both the equity and the debt (mortgage) components of that investment.

| | | | |
|---|---|---|---|
| Equity Value | (20%) | = | $160,000 |
| Mortgage Value | (80%) | = | $640,000 |
| Total Property Value | (100%) | = | $800,000 |

The capitalization rate for the debt component in a property is called the mortgage constant. The **mortgage constant** is the ratio of the loan amount (principal) to the annual sum of the individual loan payments. It is a function of the interest rate, the time length of the loan, and the frequency of loan amortization. Mortgage constants may be calculated on a financial calculator or by referring to financial tables that are discussed later in this chapter.

The capitalization rate for the equity position in a property is called the equity capitalization rate. The **equity cap rate** reflects the anticipated return on a percentage basis to the investor who owns the property and is typically reflective of the first year of the investment. Equity capitalization rates may be identified a couple of ways. One way is to divide the pre-tax cash flow of a sale by the amount of equity investment in that sale. Often this information is very difficult to confirm; however, if it is available, it is a very strong indicator. Another way is to identify the interest rates being paid on competing investments. Often the interest rates being paid on 6-month or 1-year treasury bills are the basis for estimating an equity capitalization rate.

Once the mortgage constant (debt cap rate) and the equity cap rate are identified, the overall rate indication can be calculated. The overall rate estimate generated in this manner is a composite of both the equity and debt positions in a property and is proportionally weighted by each of the property investment positions. To calculate the overall return, begin by multiplying the debt percentage of the property value by the mortgage constant. Likewise, multiply the equity percentage of the property value by the equity cap rate. Finally, add the two products together to derive the overall cap rate. The equation for calculating the overall capitalization rate using this technique looks like this:

$$\begin{array}{ll} \text{Debt Rate} & \textit{(Debt Percentage} \times \textit{Mortgage Constant)} \\ \underline{+\ \text{Equity Rate}} & \textit{(Equity Percentage} \times \textit{Equity Cap Rate)} \\ \text{Overall Cap Rate} & \end{array}$$

## Illustration

The subject property is a 50-unit apartment complex. The buyer is putting a 30% down payment on the property and can obtain financing for the remaining 70% of the property's value at 7% for 20 years fully amortized with monthly payments. Competing non-real estate investments are currently paying 12% annual interest. Using the above formula, the overall capitalization rate is computed as follows:

| Percent of Property Value | × | Cap Rate | = | Weighted Rate |
|---|---|---|---|---|
| Mortgage (70%) | × | 0.093 | = | 0.0651 |
| Equity (30%) | × | 0.120 | = | 0.0360 + |
| Overall Cap Rate | | | = | 0.1011 |

Based upon the above calculation, the overall capitalization rate is 0.1011 (10.11%)

(Note: The mortgage capitalization rate of 0.0930 is the mortgage constant for a 7% loan amortized over 20 years with monthly payments.)

## *Residual Techniques*

Real estate is divided into two components, the land, and its improvements. In income-producing properties, a portion of its total net income is attributable to its land and the remaining portion is attributable to its improvements (buildings). Similarly, there are capitalization rates that are attributable to the land and other capitalization rates that are attributable to the improvements (rarely are they the same).

> For illustration purposes, imagine a stand-alone gas station with an annual NOI of $200,000 and a cap rate of 10%. This technique says that the property improvements (building, pumps, gas reserves, etc) contribute to the NOI ($80,000) and that the land component of the property also contributes a portion (the remaining ($120,000).

> This technique subsequently states that the property's cap rate can be split to represent the rate the improvements and the rate the land contribute to the overall rate. In this case, the land-contributed cap rate is 2.2% and the improvements account for the remaining 7.8%.

If the value and the capitalization rate of one of the components are known, the net operating income attributable to that component may be deducted from the total net operating income for the property to arrive at a net operating income attributable to the other component. Capitalizing that income will result in a value indication for the unknown component. Adding the value of the two components together results in a value indication for the overall property.

Keep in mind that, for these methods to be reliable, the property must be at its highest and best use. If the highest and best use of the land is different from the highest and best use of the improvements, the residual techniques cannot accurately determine value.

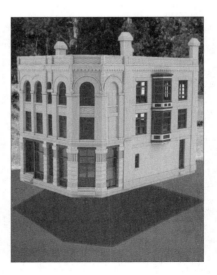

**Figure 11.4** When using a residual technique, the appraiser divides the subject property into a land component and an improvement component.

## Building Residual Technique

The value of the total property may be estimated, by using the **building residual technique** if the land value is known (or easily estimated). In the following illustration, the capitalization rates for the subject's land and building are 9% and 6% respectively.

| | |
|---|---:|
| Known Land Value | $800,000 |
| Total Net Operating Income | $225,000 |
| Less Net Operating Income Attributable to the Land | |
| (Land Value × Land Cap Rate) ($800,000 × 0.09) | − 72,000 |
| Residual Income Attributable to the Building | $153,000 |
| Building Value | |
| (Building NOI ÷ Building Cap Rate) ($153,000 ÷ 0.06) | $2,550,000 |
| Total Indicated Property Value | $3,350,000 |

In order for the building residual technique to be meaningful, the appraiser needs to have information about the current land value, net operating income information for the property, and capitalization rates for both the land and the improvements. The drawback to this method is the fact that this information may be difficult to extract from the market.

This method is used in situations where the improvements have suffered significant accrued depreciation. In some instances, accrued depreciation may be estimated by this technique when the indicated building value by this method is subtracted from the estimated building cost new.

## Land Residual Technique

The value of the total property may be estimated by using the **land residual technique** if both the total net operating income for a property and the value of the building are known. This method also assumes the appraiser has obtained information regarding cap rates for both the land and for the building. The following example illustrates this method for estimating property values.

| | |
|---|---:|
| Known Building Value | $2,550,000 |
| Total Net Operating Income | $225,000 |
| *Less* Net Operating Income Attributable to the Building | |
| (Building Value × Building Cap Rate of 6%) | − 153,000 |
| Residual Income Attributable to the Land | $72,000 |
| Land Value (Land NOI ÷ Land Cap Rate) ($72,000 ÷ 9%) | $ 800,000 |
| Total Indicated Property Value | $3,350,000 |

This method is often used where comparable land sales data is not available. It typically relies upon the cost approach to value in order to estimate the value of the improvements. As such, it relies upon the assumption that the cost to build a building is equal to its market value, which is not necessarily reflective of market realities. Like the building residual technique, the appraiser must have knowledge of the appropriate capitalization rates for both the building and for the improvements as well as information regarding the subject's total net operating income.

### *Illustration*

The subject property consists of 25 apartments. The units in this development are leased for $700 per month. There is a laundry room in the development generating approximately $5.00 per month per unit in the development. The vacancy and collection losses in this development are estimated to be 4% of potential gross income. Operating expenses are forecasted to be 35% of effective gross income. Relying upon similar sales in the subject market, an overall capitalization rate of 9.25% is used.

### Solution:

| | | |
|---|---|---|
| Rental Income | *(25 Units @ $700 per month)* | $17,500 |
| Laundry Income | *(25 Units @ $5.00 per month)* | + $125 |
| Monthly Potential Gross Income (PGI) | | $17,625 |

| | |
|---|---|
| Potential Gross Income (Annual PGI × 12) | $211,500 |
| *less* Vacancy & Collection Loss *(4% of Yearly PGI)* | – $8,460 |
| Effective Gross Income (EGI) | $203,040 |

| | |
|---|---|
| *less* Operating Expenses *(35% of EGI)* | – $71,064 |
| Net Operating Income (NOI) | $131,976 |

| | |
|---|---|
| NOI ÷ Cap Rate = Value *($131,976 ÷ 0.0925)* | = $1,426,768 |
| Indicated Value (Rounded) | $1,427,000 |

# Yield Capitalization

**Yield capitalization**, also known as discounted cash flow analysis, is a method where the value of future benefits is discounted to a present value. Future benefits include the periodic flow of income generated by a property for its owner (return on investment) as well as a reversion. **Reversion** is the lump sum amount the investor expects to receive upon sale of a property at some future point in time (return of investment).

The process where the periodic future income flows and the reversion are converted into a present value estimate is called **discounting**. Discounting is a form of capitalization that is specifically concerned with calculating present worth based upon future income. The **discount rate** is the yield rate to the investor and assumes a satisfactory return on and return of investment to the investor.

Conceptually, it is helpful to look at the property being appraised as an investment over time and note the direction of cash flow. When the initial purchase of a property is made, funds flow from the buyer to the seller. While not always the case, there is usually an expectation at this point that the property will generate funds that will flow to the investor who just bought the property. There is also an expectation that at some point in the future, the property will be sold with the investor receiving a lump sum amount of capital at that time. Yield capitalization converts these various cash flows into a value estimate.

When performing yield capitalization, the appraiser needs to perform certain steps.

1. Project the holding period of the investment. The holding period is the length of time the property will be used as an investment.

2. Estimate and forecast all the future cash flows associated with the investment. At times, monies will flow from the investor toward the investment. This is called negative cash flow. At other times, income generated by the property flows toward the owner which results in positive cash flow.

3. Identify an appropriate discount rate. The rate chosen needs to be reflective of investor's expectations and provide for an acceptable return on investment and return of investment.

4. Convert the future benefits into a present value estimate for the property.

## *Six Functions of One Dollar*

To understand yield capitalization, it is necessary to have an understanding on the time element of money. People place their funds in investments with the expectation those funds will earn interest. The investor is a "lender" and the investment is the "borrower". The individual invests (loans) capital in an investment and that investment is expected to compensate the investor with some kind of return. If an individual puts $100 into a savings account at a bank and it pays 7% per year, at the end of one year, the initial $100 investment has grown to $107. In a different light, to accumulate $107 in one year, it would be necessary to deposit $100 into an account bearing 7% interest.

There are three overall ways to look at money.

1. The future worth (amount) can be calculated based upon compounding.

2. The present worth (amount) of money may be calculated through discounting.

3. The amount of equal payments to retire a debt or to accumulate a specific amount of money may also be analyzed.

Overall, the six functions of a dollar are tied to the time element of money. These six functions are included in the following chart. With computer technology and modern financial calculators, charts like the one following this discussion have pretty much fallen into disuse. Charts like these however, are helpful to illustrate the various functions of a dollar and that is why one is included here.

The following chart includes the six functions of a dollar calculated at a 7% interest rate and projected out for 40 years. In order to use this chart, simply multiply the appropriate factor by the appropriate amount of money. The result includes the original investment plus any interest or discount.

> For example, to find out how much $250 would be worth if it were placed in a savings account untouched for 15 years, look at column 1 (Future Value of $1) for 15 years. Multiply that factor (2.759032) by $250. At the end of 15 years, the original investment of $250 will have grown to $689.76.

## Column 1, Future Value of $1

This column is used to calculate the future worth of a present amount assuming the amount invested draws interest at the rate stated at the top of the chart.

For example, the future value factor of $1.00 invested for 17 years is 3.158815. If $100 were invested for 17 years with a rate of 7% per year, the interest plus the initial investment of $100 would total $315.88.

## Column 2, Future Value of $1 per Period

This column is used to calculate the future value if regular additions of $1.00 are made every year and the interest stays constant during the investment period. In this instance, not only is interest added to the original investment amount, but additional capital is added to the investment at regular intervals as well.

If $100 is invested at the end of every year for five years and that amount earns 7% per year, the investment will build up to $575.07 at the end of the fifth year.

## Column 3, Sinking Fund Factor

This column will tell the investor how much must be invested each year to accumulate to a specific amount by the end of the stated period.

For example, if a person wants to accumulate $1,500,000 in savings over a 20-year period, an annual deposit of $36,589.50 ($1,500,000 × 0.024393) must be placed into an account bearing 7% interest every year for those 20 years.

## Column 4, Present Value of $1

This column is used to calculate the present value of a future amount.

A person who will inherit $750,000 in 5 years could sell his rights to that inheritance. If the investor buying the rights to that inheritance required a 7% return on his investment, he would pay $534,739.50 ($750,000 × 0.712986).

## Column 5, Present Value of an Annuity of $1 per Period

This column is much like Column 4, but instead of one future lump payment, it is used to discount future cash flows into a present worth.

> Assume a woman won a $20,000,000 state lottery payable at $1,000,000 per year for 20 years. If the state required a 7% discount, the woman would receive $10,594,014 ($1,000,000 × 10.594014) as a lump sum (prior to taxes).

## Column 6, Installment to Amortize $1

These columns are often used to identify the size of regular payments (annually in this case) required to pay off a debt over a specified period.

> If a homeowner obtained a 30-year, $300,000 loan at 7% to buy his house, he would have to make annual payments to the lender of $24,175.80 ($300,000 × 0.080586).

**Figure 11.5**  To convert a yearly amortized figure into a monthly payment, divide the annual payment by twelve.

The chart identifies six individual functions: columns 1 and 2 are for compounding, columns 3 and 6 are for asset accumulation or debt retirement, and columns 4 and 5 are for discounting.

| | 7.00% Annual Interest Rate | | | | | |
|---|---|---|---|---|---|---|
| | 1 | 2 | 3 | 4 | 5 | 6 |
| | Future Value of $1 | Future Value of $1 Per Period | Sinking Fund Factor | Present Value of $1 (Reversion) | Present Value of $1 Per Period | Installment to Amortize $1 |
| 1 | 1.070000 | 1.000000 | 1.000000 | 0.934579 | 0.934579 | 1.070000 |
| 2 | 1.144900 | 2.070000 | 0.483092 | 0.873439 | 1.808018 | 0.553092 |
| 3 | 1.225043 | 3.214900 | 0.311052 | 0.816298 | 2.624316 | 0.381052 |
| 4 | 1.310796 | 4.439943 | 0.225228 | 0.762895 | 3.387211 | 0.295228 |
| 5 | 1.402552 | 5.750739 | 0.173891 | 0.712986 | 4.100197 | 0.243891 |
| 6 | 1.500730 | 7.153291 | 0.139796 | 0.666342 | 4.766540 | 0.209796 |
| 7 | 1.605781 | 8.654021 | 0.115553 | 0.622750 | 5.389289 | 0.185553 |
| 8 | 1.718186 | 10.259803 | 0.097468 | 0.582009 | 5.971299 | 0.167468 |
| 9 | 1.838459 | 11.977989 | 0.083486 | 0.543934 | 6.515232 | 0.153486 |
| 10 | 1.967151 | 13.816448 | 0.072378 | 0.508349 | 7.023582 | 0.142378 |
| 11 | 2.104852 | 15.783599 | 0.063357 | 0.475093 | 7.498674 | 0.133357 |
| 12 | 2.252192 | 17.888451 | 0.055902 | 0.444012 | 7.942686 | 0.125902 |
| 13 | 2.409845 | 20.140643 | 0.049651 | 0.414964 | 8.357651 | 0.119651 |
| 14 | 2.578534 | 22.550488 | 0.044345 | 0.387817 | 8.745468 | 0.114345 |
| 15 | 2.759032 | 25.129022 | 0.039795 | 0.362446 | 9.107914 | 0.109795 |
| 16 | 2.952164 | 27.888054 | 0.035858 | 0.338735 | 9.446649 | 0.105858 |
| 17 | 3.158815 | 30.840217 | 0.032425 | 0.316574 | 9.763223 | 0.102425 |
| 18 | 3.379932 | 33.999033 | 0.029413 | 0.295864 | 10.059087 | 0.099413 |
| 19 | 3.616528 | 37.378965 | 0.026753 | 0.276508 | 10.335595 | 0.096753 |
| 20 | 3.869684 | 40.995492 | 0.024393 | 0.258419 | 10.594014 | 0.094393 |
| 21 | 4.140562 | 44.865177 | 0.022289 | 0.241513 | 10.835527 | 0.092289 |
| 22 | 4.430402 | 49.005739 | 0.020406 | 0.225713 | 11.061240 | 0.090406 |
| 23 | 4.740530 | 53.436141 | 0.018714 | 0.210947 | 11.272187 | 0.088714 |
| 24 | 5.072367 | 58.176671 | 0.017189 | 0.197147 | 11.469334 | 0.087189 |
| 25 | 5.427433 | 63.249038 | 0.015811 | 0.184249 | 11.653583 | 0.085811 |
| 26 | 5.807353 | 68.676470 | 0.014561 | 0.172195 | 11.825779 | 0.084561 |
| 27 | 6.213868 | 74.483823 | 0.013426 | 0.160930 | 11.986709 | 0.083426 |
| 28 | 6.648838 | 80.697691 | 0.012392 | 0.150402 | 12.137111 | 0.082392 |
| 29 | 7.114257 | 87.346529 | 0.011449 | 0.140563 | 12.277674 | 0.081449 |
| 30 | 7.612255 | 94.460786 | 0.010586 | 0.131367 | 12.409041 | 0.080586 |
| 31 | 8.145113 | 102.073041 | 0.009797 | 0.122773 | 12.531814 | 0.079797 |
| 32 | 8.715271 | 110.218154 | 0.009073 | 0.114741 | 12.646555 | 0.079073 |
| 33 | 9.325340 | 118.933425 | 0.008408 | 0.107235 | 12.753790 | 0.078408 |
| 34 | 9.978114 | 128.258765 | 0.007797 | 0.100219 | 12.854009 | 0.077797 |
| 35 | 10.676581 | 138.236878 | 0.007234 | 0.093663 | 12.947672 | 0.077234 |
| 36 | 11.423942 | 148.913460 | 0.006715 | 0.087535 | 13.035208 | 0.076715 |
| 37 | 12.223618 | 160.337402 | 0.006237 | 0.081809 | 13.117017 | 0.076237 |
| 38 | 13.079271 | 172.561020 | 0.005795 | 0.076457 | 13.193473 | 0.075795 |
| 39 | 13.994820 | 185.640292 | 0.005387 | 0.071455 | 13.264928 | 0.075387 |
| 40 | 14.974458 | 199.635112 | 0.005009 | 0.066780 | 13.331709 | 0.075009 |

## *Annuities*

Column 5 is the one real estate appraisers use the most frequently, and it is used to estimate the present value of an annuity. An **annuity** is regular payment of a predetermined amount. Though the term annuity technically refers to an annual amount, it applies to any kind of regular payment of a specific amount. For any income-producing property, there is the expectation that tenants will pay rent at regular intervals, usually monthly, to the property owner. Because of this, proprietors come to expect a regular amount of income generated at a predictable schedule.

Since real estate income flows in a similar pattern, it is reasonable to analyze real estate income from the point of view of an annuity. Estimating the present value of an annuity is the same process that one may use to value real estate that produces a predictable steady stream of income at regular intervals.

When discounting, the present value of an annuity is always assumed to be less than the sum total of all the cash flows during the period of the annuity. This procedure is tied to the premise that benefits received today are worth more than benefits received in the future.

The formula for calculating the present value of an annuity is rather complex and beyond the scope of this discussion. However, the factors found in the above table can be used to calculate the value of an income-producing property.

### Illustration

An income-producing property has been leased to a very reliable tenant for 18 years. The property produces a net annual operating income of $250,000 to the owners. The yield on the property has been estimated to be 7%. Though it would not work out this way in the real world, for purposes of simplicity, the net operating income is forecast to be level for the next 18 years. (This would be making the assumption that taxes, maintenance costs, management costs, etc would not go up for the next 18 years.) At the end of the 18-year lease period, the subject property's building is estimated to be at the end of its remaining economic life and will have no value at that time. Consequently, at the end of the lease period, all the value of the subject property will be solely in its land.

Current comparable land sales indicate the current value of the land at $450,000. On average, land value has historically appreciated 1% per year for the last 20 years and is forecast to increase at this rate into the foreseeable future. (The future value of a property is obviously very difficult to predict; however, this assumption is made for illustration purposes) The assignment is to estimate the current value of this property.

## Solution

To solve this valuation problem, the value of the income stream needs to be estimated as well as the value of the reversion.

1.  The value of the income stream may be estimated by multiplying the Net Operating Income (NOI) by the Present Value of an Annuity Factor at 7% for 18 years.

| | |
|---|---|
| Current annual NOI | $250,000 |
| Annuity factor (18 years @ 7%) | × 10.059087 |
| Present value of the NOI | = $2,514,772 |

2.  To estimate the value of the land, the subject's land is currently estimated to be worth $450,000. Assuming it increases in value by 1% per year, 18 years in the future it is estimated to be worth $538,300 (rounded).

| | |
|---|---|
| Current Land Value | $450,000 |
| Future Value of $1 factor (18 years @ 1%) | × 1.196147 |
| Future value of the land | = $538,266 |
| Rounded | $538,300 |

3.  The future value of the land needs to be discounted to its present value by multiplying it by the reversion factor (Column 4) for 7% at 18 years.

| | |
|---|---|
| Future Land Value | $538,300 |
| Present value of the reversion factor | × 0.295864 |
| Present value of the land | = $159,264 |
| Rounded | $159,300 |

4.  The final step is to add the present values of the income and of the reversion.

| | |
|---|---|
| Present value of the NOI | = $2,514,772 |
| Present value of the land (rounded) | $ 159,300 |
| Present value of the reversion | $2,674,072 |
| Rounded | $2,675,000 |

# Summary

The **income approach to value** is for properties that produce income and is based on the premise that a property is worth the amount of money it produces, or is expected to produce. Most beginning appraisers need not concern themselves with the more complex formulas for converting income into value, but it is worthwhile to be familiar with the basic three methods: **gross income multiplier**, **direct capitalization**, and **yield capitalization.**

The first step in each of the methods is to determine the subject's income. This usually takes several steps and different levels of analysis. The appraiser can estimate the **potential gross income** with relative ease. However, since this factor is the least indicative of the market, an appraiser will want to calculate (or estimate) the property's **effective gross income** and **net operating income**. The first is done by subtracting an allowance for **vacancy and collection losses**. Once the effective gross income has been calculated, the net operating income can be calculated by subtracting the **operating expenses** from the effective gross income.

Operating expenses fall into three broad categories. **Fixed expenses** are expenses more or less permanent to the property and do not vary with the property's occupancy or income. **Variable expenses** are those expenses that do vary with the property's income and occupancy level, such as management, marketing, maintenance, and utility expenses. **Replacement for reserves** are funds that are set aside to pay for major component and fixture replacement.

When totaling a property's expense report, there are certain expenses that should not be counted by the appraiser. The expenses to avoid are financing expenses, expenses associated with income taxes, book depreciation, capital improvements, and some insurance expenses.

Once the appraiser has determined the different incomes, he or she can then convert them into a value. The gross income and gross rent multipliers are the simplest methods. By multiplying the property's annual income or rent by a multiplier extracted from the market, the appraiser can quickly project the property's value. Though this method is the easiest and quickest, it is also the least accurate.

**Direct capitalization** is a more accurate method that involves applying a **capitalization rate** to a property's net operating income. The cap rate is a figure that expresses the relationship between a property's income and value and can be estimated in several ways.

**Extracting a cap rate from comparable sales** is the preferred method when enough market data is available. To do this the appraiser simply divides a comparable property's NOI by its sales price. After enough properties have been analyzed, the appraiser can extract a suitable cap rate to apply to the subject property's income.

The **band of investment method** is a method that accounts for both participants in an investment, the buyer and the lender. Since hardly any property is purchased without a loan, this method is applicable in almost all cases.

When an appraiser only knows one component of value, either the land or building, he or she can convert this value and NOI into an overall value by using one of the residual techniques. These techniques divide the property income into its component parts and capitalizes them separately, before adding them back together into a total property value.

**Yield capitalization,** the most complex and accurate technique, accounts for the present worth of future benefits. Basically, yield capitalization will condense forecasted future income streams into a singular, present day value. In order to do this, the appraiser must be familiar with the **six functions of a dollar**. These functions can be calculated using a scientific calculator or a spreadsheet program. Hard copy charts are available as well.

# Review Exercises

## Matching Exercise

**Instructions:**  Look up the meaning of the terms in the Glossary, then write the letter of the matching term on the blank line before its definition.  Answers are in Appendix B.

### Term

A.  annuity

B.  capitalization rate

C.  debt capital

D.  discount rate

E.  discounting

F.  effective gross income

G.  equity cap rate

H.  equity capital

I.  fixed expenses

J.  mortgage constant

K.  net operating income

L.  net operating income ratio

M.  operating expense ratio

N  operating expenses

O.  potential gross income

P.  rental survey

Q.  replacement reserves

R.  reversion

S.  variable expenses

T.  yield capitalization

### Definitions

1. _____ The maximum income a property could generate.

2. _____ The property's income after allowances for vacancy and collection losses are deducted from the estimate of potential gross income.

3. _____ The income remaining after the operating expenses are subtracted from the effective gross income.

4. _____ Expenses necessary to maintain the property and to help ensure the continued production of effective gross income.

5. _____ Operating expenses that vary based on numerous criteria such as the level of occupancy, the income a property generates, and the amount of services provided by the owner to the tenants.

6. _____ Funds set aside by the property owner to pay for the replacement of certain building components and fixtures that periodically wear out in a property.

7. _____ A market-derived ratio reflecting the relationship between the net operating income a property generates and its value.

8. _____ The ratio calculated by dividing the property's operating expenses by its effective gross income.

9. _____ The amount a buyer invests into a property.

10. _____ The amount borrowed by the buyer to purchase a property.

11. _____ Reflects the anticipated return on a percentage basis to the investor who owns the property and is typically reflective of the first year of the investment.

12. _____ A method where the value of future benefits is discounted to a present value.

13. _____ The lump sum amount the investor expects to receive upon sale of a property at some future point in time.

14. _____ The yield rate to the investor assuming a satisfactory return on and return of investment to the investor.

15. _____ Regular payment of a predetermined amount.

## Multiple Choice Questions

**Instructions:** Circle your response and go to Appendix B to read the complete explanation for each question.

1. The main principle behind the income approach is:
   a. anticipation.
   b. production.
   c. multiplication.
   d. supplication.

2. Potential gross income includes income from:
   a. rent.
   b. parking fees.
   c. laundry and vending machines.
   d. all of the above.

3. The purpose of a rental survey is to:
    a. find out if tenants think the rent is reasonable.
    b. identify the amount of income the subject property can be expected to generate.
    c. determine how many comparable properties are currently rented.
    d, determine vacancy losses.

4. Over the last year, a 10-unit apartment complex had 2 units that were each vacant for 1 ½ months.  What was the vacancy loss?
    a. 2.5%
    b. 5%
    c. 15%
    d. 20%

5. Which of the following is an example of a fixed expense?
    a. Marketing fees
    b. Cleaning expenses
    c. Property taxes
    d. None of the above

6. An accountant has provided the appraiser with the subject property's operating statement.  It included the following list of expenses.

| | |
|---|---|
| Utilities | $2,150.00 |
| Repairs | 1,075.00 |
| Management | 3,000.00 |
| Property taxes | 4,000.00 |
| Mortgage – principal and interest | 12,000.00 |

From the appraiser's perspective, the operating expenses total:
    a. $3,225.00.
    b. $7,225.00.
    c. $10,225.00.
    d. $22,225.00.

7. If a property rents for $1025/month and the gross rent multiplier is 240, what is the value of the property?
   a. $246,000
   b. $258,300
   c. $634,050
   d. $2,952,000

8. If a property's net operating income is $92,250 and the estimated cap rate is 9%, what is the value of the property?
   a. $100,553
   b. $1,025,000
   c. $1,206,630
   d. None of the above

9. Safe investments would have a:
   a. low capitalization rate and low value.
   b. low capitalization rate and high value.
   c. high capitalization rate and high value.
   d. high capitalization rate and low value.

10. A property has a effective gross income of $100,000 and operating expenses totaling $15,000. Which of the following statements is true?
    a. The operating expense ratio is .15. The net operating income cannot be determined.
    b. The operating expense ratio is .18. The net operating income cannot be determined, but the net operating income ratio must be .82.
    c. The operating expense ratio is .15. The net operating income is $85,000 and the net operating income ratio is .85.
    d. None of the above

11. In the band of investment method, the mortgage constant is:
    a. a market derived percentage of the debt capital.
    b. the pre-tax cash flow divided by the amount of debt investment.
    c. an amount that is deducted from a property's income to account for the mortgage payments that a typical owner would make.
    d. the ratio of the loan amount to the annual sum of the individual loan payments.

12. The building residual technique is used when:
    a. the building value is known.
    b. the land value is known.
    c. comparable land sales data is not available.
    d. a building has burned down and the appraiser must determine the value of the remaining structural elements.

13. All of the following are steps in the yield capitalization process, except:
    a. projecting the holding period of the investment.
    b. estimating and forecasting all the future cash flows associated with the investment.
    c. identifying an appropriate discount rate.
    d. determining the gross income multiplier.

14. Bob, a property owner, needs to set aside money for replacement reserves. He plans to invest money regularly in an account that gives 5% interest, and he wants to accumulate $16,000 to replace the roof of the apartment complex 3 years from now. Which function of one dollar would he use to determine how much he has to invest each year?
    a. Column 2, Future Value of $1 per Period
    b. Column 3, Sinking Fund Factor
    c. Column 4, Present Value of $1
    d. Column 6, Installment to Amortize $1

15. Which function of one dollar is most commonly used by appraisers?
    a. Column 1, Future Value of $1
    b. Column 2, Future Value of $1 per Period
    c. Column 3, Sinking Fund Factor
    d. Column 5, Present Value of an Annuity of $1 per Period

# Chapter 12

# Cost Approach: Reproduction of Improvements

## Introduction

The cost approach recognizes the two major components in real estate: land and improvements. Land includes the ground itself and the rights inherent in the use of that ground. Improvements are buildings or other structures that are permanently attached to the land. Houses, detached garages, barns, office, and retail buildings are all examples of improvements. Other improvements such as sidewalks, curbs, drainage structures, retaining walls, grading, streets, and utility hook-ups are commonly called site improvements and need to be analyzed in this approach as well.

Estimating land value is straightforward. In Chapter 8, we discussed site characteristics that may influence land value. In this chapter, we cover six different methods to determine the value of a site.

Estimating the value of improvements is a little more complex. Using the cost approach, appraisers first estimate the cost to build the improvements, as if new. However, buildings do not stay new; they **depreciate**, or lose value over time. Determining depreciation is the subject of the next chapter.

## Learning Objectives

After reading this chapter, you will be able to:

- identify the techniques that are commonly used to value land.

- recognize the difference between reproduction and replacement cost.

- identify the four major methods used to estimate replacement cost.

- discuss the applications and limitations of each method.

- describe entrepreneurial profit.

- identify items that qualify as on-site improvements.

# Overview of the Cost Approach

Like the sales comparison approach, the cost approach is based on the principle of substitution.  However, in this case, the substitute is not purchasing another similar property.  The substitute is building one.  When using the cost approach, the appraiser is comparing the value of the subject property with the cost of building a similar property.

## Applications of this Approach

The cost approach is of particular value when appraising:

- new properties.

- properties with unique improvements.

- properties that cannot be analyzed using the other approaches to value, i.e. not enough comparables and no income produced.

- special use properties.

This valuation method can have much use in appraising unique homes, church buildings, schools, museums, public buildings, and special use properties.  When appraising single-family residences using the sales comparison approach, appraisers also use this approach to support the value conclusion reached.

In some instances, the cost approach is the only reliable indicator of value in an assignment.  Variations on this approach are often useful in identifying market reactions when appraising oddball properties that have unique designs and characteristics.

**Figure 12.1** The cost approach to value is applicable for unique properties and special-use properties like a stadium.

## Limitations of this Approach

Like the other two approaches to value, the cost approach to value is not applicable to every appraisal assignment. The cost approach to value is usually not applicable when appraising:

- properties with older improvements.

- properties in a market where there are minimal land value indicators.

- properties that are not at their highest and best use.

This approach is also limited in other ways. The cost approach assumes that the cost to build an item is equal to its value in the market, but that is not always the case. Also, depreciation can be difficult to determine accurately. At times, estimating accrued depreciation may have to be based on subjective reasoning which lessens the applicability of this approach. **Accrued depreciation** is the difference between the cost to replace the property and the property's current appraised value.

**Figure 12.2** The cost approach is inapplicable when appraising older buildings because it is difficult to accurately measure the depreciation.

In certain assignments, like appraising vacant land or a condominium, the cost approach to value is completely inappropriate. This is because the cost approach requires both an estimate for land and an estimate for improvements. Vacant land is, of course, missing improvements, and the condominium form of ownership does not include the land but rather airspace and its contents.

Because of these limitations, the cost approach to value is often omitted in an assignment. When it is developed, the primary role of the cost approach to value is to lend support to the value estimates derived by the sales comparison approach or the income approach.

## Steps in Cost Approach

When applying the cost approach, appraisers:

1. estimate the value of the land component of the subject property as though vacant and available to be put to its highest and best use.

2. estimate the reproduction or replacement cost new of the building improvements on the subject site as of the effective date of the appraisal.

3. add entrepreneurial profit, when appropriate, to the building improvements' estimated reproduction or replacement cost.

4. estimate accrued depreciation from all sources (physical, functional, or external), and deduct from estimated reproduction or replacement cost.

5. estimate "as-is" value of additional site improvements, if necessary.

6. add the land value estimate, the depreciated value of the improvements, and the value of the site improvements together to calculate the property value by the cost approach.

| COST APPROACH TO VALUE (not required by Fannie Mae) | | | | | |
|---|---|---|---|---|---|
| Provide adequate information for the lender/client to replicate the below cost figures and calculations. | | | | | |
| Support for the opinion of site value (summary of comparable land sales or other methods for estimating site value) | | | | | |
| | | | | | |
| | | | | | |
| ESTIMATED ☐ REPRODUCTION OR ☐ REPLACEMENT COST NEW | OPINION OF SITE VALUE............................................................... = $ | | | | |
| Source of cost data | Dwelling | Sq. Ft. @ $ | ................... =$ | | |
| Quality rating from cost service            Effective date of cost data | | Sq. Ft. @ $ | ................... =$ | | |
| Comments on Cost Approach (gross living area calculations, depreciation, etc.) | | | | | |
| | Garage/Carport | Sq. Ft. @ $ | ................... =$ | | |
| | Total Estimate of Cost-New | | ................... = $ | | |
| | Less            Physical | Functional | External | | |
| | Depreciation | | | =$(              ) | |
| | Depreciated Cost of Improvements............................................ =$ | | | | |
| | "As-is" Value of Site Improvements......................................... =$ | | | | |
| | | | | | |
| Estimated Remaining Economic Life (HUD and VA only)                    Years | Indicated Value By Cost Approach ............................................ =$ | | | | |

**Figure 12.3** The Cost Approach section of the URAR form.

The Cost Approach section of the standard **Uniform Residential Appraisal Report** (URAR) has a space for each of these calculations.

The steps in the cost approach follow a logical sequence. First, the appraiser determines the value of the land (site). Then, the cost to reproduce the structure is calculated. These figures, added together, give the estimated cost of the new subject property. However, a new structure is not being appraised. Once a hypothetical replica of the subject has been established, the appraiser must account for the percentage of usefulness that has elapsed. This is called depreciation. Additional items of value may need to be calculated. For example, swimming pools, fences, or landscaping add value to the property.

The rest of this chapter is devoted to discussing the first three steps in the cost approach.

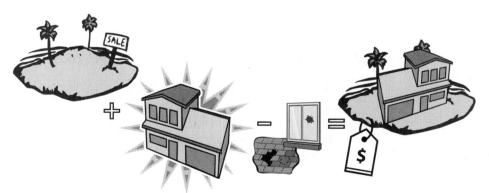

**Figure 12.4** The steps in the cost approach: a property's value is equal to the value of the land component, plus the cost of the improvements new, minus the accrued depreciation. If applicable, the appraiser must add entrepreneurial profit and the "as-is" value of site improvements.

# Estimating Land Value

The principles of supply and demand, change, anticipation, substitution, and balance all influence land value. All of these principles need to be considered in estimating the value of land.

> For example, as stated in an earlier chapter, the principle of anticipation causes value to be created in anticipation of benefits that may be derived at some point in the future. Buyers acquire properties in anticipation of what may be done with that property in the future, not necessarily what may be economically done immediately upon acquisition. The competition among buyers creates a price level for land that may have little, or nothing, to do with its current use.

Appraisers may use numerous techniques in order to identify the land value for the subject. It is important to recognize that the following techniques produce estimates of the fee simple interest in land. If there is another interest in land required in an assignment, such as a leasehold, leased fee, or reversionary interest, the land value estimate will need to be adjusted.

Six methods are commonly used to estimate land value. These procedures are the:

- sales comparison method.

- allocation method.

- extraction method.

- subdivision development method.

- land residual method.

- ground rent capitalization method.

## Sales Comparison Method

The **sales comparison method** is the most commonly used method for valuing land and is preferred over the other methods. When using this technique, the appraiser compares the subject site with other vacant land sites that have been sold recently.

The appraiser follows the steps for the sales comparison approach that were covered in Chapter 10. The appraiser collects data, selects the most appropriate comparable sites, and verifies the information gathered. He or she analyzes sales of vacant land that are comparable to the subject, and applies adjustments to the comparable sales to reflect differences between the subject site and the comparable vacant land sales used. Elements of comparison, including such items as property rights, legal and physical characteristics, utilities, zoning, highest and best use, financing, etc., are identified on both the subject and the comps. The sales prices of the comparable vacant land sales are adjusted to reflect the market's reaction for any dissimilarity between the subject and the comps. After adjusting a representative number of comparable sales, the adjusted prices indicated by the comparable sales are reconciled into an estimate of value. When performing the reconciliation process, the sales requiring the least amount of adjusting tend to be the strongest indicators of value.

When valuing land, the appraiser must be sure to use the same units of comparison. **Units of comparison** are the components the property is divided into for purposes of comparison. The units of comparison for land may be per acre, per square foot, per front foot, etc.

As in other instances where the sales comparison analysis is performed, comparable sales used in valuing land should be as similar as possible to the subject. Zoning is often the most important criterion when selecting comparable sales for the subject because it may create limitations on how a lot may be used, making it inappropriate for comparison with another lot. One lot may have available utilities, where another does not, thus limiting its comparability. The appraiser must use research to detect all similarities and differences in characteristics and qualities of sites. As a rule, the greater the amount of dissimilarity between the subject and the comparable sales, the greater the potential there is for error and distortion in this approach to value.

Although this approach is the most commonly used, there are situations where it does not apply. In some instances, the subject property may be in a heavily developed area with very few vacant sites and even fewer vacant land sales. Similarly, in some rural areas, vacant land sales may occur so seldom that the available data is inadequate to develop a credible estimate of the land value using the sales comparison method.

## Allocation Method

The **allocation method** is based upon the principle of balance as well as on the concept of contributory value. The basic assumption of this method is that there is a typical ratio between the land value of a property and the value of its improvements. Historically, this has been the case in many areas. The ratio varies by area, so the appraiser must extract the ratio from the local market. Then, he or she can apply it to other improved sales in the subject's neighborhood in order to establish the land value.

For example, assume that there have been no recent sales of vacant land in the subject's neighborhood. Appraiser John has found that houses in a nearby neighborhood sell for prices ranging from $200,000 to $300,000. He found a property in that same area where the developer purchased lots for $100,000 and built houses that sold for $300,000 upon completion. In this case, the value of the land ($100,000) represents 33.3% ($100,000 ÷ $300,000) of the overall value of that property.

John then finds a sale of an improved property with a site virtually identical to the subject. This property sold for $360,000. Applying the ratio to this sale, he estimates that the land is worth $120,000 (33.3% × $360,000).

While this method does not produce conclusive value estimates, it can be used to establish land values in situations where recent comparable land sales are scarce or non-existent. The weakness of this method is that it does not take into account individual property differences.

**Figure 12.5** The allocation method holds that the property value is composed of a typical ratio of land to improvements.

## Extraction Method

The **extraction method,** also known as the abstraction method, is a variation on the allocation method and is based on the same principles.

Using this method, appraisers derive the land value of a comparable property by deducting the depreciated costs of the improvements on that property from the property's known sale price. The remaining value represents value attributable to the land.

This method may be best applied in situations where the improvements contribute a relatively small amount of value to the overall property.

## Land Residual Technique

As we discussed in Chapter 11, the **land residual technique** is based upon the premise that the income of a property is generated by both the land and the improvements, and that there is a relationship between the income a property produces and the value of that property.

If an appraiser knows or can reliably estimate the income for the whole property, the appraiser can subtract the portion of that income attributable to the improvements to determine the income attributable to the land. The income attributable to the land is converted into a land value by applying a capitalization rate. The **capitalization rate** is the interest rate that is considered a reasonable return on the investment.

This technique may be used where building value is known or can be accurately estimated and is valuable in situations where there are few comparable sales available. However, when using this analytical technique, the forecasted income must be at the property's highest and best use. Estimating this income upon some other use will provide a less than accurate indication of value.

## Ground Rent Capitalization Method

In some instances, property owners lease out their land to tenants who chose to build upon that site. In these situations, the tenant owns the building with a leasehold interest in the land. The owner retains the **leased fee** interest in the land. In these situations, the lease is usually long-term (sometimes up to 99 years) and is called a **ground lease**. **Ground rent** is the rent that is payable under a ground lease.

In order to estimate value for the subject property, the annual ground rent is divided by a market-derived capitalization rate. The calculation under this method is similar to that used in the land residual method. However, using this method, the income is determined by the land lease amount rather than calculating the residual of the whole property's income. Variations in the terms of the lease such as renewal options and escalator clauses need to be considered in this analysis.

This technique is useful in situations where comparable sales of leased land are available, and the terms of those leases are known.

## Subdivision Development Analysis

Also called the land development method, this method may be used to value land when subdivision and development of the subject site represents the highest and best use of the property and sales information for finished lots is available. This analysis may be applied to all kinds of land including residential, commercial, recreational, or industrial. It requires accurate forecasting of market demand and risk factors.

In performing this analysis, the appraiser estimates the number, size, and price of lots that may be created by subdividing the subject property. While it may be impossible to determine this information precisely without performing surveys or engineering studies, analyzing zoning and subdivision requirements may enable the appraiser to formulate a reasonable estimate. The appraiser may also estimate the subdivision potential of the subject property by analyzing the number of lots created in other nearby subdivisions.

> For example, an appraiser estimates that a parcel can be subdivided into 50 lots of the same size. From market data, the appraiser determines that this size lot is are worth approximately $30,000. The total projected gross income from lot sales once developed is $1,500,000 total.

After the development potential of the subject property is estimated, the time required to develop the subject into individual sites needs to be estimated.

Similarly, the period required to sell all these newly developed lots created from the subject property, called the absorption rate, needs to be calculated.

> For instance, if the subject is developed into 50 single family residential lots, the absorption forecast may project that the first 20 homes will sell in the first year for $300,000 each, the second 20 for $330,000 in the next year, and the final 10 for $375,000 in the third year.

The owner will incur many different costs in the process of subdividing the land into individual lots, developing the lots, and marketing them. All these costs need to be deducted from the sum of the projected sales prices for the sites. Then, the projected net proceeds from these sales are discounted to their present value in order to arrive at an indication of the land's present value in its raw state.

The subdivision method is useful in situations where comparable sales are scarce or non-existent. It is also useful in developing feasibility studies. However, it is often necessary to make speculative assumptions when performing this approach, which lessens the reliability of this technique. While the complexity of this technique may cause appraisers to use it less than other methods, it is useful when others are not available.

# Estimating Building Costs

After estimating the land value, the next step is to determine the cost to reproduce or replace the improvements. Reproduction cost and replacement cost are calculated differently, and it is important to understand the difference.

## Reproduction vs. Replacement

The decision to use replacement cost or reproduction cost is usually related to the intended use of the appraisal. Fannie Mae and Freddie Mac require reproduction cost estimates in appraisals for loans they purchase. For insurance purposes, replacement cost may be desired.

### *Reproduction Cost*

**Reproduction cost** is the dollar amount required to construct an exact replica of the property being appraised. This cost estimate assumes the cost of using like kind and quality of materials, identical construction and workmanship standards, as well as identical design and layout. It reflects construction prices current as of the date of the appraisal.

When performing a reproduction cost estimate, the appraiser estimates the costs using the exact same building materials, construction standards, floorplan/layout, and quality of workmanship existing in the property being appraised. This option is more suited to estimating unique or historical structures, when an exact replica is requisite.

In some instances, reproduction cost is difficult, if not almost impossible, to estimate accurately because identical building materials may no longer be available and construction standards may have changed.

> For example, asbestos was used widely used for siding and insulation in years past. Today it is virtually impossible to buy building materials containing asbestos.

> Similarly, in years past, 60-amp electrical service using "knob and tube" wiring was the standard for most homes. This kind of electrical system is no longer compliant with building codes.

In such instances, the appraiser estimates costs using substantially equal building materials and construction methods.

### *Replacement Cost*

Since estimating the reproduction cost of an existing structure is not always feasible, it may be more reliable and more prudent to estimate the cost to replace the existing improvements. **Replacement cost** is the dollar amount required to construct improvements having the same utility and quality as the subject property using current construction materials, methods, and techniques. Like reproduction cost, replacement cost reflects construction prices current as of the date of the appraisal.

To estimate the replacement costs for an older subject property, the appraiser may find the costs of newer homes with similar bedroom and bath counts, similar gross living area, and similar room sizes. Generally, similar-sized structures, of similar quality construction and similar utility will have very similar values. An exact replica is not necessary to achieve the same value in the marketplace, and it may not even achieve maximum value if depreciation due to excess construction offsets perceived worth in the marketplace. Because of this, residential appraisers are mostly concerned with replacement cost, and this textbook focuses on replacement cost.

## Data Sources

Throughout this textbook, we have discussed data that the appraiser collects. When using the cost approach, the most important data for the appraiser to collect is information on the building area and construction costs.

### *Building Area*

The methods used in the cost approach require a very accurate measurement of the improvements. In Chapter 9, we discussed inspecting the property and measuring the improvements. Measuring the subject property is just one of the tasks performed during the property inspection. The appraiser at that time will also identify the other physical characteristics of the subject including its quality, condition, effective age, physical characteristics, and other amenities that will need to be considered in all three approaches to value.

Depending upon the scope of work being performed in an assignment, building area may be identified in a number of ways.

The size of the improvements may be estimated based upon information available from local county tax assessor's records. The appraiser may obtain measurements from previous appraisals if provided by the client. Improvement size may also be obtained from sales brochures, owner sketches, or blueprints. The square footage of the building(s) being appraised may also be determined by personally inspecting and measuring the improvements.

If the appraiser relies on third party sources, the appraiser increases his risk of producing a misinformed appraisal. By personally measuring the improvements, the appraiser avoids the need to make an extraordinary assumption regarding the size of the improvements and lessens the risk of poorly appraising the property.

## *Construction Costs*

Appraisers need to rely upon credible and reliable cost data in order to formulate the cost approach. As such, gathering and identifying this information is essential.

Some of the best indicators of cost are construction contracts for buildings that are similar to the one being appraised. While these are not often available, they provide a very strong foundation upon which to base a cost estimate.

Data sources such as Marshall & Swift/Boeckh, R.S. Means Company, and Craftsman Book Company all are sources of construction cost data. Computer assisted cost estimator programs as well as Internet based cost estimator resources are also available to the appraiser.

Discussions with builders and cost estimators are also a very good way to determine local building costs to incorporate into appraisal assignments.

Some appraisers maintain extensive records which include the costs of various kinds of buildings they have appraised. While this method is very reliable, the appraiser needs to maintain confidentiality according to USPAP.

It is prudent for the appraiser to compare data obtained from different sources, such as contractors and cost estimators, in order to verify the accuracy of the information provided. If significant discrepancies are found when comparing one data source to another, additional investigation needs to be performed by the appraiser to identify why the discrepancy exists.

### Direct Costs and Indirect Costs

Cost estimating services all provide direct cost estimates; however, they vary in their levels of accurately identifying indirect costs. **Direct costs** or hard costs refer to costs directly related to labor and materials. **Indirect costs** or soft costs include all other costs, such as building permit fees and interest on a construction loan. The appraiser needs to be certain if the cost information obtained from other sources includes indirect costs or not. If not, indirect costs need to be added into that cost estimate.

Examples of costs that are directly involved with construction include:

- building materials, products, and equipment used in construction.

- labor used to construct the building(s).

- contractor's profit and overhead including both project and worker supervision, worker's compensation, fire, liability, and unemployment insurance, as well as performance bonds.

- equipment rental, including an on-site temporary office, material storage facilities, security fencing, barricades, and portable toilets.

- temporary power, water, phone service, and utility costs.

- security, including guards and video monitoring.

- temporary construction easements.

**Figure 12.6** Direct costs include those costs directly associated with construction such as materials and labor.

Indirect costs, on the other hand, are costs for items not directly linked to construction which are still incurred in the overall process. They include:

- professional fees such as architect's fees, surveyor's fees, civil, geotechnical, mechanical, electrical, and structural engineering fees.

- environmental and building permit fees including plan check fees.

- building construction inspector fees.

- zoning change, conditional use permit, and environmental consultant's fees.

- accounting, legal, and appraisal fees.

- financing fees, including costs and interest paid on construction loans, and also permanent financing costs, processing fees and service charges.

- lease-up, marketing, and sales costs including commissions, sales incentives, and administrative costs.

- escrow, title insurance and recording fees.

- insurance and property taxes during construction.

Some of the indirect costs listed above are calculated as a percentage of the direct costs.  Others are calculated as a lump-sum amount to the overall cost since they are not related to the size or direct costs of the building(s) being constructed.

Obviously, not all of the direct and indirect costs listed above would be incurred in every instance.  Constructing a high-rise office tower would incur different costs than those incurred when building a detached, single-family home.  The appraiser must be careful to be sure that the cost estimate in an appraisal reflects the costs likely to be incurred by an owner/developer.

## Methods Used to Estimate Cost

The four ways commonly used to estimate building costs are the:

- index method.

- comparative unit method (also frequently called the square-foot method).

- unit-in-place method.

- quantity survey method.

The **index method** and **square-foot method** are the quickest and easiest to calculate.  However, they also tend to be the least accurate of the methods used for cost estimation.  The **unit-in-place method** is a more in-depth cost estimate that provides more detail than the square-foot or index method.  The **quantity survey method** is the most in-depth and detailed of the commonly used processes for estimating costs, but it also is the most time-consuming and arduous of the four.  It is the method least used by appraisers.

Once the size of the improvements is determined, that information is incorporated into the cost approach using any of the four commonly used methods.

> **Review — The four methods for estimating cost are the:**
> - index method.
> - comparative unit method.
> - unit-in-place method.
> - quantity survey method.

## Index Method

Many of the **cost services** include information regarding cost trends. Cost-index trending involves converting known historical costs into current cost estimates. Usually, the cost reporting service such as Marshall & Swift/Boeckh keeps track of building cost trends over time. The reporting service assigns a numerical index to a cost relative to a base year. By comparing the current cost index with the cost index when a property was constructed, an estimate for current costs may be obtained.

To update the known historical cost to the current date of valuation, it is necessary to divide the present index by the historical index at the time of construction and multiply that result by the original cost of construction. The following equation illustrates this concept:

$$\frac{\text{Current cost index}}{\text{Historical cost index}} \times \text{Historical cost} = \text{Present cost estimate}$$

The following example shows how simple this method is.

> Appraiser Joe is appraising a single-family detached home that was constructed in 1973. From his research, he identified the historical cost index figure at 177. He also identified the cost to construct the subject property at $64,000 from examining the contractor's records. The current cost index is 587. To estimate the current replacement cost of the subject property, Joe uses the above formula to calculate the cost:
>
> 587 ÷ 177 = 3.32 (rounded)
>
> $64,000 × 3.32 = $212,480

## Limitations of this Method

There can be problems with estimating costs using this method:

- Historical costs do not always indicate typical costs for that period.

- Historical data does not always correspond in its individual components with current costs.

- Construction methods at the time of the historical cost may differ from the methods at the time of the appraisal.

Cost-index trending is rarely accurate when used as the only method of estimating current costs. Used alone, this method is not a reliable replacement for more traditional cost estimating methods. It may be used to help verify one of the other ways costs are estimated, however, and give further support to the final cost estimate.

## Comparative Unit Method

The **comparative unit** or **square-foot method** is based upon costs of similar structures computed on a unit of measurement. The comparative unit method is a relatively uncomplicated way of estimating costs and is widely used. The cost to build a building is multiplied by the area of the building being appraised.

### Unit of Measurement

The two **units of measurement** that are most commonly used are square foot and cubic foot. A **square foot** is an area equal to one foot by one foot square. A **cubic foot** is a measurement for volume. It is an area one foot long, by one foot wide, by one foot high.

When appraising residential property, the cost approach is typically calculated on a per-square foot basis. This is a measurement of a building's area.

Sometimes the unit used in this method is a cubic foot. This is useful in identifying the volume of a building. Cubic foot measurements are typically used when appraising commercial, industrial, or special use buildings, when the heights of floors within a structure are varied and a simple square foot measurement would not accurately account for all the materials used in the structure. Cubic foot measurements are also used for structures like warehouses or silos that are very tall with no floors other than the ground floor. Obviously, a square-foot measurement would not account for all the materials used in the height of the walls.

Even though both units of measurement are used, the remainder of this section concentrates on using the cost-per-square foot as the comparative unit. In either case, the process is overall the same.

### Basic Process

As mentioned earlier, the appraiser must first collect the necessary data. The cost to construct a property on a per square-foot basis may be obtained from cost estimate services such as Marshall & Swift/Boeckh or may be obtained from developers or contractors who have built other similar properties.

When appraising single-family properties, the cost to build a structure on a per-square-foot basis is multiplied by the gross living area of the building being appraised. The cost of additional components, such as garages, basements, driveways, pools, patios, etc., is added to this calculation to arrive at the total cost estimate. This method applies whether calculating replacement cost or reproduction cost.

> For example, an appraiser contacts a contractor who just built a brand new tract about four blocks away from the subject. The new complex averaged about $105 per square foot of construction and contained both two and three bedroom homes. The subject is a three-bedroom house and has 2,124 square feet of living area. Using the comparative unit method, the appraiser estimates that it would cost approximately $223,000 to rebuild the subject property (2,124 sq. ft. × $105).

The above example, of course, is over-simplified. An appraiser, typically, has to account for a multitude of variables. In addition, he or she must make adjustments to those variables.

## Adjustments

Cost estimating services typically generate the cost-per-square-foot estimate starting with a base price, which is usually reflective of the subject's quality and size. This base cost estimate is adjusted up or down depending upon features found in, or lacking from, the subject property.

In a middle-income area where homes are built in subdivisions and floors are linoleum, the quality of construction might be called average. In a high-end area of luxury and custom homes, where the floors are marble and the kitchens have polished granite counter tops, a higher quality of construction would be encountered and a higher price per square foot would be used. When using costs obtained from similar buildings, appraisers need to apply adjustments to reflect the differences between the costs to build those similar properties and the subject.

> For example, assume homes that are similar to the subject are being built at a cost of $110 per square foot and have average-quality kitchen cabinetry and equipment. The subject may be estimated to cost $115 per square foot if it has superior kitchen cabinetry and equipment.

Additionally, appraisers usually need to apply regional and local cost multipliers to the subject's base cost, because the same house built in Los Angeles and Des Moines will have different costs associated with the project. Regional and local cost multipliers account for the differences in regional median wages, materials that have regional cost differences due to supply or transportation costs, as well as regional building requirements. These adjustment figures and locational multipliers are also supplied by the cost estimating service.

Be careful when identifying building costs in this manner. For instance, some developers build so many homes that they are able to take advantage of economies of sale and spend much less money building properties than it costs others. Building costs should be reflective of the cost to build one unit, not one of many units.

Similarly, costs on a per-square-foot basis vary with size. All other things being equal, it typically costs less to build a larger building on a per-square-foot basis than to build a smaller building. First, this is due to **economies of scale;** larger quantities of building materials typically cost less, on a per unit basis, than smaller quantities of the same materials. Second, certain items, such as heating, plumbing, doors, windows, elevators, and insulation, do not cost proportionately more to install in a larger building than in a smaller one.

## Other Improvements

Costs on a per-square-foot basis also vary depending on the type of structure. Residential appraisers will notice that costs vary depending on whether the structure is finished or unfinished. Finished structures, like the house, will require a higher cost per square foot. Unfinished structures, like the garage or carport, will require a lower cost per square foot.

Construction within a home will include insulation, fine carpentry, and finishing of all surfaces, carpeting, and so forth. In contrast, the price per square foot for primarily unfinished structures like a garage will be much less, lacking the details and added costs of the dwelling. The garage usually is a shell, lacking flooring, insulation, and drywall. It is therefore calculated separately from the calculation for the gross living area of the single-family residential property.

## Entire Process

Once the appraiser has determined all the costs, he or she adds the adjusted base cost of the subject's gross living area to the costs of the garage and any other improvements.

To illustrate this process, the following simplified example is used.

> Assume the property being appraised is a single-family residence that has 1,565 square feet of gross living area. The reproduction cost of the gross living area is estimated to be $81.00 per square foot. The subject has a tile roof that, according to the cost estimating service, adds $6.25 per square foot to the base cost. The subject property is two stories tall which lowers the overall cost $7.50 per square foot. The subject has no basement; however, it does have a 420-square-foot garage that is estimated to cost $19.50 per square foot to build. The regional multiplier supplied from the cost service is 1.05.

The following table illustrates the reproduction cost estimate for the above example.

| | | |
|---|---|---|
| **House** | Base Cost<br>Tile Roof Premium<br>Two-Story Design | $81.00<br>+ $ 6.25<br>− $ 7.50 |
| | Cost per Square Foot<br>Gross Living Area | $79.75<br>1,565 ft.$^2$ |
| | Reproduction Cost | $124,808.75 |
| **Other** | Garage Cost per Sq Foot<br>Garage Area | $19.50<br>× 420 ft.$^2$ |
| | Garage Reproduction Cost | $8,190.00 |
| Reproduction Costs Subtotal<br>Regional/Local Multiplier | | $132,998.75<br>× 1.05 |
| Total Reproduction Cost | | $139,648.69 |
| **Rounded Estimate** | | $139,600.00 |

With experience, the appraiser becomes accustomed to what price per square foot is appropriate for which type of construction in the area, and does not have to perform such laborious research for each appraisal. The appraiser, however, should always be aware of any economic changes in the area that could cause building costs to increase or decrease. The appraiser must be in touch with the market for all relevant data, including cost data. Consulting available cost handbooks, as well as builders, contractors, and other appraisers in the area is necessary.

## Unit-in-Place Method

The **unit-in-place method**, sometimes called the segregated cost method, is more precise overall than the comparative unit method. Since it is more in-depth than the comparative unit method, it is considered a more accurate way to calculate building costs since every building component must be identified. However, it is also much more time-consuming than the comparative unit method.

In this method, the costs of the various building components, as installed, are calculated separately and then added together into a single value estimate. Building components would include such items as the foundation, exterior walls, interior walls, roof structure, ceiling, electrical system, plumbing system, kitchen cabinetry, kitchen equipment, windows, doors, mechanical systems, stairways, etc.

The costs to build each of these component parts in place is calculated then added together with the cost of the other component parts in order to estimate the value of a property. The individual costs estimated for each of the building components required in this method are in terms of the standardized units typically used for the individual building component.

> For example, concrete for a foundation is measured in dollars per cubic yard. Roofing may be calculated in terms of a **square**, which equals 100 square feet. The cost of a raised foundation made of concrete block may be expressed as dollars per linear foot. Carpeting may be calculated in terms of square yardage.

Cost estimates for the individual components need to include a proportionate share of all direct costs including labor, contractor's profit, etc. Indirect costs are usually calculated separately when using this method.

As in the comparative unit method, costs to perform the unit-in-place method may be obtained from local developers and contractors. The unit-in-place estimates may be calculated with cost estimating services. Even though cost information obtained from developers and contractors may be more accurate, it is more time consuming.

## Limitations of this Method

This method breaks down the cost of a building into the cost of its component parts. Unfortunately, the market is not always reflective of valuing a property on this basis. The knowledge about costs concerning materials, equipment, labor, and contractor's profit associated with every component of a building, or buildings, on a site may be very difficult to estimate. Additional specialized knowledge may be required to perform this procedure accurately.

## *Quantity Survey Method*

The **quantity survey method** is the most thorough and accurate method of estimating building costs. This means that it is also the most time-consuming and intricate method available for estimating cost. The quantity survey method accounts for every inch of material used, every man-hour put in, every dollar spent on insurance, etc.

**Figure 12.7** The quantity survey method is the most comprehensive way to estimate cost new and it accounts for all materials used.

As the most comprehensive way to estimate costs, the quantity survey method duplicates a contractor's method of developing a bid for construction. When employing this method, the quality and quantity of all the materials used and all labor associated with building the structure is identified and estimated. For example, the number of bricks used in construction are identified, the number of yards of concrete needed are determined, the amount and type of electrical wire calculated, the number and type of plumbing fixtures counted, and the number of hours associated with each category of labor necessary to construct the building are estimated. The cost of each of these items is then calculated and the labor associated with assembling and building all these items is calculated.

An in-depth quantity survey identifying costs may encompass many pages and be precise enough to identify how many gallons of paint are needed, how many cases of nails are required, and how many hours an electrician will require to complete the electrical system in the property. The cost of waste normally associated with construction is also calculated.

The quantity survey method breaks down the indirect costs in an in-depth manner as well. Permit fees, taxes, insurance costs, surveys, financing fees and interest, and developer's profit are all calculated in as precise a manner as possible.

### Limitations of this Method

This method for estimating costs is very precise when properly execut-ed.  However, it is also very time-consuming and costly to perform. Most often, an appraiser will lack the expertise necessary to perform this kind of cost estimate.  Usually, this method requires the services of a professional construction cost estimator.  Due to the level of expert-ise required and the costs and time required to develop this method properly, the quantity-survey method is not often used.

## Estimating Entrepreneurial Profit

No matter which method the appraiser chooses to use for reproducing the cost estimate of the subject, the entrepreneurial profit must also be estimated.  **Entrepreneurial profit** is the compensation the owner or developer expects to gain from the undertaking.  It is typically reflect-ed as the property value once construction is completed minus the developer's costs (including direct and indirect costs) and the land value.

Entrepreneurial profit is a necessary element of the cost approach esti-mate.  It is based upon the principle of anticipation and reflects the usual motivation within the market.  If the value of a property were only equal to its cost plus its land value, there would be no incentive for an owner to build.  While there are some individuals who may build with the intention of making no profit, the overwhelming majority of developers expect to be compensated for their efforts.

When applying the cost approach, appraisers must estimate the appro-priate amount to allow for entrepreneurial profit, since cost estimator services like Marshall & Swift/Boeckh do not include entrepreneurial profit in their listed costs.  Estimating entrepreneurial profit is done differently in different markets.  It may be calculated as a percentage of cost, a percentage of cost plus land value, or a percentage of the final estimate of value.

Different classes of developers have different levels of expectation regarding the profit they anticipate, which makes it more difficult to determine the amount of entrepreneurial profit.  A developer of large housing tracts would most likely expect a higher overall profit on a per-centage basis than an individual who builds a single house.  In these instances, the large developers typically take advantage of economies of scale, which serves to lower their overall costs (both direct and indi-rect) while the small builder cannot take advantage of these benefits. Though these developers may build houses that are worth the same amount, the amount of profit the large developer stands to gain may be significantly more that that of the small developer.

Surveying builders for both their costs and their profits is typically how entrepreneurial profit is determined. When estimating entrepreneurial profit, the appraiser needs to consider expectations within the subject's market.

## Estimating the Value of Site Improvements

Although adding the value of on-site improvements is one of the final steps in the cost approach, it will be addressed here before we cover depreciation since on-site improvements are typically valued "as-is", and the value of the site improvements is not depreciated. Items like landscaping, sprinkler systems, driveways, brickwork, fences, etc. fall into the category of site improvements. The appraiser uses market data to determine the "as-is" value.

This method is used because the cost to install site improvements new does not necessarily equal the value they contribute to the site. A swimming pool, for example, may cost $35,000 to install, but only add $10,000 to the value of the property. This has to be determined by a paired sales analysis or by other appropriate market abstraction. Other items of site improvements may add more value to the property than their cost to install. Landscaping, for example, may cost $3,000, but add $5,000 to the value. This, too, must be referenced to data from the marketplace.

**Figure 12.8** Site improvements like decorative landscaping are valued "as-is" and are added to the property value after improvement depreciation.

For some properties, the contribution of site improvements to value is negligible. In other situations, it is significant. The appraiser must be alert to examine thoroughly all site improvements and all contributions to value, read the marketplace accurately, and incorporate appropriate estimates of value.

After the appraiser has determined the land value, and developed a depreciated value of improvements, those two factors are combined with the value of site improvements to create an entire property value based on the cost approach to value.

# Summary

The **cost approach** to value is not as commonly used as the sales comparison or income approaches.  However, there are situations where the cost approach is the only way to estimate reliably a property's value.

The first step in the cost approach is to determine the value of the **site**. Land value can be estimated using the **sales comparison method, allocation method, extraction method, land residual technique, ground rent capitalization method,** or **subdivision development analysis.**

Once the appraiser has determined the land value, the next step is to estimate the **reproduction cost** or **replacement cost** of the subject property.  This includes researching costs through cost estimating services or by contacting developers or contractors, and choosing an appropriate method to use.

The four methods used to estimate cost are the **index method,** the **comparative unit method,** the **unit-in-place method,** and the **quantity survey method.**  They vary in complexity and reliability.  In this chapter, they are presented in order — the least complex and least reliable is the index method, and the most complex and most reliable is the quantity survey method.  The **comparative unit method** is the one most widely used when appraising residential properties.

As a part of calculating the cost-new for the subject, the appraiser must also account for the **entrepreneurial profit** when necessary. Estimating the "as-is" value of other site improvements is another separate step.

Once the appraiser has determined the cost to build the improvements, he or she is only half-way there.  Because the subject property is almost never brand new, the appraiser must examine the property and decide how much the improvements have depreciated, which is the subject of the next chapter.

# Review Exercises

## *Matching Exercise*

**Instructions:** Look up the meaning of the terms in the Glossary, then write the letter of the matching term on the blank line before its definition. Answers are in Appendix B.

### Terms

A. direct costs

B. entrepreneurial profit

C. ground rent

D. index method

E. indirect costs

F. quantity-survey method

G. replacement cost

H. reproduction cost

I. square

J. unit-in-place method

### Definitions

1. _____ The compensation the owner/developer expects to gain by supplying the necessary funds to begin and maintain the project as well bearing the risks associated with the development.

2. _____ Rent that is payable under a ground lease.

3. _____ The dollar amount required to construct an exact replica of the property being appraised.

4. _____ The dollar amount required to construct improvements having the same utility and quality as the subject property using current construction materials, methods, and techniques.

5. _____ The construction costs that are not counted as labor or materials.

6. _____ The cost calculation method where the costs of the various building components, as installed, are calculated separately and then added together into a single value estimate.

7. _____ Equals 100 square feet.

# *Multiple Choice Questions*

**Instructions:**   Circle your response and go to Appendix B to read the complete explanation for each question.

1. The cost approach recognizes that there are two major components in real estate. They are:
   a. cost and value.
   b. land and improvements.
   c. supply and demand.
   d. income and expenses.

2. Regarding the cost approach to value, which of the following statements is true?
   a. It is the best approach to appraising new condominiums.
   b. The cost to build an item usually equals its value.
   c. It is best suited for older buildings because of its reliance on depreciation.
   d. Like the other two approaches to value, the cost approach to value is not applicable to every appraisal assignment.

3. Which method of valuing land is most like the market-data approach of appraising?
   a. Sales comparison method
   b. Allocation method
   c. Extraction method
   d. Land residual method

4. In Anytown, the ratio of land value to improvement value is historically 2 to 1. If a typical improved comp value is $300,000, what is the typical lot value?
   a. $100,000
   b. $150,000
   c. $200,000
   d. Cannot be determined

5. Linda must identify the value of the land component for a developed property. The property sold recently for $500,000 and she has determined the improvement value, through the cost approach, to be $289,000. Thus, the land value must be $211,000. Linda used which method of land valuation?
   a. Allocation
   b. Abstraction
   c. Sales comparison
   d. Land residual

6. The dollar amount to replicate an improvement using like kind and quality of materials, identical construction and workmanship standards is known as the:

    a. replacement cost.

    b. reproduction cost.

    c. index cost.

    d. entrepreneurial cost.

7. Which of the following is the most in-depth method for estimating cost?

    a. Index

    b. Square-foot

    c. Unit-in-place

    d. Like-quality

8. In 1984, a three bedroom, two bath single-family detached home cost $65,000 to construct in Anytown, Arizona. The historical cost index for that area is 220 and currently is 378. Using the index method, what is the current replacement cost for this structure?

    a. $112,000

    b. $378,000

    c. $ 37,800

    d. $ 78,000

9. According to a costing service, a two thousand square foot office building cost $300,000 to build. What is the cost per square foot?

    a. $140

    b. $150

    c. $160

    d. $660

10. A starter home that Earl is appraising contains 978 square feet of above grade improvements and a garage that contains 168 square feet. Earl estimates the land value at $75,000 from recent comparables. If the cost estimating service Earl uses has a base cost of $81 per unit of above grade improvements and $23 per unit for below grade improvements and a regional multiplier of 1.19, what is the reproduction estimate for the subject home?

    a. $ 98,868

    b. $173,867

    c. $ 83,082

    d. $141,829

11. Which method of cost estimation would use the following list?
    Foundation - $30 per linear foot, Floor Construction - $3.60 per sq. ft.,
    Framing - $4.50 per sq. ft. of support area, Roof Construction - $3.70,
    Exterior Walls - $10.20 per sq. ft., Windows - $14.20 per sq. ft.
    a.  Index method
    b.  Comparative unit method
    c.  Unit-in-place method
    d.  Quantity survey method

12. Which of the following is not considered a direct cost?
    a.  Site utility costs
    b.  Labor
    c.  Financing costs
    d.  Portable toilets

13. In the context of the cost approach to value, an appraisal fee would be
    considered:
    a.  entrepreneurial profit.
    b.  a direct cost.
    c.  an indirect cost.
    d.  necessary cost.

14. Entrepreneurial profit is based on the principle of:
    a.  depreciation.
    b.  anticipation.
    c.  reproduction.
    d.  substitution.

15. Items which are not attached to the main structure of the property, but still
    add value are:
    a.  added to the depreciated value of improvements and land value.
    b.  not depreciated.
    c.  site improvements.
    d.  all of the above.

# Cost Approach: Depreciation of Improvements

## Introduction

After estimating the reproduction or replacement cost of a structure, the appraiser's next step is to determine the depreciation amount. This step is required to determine the present value of the structure.

To better understand and utilize the concept of depreciation, the appraiser must fully comprehend the different causes of depreciation and the different ways to calculate it. An estimation of value by the cost approach is not complete until the depreciation of the improvements has been deducted.

### Learning Objectives

After reading this chapter, you will be able to:

- discuss the different causes of depreciation.
- identify the different methods of depreciating improvements.
- describe how the processes of estimating reproduction costs and determining depreciation combine to create a final value estimate.

# Depreciation

Depreciation is a loss in value to a property due to any cause. **Accrued depreciation** is depreciation that has already occurred. This loss in value is equal to the difference between the replacement cost-new of the improvements and their market value. Depreciation may be due to the physical wearing out of a building, functional problems, or locational problems affecting the property. Once the appraiser has estimated accrued depreciation, he or she deducts the depreciation from the replacement cost of the building(s) on a property. The resulting figure is the depreciated cost of the improvements.

# Effective Age and Economic Life

Before exploring the different types of depreciation, the appraiser must have a sound understanding of certain terms related to a structure's age and life.

## Effective Age

The chronological age of the structure is its **actual age**. However, properties often appear younger or older than the structure's actual age and have an effective age that varies from its actual age. **Effective age** describes the age of a structure based on its condition and usefulness.

The appraiser should always use effective age instead of chronological age because properties physically depreciate at different rates based on the quality of materials, maintenance levels, and workmanship. Effective age is a more accurate representation of the desirability of the property in the marketplace.

The appraiser estimates effective age based on experience. Although not an exact science, an experienced appraiser can produce a very meaningful figure with effective age. Appraisers usually express effective age in five-year increments, reflecting that it is just an estimate. When effective age is expressed as six years, or 11.5 years, the estimate becomes too defined to have much meaning. Effective age is just a tool, and it should be used in the most meaningful way possible.

## Economic Life

Buildings have a certain useful life in which a property's improvements contribute to property value. For residential properties, the structure's utility and physical appeal contribute to its useful life. For income-producing properties, the estimated period during which the structure will profitably produce income is its **economic life**. The difference between the structure's estimated economic life and its effective age is the **remaining economic life**.

There are many structures in urban areas that have just about used up their economic life. Movie theaters today are contained in large complexes, yet there are still some old buildings in existence that may have one or two theaters. These buildings are not supporting the movie industry, and they are not competing by showing recent releases. Instead, they tend to show older movies at reduced prices. Sometimes they show a particular genre of film, and have an eclectic following. Often, their use is entirely different from the original intent. Perhaps churches or live theater groups have taken over their use. At some point, however, the owners of such buildings may have to conclude that they cannot make enough money by operating these buildings to justify continuing to use them. They are no longer an asset to the land. They have become a burden that will soon have to be demolished.

Old gas stations are another example. Once called service stations because you could actually have your car serviced at these facilities, today, the majority of these structures have been transformed into mini-marts. The customer can buy gas on a self-serve basis, but a huge profit center is the little store inside that has practically all the products of a downsized supermarket. The old service station buildings have worn out their usefulness and been torn down.

**Figure 13.1** Structures that have used up their economic life should be demolished.

A new appraiser will learn what economic life is acceptable in a particular marketplace for a specific type of property. Commercial property, due to dependence on the ability to produce income, generally has a shorter economic life than that of a residential property. In fact, the economic life of residential properties has expanded in some areas from 60 to 75 years.

Typically, an appraiser uses the comparison method to identify what length of economic life to use. This means talking to other appraisers and comparing data. Economic life usually is shorter than physical life, as a structure generally will still physically exist but not be viable in the marketplace.

# Types of Depreciation

There are three types of depreciation: physical deterioration, functional obsolescence, and external obsolescence. **Physical deterioration** of a building and its equipment includes physical wear and tear, disintegration, decay or rot, or physical damage of any kind caused by the elements. **Functional obsolescence** refers to deficiencies, superadequacies, or simply undesirable features found in a building. **External obsolescence** is attributable to external adverse conditions that affect a property.

A property may suffer from any combination of the three types of depreciation, or it may not suffer from any depreciation at all. However, unless brand new, a building will probably have incurred some degree of depreciation. Like a brand new car driven off the showroom floor, a structure begins to lose value the moment it is built.

## Curable and Incurable

Adverse physical, functional, and locational influences cause property improvements to depreciate. Physical deterioration and functional obsolescence are further divided into two sub-categories: curable and incurable.

**Curable depreciation** refers to a loss in value that is economically feasible to correct. In other words, the cost to fix the problem is less than the loss in value, so fixing the problem makes economic sense.

> Example: If a house is estimated to have $2,000 worth of depreciation due to poor exterior paint and the cost to repaint is $1,500, then it is economically feasible to do so. This is an example of curable physical deterioration.

**Incurable depreciation** refers to items of depreciation that either are physically impossible to cure or are too expensive to be worth curing. If the cost to fix the problem exceeds the loss in value caused by the problem, then it does not make economic sense to repair it.

> Example: A house with a seriously cracked foundation can be repaired, but it typically costs far too much to take the necessary steps to properly fix a damaged foundation. In fact, depending on the cost of the repairs, it makes more sense from an economic standpoint to simply raze the structure than to try and repair it. This is an example of incurable physical deterioration.

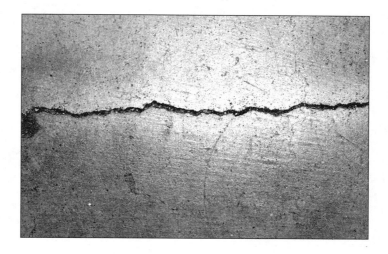

**Figure 13.2**  A cracked foundation is repairable, but the cost to cure may outweigh the benefit.

## Physical Deterioration

As stated earlier, physical deterioration can take the form of wear and tear, disintegration, decay or rot, or physical damage by the elements. It can come from any of a number of sources.

Physical wear and tear through use will help to wear out a building. People walking on carpeting will eventually wear out that carpeting. Heating and cooling systems eventually wear out too. Sometimes naturally occurring elements, such as ultraviolet sunlight, wind, and water wear on a property. Storms, extreme temperatures, earthquakes, termites, carpenter ants, and floods all work in varying degrees to affect properties physically. Fire, explosion, vandalism, and neglect also have a detrimental physical effect upon properties. The wear and tear from these various elements on a building accounts for the physical deterioration affecting that building.

Property components that exhibit curable physical deterioration can be repaired or replaced economically. This includes deferred maintenance and easily repairable items. **Deferred maintenance** refers to items that are in need of repair due to lack of upkeep. Items such as a roof repair or replacement, painting, building maintenance, floor covering replacement, and forced air heater replacement are items that are typical examples of curable physical deterioration.

**Figure 13.3** Repairing items of deferred maintenance like broken windows and flaking paint is relatively easy and is economically feasible.

Physical items that are incurable cannot be replaced or repaired economically. Incurable physical deterioration typically occurs with structural components that are expected to last for the life of the entire building. For example, items such as foundations, framework, walls, masonry, and ductwork usually have long physical lives and often are considered incurable. When incurable physical deterioration is evident, it may make more sense from an economic standpoint to tear down the building rather than to try to repair it.

Appraisers classify physical deterioration of components based on economic considerations. Since structural components rarely depreciate at similar rates, appraisers also classify them on the length of time they are expected to last — either as short-lived or long-lived. **Short-lived** items are expected to be replaced or repaired on a consistent basis throughout the life of the structure. **Long-lived** items need replacement less frequently, and sometimes never. For instance, walls will typically need repainting more frequently than the roof will need re-shingling. Therefore, the paint on the wall is considered short-lived, and the shingles are considered long-lived.

# Functional Obsolescence

Functional obsolescence is depreciation that is attributable to an item or feature within the subject property that is no longer useful or functional. This impaired feature results in loss of value (depreciation) for the entire property. Functional obsolescence is caused in part by changing market requirements and can appear in several different forms, including construction style preferences and outdated architecture, design or layout problems, lack of modern facilities, and superadequacy.

## *Outdated Architecture or Construction Style Preferences*

Historically, some interesting construction style changes have taken place.

A hundred years ago, a trip to the bathroom necessitated a walk outside the main dwelling to a distant place in the backyard. As advances in plumbing and sewer lines were made, bathroom facilities were placed inside the house. Once this was possible, demand for houses without this modern convenience practically disappeared.

Not too long ago, a one-car garage was perfectly adequate because families typically owned one car. Today, old homes with one-car garages can still be found, but usually sell for less than similar homes with two-car garages.

Today, our society is in the midst of some notable changes. Computers dominate every aspect of our lives, and the Internet is here to stay. Smart houses, which have operating systems for the house being run by computers, are under construction. In the next 15 years, it is probable that new houses will be built with fiber optics, which would allow computers to be hooked up to the Internet 24 hours a day in every room of the house. Any house built without computer and Internet capabilities would be considered functionally obsolete.

## *Design or Layout Problems*

Outmoded features and equipment also are examples of functional obsolescence. Appraisers must recognize that the tastes and preferences of society change over time. A house built 50 years ago may have been appealing to people at that time, but today, the style may be considered outdated and tiresome. Ornate molding and sculpting may have been desirable in the past, but may be considered outdated today.

### *Lack of Modern Facilities*

Today's marketplace demands certain modern facilities to maximize value. Kitchens and bathrooms are two areas where consumers prefer luxury and convenience. Older homes often do not contain a dishwasher. A house without a dishwasher will sell, but will sell for less. If installation costs are less than what the dishwasher will contribute, then the obsolescence is curable. If more, it is incurable.

Air conditioning, as a modern convenience, must be measured within the context of its marketplace. In the desert, a house lacking air conditioning is definitely at a disadvantage. However, at the beach, air conditioning is not as essential.

Lack of modern facilities most often is curable, but the cost to cure must be measured against the benefit to property value. When adding modern facilities that are valued in the marketplace, it is believed that the enhancement to value usually will more than offset the cost of installation.

### *Superadequacy*

**Superadequacies** or **over-improvements** are features that are too large or of a higher quality than needed for a property. The cost to add features of this type is greater than the value contributed by the features. Building a 10,000-square-foot home in the middle of a tract of homes ranging in size from 1,200 to 1,800 square feet is an example of a superadequacy. An excessive number of bedrooms or 1-foot thick, wood-framed exterior walls also qualify as over-improvements.

**Figure 13.4** Both over-improvements and under-improvements have a negative impact on value.

## External Obsolescence

External obsolescence takes place when influences that are external to property adversely affect that property. These external influences can be categorized as locational or economic.

**Locational obsolescence** is caused by the physical location of the subject property and its proximity to a negative influence. Heavy traffic noise such as that generated by freeways and airports may cause locational obsolescence. Recurring smoke, dust, and noxious odors from sources external to a property, like a dairy farm or sewage plant, also tend to have an adverse influence on the value of a property.

**Figure 13.5** Any loss in value from sources outside the property is classified as external obsolescence.

**Economic obsolescence** occurs when changes in the local economy affect the subject property's value. Some cities rely on one major industry or employer. If the industry shuts down or the employer ever moves, a devastating impact on real estate values would result.

Unfavorable zoning ordinances, environmental restrictions, or other legislative decisions that restrict use can also cause external obsolescence. Since these factors originate externally to the property itself, they are considered external obsolescence.

External obsolescence is incurable in virtually all cases since the adverse condition(s) affecting the property are exterior to the subject and few owners are willing or able to spend money to change adverse conditions that are not located on their own property. Changes such as relocating a freeway or a nearby airport simply make no economic sense and are well beyond the financial means of most property owners.

# Methods of Calculating Accrued Depreciation

An estimate of value developed through the cost approach is no more accurate than the measure of depreciation calculated as a part of that approach to value. It is through depreciation that cost estimates are converted into a measure of value.

Remember that accrued depreciation is calculated for improvements only, because land does not depreciate. Land is factored into the cost approach at its market value. Since the value of the land is already at market value, making additional deductions to the land value would cause it to be doubly penalized for any condition adversely affecting value.

There are both complex and simple methods used to calculate accrued depreciation. As with calculating replacement costs, the more complex methods of estimating accrued depreciation tend to be the more accurate. The appraiser should always use the most appropriate method for the particular property he or she is appraising.

Ways of calculating accrued depreciation include the cost to cure method, economic age/life method, modified age/life method, breakdown method (or observed condition method), market extraction using sales comparison techniques, and income capitalization method.

## Cost to Cure Method

The **cost to cure method** is the most basic and straightforward method to calculate accrued depreciation. It is based on observed deferred maintenance and the application of current building costs at the time of the appraisal. Its basic premise states that the cost required to replace an item is the amount lost due to accrued depreciation.

It is relatively easy to estimate physical deterioration using this method. If certain items wear out on a building, such as the floor coverings, estimating the cost to repair or replace these items often gives a credible estimate of the physical deterioration. If a stairway needs to be replaced, the amount of accrued depreciation is the cost to accomplish that. If a roof needs to be replaced, the amount of accrued depreciation is the cost to do it, labor and materials.

This method is used to calculate curable functional obsolescence. Generally, if the functional problem involves a new or newer property, the cost to cure the functional problem is used as the estimate. In an older property, the cost to cure minus the remaining value of the item being replaced is a way to determine the loss.

## *Limitations of this Method*

This simplistic method only allows for a 100% depreciation of any item. The cost to cure method is not very useful when dealing with items that have partial depreciation, like a roof that is not brand new but still has years left before it needs replacement.

## Economic Age/Life Method

The **economic age/life method** of calculating accrued depreciation is conceptually one of the easiest to use and to understand. This method compares a structure's effective age to its economic life. Also known as the **straight line method** or just simply as the **age/life method**, this is the method most residential appraisers most frequently use. With this method, an equal amount of accrued depreciation is attributed to each year of the economic life of the structure. An effective age is estimated and assigned to the structure, and the remaining economic life is determined.

In the age/life method, the ratio of the improvements' effective age to its total economic life is multiplied by the current reproduction or replacement cost of those improvements. The resulting number is the accrued depreciation of the subject property.

The following equation illustrates how to calculate accrued depreciation using this method.

$$\frac{\text{Effective age}}{\text{Economic life}} \times \text{Replacement/reproduction cost} = \text{Accrued depreciation}$$

In order to understand the concept of economic life, effective age, and the straight line method, examine the following example:

> The subject property is a 50-year-old house with an economic life of 70 years. After close inspection, the effective age of the structure is determined to be only 15 years. The cost to reproduce the structure is $200,000. In this example, the structure is only 21% depreciated, despite its chronological age of 50 years (15 ÷ 70). Multiplying the reproduction cost of the improvements by the depreciation percentage, $200,000 × 21%, the accrued depreciation is calculated at $42,000, and the depreciated value of the improvements at $158,000 ($200,000 – $42,000).

With an effective age of 15 years, and an economic life of 70 years, despite the chronological age of 50 years, the structure can be said to have a remaining economic life of 55 years. This structure still has a long, useful life remaining.

Sometimes, not all the variables are expressly provided. A skilled appraiser, with a complete understanding of effective age and economic life, is able to extract the needed variable from the provided information, as in this following example.

> Suppose a commercial office building is 20 years old, has a remaining economic life of 25 years, and an effective age of 15 years. The cost to reproduce the improvements is $350,000.

In this example, the total economic life is not expressed, but can be determined easily by adding the effective age of 15 years to the remaining economic life of 25 years for a total economic life of 40 years. Since the effective age is 15 years, the percentage of accrued depreciation to the building is 38% (15 ÷ 40). If the cost to reproduce the building is $350,000, the accrued depreciation is $133,000 ($350,000 × 38%) and the depreciated value of the improvements is $217,000 ($350,000 − $133,000).

## *Limitations of this Method*

While the economic age/life method is relatively simple to calculate, it tends to obscure the overall accrued depreciation estimate since it lumps all items of accrued depreciation together. A significant weakness in this method is that curable items of accrued depreciation are not treated separately from incurable items of accrued depreciation. It also does not recognize that certain items in a building have a shorter remaining economic life than the total economic life of the structure. This method accounts for physical, functional, and locational obsolescence, but it does not differentiate between the different kinds of accrued depreciation.

## Modified Age/Life Method

In the **modified age/life method**, curable physical and functional items of accrued depreciation are identified. The cost to cure all these items is deducted from the reproduction or replacement cost of the improvements. The ratio derived from the age/life method is then multiplied by the remaining cost to arrive at an estimate of accrued depreciation from all other causes.

> Example: the subject property's reproduction cost is estimated at $550,000. Items that can be cured economically include the roof, the carpet, and several bathroom fixtures, and total $20,000 in expenses. The remainder of the structure is estimated to have 50 years of useful life remaining of an 85-year economic life. The appraiser would first subtract the curable items from the cost estimate, and then apply the age/life ratio to the remaining cost.

| Mathematically, it would look like this: | |
|---|---|
| Replacement cost new | $550,000 |
| Less curable items | − $20, 000 |
| Remaining cost | $530,000 |
| Age/life ratio (35 ÷ 85) | × 41% |
| Less amount of accrued depreciation | $217,300 |
| **Current building value** | **$312,700** |

## *Limitations of this Method*

Although curable items are recognized by this method, it still does not account for differences in the remaining economic life of the other building components. This method is a little more accurate, but it is based upon the same assumption as the economic age/life method. Both methods assume that a single age/life ratio can be applied to every component of the improvements.

## Breakdown Method

In the **breakdown method**, also known as the **observed condition method**, an appraiser analyzes each type of accrued depreciation separately, measures the amount of each, and totals the individual estimates to determine the total accrued depreciation. Then, the total accrued depreciation is deducted from the reproduction or replacement cost.

If the accrued depreciation is deducted from replacement cost, some kinds of functional obsolescence, such as that attributable to outdated equipment or materials, are not to be deducted since, upon replacement, current equipment and materials would be used.

As the name implies, the appraiser observes the condition of various component parts of the structure, observes the percent of deterioration or loss in value as-is, in comparison to a new properly planned structure not suffering from any loss in value. Physical deterioration and functional obsolescence can be measured in this way, although success with this method requires experience and an up-to-date knowledge of current building costs on the part of the appraiser.

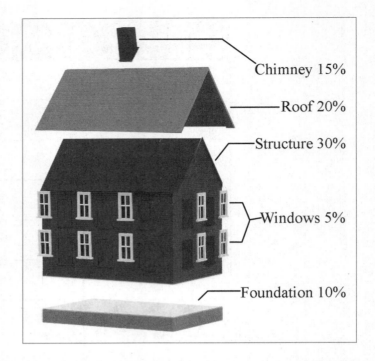

Chimney 15%

Roof 20%

Structure 30%

Windows 5%

Foundation 10%

**Figure 13.6** The breakdown method depreciates each item separately.

The following table shows the observed condition method applicable to physical deterioration estimates of accrued depreciation for a property that would cost $400,000 to replace at current market conditions.

| Item | Item Reproduction Cost | Observed Deterioration | Dollar Amount of Deterioration |
|---|---|---|---|
| Foundation | $17,500 | 5% | $875 |
| Basic Structure | $125,000 | 25% | $31,250 |
| Finished Floors | $18,500 | 20% | $3,700 |
| Electrical | $10,000 | 20% | $2,000 |
| Heating/AC | $16,000 | 25% | $4,000 |
| Kitchen Cabinets | $10,000 | 20% | $2,000 |
| Plumbing | $18,000 | 30% | $5,400 |
| Fireplaces/Chimneys | $14,000 | 20% | $2,800 |
| Insulation | $5,000 | 5% | $250 |
| Total | $234,000 | | $52,275 |

The following table shows the observed condition method applicable to functional obsolescence estimates of accrued depreciation, both curable and incurable for the same property.

| Curable | |
|---|---|
| Remodel Kitchen | $12,750 |
| Replace Obsolete Lighting Fixtures | $1,600 |
| Total Curable Accrued Depreciation | $14,350 |
| **Incurable** | |
| Estimated Loss Due to Obsolete Floor Plan (3% of Cost New) | $12,000 |
| Estimated Loss Due to Excessive Ceiling Heights (1.5% of Cost New) | $6,000 |
| Total Incurable Accrued Depreciation | $18,000 |
| Estimated Total Functional Obsolescence | **$32,350** |

If there is no accrued depreciation due to economic obsolescence, the appraiser's next step is to subtract $84,625, a figure that represents all losses attributable to accrued depreciation ($32,350 + $52,275) from the reproduction cost of the improvements to obtain the current market value of the improvements, $315,400 rounded ($400,000 – $84,625).

## Market Extraction Using Sales Comparison Techniques

Another method used to estimate accrued depreciation is to extract the accrued depreciation by applying techniques used in the sales comparison approach. Care needs to be exercised by the appraiser when applying market extraction techniques to ensure that all the sales prices of all the comps are truly indicative of the market. Seller incentives such as loan discount points, prepaid homeowner's association fees, rebates, seller-paid closing costs, personal property included in the sale, etc., usually have an effect upon sales prices and can significantly affect results obtained from the following two techniques.

Accrued depreciation may be extracted from the market by performing sale-resale analysis, by paired sales analysis, and by extraction.

### Sale-Resale Analysis

In a **sale-resale analysis**, a property that sells and resells in a relatively short period of time is analyzed. By finding properties in a stable market that had two open market, arm's-length sales in a relatively short period of time, any difference in price would logically be attributable to changes to that property.

> For example, a property in a stable market had deferred maintenance when originally purchased. The purchaser remodeled the building, so the subsequent sale would be reflective of the market's reaction to that remodeling. In this scenario, if the cost of the remodeling is known, the difference between cost and value can be used to identify any functional obsolescence attributable to the remodel. If the market has been increasing or decreasing, a time adjustment would be warranted. After any time adjustments have been applied, any difference would still be attributable to changes affecting that property. If the changes to the property are known, market reaction may be identified.

Similarly, a sale-resale analysis may be employed to determine external economic obsolescence if the adverse influence was present during the time of one transaction and not the other.

### Paired-Sales Analysis

In a **paired sales analysis**, two similar properties that sell during the same time period in the same market are analyzed. If the sales are open market, arm's-length transactions, any difference in price could be attributable to differences between the two properties. If that difference can be identified, the market reaction to that difference may be identified.

> For example, imagine there are two homes with the same floor plan within the same development. One house is near the complex's main entrance, and thus closer to a busy thoroughfare. The other house is nestled deep inside the development and is shielded from external obsolescence. Both homes sold within one week of each other, but the one near the entrance sold for $3,000 less. From this paired sales analysis, an appraiser could conclude that, within this particular neighborhood, the external obsolescence caused by traffic is approximately $3,000. Taking this concept one step further, he or she could convert this dollar amount to a percentage so that it could be applied to properties of different size and quality in the area.

## *Extraction Method*

Similar to the method of the same name used for calculating land value, the **extraction** method enables the appraiser to determine the depreciated value of the improvements of the subject property by estimating the cost-new of recently sold comparables, minus the sales price of those comparables, and minus the value of the land in the transaction.

Extraction is an accurate way of reading the marketplace, because arm's-length transactions reveal the amount of accrued depreciation recognized by purchasers. The more samples that can be extracted from the marketplace, the more reliable the assembled data. Among the comparable sales that are analyzed, correlations should be made to arrive at appropriate percentages. With similar comparable sales, the percentage of accrued depreciation can be directly applied to the subject property.

Because the appraiser is simply reading the marketplace with this method, all sources of accrued depreciation are included — physical deterioration, functional obsolescence, and economic obsolescence. If it were necessary to separate out one source of accrued depreciation, a further application of the abstraction method could be used. The appraiser could estimate accrued depreciation attributed to two of the sources by other appropriate methods, and then subtract the amount of accrued depreciation attributed to those sources from the total amount of accrued depreciation. The difference will be the accrued depreciation belonging to one isolated source.

The following example will estimate accrued depreciation of a sold comparable property. Where differences exist in the subject property from any of the recognized sources of depreciation, adjustments should be made. The following demonstrates how one comparable could be used to abstract depreciation.

| | |
|---|---|
| Estimated cost-new of comparable structure | $275,000 |
| Sales price of comparable property | $225,500 |
| Market value of comparable land | – $45,000 |
| Less current value of comparable structure | $180,500 |
| Total Accrued Depreciation | $94,500 |

Percentage of Accrued Depreciation = 34% *($94,500 ÷ $275,000)*

## Income Capitalization Method

Income-producing properties are treated differently from non-income properties in regards to depreciation. Instead of totaling dollar amounts of depreciation and then subtracting that amount from the estimated cost-new, appraisers formulate an estimate based upon a loss of income attributable to the item(s) causing the depreciation. In order for this technique to work, the subject needs to be an income-producing property.

The **income capitalization method** is like the market extraction method because it is necessary to find similar income-producing properties both with and without the same influencing defects. Once these properties are isolated, the influence of the defects can be analyzed to determine how it causes the accrued depreciation. This method takes it a step further, though, by applying a market-derived capitalization rate to that income to estimate the overall loss in value.

> For example, a four-bedroom, two-bath house in Marketplace Z rents for $1,200 per month. A four-bedroom, one-bath house in the same marketplace rents for only $1,100 per month. This factor of functional obsolescence (less one bath) costs $100 per month in income for the second house. If the appraiser has determined that the appropriate monthly gross multiplier for the area is 150, the loss in value caused by functional obsolescence is $15,000 (150 × $100). If this condition is incurable, that is, there is no room to add a second bathroom or it is not economically feasible, the amount of accrued depreciation for this item is $15,000.

> However, if the item is curable and the cost to cure is only $12,000, an appraiser would use the $12,000 figure to represent accrued depreciation.

The above example determines accrued depreciation based on functional obsolescence. The following example demonstrates how the same method is applicable to economic obsolescence

> A three-bedroom, two-bath house rents in a particular marketplace for $925 per month. Another three-bedroom, two-bath house in the same marketplace rents for only $850 per month because of a less favorable location, backing up to a main street and suffering excessive traffic noise. The difference in rental income is $75 per month. If the appropriate monthly gross multiplier is 130, the loss in value is $9,750 ($75 × 130). Since the external obsolescence is incurable, $9,750 is the amount of the accrued depreciation charged against the subject property.

# Putting it all Together

When all of the causes of depreciation are calculated and deducted, the depreciated value of the improvements will be known.

Now we are ready for the last step in the cost approach process:

1. Estimate the value of the land component of the subject property as though vacant and available to be put to its highest and best use.

2. Estimate the reproduction or replacement cost new of the building improvements on the subject site as of the effective date of the appraisal.

3. Add entrepreneurial profit, when appropriate, to the building improvements' estimated reproduction or replacement cost.

4. Estimate accrued depreciation from all sources (physical, functional, or external), and deduct from estimated reproduction or replacement cost.

5. Estimate "as-is" value of additional site improvements, if necessary.

6. Add the land value estimate, the depreciated value of the improvements, and the value of the site improvements together to calculate the property value by the cost approach.

The following example will tie all the steps of the cost approach to value together and demonstrate how each step is vital to the final value conclusion.

> The subject is a single-family residence in an average subdivision in Anytown, America. The house is 1,800 square feet with a 360-square foot garage. The cost of construction for homes in this area has been determined to be $70 per square foot and $25 per square foot for garages. The improvements sit on a 5,000-square-foot lot, valued at $45,000, which is typical for the area and the subdivision. The lot is surrounded on three sides by a block-wall fence, worth approximately $5,000. The house backs to a main street and suffers from traffic noise. The market shows that similar houses with similar external obsolescence lose roughly $3,000 in value. The house is 12 years old with an effective age of 7 years, and its estimated economic life is 70 years.

| | |
|---|---|
| Estimated Site Value | $45,000 |
| Estimated Reproduction Cost New of Improvements | |
| Dwelling 1,800 sq. ft. × $70 per square foot | $126,000 |
| Garage: 360 sq. ft. × $25 per square foot | $9,000 |
| Total Estimated Cost New | $135,000 |
| Less Depreciation | |
| Physical  10% of Total Cost New | $13,500 |
| Functional  0% | $0 |
| External  (from market) | $3,000 |
| Total Depreciation | $16,500 |
| Depreciated Value of Improvements | $118,500 |
| Value of Site Improvements | $5,000 |
| Indicated Value by Cost Approach | $168,500 |

In this cost approach analysis, the indicated value is $168,500.

If the property appraised at $165,000 using the market data approach, the indicated value by the cost approach would support that value, since the consensus among appraisers is that the cost approach represents the upper limits of value. The rationale behind this is that a buyer would have no reason to pay more for a property than it would cost him to purchase land and build a similar structure. There is an exception, however. The exception is time and convenience. It could take a year or more for a buyer to acquire the land, get plans approved and build the structure. If a buyer could find a similar property that met his or her needs and be using that property in 45 days, the buyer might, in fact, be willing to pay more for that property. So the old adage does not always hold true.

# Summary

After determining the **cost new of the improvements**, the appraiser must calculate the **accrued depreciation**. Depreciation can be **curable** or **incurable** and is categorized as **physical deterioration, functional obsolescence,** or **external obsolescence**. There are several different methods that appraisers can use to calculate accrued depreciation. These methods vary in their complexity and in the amount and type of data that they require. Appraisers choose which method to use based on the particular assignment they are completing.

Once the accrued depreciation has been determined, the appraiser can determine the depreciated value of the improvements by adding the cost-new of the improvements to the **entrepreneurial profit** and then subtracting the accrued depreciation. When the land value is added to the depreciated value of the improvements and the **"as-is" value** of the additional on-site improvements, the resulting number is a value estimate for the subject property.

# Review Exercises

## Matching Exercise

**Instructions:** Look up the meaning of the terms in the Glossary, then write the letter of the matching term on the blank line before its definition. Answers are in Appendix B.

### Terms

A.  accrued depreciation

B.  age/life method

C.  chronological age

D.  curable depreciation

E.  deferred maintenance

F.  economic life

G.  effective age

H.  external obsolescence

I.  functional obsolescence

J.  incurable depreciation

K.  long-lived items

L.  physical deterioration

M.  remaining economic life

N.  short-lived items

O.  superadequacies

### Definitions

1. _____ A loss in value to a property due to any cause as of the effective date of the appraisal.

2. _____ A loss in value that is economically feasible to correct; it adds value equal to or greater than the cost of curing the item.

3. _____ Deficiencies, superadequacies, or undesirable features found in a building.

4. _____ Almost always considered to be incurable, conditions affecting a property that are external to that property.

5. _____ Items that are in need of repair due to lack of upkeep.

6. _____ Items that are expected to be replaced or repaired on a consistent basis throughout the life of the structure.

7. _____ A method that uses a ratio of the building's age to its expected life.

8. _____ Features that are too large or of a higher quality than needed for a property and have a negative effect on property values.

9. _____ Physical wear and tear, disintegration, decay, rot, or physical damage of any kind caused by the elements.

10. _____ Actual age of structure.

11. _____ Time in which the property's improvements contribute to property value.

12. _____ The difference between the structure's estimated economic life and its effective age.

## *Multiple Choice Questions*

**Instructions:** Circle your response and go to Appendix B to read the complete explanation for each question.

1. The difference between the improvements' market value and the cost to build them new is called:

   a. deferred maintenance.

   b. future depreciation.

   c. accrued depreciation.

   d. internal obsolescence.

2. A house in a middle-income neighborhood is under-valued by $20,000 due to extreme deferred maintenance. The cost to paint, re-floor, replace the broken windows, repair the fixtures, and patch the roof is approximately $15,000. This scenario describes:

   a. curable physical deterioration.

   b. incurable functional obsolescence.

   c. curable external obsolescence.

   d. short-lived economic obsolescence.

3. A house's value suffers because of its proximity to an airport. An appraiser would identify this as:

   a. curable.

   b. incurable.

   c. deferred.

   d. long-lived.

4. A furnace would qualify as a(n):

   a. incurable item.

   b. short-lived item.

   c. long-lived item

   d. superadequacy.

5. When constructed, an office building was projected to last 80 years. It is currently 24 years old. Using the square foot method, the appraiser concludes that the building new would cost $500,000. Using the age/life method, estimate the office building's current value.

    a. $150,000

    b. $166,666

    c. $333,333

    d. $350,000

6. A house located in an area where the recommended insulation is R–19 has insulation rated at R–42. This home suffers from:

    a. superadequacy.

    b. external obsolescence.

    c. internal obsolescence.

    d. none of the above.

7. A property valued at $300,000 contains a single-car garage in a neighborhood that predominately contains two-car garages. The typical house value in the neighborhood is $310,000. A contractor estimates the cost of converting the single car garage into a two-car at $15,000. This is an example of:

    a. incurable subadequacy.

    b. curable economic obsolescence.

    c. incurable functional obsolescence.

    d. single-car deficiency.

8. Which of the following is **not** a type of depreciation?

    a. Incurable functional obsolescence

    b. Curable external obsolescence

    c. Deferred maintenance

    d. Physical deterioration

9. What is the best way to depreciate the value of land?

    a. Cost to cure

    b. Age/life method

    c. Breakdown method

    d. None of the above

10. What is the biggest weakness of the cost to cure method of estimating depreciation?

    a. Cost does not equal value.

    b. It does not allow for partially depreciated items.

    c. It does not account for fully depreciated items.

    d. Curing is not always economically viable.

11. A barn was built 40 years ago; however, it has been abandoned and looks 20 years older than it actually is. What is its effective age?

    a. 20

    b. 40

    c. 50

    d. 60

12. A strip mall was built with the expectation that it would be economically viable for 99 years. Currently, it is 40 years old. The property management company and tenants have exceptionally managed and maintained it and local architectural tastes have not changed. An appraiser concludes that the property has an effective age of 25 years. What is the strip mall's remaining economic life?

    a. 15 years

    b. 59 years

    c. 74 years

    d. 25%

13. A duplex is 30 years old, has a remaining economic life of 75 years and an effective age of 20 years. The current cost to reproduce the improvements is $450,000. How much depreciation should be charged against this structure?

    a. $120,000

    b. $330,000

    c. $95,000

    d. $180,000

14. Which of the following is **not** a market extraction technique for estimating depreciation?

    a. Abstraction

    b. Sale-resale

    c. Paired-sale

    d. Extraction

15. An office building was renting space for $25 per square foot per month but the recent installation of a nearby dump has forced the price down by $4. If the building has 28,000 square feet of rentable space, how much income is being lost each year due to external obsolescence?

    a. $1,344,000

    b. $7,056,000

    c. $112,000

    d. $588,000

# Chapter

# 14

# Reconciliation and Reporting

## Introduction

The final steps in the appraisal process are reconciliation and reporting. After the appraiser has analyzed the subject and other data critical to the appraisal, he or she will have a range of value or several values that have been calculated from the three approaches. **Reconciliation** is the process of refining the range or set of values into a single supportable value opinion, called the **final value estimate**.

Once the appraiser has reconciled all of the work into a value, he or she must then report it to the client. The detail and format will depend on the client's needs, but there are many options available to the appraiser.

## Learning Objectives

After reading this chapter, you will be able to:

- recognize the definition and process of reconciliation.
- identify the strengths and weaknesses of each approach to value.
- recognize of the appraiser's need to recertify data and the methods used.
- identify types and styles of appraisal reports available to the appraiser.

# Reconciliation and Final Value Estimate

In a perfect world, each approach would be flawless, and each would result in the exact same value for the subject property. However, in practice, each approach has so many variables that there is a very small chance that the value derived using one approach will ever exactly match the value derived using another approach. In fact, the chance of arriving at the same value conclusion from two or three different approaches is so remote that, if it did occur, it should be considered a major red flag.

Since an appraiser will arrive at different values from each approach, he or she will have to examine the choices carefully, weigh each one against the other, and then arrive at a single supportable value conclusion. This process is reconciliation.

Ideally, all three approaches should be used on every assignment, but sometimes an approach is inapplicable, unwanted by the client, or lacks enough supportable data to apply.

For example, when appraising vacant land, there is no physical way the cost approach can be used. Because the land is vacant and the cost approach requires the valuing of improvements, the method is inapplicable.

The client's wishes may also determine which approaches are or are not used. The most common example of this occurs when the client, i.e. the lender, asks the appraiser to use Fannie Mae Form 2055. This form only allows room for the sales comparison approach. The appraiser could include the other approaches in an addendum, but the lender's request to use Form 2055 typically means that the lender only wants the one approach used. The appraiser has to make this decision based upon the type of property and his or her experience. If the appraiser thinks that market value can be estimated accurately using only the sales comparison approach, then that is all he or she will use. However, if the appraiser determines that other approaches are needed, he or she must notify the client.

In other situations, there simply may not be enough data to apply a particular approach. For instance, when appraising a single-family home, the income approach may be unnecessary, especially when there is no rental data in the area for that type of property. Similarly, an instance may occur when the sales comparison approach does not have enough supportable data to be applicable to a single-family residence, even though it is commonly thought of as the strongest indicator of value for that type of property.

**Figure 14.1**  An appraiser makes decisions based on the client's needs and the appraiser's understanding of the assignment.

How the appraiser decides which approaches are appropriate for an assignment depends on the client's needs coupled with the appraiser's understanding of the nature of the property and the purpose of that particular assignment.   It is an assignment-by-assignment decision.

Reconciliation not only includes analyzing the different values derived from the appraisal approaches, it also includes revisiting the steps in the appraisal process, and re-verifying that the value defined and the data collected were both valid and relevant.   In addition, the appraiser must weigh the strengths and weaknesses of each approach used, and consider how those approaches are pertinent to the process as a whole, and to the subject property.

## Reviewing the Approaches

When reviewing the approaches chosen for an assignment, an appraiser considers the validity and reliability of each approach.   He or she is also reviewing the quantity, quality, appropriateness, and accuracy of data for each approach that is used.   In order to do this properly, the appraiser should be aware that each approach has certain limitations and advantages.

The strengths and weaknesses of each approach were discussed in previous chapters.   The following section summarizes the strengths and weaknesses for the three major approaches, and lists the items an appraiser should reexamine in the reconciliation process.

## Sales Comparison Approach

When using the sales comparison approach in the assignment, the appraiser should carefully verify that:

- the comparables are significantly comparable to the subject property.

- there is an adequate amount of sales data.

- the sales data is both accurate and reliable.

- the adjustments made to the comps are logical and in good order.

- the adjustments are mathematically correct.

- the value conclusion drawn from the adjusted comparables is legitimate.

This approach has both advantages and limitations. Its simplicity is an advantage. It is easy to understand how adjusted comparables can represent a current value for the subject. When available, sales information is usually easy to obtain. In addition, the sales comparison approach is the best determinate for frequently sold property types, namely residential properties.

The sales comparison approach is a terrible indicator of value for infrequently sold properties and properties that are unique. It is not as useful with insufficient or inaccurate data. Finally, its reliance on historical data can be a limitation, because while information might be easy to gather, it may be outdated or completely erroneous.

## Cost Approach

When using the cost approach in the assignment, the appraiser should verify that:

- the sites used to determine the subject's site value are comparable to the subject.

- any adjustments made to comparable sites are logical and accurate.

- reproduction or replacement cost is correctly identified.

- the unit chosen for the comparative-unit method is appropriate.

- data obtained for the unit-in-place or quantity survey method is current and accurate.

- accrued depreciation was deducted properly, without under-depreciating or double-depreciating certain items.

- external influences researched include all possible ones.

The cost approach is very precise for newer buildings. Also, it is the best indicator of value when the building is specialized or there is a lack of comparable properties.

On the other hand, the older the building becomes, the more difficult it is to calculate its accrued depreciation accurately. This approach is a more complicated approach. Unless the appraiser is dutiful and organized in his or her systemization of component costs, the cost approach lends itself to multiple errors because of the sheer number of calculations. Lastly, the cost approach tends to identify the upper levels of the value range for a property. If all three approaches are applied to a property, the value derived by the cost approach analysis would most likely be the highest, and therefore is not entirely representative of what that property may sell for on the open market.

The cost approach to value probably has more limitations than benefits. As a result, the cost approach is best suited as a very valuable support approach to the other two major approaches, unless special circumstances dictate otherwise.

## Income Approach

When using the income approach in the assignment, the appraiser should verify that:

- the market rents are mathematically accurate.
- the reconstructed operating statement is accurate.
- the gross income estimate is mathematically accurate.
- the net income estimate is mathematically accurate.
- the capitalization rate (GRM or direct cap rate) is mathematically accurate.
- the comparable sales are sufficiently comparable to the subject property.
- there is an adequate amount of rental data available from the subject market.

As the name implies, the income approach to value is solely dependant on a property's income, real or potential. Therefore, this approach is the best indicator of value for income-producing properties. Even if the property is not currently producing income, this approach can convert its potential income into a current value.

The income approach will require current market data for rentals of like properties as well as a careful analysis of the operating statements. Sometimes these pieces of information are difficult to obtain and analyze. In addition, determining the appropriate capitalization rate is very difficult, and at times, can become very complex.

# Weighing the Choices

After the appraiser has revisited all of the information used during the appraisal process, he or she then has to conscientiously weigh the approaches and determine which one best indicates value.

Typically, one of the approaches to value is determined to be the best value for the subject property. At times, the final reconciled value may be a combination of two or three approaches. In addition, the appraiser must be aware of factors that may weaken an approach's validity. For example, even though the comparison approach is usually the best indicator for residential property, if the market is unstable, this approach may become less reliable than if it were located in a stable market. In this instance, the appraiser should not simply discard the sales approach analysis, but should depend more heavily on the cost and/or income approaches.

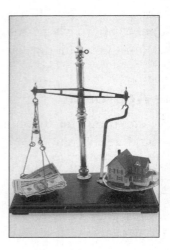

**Figure 14.2** A major step in the reconciliation process is to weigh the appropriateness of each approach to value.

## Case Study

Jill is appraising a single-family residence in a neighborhood near a college. Because of the need for student housing, many similar properties in the area are rented. Additionally, because of the nature of this type of tenancy, the neighborhood is in decline. The neighborhood as a whole suffers from excessive deferred maintenance as well as negative external influences like noise pollution.

From the sales comparison approach, Jill estimates the subject's value at $251,000. From the cost approach, she arrives at an estimate of $260,500, and from the income approach $255,800.

Based on the information provided above, Jill sees a range of value from $251,000 to $260,500. This range of $9,500 is relatively narrow considering all of the factors that affect the subject and its neighborhood. Jill's next step is to analyze and weigh these three value determinates and arrive at a single value conclusion that is supported by them. She should be comfortable with any conclusion reached that falls in the range of the three estimates, from $251,000 to $260,500. In addition, the final value may reflect one approach's estimate exactly, or may be a hybrid of two or three of them.

Jill knows that because of the age of the subject property and its excessive deferred maintenance, her calculation of accrued depreciation may not be the most accurate. She also knows that the cost approach tends to flank the higher end of the value range. Therefore, she decides to give the cost approach the least amount of weight.

In her analysis of the result based on the sales comparison approach, Jill recognizes that while this approach is typically the best indication of value for this type of property, in this instance, the neighborhood is in serious decline and, therefore, the sales comparison approach may lose some of its credibility. That said, she is still convinced that the value derived from her comparison analysis reflects current market value of the subject property. She double-checks her comps and determines that all of the comps used in her sales comparison analysis are legitimately comparable to the subject and none need extensive adjustments.

Finally, Jill reviews the income approach to value and carefully reexamines all of the information and data used in arriving at her conclusion. She determines that this approach seems to be a strong indicator of value and gives it the most weight. This is because her analysis of the neighborhood revealed several similar rental houses. The rentals are all on a month-to-month basis and are all very competitive. Therefore, they are representative of current market rent.

Jill's final analysis comes down to a value somewhere in between the sales comparison value of $251,000 and the income value of $255,800. She could pick one of the values and use it as the final value estimate for the property, but this does not satisfy her. She determines that the income estimate receives the strongest consideration, but cannot completely discount the sales comparison estimate because it is typically the best indicator of value for single-family detached residences. Jill finally reconciles that the market value for this type of property in this neighborhood is $255,000. She chose to round the income estimate figure down instead of rounding up, which she would typically do in most other circumstances, to account for the influences and disparity from the comparison analysis.

An appraiser should round the final value estimate to the nearest thousand to emphasize the fact that it is indeed an estimate. If Jill were to become too finite in her estimation, say by stating the final value at $254,654, it would be too exact for the marketplace.

# What Reconciliation is Not

Reconciliation is often not clearly understood. Although the reconciliation process is strongly rooted in factual data and mathematics, it is subjective, and there is no one set of rules that will apply to any or all appraisal assignments.

Reconciliation is not a mathematical process. If the appraiser has three different values derived from the major approaches to value to consider, appraisers should never simply add the values together and divide by three. Instead, appraisers should carefully analyze them and use their judgment. If Jill would have averaged the three approaches in her analysis, she would have ignored the cost approach's inadequacy due to excessive deferred maintenance, and she would not have considered the market conditions that weakened the sales comparison approach.

**Averaging**, as well as applying other statistical functions to the approaches, may be used as a check and balance and is an excellent way to analyze the figures used throughout the appraisal. However, averaging should never determine the result. Mathematical formulas cannot account for the appraiser's opinions or any other intangibles. Averaging implies that each approach receives equal weight, and this just is not the case because, as stated earlier, certain approaches typically are better indicators for certain types of properties.

Reconciling the three value determinates is not a way to fit the conclusion into a preconceived value. Appraisers should always be independent, open minded, and objective. If, at some point in the analysis, the appraiser gets the feeling that the subject property will probably be worth about so much, he must be open to other alternatives that may develop during the final value reconciliation. Of course, an experienced appraiser may have a feeling during the appraisal that comes to fruition in the reconciliation. However, the appraiser must not use the process of reconciliation to bend the three values into a single matching value.

Finally, reconciliation is not the narrowing of the range of value estimates. This means that when reconciling, you do not make changes to the three separate value estimates so that they all match. As we mentioned earlier, all value estimates will probably be different, and the appraiser must report them that way. The only reason to make changes to a value previously derived is if an error was discovered in the data or process used to arrive at that value. Remember, reconciling is weighing the choices and using expertise and analysis to determine a final value based on each approach. The thought process used in reconciling the value will require explanation so that the client can see exactly how the appraiser arrived at the value. Therefore, the three separate values need to be included in the report.

# Appraisal Reports

The type of report chosen does not determine the amount of work put into the actual appraisal process. Whether the client requests a detailed report or just a summary, the steps, methods, and amount of work should be identical. The report type chosen only affects how much detail the appraiser uses when communicating his or her findings to the client.

The Uniform Standards of Professional Appraisal Practice (USPAP) list the type of reports an appraiser can use. It is the appraiser's responsibility to understand the designated types of reports, to apply the correct type of report to the appropriate appraisal assignment, and to compose the report correctly. The three types of real property appraisal reports recognized by USPAP are the:

- Self-Contained Appraisal Report.
- Summary Appraisal Report.
- Restricted-Use Appraisal Report.

An appraiser must carefully decide which type of report to use. Appraisal standards set minimum requirements for the content and level of information in each type of report. The final report is presented in either a short-form style or narrative style. Appraisals are valid on the date that the appraiser signs and dates the report.

## Self-Contained Report

The **Self-Contained Report** is the most elaborate report and contains the most detailed information. Self-contained means that everything the user of the report needs to fully understand it is contained within the report. The user does not have to rely on the appraiser's workfile like in the other report options.

A Self-Contained Report could be as many as 300 pages long, or more. Appraisers typically do not use this type of report for single-family residences. Rather, it is more common for income-producing properties, like apartment complexes, office buildings, hotel resorts, and so forth. Since these kinds of properties are valued based on the income they produce, the report must show all pertinent information about the subject property that influences the value, as well as all pertinent information about the economy of the area that drives the income.

The main thing that distinguishes the Self-Contained Report from the others is what USPAP terms as "describe". When an appraiser describes information, it is presented in a more elaborate level of detail than "summarizing", or "stating". In a Self-Contained Report, the appraiser would describe:

- the real estate to be appraised.

- the value to be estimated.

- the information considered.

- the appraisal procedures followed.

- the reasoning that supports the analyses, opinions, conclusions.

- the appraiser's opinion of the highest and best use of the real estate when appropriate.

- any additional information that may be suitable to show compliance with, or clearly identify and explain, permitted departures from the specific guidelines of STANDARD 1 of USPAP.

The Self-Contained Report must include sufficient information to indicate that the appraiser complied with the requirements of STANDARD 1, including the requirements governing any permitted departures from the appraisal guidelines. USPAP states that the amount of detail required will vary with the significance of the information to the appraisal.

The Self-Contained Appraisal Report includes the identity of the client and any intended users (by name or type), the intended use of the appraisal, the real estate involved, the real property interest appraised, the purpose of the appraisal, and dates of the appraisal and of the report. It also describes work used to develop the appraisal, the extraordinary assumptions and limiting conditions, the information that was analyzed, the procedures followed, and the reasoning that supports the conclusions. The report states the current use of the real estate and the use reflected in the appraisal, the support for the appraiser's opinion of the highest and best use, and any departures from the Standards. It also includes a signed certification.

Note that the length of the report does not dictate which type it is. An appraiser can create a one-hundred-page report, but if it does not contain the proper detail, it will not be a Self-Contained Report.

**Figure 14.3** Appraisals can be delivered in a traditional written format or orally.

## Summary Report

The **Summary Report** contains less detail than a Self-Contained Report, but more than the Restricted-Use Report. It is also the most commonly used report option. Instead of describing the information in detail, the appraiser would summarize (as the name implies) the following:

- the extent of the process of collecting, confirming, and reporting data.
- the information considered.
- the appraisal procedures followed.
- the reasoning that supports the analyses, opinions and conclusions, including the appraiser's opinion of highest and best use of the real estate when appropriate.
- any additional information that may be relevant to show compliance with, or clearly identify and explain permitted departures from, the specific guidelines of STANDARD 1 of USPAP.

To summarize is to elaborate but not provide every detail required to reach that conclusion. For example, the Uniform Residential Appraisal Report (URAR) is a Summary Report. It contains many fields of information in organized categories, and allows for proper summarizing statements and even an addendum to support and clarify concepts when necessary. Most residential appraisals would be done on this standardized form, and would be considered Summary Reports.

The Summary Appraisal Report covers the same categories as the Self-Contained Appraisal Report, but where the Self-Contained Appraisal Report includes descriptions, the Summary Appraisal Report contains summaries.

# Restricted-Use Report

The **Restricted-Use Appraisal Report** is the briefest presentation of an appraisal and contains the least detail.  This type of report is called restricted-use because there can only be one intended user of the report.

Normally, the term **intended user** includes the client and any other party identified by the appraiser as users of the appraisal report.  However, for the Restricted-Use Appraisal Report, the client is the only intended user.  Since the appraiser always has the responsibility to include enough information that the intended user(s) can understand the report, the appraiser should only complete this type of report when the client is very familiar with the property, and therefore able to understand such a brief report.  Anyone else who tries to use a Restricted-Use Report is an unintended user.

Restricted-Use Appraisal Reports are used only when they convincingly meet the client's needs, and the client clearly understands their restricted use.  The Restricted-Use Appraisal Report covers the same categories as the other two reports with the following differences:

- only the client is named because there are no other users.
- the use of the report is limited to the client.
- the report refers to the appraiser's workfile as the source of necessary additional information about the appraisal.

Much of the information in a restricted report is just stated, which is the briefest method of presenting information.  There is no elaboration when information is stated.  For example, to state the zoning, simply indicate R-1 (residential – one unit).

Because of the restricted report's brief nature, the appraiser should describe the extent of the process of collecting, confirming, and reporting data.  The appraiser must also include a prominent use-restriction that limits reliance on the report to the client, and warns that the report cannot be understood properly without additional information in the workfile of the appraiser.

Information stated in a restricted report would include:
- the real property interest being appraised.
- the purpose and intended use of the appraisal.
- the effective date of the appraisal and date of the report.
- assumptions and limiting conditions that affect the analyses, opinions, and conclusions.
- the appraiser's opinion of highest and best use.
- a definition of the value to be estimated.
- the exclusion of any of the usual valuation approaches.
- the appraiser's opinion of value.

## Report Styles

A distinction needs to be made between the different report types (discussed above) and the styles in which the reports are presented.

All three types of reports can be presented as a form report, in a narrative style, or even verbally. **Form style report** means that the appraiser is presenting the report using preprinted forms. Fannie Mae Form 1004, called the **Uniform Residential Appraisal Report (URAR)**, exemplifies the form report. A **narrative style report** does not use a form. Instead, it is an account of the particulars of the appraisal, usually written in a free-form style. **Oral reports** are usually reserved for litigation purposes, but may be used at anytime if requested by the client. According to USPAP, an oral report should have a workfile that is as complete as the file for a written report. Additionally, a written summary of the oral appraisal report must be added to the workfile within a reasonable time.

Routinely, the client that requires the Summary Report wants it to be in form style. Because of its length, a Self-Contained Appraisal Report is best suited for the narrative style. However, this certainly does not disqualify an appraiser from using a narrative report for either of the other two report types, nor creating a form that can contain all of the detail required to qualify it as a Self-Contained Report.

## Summary

The appraiser will spend countless hours collecting and verifying data, analyzing that data, and then using it to implement one, two, or three approaches to value. Once these separate approaches to value have been successfully applied, the final step in the appraisal process is to reconcile these separate values into a singular supportable value. This is known as **reconciliation.**

A great deal of effort is put into the reconciliation process. Besides weighing and scrutinizing the different values, the appraiser has to revisit the data, methods, and computations used while arriving at those value opinions. He or she must also analyze the different value conclusions in comparison with each other, as well as in the context of the subject property and its neighborhood.

Once this process is completed, the appraiser has a **final value estimate** to present to the client. Depending on the client's needs, the appraiser may have to include every possible detail of the appraisal process or just merely summarize or state the pertinent information. This can be done in a **form report**, a **narrative report**, or an **oral report**. Whichever report type and style is chosen, the appraiser has a responsibility to clearly and accurately communicate his or her analyses, opinions, and conclusions to the client in a credible, comprehensible report.

# Review Exercises

## *Matching Exercise*

**Instructions:**   Look up the meaning of the terms in the Glossary, then write the letter of the matching term on the blank line before its definition.   Answers are in Appendix B.

### Terms

A. final value estimate

B. form style report

C. intended user

D. narrative style report

E. oral reports

F. reconciliation

G. Restricted-Use Appraisal Report

H. Self-Contained Report

I. Summary Report

J. Uniform Residential Appraisal Report

### Definitions

1. _____ The process of refining the range or set of values into a single supportable value opinion.

2. _____ A single supportable value opinion.

3. _____ The most elaborate report which contains the most detailed information.

4. _____ The most commonly used report option.

5. _____ The briefest of the appraisal reports.

6. _____ The client and any other party identified by the appraiser as a user of the appraisal report.

7. _____ A report that is presented using preprinted forms.

8. _____ An example of a form style report.

9. _____ A report that is an account of the particulars of the appraisal, usually written in a free-form.

10. _____ Type of report usually reserved for litigation purposes.

## *Multiple Choice Questions*

**Instructions:** Circle your response and go to Appendix B to read the complete explanation for each question.

1. Which of the following statements is true regarding the process of reconciliation?
   a. Every approach is applicable in all assignments.
   b. Applying the three appraisal approaches to value to the same property will typically produce the same figure.
   c. The most credible reconciliation uses the average of the different three values derived from the three approaches.
   d. Identical values produced from different approaches are a red flag.

2. Which of the following is an instance where an approach is definitely inapplicable?
   a. Cost approach not listed on the appraisal form
   b. Income approach on a residential subject
   c. Cost approach for vacant land
   d. Sales comparison approach on a strip mall

3. When using the sales comparison approach, an appraiser should:
   a. ensure there is an adequate number of comparable sales.
   b. double-check all mathematics used.
   c. re-verify that comparables used are in fact comparable to the subject.
   d. do all of the above.

4. Out of the different approaches to value, which would most likely yield the highest value?
   a. Sales comparison approach
   b. Cost approach
   c. Income approach
   d. They will all yield the same value.

5. The income approach applies to:
   a. income-producing properties only.
   b. any property type.
   c. any property that has income potential.
   d. special-purpose properties that produce income.

6. Why should an appraiser round the final value estimate?
    a. Because numbers confuse clients
    b. Because exact figures cease to be an estimate
    c. To make the estimate easier to read
    d. To allow more room for error

7. While reconciling a final value conclusion, an appraiser should never:
    a. reduce the process to a mathematical calculation.
    b. bend the values to fit a preconceived notion.
    c. make changes to values, calculations, or data unless a genuine mistake was discovered.
    d. do all of the above.

8. Regarding appraisal and appraisal reporting, which of the following is true?
    a. An appraisal with a summary report requires more work than an appraisal with a restricted-use report.
    b. Self-contained appraisals require the most work out of all appraisals.
    c. Appraisal reports dictate the amount of detail conveyed to the client, but have no bearing on the amount of work put into an appraisal.
    d. All of the above

9. Which is the most elaborate of the appraisal report options?
    a. Narrative-form
    b. Summary
    c. Self-contained
    d. Restricted-use

10. When is a workfile required?
    a. When using a restricted-use report
    b. When using an oral report
    c. When using the narrative style
    d. Anytime an appraisal is performed

# Chapter 15

# *Appraisal Statistical Concepts*

## Introduction

This chapter will explain the basic mathematical procedures you will need in order to be successful in your real estate appraisal career. Many people are intimidated by the word "math", but in this case, the concepts presented here are mainly a review of knowledge you already possess—and probably use in your daily life. An understanding of the principles and formulas explained in this chapter will help you as a licensee solve the math problems you will encounter regularly.

### Learning Objectives

After reading this chapter, you will have a basic understanding of algebra and geometry and will review:

- working with percentages, fractions, and decimals.

- inconsistent measurements and measurement conversions.

- calculating perimeter, area, and volume.

- basic interest, word problems.

- statistical measurements.

# Basic Math Principles

As we cover basic math principles, numerous examples are used. Keep in mind that there are several ways to solve each example. We have attempted to be consistent in our explanations for the beginner. Some students will recognize the algebraic solutions presented, and will use their own techniques for solving the problems.

## Calculators

For most appraisal math, a basic calculator can make all of the necessary computations, and if properly used, it will cut down on mistakes in calculations. A basic calculator will be vital to the beginning appraiser, especially for testing purposes. For the purposes of this text, as well as testing purposes, we recommend a basic four-function calculator. The functions on a basic calculator are add ( + ), subtract ( − ), multiply ( × ), divide ( ÷ ), percent ( % ), and square root ( √ ). Try to get a calculator that runs on batteries and is noise free, because the testing centers may not have the necessary light that solar calculators require.

Once you begin to work more with income-producing properties, you may want to purchase a financial calculator. A financial calculator provides many benefits to the appraiser, including the Six Functions of 1 Dollar tables at a touch of a button. However, a basic calculator is sufficient for these problems, so it is not necessary to purchase a financial calculator now. They are rather expensive, are very elaborate, and may create more problems than they solve.

The following problem-solving techniques are explained for beginning math students and for individuals who have not used math techniques for quite some time and need a little practice to become proficient.

## Decimals, Fractions, and Percentages

Before starting to study various mathematical problems, it will be helpful to review the concept of decimals. The period that sets apart a whole number from a fractional part of that number is called a **decimal point**. The position of the decimal point determines the value of the number.

Any numerals to the right of the decimal point are less than one. The 10th position is the first position to the right of the decimal point, the 100th position is the second to the right of the decimal point, the 1,000th position is the third to the right of the decimal point, and so forth.

The whole numerals are to the left of the decimal point. The ones are in the first position to the left of the decimal point, the 10s in the second position to the left of the decimal point, the 100s in the third position to the left of the decimal point, the 1,000s in the fourth position to the left of the decimal point, and so forth.

| Decimal | Fraction | Percentage |
|---------|----------|------------|
| 0.045 | 1/22 | 4 1/2% |
| 0.0667 | 1/15 | 6 2/3% |
| 0.10 | 1/10 | 10% |
| 0.125 | 1/8 | 12 1/2% |
| 0.1667 | 1/6 | 16 2/3% |
| 0.25 | 1/4 | 25% |
| 0.33 | 1/3 | 33 1/3% |
| 0.5 | 1/2 | 50% |
| 0.667 | 2/3 | 66 2/3% |
| 0.75 | 3/4 | 75% |
| 1.00 | 1/1 | 100% |

## Converting Fractions into Decimals

**Fractions** are always composed of two numbers, one on top, and one on bottom. The top number is the **numerator**, and the bottom number is the **denominator**. These numbers are related as a part to the whole, where the numerator (top) is the part of the denominator (bottom) whole. Examine 1/2 for example, probably the simplest fraction. There are two equal parts that make up the whole, and 1/2 represents one of those two parts.

To convert the fraction into a decimal, simply divide the top number (numerator) by the bottom number (denominator). You can do this manually, but using a calculator will simplify the process:

To convert 1/2,  $1 \div 2 = 0.5$

To convert 3/4,  $3 \div 4 = 0.75$

To convert 3/10,  $3 \div 10 = 0.3$

## Converting Decimals to Percentages

To convert a decimal to a percentage move the decimal point two places to the right and add a percent symbol. When no decimal is present (in whole numbers), assume the decimal is to the very right of the number (for example, 10 is the same as 10.0). So, when converting a decimal to a percentage, 1 becomes 100%, 0.02 becomes 2%, 0.57 becomes 57%, 0.058 becomes 5.8%, and 9.02 becomes 902%.

## Converting Percentages to Decimals

Reverse the above process to convert a number expressed as a percentage to a decimal. Again, when working with numbers like 10% or 20%, the decimal point is assumed to be on the right side of the number. Move the decimal point two places to the left and remove the percentage sign. Thus 6% becomes 0.06, 30% becomes 0.30, 2.3% becomes 0.023, and 210% becomes 2.10.

## Addition of Decimal Numbers

All numbers must be in a vertical column when adding numbers with decimals. Always be sure to line up the decimals vertically. If it helps, use zeros as placeholders. A **placeholder** will help line up the decimals and is a meaningless zero. Only one rule applies: a placeholder can only be added to the right of the last decimal position. 6.70000 is mathematically identical to 6.7. So when adding these figures together — 902.36, 2.053, 387.1 it will look like this:

$$
\begin{array}{r}
\text{Formula:} \quad 902.360 \\
2.053 \\
+\ \ 387.100 \\
\hline
1{,}291.513
\end{array}
$$

## Subtraction of Decimal Numbers

In subtracting numbers with decimals, use the same process, making sure to line up the decimals vertically.

$$
\begin{array}{r}
\text{Formula:} \quad 43267.23 \\
-\ \ 235.10 \\
\hline
43032.13
\end{array}
$$

## Multiplication of Decimal Numbers

After multiplying the numbers just as you would in a non-decimal problem, count the total number of decimal places in the numbers being multiplied and place the decimal point in the answer that many places from the right.

Formula :

$$\begin{array}{r} 4.327 \\ \times\ \ 82.2\ \ \ \\ \hline 355.6794 \end{array}$$

3 decimal places
1 decimal place
4 total decimal places

## Division of Decimal Numbers

The decimal point must be removed before solving the problem when there is a decimal in the divisor.  Move the decimal point in the divisor to the right, and then move the decimal point in the dividend the same number of places to the right.  Add zeros to the dividend if it has fewer numerals than are needed to carry out this procedure.  Put the decimal point in the answer directly above the new decimal point in the dividend.

Formula:

$$0.021\,\overline{)\,840\,}$$

$$\overset{40.000}{21\,\overline{)\,840.000}}$$

When there is no decimal point in the divisor, put the decimal point in the answer directly above the decimal point in the dividend.

Formula :

$$\overset{00.196}{94\,\overline{)\,18.43}}$$

## Rounding

Rounding a number means making it the closest whole number or other designated position, i.e., rounding 5.8 up to 6 or rounding $392 up to the nearest hundred ($400).  A few rules of thumb are in order when rounding numbers.

If the number is greater than or equal to half of the place you are rounding to, round up; if it is lower, round down.  This will depend on the position to which you are rounding.  For example, if rounding to the nearest hundred, when the number is 50 or above round up; if it is below 50 round down.

Examples:

| | | |
|---|---|---|
| 0.66666 | Rounded to hundredth | 0.67 |
| 10,550 | Rounded to hundred | 10,600 |
| 24 | Rounded to ten | 20 |
| 5.167 | Rounded to tenth | 5.2 |
| 321.568 | Rounded to whole | 322 |
| 321.444 | Rounded to whole | 321 |

Typically, as an appraiser, you will be working with large monetary figures as well as miniscule percentages. The second rounding rule is do not round until you get to the final answer.

The exception to this rule is percentages. Generally, percentages do not need to exceed the hundredth place, but be sure not to over-round to the tenths or a whole percentage, as the result will vary.

| **No rounding** | **Rounding 100ths** |
|---|---|
| $\dfrac{\$39{,}956}{8.5699\%} = \$466{,}236.47$ | $\dfrac{\$39{,}956}{8.57\%} = \$466{,}231.03$ |

When the rules above are followed, the rounded final answer (to the closest hundred) is the same, $466,200. However, if you over-round, the final answer can change significantly.

$$\frac{\$40{,}000}{9\%} = \$444{,}444.44$$

When tallying multiple figures, the rounding principle becomes more important because combining the disparities caused by over-rounded figures will significantly affect the analysis. In the above example, the disparity was a couple hundred dollars. Imagine if five samples were added together and each had a disparity of $200 to $300. The final answer could be off by $1,000 or more. Moreover, if you had to apply that answer elsewhere, the result of that calculation would be affected even more. The possibility of the snowball effect due to excessive rounding is clear.

# Working with Algebra

The following basic algebraic principles can help the beginning appraiser solve for an unknown variable, whether working with percentages (usually capitalization rates or interest rates), dollar figures, or both. Typically, each problem has three variables and in any given problem, two of the three are known. Problems that are more complex really are just comprised of multiple smaller problems and merely need to be broken down into their components.

## Basic Formula

With a basic understanding of algebra, anyone can manipulate the basic formula to calculate the unknown: $x \ (\pm \ or \ \times / \div) \ y = z$

The key to this principle is that whichever operation is in the formula, whether it be $+$, $-$, $\times$, or $\div$, use the opposing operation and apply it to both sides of the equals sign ( $=$ ). The following problems should clarify:

$x + y = z$
if $x = 4$ and $y = 3$, to solve for $z$ simply add 4 to 3
$4 + 3 = 7$

However, in instances where the unknown variable is not isolated on one side of the equals sign, steps can be taken to isolate it. Complete the following using the same formula from above:

Solve for $y$ when $x = 2$ and $z = 5$

First, plug the numbers into the formula

$2 + y = 5$

To calculate the value of $y$, isolate the unknown variable ($y$) by applying the opposing operation ($+/-$ or $\times/\div$) to the numeral that accompanies the unknown variable. In this case, subtract 2 from both sides of the equation ( $=$ ).

$2 \ (-2) + y = 5 \ (-2)$
$[2 - 2] \ + y = 5 - 2$
$y = 5 - 2$
$y = 3$

On the left side of the equation the $+2$ and $-2$ cancel each other out, leaving only the unknown variable. On the right side of the equation, the negative 2 is added to the 5 (or subtract 2 from 5) and the result is 3. This will work with subtraction, multiplication, and division problems as well. Remember, though, that you need to apply the opposing operation.

Another example:

> Formula: $x - y = z$
> Solve for x when $y = 10$ and $z = 5$
> $x - 10 = 5$
> $x - 10 \, (+10) = 5 \, (+10)$
> $x \, [-10 + 10] = 5 + 10$
> $x = 15$

A multiplication example:

> Formula: $x \times y = z$
> Solve for y when $x = 25$ and $z = 100$
> $25 \times y = 100$
> $25 \, (\div 25) \times y = 100 \, (\div 25)$
> $[25 \div 25] \times y = 100 \div 25$
> $y = 4$

In the above multiplication problem, the opposing operation is division, and the 25 divided by itself cancels itself. The same occurs in reverse when working with division problems.

> A division example:
> Formula: $x \div y = z$
> Solve for x when $y = \$400$ and $z = 8\%$
> $x \div \$400 = 8\%$
> $x \div \$400 \, (\times \$400) = 8\% \, (\times \$400)$
> $x \, [\div \$400 \times \$400] = 8\% \times \$400$
> $x = \$32$

## Word Problems

The above algebraic principles are useful when working with word problems. The key to word problems is knowing how to decipher the information as well as knowing where the variables fit into the formula. The most important thing regarding word problems is to read the problem carefully and know what is being asked. Often, extra information is included. Other times all the variables are not included, rather information is included that will allow you to determine the needed variables. Using the basic algebraic formula for computing percentage problems (an $x \times y = z$ problem), solve the following simple word problems

Formula   $\underline{\text{Whole}}$   $\times$   $\underline{\text{Percentage}}$   $=$   $\underline{\text{Part}}$
$\quad\quad\quad\quad$ (x) $\quad\quad\quad\quad\quad$ (y) $\quad\quad\quad\quad\quad$ (z)

## Dollar-Off Problems

A freeway was constructed next to a home that was previously valued at $500,000. Since the construction of the freeway, the property's value has dropped by 35%. How much value did the property lose?

**Solution**

By plugging in the factors into the formula, this word problem is relatively uncomplicated to solve:

Whole   $\times$   Percentage   $=$   Part

$500,000 $\times$ 0.35 (35%) $=$   $175,000, the dollar amount of value
$\quad\quad\quad\quad\quad\quad\quad\quad\quad\quad\quad\quad\quad\quad$ lost due to the freeway.

If the same problem instead asked what the property is worth after the freeway construction, you could go through the steps above, and then subtract the result from the whole:

$\quad\quad$ $500,000 $-$ $175,000 $=$ $325,000

Alternatively, you could multiply the whole by the percentage remaining of the value.

$\quad\quad$ $500,000 $\times$ 0.65 (100% - 35%) $=$ $325,000

If this confuses you, consider the following:

> In retail, the retailer typically marks the sale price as a percentage off — for example, a pair of $120 sneakers is 40% off. Consider viewing it in this manner, however. Instead of taking 40% off, are you not just paying 60% of the regular price? Therefore, it can be mathematically expressed as $120 − ( $120 $\times$ 40% ), or $120 $\times$ 60%. In either case, the sales price is $72.

## Percentage-Off Problems

Sometimes, you will get word problems that are similar to the shoe example above, but instead of wanting to know the sales price, the problem will ask how much the percentage-off is.

Parents just sold their home to their daughter for $300,000. The appraiser concludes that it was not an arm's-length transaction and determines its actual market value is $400,000. What was the daughter's percentage of savings?

**Solution**

To solve this, use the same formula from above:

**Whole** × **Percentage** = **Part**
$400,000 × % = $100,000

Apply the opposing operation by dividing both sides by $400,000

Percentage = $100,000 ÷ $400,000 which equals 0.25 or 25%

In this problem, in order to solve for the percentage of savings, the Part used must be the dollar amount saved, which is not provided but can easily be calculated ($400,000 − $300,000). If you instead use the below market value, which is a common mistake, you are solving for the percentage below-market that the daughter paid.

$300,000 ÷ $400,000 = 0.75 or 75%

As you can see each result is complementary to the other (25% and 75%), and added together, they will equal 1 or 100%. If you do make the mistake of solving for the percentage below-market, simply subtract this figure from 100% to calculate the correct answer.

## Miscellaneous Problems

When you are asked to find an amount resulting from an interest rate, it will usually be an annual number. If not otherwise specified, make sure you annualize, that is convert any monthly figures to annual or yearly figures by multiplying the monthly figures by 12.

Steve has a savings account and wants to earn $100 per month in interest. If the account pays 4% interest, how much should Steve keep in the account?

Whole × Percent (0.04) = Part ($1,200 per year = $100 × 12 months)

Isolate the unknown Whole by dividing both sides of equation by 0.04.

Whole = $1,200 ÷ 0.04, or $30,000

Mitch bought a house for $145,000. The house was later sold for $165,000. What is the rate (%) of profit Mitch made on this sale?

Again, the problem is asking you to solve for something that is not included in the problem, the profit. However, it is easily calculated by subtracting the price paid from the price sold, $165,000 – $145,000 = $20,000. Then you can plug the correct variables into the Whole/Percent/Part problem:

Whole ($145,000) × Percent = Part $20,000

Percent = $20,000 ÷ $145,000 or percent of profit equals 13.8%

## Interest and Loan Problems

The charge for the use of money is called **interest**. The rate of interest that is charged will determine the total dollar amount of the payments. When money is borrowed, both the principal and interest must be paid back according to the agreement between the borrower and lender.

The formula for interest and loan problems is a variation of the *xyz* formula introduced earlier in the chapter. However, this one contains a fourth variable. It is treated the same, but there is one more step to isolate the unknown. The terms needed for calculating this type of problem are:

**Interest** (I):   the dollar amount charged for the use of money
**Principal** (P):  the dollar amount of money borrowed
**Rate** (R):       the percentage of interest charged
**Time** (T):       duration of loan in years
**Formula: I = P × R × T**

---

**Problem**
Andrea borrowed $6,000 for one year and paid $520 interest. What interest rate did she pay?

**Solution**:   First, plug in the variables.
$520 = $6,000 × R × 1
Then solve by isolating the unknown variable.
$520 ÷ $6,000 = R, or R = .08666 (8.67% rounded).

---

The above problem had a fourth variable of 1. When multiplying or dividing by 1, there is no effect on the outcome. Multiply or divide the answer by 1 on your calculator and see for yourself.

If all other variables remain the same and the years double, you would calculate the same problem as follows:

$$\$520 = \$6,000 \times R \times 2$$
$$\$520 = \$12,000 \ (\$6,000 \times 2) \times R$$
$$\$520 \div \$12,000 = R, \text{ which equals } 4.33\%$$

In the above scenario, Andrea borrowed the same amount and paid the same amount of interest, but had two years instead of one to pay it, thus cutting her effective rate in half. Try the following problem using the $I = P \times R \times T$ formula.

**Problem:**
If one month's interest is $50 on a five-year, straight interest-only note, and the interest rate on the note is 10% per year, what is the amount of the loan?

**Solution:** $\quad \$600 \ (\$50 \times 12 \text{ months}) = P \times 10\% \times 1$
$\qquad\qquad\quad \$600 \div 0.1 = \$6,000$

One final example will demonstrate how to manipulate the formula in a similar fashion to what was shown in the Word Problem section.

**Problem:**
Chuck has paid $600 total in equal payments of interest so far on a loan of $40,000. His terms were 6% over 2 years. How many payments does he have left?

**Solution:**
This question is a little tricky and will take several steps. First, determine how much interest Chuck should pay by the end of the term and then compare it to how much he has paid already.

I = $40,000 × 6% × 2, or a total of $4,800 in interest.

There are 24 months in two years. To figure how much his monthly payments are, divide his total interest by the 24 payment periods to get $200 per month ($4,800 ÷ 24). Then divide the amount of interest he has paid thus far on the loan by the amount per payment to calculate how many payments have been made ($600 ÷ $200 = 3). Then subtract the number of monthly payments already made from the total payment periods to calculate the answer to the question (24 – 3 = 21 payments).

# Area and Volume Calculations

On the state exam, you will most likely be asked to solve problems regarding area and volume. In actual practice, you will calculate the area of lots, buildings, and garages, and the volume of structures like warehouses. These types of calculations will require a basic understanding of geometry.

These days, computer programs and specialized measuring devices do most of the work when it comes to determining area and volume. However, it is always good to know the basics. That way, you can check the computer-generated answers and make sure they are reasonable. This keeps you from blindly relying on a computer or calculator and will help you catch the problem if you make a mistake inputting information.

Therefore, in addition to the basic algebra lesson, there will also be a basic geometric lesson. The following chart summarizes the formulas an appraiser may need in daily life.

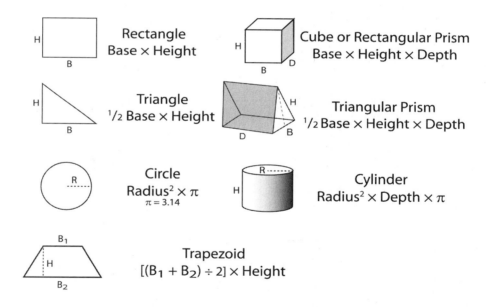

Before areas and volumes are further explored, certain clarifications need to be addressed. We live in a three dimensional universe, and as such, these dimensions are reflected in an appraiser's measurements and calculations.

The most basic measurement is a linear measurement. A linear measurement is a measurement of distance and can be straight, curved, or angled. Examples of linear measurements include the length of the property's front boundary, the perimeter (or distance around) a grain silo, or the drive from Los Angeles to Las Vegas. This measurement will be expressed in linear terms, i.e. an inch long, a foot deep, or a mile wide.

When a second dimension is included in the equation, the measurement becomes an area measurement instead of a linear one. **Area** articulates the amount of space covered, whether by a real object or theoretical shape, and is always expressed in terms of square measurements. This is because the most basic area measurement is a square, but this does not preclude other shapes. Typical area measurements an appraiser will encounter include the floor area of a bedroom, a lot size, and the area of a wall the window occupies. To compute a square measurement, one simply needs to multiply two linear measurements together. Examine the following for clarification:

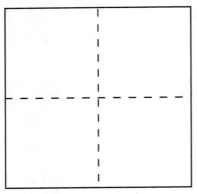

This square is two inches by two inches, meaning that every side on it measures two inches.

Its area equals four square inches, meaning that the space it covers is equal to four one-inch square sections.

2 in. x 2 in. = 4 square in.

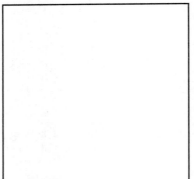

Measure the perimeter of the same square. Perimeter measures the distance around instead of the space covered.

If each side measures two inches, its perimeter equals eight inches. If you walked around the square, you would have walked eight inches.

2 in. + 2 in. + 2 in. + 2 in. = 8 in.

When a third dimension is added, **volume** is being quantified, that is the amount of space being occupied. When a three-dimensional object is measured in terms of volume, like an Olympic-sized swimming pool for instance, it consists of three measurements: the width, the length, and the depth (or height). When these three measurements are multiplied, the resulting figure is a cubic measurement.

Take that Olympic- sized pool for example. According to the Olympic committee, the pool must measure 50 meters in length, 25 meters in width, and must be at least 2 meters deep. Using the formula for a cube, the volume of the pool is calculated at 2500 cubic meters (50m $\times$ 25m $\times$ 2m).

## *Working with Odd Shapes*

Unfortunately, lots and rooms are not always perfect rectangles, and warehouses and other industrial buildings are not always perfect cubes or rectangles. When you have to calculate area for an irregular lot or building, treat it like a complicated word problem, by breaking it down into its component parts.

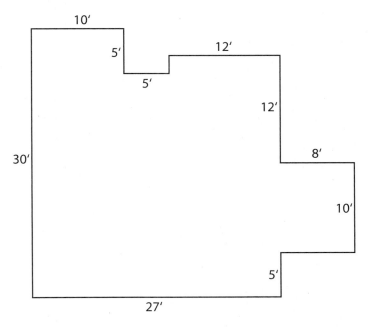

Certainly, the above floorplan is not a perfect rectangle. However, all you need to do is separate it into smaller shapes that are easier to compute. Then add all of the figures together to achieve the final answer. There is no one right way to divide this shape into several smaller shapes. Ideally, make it as uncomplicated as possible. The fewer shapes you must calculate, the less potential for mistakes.

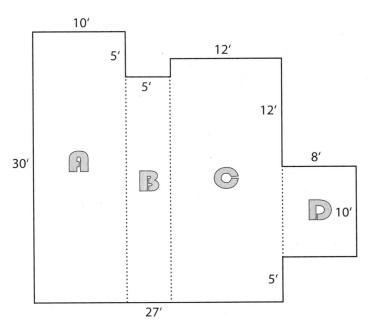

Once it is broken into smaller, more manageable rectangles, the area becomes much easier to compute.

Rectangle A   10' × 30' = 300 sq ft
Rectangle B   5' × 25' = 125 sq ft
Rectangle C   12' × 27' = 324 sq ft
Rectangle D   8' × 10' = 80 sq ft
Floorplan total area = 829 square feet

Another way to approach this figure is the cutaway method. This involves transforming the irregular shape into a perfect shape (a rectangle in this case) and then subtracting the cutaway areas from the larger rectangular area. The following should illustrate.

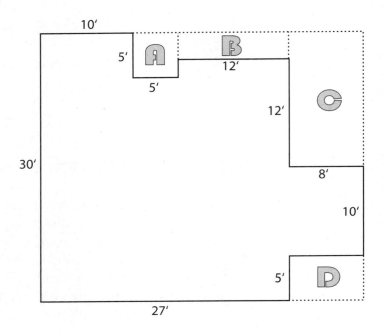

Rectangle     30' × 35' = 1,050 sq ft
Cutaway A     5' × 5' =    – 25 sq ft
Cutaway B     3' × 12' =   – 36 sq ft
Cutaway C     15' × 8' =   – 120 sq ft
Cutaway D     5' × 8' =    – 40 sq ft
Floorplan total area = 829 square feet

Either method results in the same answer. There are still other possibilities as well. Whichever method you choose, be careful and precise in your calculations.

## *Volume Calculations*

When measuring volume, a similar instance may occur. While some warehouses are rectangular, some may have a gable roof, or some other feature that complicates the calculations. Again, break the object into its simpler component parts and determine the volumes separately before you add them all together for a final computation.

In the following figure, the industrial building pictured is 80' × 100' × 30'. The height of the eaves is measured at 18'.

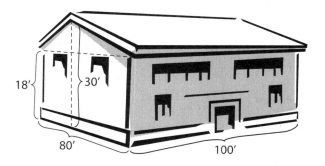

To solve for the volume of this building, divide the shape into a rectangular prism that measures 80' × 100' × 18' and a triangular prism that measures 100' × 80' × 12'. Then calculate the volume for each and add the two figures together for the entire building's volume.

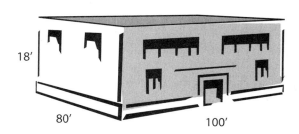

Rectangle 80' × 100' × 18' = 144,000 cu. ft.

Triangle 100' × 80' × 12' ÷ 2 = 48,000 cu. ft.

Warehouse total area = 192,000 cubic feet

## Conversions

Often figures are not presented to you in like measurements, so knowing how to convert inches to feet, and feet to yards, and yards to miles or acres is invaluable. It is very important to use like measurements when working through computations or else answers will be wrong.

For example, Jane bought a Jacuzzi and was about to install it in her backyard when the contractor came across a CC&R that prohibited any excavation of surface ground exceeding an area of 30 square feet total. The measurements of her Jacuzzi are 5 foot 10 inches by 5 foot 4 inches. Will her Jacuzzi fit?

Once converted to all inches (70 in × 64 in) or all feet (5.83 ft × 5.33 ft) she would see that the Jacuzzi covers an area of just over 31 square feet.

Following is a chart that lists many different conversions with which an appraiser should be familiar.

| Linear | Square | Cubic |
|---|---|---|
| 12 inches = 1 foot | 144 square inches = 1 square foot | 1,728 cubic inches = 1 cubic foot |
| 3 feet = 1 yard | 9 square feet = 1 square yard | 27 cubic feet = 1 cubic yard |
| 1,760 yards = 1 mile | 36 sections = 36 square miles | 46,565 cubic inches = 1 cubic yard |
| 1 mile = 5,280 feet | 23,040 acres =36 square miles | 1 board foot = 144 cubic inches |
| 1 mile = 63,360 inches | 640 acres = 1 section | |
| 1 yard = 36 inches | 43,560 square feet = 1 acre | |
| 1 section's perimeter = 21,120 feet | 1 township = 36 square miles | |

An acre is not a particular shape. Rather, an **acre** is a measure of area that covers 43,560 square feet, no matter the form. What this means is that an acre could be a perfect square with sides measuring 208.71 feet or it could be a narrow rectangle that is one foot wide and 43,560 feet long. As long as a shape contains 43,560 square feet it will be measured as an acre. As an appraiser, you will need to be very familiar with acreage.

A similar, but less frequently used, cubic measurement is the board foot. A **board foot** always measures 144 cubic inches; any measure of volume containing 144 $in^2$ is considered a board foot. A piece of lumber that is 2 inches by 6 inches by 12 inches long contains a board foot, just as a box that measures 6 inches by 6 inches by 4 inches contains a board foot.

# Practice Problems

The following problems combine elements of the preceding chapter into semi-complex problems. Read each carefully and learn how to decipher the word problems and break the equations into smaller, manageable steps.

1) Felix owned four acres of land with a front footage of 500 feet along Old Bucket Country Road. What is the depth of the land?

First, convert the acres to square feet

43,560 square feet $\times$ 4 = 174,240 square feet.

If necessary, draw a rectangle representing the land and plug the variables into the formula H $\times$ W = Area

500 $\times$ W = 174,240

W = 174,240 $\div$ 500

W = 348.48, or 350 ft (rounded).

2) Jack is appraising a warehouse that is 90 ft by 90 ft by 30 ft. His market analysis reveals that the monthly GRM for this type of structure is 54 and the comparative unit is $11.10 per cubic yard. If Jack assumes the reproduction value and income approach value are identical, how much should the subject rent for per month?

This is an overly complicated problem, but working through it will certainly help you when test time comes because sometimes a convoluted problem or two will show up. Follow the solution if you can. First, calculate the dimensions and reproduction value.

90 ft $\times$ 90 ft $\times$ 30 ft = 243,000 cubic feet

243,000 cubic feet $\div$ 27 = 9,000 cubic yards

9,000 cubic yards $\times$ $11.10 = $99,900

Since the reproduction value is equal to the monthly income capitalized, and a gross rent multiplier is applied to rent to determine value, divide the value by the multiplier to calculate the rent.

$99,900 $\div$ 54 = $1,850 rent per month.

3)  Carlos bought a triangular lot for $800,000 that measures 450 feet at its widest point and 350 feet at its longest point. How much did Carlos pay for his property per acre?

450 ft × 350 ft ÷ 2 = 78,750 square feet (remember the formula for triangles)

78,750 ft$^2$ ÷ 43,560 ft$^2$ = 1.81 acres

$800,000 ÷ 1.81 = $441,988 or $442,000 per acre (rounded)

4)  Cliff owns a four-acre lot that is 80 feet deep. He originally paid $1,000 per acre 2 years ago. He is in the process of purchasing a neighboring lot that contains two more acres with the same depth for $3,300. He wants to assemble the lots and then subdivide them into 27 equal neighboring lots so he can sell them. His appraiser notified him that he could expect to make $14 per front yard per lot. How much can he expect to make in profit?

First, determine the size and dimensions of the four- acre and two-acre lot combined before subdivision.

6 acres × 43,560 ft per acre = 261,360 square feet

261,360 ÷ 80 foot depth = 3,267 length

The size and shape of the lot is known – a rectangle that measures 80 by 3,267 feet, and covers an area of 261,360 square feet. Next, figure out the front footage of the individual lots once subdivided for sale.

3,267 ÷ 27 = 121 feet

Once divided, he will have 27 lots for sale that are 121 feet long and 80 feet deep. To finish the problem, compute the gross sales then subtract the amount he paid for the properties. Since the sale value is in yardage, the first thing to do is convert the frontage measurement into yardage.

121 ÷ 3 = 40.33 yards

40.33 × $14 = $564.62 per lot

$564.62 × 27 lots = $15,245 (rounded)

$4,000 for original lot + $3,300 for second lot = $7,300

Profit equals projected income minus lot expense.

$15,245 – $7,300 = $7,945

# Statistics

**Statistics** is the science of gathering, categorizing and interpreting data. Statistical analysis has become a very useful tool to the appraiser, especially with the advances in desktop computers. Complicated programs exist that analyze thousands of bits of information in the blink of an eye, but in this chapter, only the most basic statistical concepts will be covered. While appraisers make use of these tools, statistics alone should never be solely relied on for value conclusions. Rather, statistical analysis should outline parameters and assist an appraiser in developing his opinion.

When analyzing statistical data, appraisers will work with a sample of a population, or a defined group within the whole. For example, if the population is Ford manufactured cars, a sample might be all Ford trucks manufactured in the year 1998. If referring to one truck, in statistical terms, you are referring to a variate. A **variate** is a single item in the group. **Parameters**, or further definitions, can also be applied, like refining the sample to all blue trucks manufactured in 1998. When all the blue Ford trucks manufactured in 1998 are accounted for, the total is known as the **aggregate**.

Now that we have introduced the terminology, we can delve into how to organize and categorize statistical information. In order to keep it simple, we will use a small sample for all of the following demonstrations. Assume that you are appraising a 3-bedroom 2-bath house. After market research, you pull a list of ten comps that are nearly identical in size and amenities. This is the MLS price list:

| | |
|---|---|
| 560 Planter Lane | $320,000 |
| 211 Planter Lane | $305,000 |
| 1010 Fascia Avenue | $299,500 |
| 1099 Fascia Avenue | $305,000 |
| 4256 Fascia Avenue | $310,000 |
| 14 United Boulevard | $300,000 |
| 27 United Boulevard | $305,500 |
| 898 Falconcrest | $312,000 |
| 787 Belvue | $308,500 |
| 2 Bonaventure Street | $301,000 |

When analyzing statistical data, the numbers (sales prices) are the most important. In order to make the figures more workable and organized, the first step is to place the sales prices into an array. You do this by sorting the list from lowest to highest or highest to lowest:

| | |
|---|---|
| 1010 Fascia Avenue | $299,500 |
| 14 United Boulevard | $300,000 |
| 2 Bonaventure Street | $301,000 |
| 1099 Fascia Avenue | $305,000 |
| 211 Planter Lane | $305,000 |
| 27 United Boulevard | $305,500 |
| 787 Belvue | $308,500 |
| 4256 Fascia Avenue | $310,000 |
| 898 Falconcrest | $312,000 |
| 560 Planter Lane | $320,000 |

The figures vary from $299,500 up to $320,000, which is not a huge disparity, but the sales are not identical either. To analyze this sample further, appraisers apply what are known as the measures of central tendency.

## Measures of Central Tendency

There are three common statistical measures — the mean, the median, and the mode. All three are used to measure central tendency and to identify the typical variate in a sample or population.

### *Mean*

The **mean**, which is commonly known as the average, is calculated by adding all of the variates together and then dividing by the number of variates. The result will provide a single figure that accounts for all variates, even ones that are significantly lower or higher than the majority.

For example, the variates are 4, 5, 6, and 7. Add them together and divide by four (the number of variates): $22 \div 4 = 5.5$. However, if the variates are changed and are now 4, 5, 6, and 13, the mean for this sample changes from 5.5 to 7. The majority of the variates are clustered around 5, but since one variate is significantly higher, it influences the conclusion significantly.

Determine the mean for the 3bd/2ba sample.

| | |
|---|---|
| 1010 Fascia Avenue | $299,500 |
| 14 United Boulevard | $300,000 |
| 2 Bonaventure Street | $301,000 |
| 1099 Fascia Avenue | $305,000 |
| 211 Planter Lane | $305,000 |
| 27 United Boulevard | $305,500 |
| 787 Belvue | $308,500 |
| 4256 Fascia Avenue | $310,000 |
| 898 Falconcrest | $312,000 |
| 560 Planter Lane | $320,000 |
| Total | $3,066,500 |
| Mean ($3,066,500 ÷ 10) | $306,650 |

Therefore, while the sample ranges from $299,500 to $320,000, the average or mean house price for this sample is $306,500.

## *Median*

The second measure of central tendency is called the **median**, which provides a figure that is directly in the middle of the population. Unlike the mean, the median is not significantly affected by one unusually high or low number. Finding the median is like lining up all of your favorite photos in order of favorite to least favorite, and then picking the photo in the middle of the line.

To do this, divide a sampling into two equal groups. The number in the middle is the median and will provide a figure that is truly the midpoint. With a sampling of 12, 3, 6, 15, and 9, first place the numbers into an array: 3, 6, 9, 12, 15, and then divide them into equal groups:

(3, 6) 9 (12, 15). Since 9 is in the middle of the list, it is the median.

If the number of variates is an even number, as is the MLS sample with which we have been working, there will not be a single variate directly in the middle. In situations where there is an even number of variates, find the mean of the two numbers on either side of the midpoint.

| | |
|---|---|
| 1010 Fascia Avenue | $299,500 |
| 14 United Boulevard | $300,000 |
| 2 Bonaventure Street | $301,000 |
| 1099 Fascia Avenue | $305,000 |
| 211 Planter Lane | $305,000 |

The middle – add these two and divide by 2 ↕

| | |
|---|---|
| 27 United Boulevard | $305,500 |
| 787 Belvue | $308,500 |
| 4256 Fascia Avenue | $310,000 |
| 898 Falconcrest | $312,000 |
| 560 Planter Lane | $320,000 |

$305,000 + $305,500 = $610,500. $610,500 ÷ 2 = $305,250

$305,250 is the median in this sample.

## *Mode*

The final measure of central tendency is called the mode. This **mode** is the number that occurs the most frequently, and when analyzing comparable sales, the most frequently occurring sales price definitely warrants consideration.

| | |
|---|---|
| Once | $299,500 |
| Once | $300,000 |
| Once | $301,000 |
| Twice | $305,000 |
| Once | $305,500 |
| Once | $308,500 |
| Once | $310,000 |
| Once | $312,000 |
| Once | $320,000 |

From the array above, the most frequently occurring variate is $305,000.

In analyzing this sample of comparable sales, the sales range from $299,500 to $320,000 with a mean of $306,650, a median of $305,250, and a mode of 305,000. An appraiser could make an argument for any value within the range. However, after further analysis, there is a better argument for a value that fits the central tendencies.

## Measures of Dispersion

Sometimes, the measures of central tendency are not adequate for the statistical analysis. In order to determine if the variates of the sample are clustered together or spread out, apply the three measures of dispersion: range, average deviation, and standard deviation. While less frequently used, they are another tool in the appraiser's bag.

### *Range*

The **range** is simply the difference between the highest and lowest variate. The lower the range, the more clustered the grouping, and conversely, the higher the range, the more spread out they are. The range for the MLS sample list that we have used through this section can be found by subtracting $299,500 from $320,000. The range equals $20,500. While this certainly is a lot of money, it is not a huge difference when put into the context of the housing market.

### *Average Deviation*

All of these variates differ from the central tendency to some degree; and **average deviation** will measure their combined average dispersion. For this, the mean is needed. Once the mean of the sample is known, add the difference of each variate in relation to the mean together and then divide the sum by the number of variates in the sample.

For this, it may help to imagine a numberline, which is a line with equally spaced tick marks representing a different sequential number.

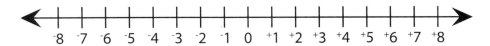

In the above numberline, both +1 and −1 are the same number of positions, one, from the mean of 0. When counting deviation, it is important to disregard the positive or negative attributes of the deviations because, whether positive or negative, they are a certain measure from the mean. If the average income is $50,000 and Joe makes $45,000 and Jane makes $55,000, both are $5,000 from the mean.

Before this is applied to the sample of houses, examine this demonstration on a smaller scale. If the sample is 14, 5, 26, 7, 38, 9, 1, and 4, the mean is 13. To calculate the average deviation, find the number of places that each variate is different from the mean, like so:

| Mean | Variate | Difference +/– | Difference |
|------|---------|----------------|------------|
| 13 | 1 | -12 | 12 |
| 13 | 6 | -7 | 7 |
| 13 | 5 | -8 | 8 |
| 13 | 7 | -6 | 6 |
| 13 | 9 | -4 | 4 |
| 13 | 14 | 1 | 1 |
| 13 | 26 | 13 | 13 |
| 13 | 38 | 25 | <u>25</u> |
| | | Sum of differences | 76 |

Finally, divide the sum of differences by the number of variates. The average deviation is 9.5. Again, as with the measure of range, the more spread out the sample is the higher the deviation figure will be.

Apply this concept to the price list of 10 variates.

| Mean | Variates | Diff +/- | Difference |
|------|----------|----------|------------|
| $306,650 | $299,500 | $7,150 | $7,150 |
| $306,650 | $300,000 | $6,650 | $6,650 |
| $306,650 | $301,000 | $5,650 | $5,650 |
| $306,650 | $305,000 | $1,650 | $1,650 |
| $306,650 | $305,000 | $1,650 | $1,650 |
| $306,650 | $305,500 | $1,150 | $1,150 |
| $306,650 | $308,500 | -$1,850 | $1,850 |
| $306,650 | $310,000 | -$3,350 | $3,350 |
| $306,650 | $312,000 | -$5,350 | $5,350 |
| $306,650 | $320,000 | -$13,350 | <u>$13,350</u> |
| | | Sum of differences | $47,800 |

The average deviation for the price list sample is $4,780 ($47,800 ÷ 10).

**Standard deviation** is even more complex than average deviation, but will produce a useful and credible analysis by statistical means. With this method, before adding the deviations from the mean, they must be squared.

**Squaring** a number means multiplying the figure by itself. Once the deviations are squared, the square root ( $\sqrt{\phantom{x}}$ ) of their mean is taken, and that figure represents the standard deviation of the sample.

If you do not know what a **square root** is, it is the inverse of squaring. If squaring 3 equals 9 (3 × 3 is 9), then the square root of 9 is 3. You do not have to figure this out by hand. Simply punch into your calculator whatever number you need to find the square root of and hit the [ ⁻ ] button.

Perhaps a visual illustration will help. Using the same practice sample as we did in average deviation:

| Mean | Variates | Difference | Diff Square | |
|------|----------|------------|-------------|---|
| 13 | 1 | 12 | (12 × 12) | 144 |
| 13 | 6 | 7 | (7 × 7) | 49 |
| 13 | 5 | 8 | (8 × 8) | 64 |
| 13 | 7 | 6 | (6 × 6) | 36 |
| 13 | 9 | 4 | (4 × 4) | 16 |
| 13 | 14 | 1 | (1 × 1) | 1 |
| 13 | 26 | 13 | (13 × 13) | 169 |
| 13 | 38 | 25 | (25 × 25) | 625 |
| Sum of differences squared | | | | 1104 |
| Mean of differences squared | | | (1104 ÷ 8) | 138 |
| Square root of mean | | | ( √ 138) | 11.75 |

The standard deviation is 11.75.

In our final example, we will calculate the standard deviation for the list of comparables.

| Mean | Variates | Difference | Diff Squared |
|------|----------|------------|--------------|
| $306,650 | $299,500 | $7,150 | $ 51,122,500 |
| $306,650 | $300,000 | $6,650 | $ 44,222,500 |
| $306,650 | $301,000 | $5,650 | $ 31,922,500 |
| $306,650 | $305,000 | $1,650 | $ 2,722,500 |
| $306,650 | $305,000 | $1,650 | $ 2,722,500 |
| $306,650 | $305,500 | $1,150 | $ 1,322,500 |
| $306,650 | $308,500 | $1,850 | $ 3,422,500 |
| $306,650 | $310,000 | $3,350 | $ 11,222,500 |
| $306,650 | $312,000 | $5,350 | $ 28,622,500 |
| $306,650 | $320,000 | $13,350 | $178,222,500 |
| Sum of differences squared | | | $355,525,000 |
| Mean of differences squared | | | $ 35,552,500 |
| Square root of mean | | | $ 5,963 |

The measures of dispersion may seem convoluted, but they convey useful information to the appraiser. Consider our list of comparables. If an appraiser were using this list to determine the subject's value, he or she would certainly want to make sure that the indicated value fell within the range. In addition, a good value check is to make certain that the chosen value does not deviate from the mean by being greater than the standard and average deviations, at least not without reasonable explanation.

Statistical analysis cannot be the sole indicator of value. For instance, with the list we have been using, the data indicates that the subject's value should be around $305,000 and no more than $6,000 higher or lower than that number. This analysis of the numbers does not take into account any non-quantifiable characteristics of the subject or comparables like condition, quality, and other amenities like landscaping or customization. This is where appraising becomes more than just number crunching; it becomes an art.

However, if the appraiser does choose a value outside of the range supported by a statistical analysis, he or she may need to go back and verify the information and be certain that he or she is using appropriate comparables.

## Summary

Math is a major component of the appraisal process. Appraisers need to know how to **calculate areas and volumes** as well as **interest** and **capitalization rates**, among others. It will be of tremendous use both in the practical world and in testing conditions to know when to **round**, how to **convert percentages to decimals,** and how to convert **units of measurement**.

Knowing how to analyze statistical data will be very practical as well. Though appraisers cannot rely solely on **statistical analysis**, it is a good tool to add greater support to or assist the appraiser in his or her analysis.

# Review Exercises

## *Matching Exercise*

**Instructions:** Look up the meaning of the terms in the Glossary, then write the letter of the matching term on the blank line before its definition. Answers are in Appendix B.

### Terms

A. acre

B. aggregate

C. area

D. average deviation

E. decimal point

F. interest

G. mean

H. median

I. mode

J. parameter

K. range

L. square root

M. squaring

N. standard deviation

O. statistics

P. variate

Q. volume

### Definitions

1. _____ The amount of space covered in two dimensions.

2. _____ The amount of space being occupied in three dimensions.

3. _____ 43,560 square feet.

4. _____ The science of gathering, categorizing, and interpreting data.

5. _____ A single item in the group, statistically.

6. _____ The charge for the use of money.

7. _____ The statistical total.

8. _____ The average.

9. _____ The figure that is directly in the middle of the population.

10. _____ The most frequently occurring number.

11. _____ The difference between the highest and lowest variate.

12. _____ A measure of combined average dispersion.

13. _____ A measure of the dispersion or variation in a distribution using the squares of the mean.

14. _____ Multiplying a number by itself.

15. _____ A number, that when multiplied by itself, will result in a
given number.

## Multiple Choice Questions

**Instructions:**   Circle your response and go to Appendix B to read the complete explanation for each question.

1. The dot in 425.9056 is called a:
    a.   period.
    b.   point.
    c.   decimal point.
    d.   decibel point.

2. In the number 425.9056, the 9 is in which position?
    a.   10
    b.   1
    c.   10th
    d.   100th

3. 240% expressed as a decimal is:
    a.   2,400.
    b.   2.4.
    c.   0.24.
    d.   240.

4. 5/2 expressed a percentage is:
    a.   10%.
    b.   250%.
    c.   4%.
    d.   400%.

5. Meagan found three comps that recently sold.  After applying a market derived cap rate, the market value for these comps is as follows:  $574,511; $499,996; and $525,444.  Rounded to the nearest thousand, the final comparable values are:
    a.   $500,000; $525,000; $575,000.
    b.   $499,000; $525,000; $574,500.
    c.   $500,000; $526,000; $575,000.
    d.   $500,000; $524,500; $570,000.

6. Since Rebecca purchased her home one-year ago, property values in the area have increased by 30%. Her property is currently valued at $390,000. How much equity has she earned in the last year?
    a. $117,000
    b. $90,000
    c. $113,000
    d. $11,700

7. Melissa found a property selling for $210,000 that she really liked but could not afford. After sitting on the market for 45-days, the seller offered a $30,000 rebate to facilitate the sale. At that time Melissa decide to purchase the property. What percentage of savings is she receiving?
    a. 85.7%
    b. 63%
    c. 14.3%
    d. 16.7%

8. Sherri is considering buying two adjoining lots and assembling them and then reselling the single lot for a profit. Lot 1 is priced at $30,000 and Lot 2 is priced at $55,000. A contractor estimates the cost to demolish the structures on the sites at $15,000 and Sherri's appraiser estimates the value of the combined lot at $115,000. What would Sherri's rate of return if she goes forward with this?
    a. 10%
    b. 13%
    c. 15%
    d. 30%

9. Ramon took out a one-year interest only loan of $10,000 at 9%. If his final monthly payment must include the last interest payment and the loan balance, how much will it be?
    a. $10,900
    b. $10,075
    c. $908.33
    d. $874.51

10. Which type of measurement is produced when you multiply width by depth?
    a. Inches
    b. Area
    c. Volume
    d. Feet

Use the following figure for questions 11 – 13.

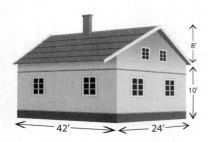

11. What is the perimeter of the house?
    a. 1,008 feet
    b. 132 square feet
    c. 1,008 square feet
    d. 132 feet

12. What is the square footage of the first floor of the house?
    a. 1,008 square feet
    b. 1,008 feet
    c. 132 square feet
    d. 18,144 feet

13. What is the volume of the house?
    a. 18,144 feet
    b. 14,112 cubic feet
    c. 18,144 cubic feet
    d. 9,072 feet

14. What is the GLA of the following floorplan?

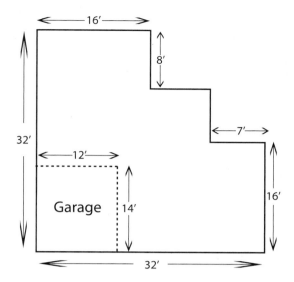

    a.  816 feet

    b.  137 square feet

    c.  672 square feet

    d.  616 feet

15. Which of the following is a larger measurement?

    a.  3 acres

    b.  15 square yards

    c.  1/128 of a section

    d.  ½ mile square

16. Sue owns a 6-acre parcel that is 396 feet deep that she would like to subdivide and sell off as separate lots.  If she creates lots that are 60' × 44' and sells them for $20,000 apiece, how much money will she make?

    a.  $1,980,000

    b.  $5,280,000

    c.  $180,000

    d.  $133,333

17. A rural lot starts at the southwest corner of the intersection of Rural Route 8 and Old County Road. The northern property line follows RR-8 100 yards west, thence southeasterly 175 yards until it meets the western border of Old County Road, thence follows Old County Road northerly 432 feet until it meets the point of origin. How many acres is this parcel?

    a. 105

    b. 87

    c. 1.5

    d. 0.6

18. Beth is using the unit-in-place method on a newer home. She measures the foundation at 36'4" by 38'10". A contractor tells her that the cost of a foundation in the subject neighborhood is $18.63 per linear foot. What is the total cost of the foundation?

    a. $26,280

    b. $2,800

    c. $1,397

    d. $25,837

19. As part of his first farm appraisal, Sal must appraise a grain silo. From research and talking to local appraisers, he learns that the traditional method is the cubic foot method. After inspection, Sal concludes the following: It measures 41 feet tall and has a radius of 9 feet. The comparative unit is $15.00 per cubic foot, with a regional multiplier of 0.98. The silo has 90 years of economic life remaining on an expected life of 100 years. What is Sal's opinion of value for the silo?

    a. $138,000

    b. $48,800

    c. $44,000

    d. $15,300

For questions 20-26 use the following 3 bedroom/2 bath sample from Keokuk, Iowa.

| | |
|---|---|
| 8181 High St. | $15,000 |
| 122 Kenny St. | $103,000 |
| 211 Road Blvd. | $99,900 |
| 214 Burk Ln. | $67,500 |
| 706 Hazelnut Hwy. | $95,000 |
| 743 Eicher Way | $95,000 |
| 1031 N 26th Ave. | $66,000 |
| 2050 7th Ave. | $33,000 |
| 7107 Oceans Ave. | $74,900 |

20. What is the mean house price for a 3br/2ba home in Keokuk, IA?
    a. $72,144
    b. $74,900
    c. $88,000
    d. $95,000

21. What is the median house price for a 3br/2ba home in Keokuk, IA?
    a. $72,144
    b. $74,900
    c. $88,000
    d. $95,000

22. Which 3br/2ba home in Keokuk, IA is the mode?
    a. $72,144
    b. $74,900
    c. $88,000
    d. $95,000

23. What is the range of the sample of 3br/2ba homes in Keokuk, IA?
    a.  $72,144
    b.  $74,900
    c.  $88,000
    d.  $95,000

24. What is the average deviation of the sample population of 3br/2ba homes in Keokuk, IA?
    a.  $29,120
    b.  $103,000
    c.  $23,795
    d.  $87,361

25. What is the standard deviation of the sample population of 3br/2ba homes in Keokuk, IA?
    a.  $649,300
    b.  $30,886
    c.  $23,795
    d.  $29,120

# Appendix A
# *The Professional Appraiser*

## Introduction

Professional real estate appraisers specialize in estimating the value of property. They typically work in an office setting. However, they leave the office frequently to inspect properties. This involves walking around buildings, measuring, taking photos, and climbing stairs or crawling behind bushes as needed. Appraisers use their mathematical knowledge and communication skills when they are analyzing data and preparing their reports.

As mentioned previously, appraisals are needed in many different situations. This appendix covers some of the job opportunities and types of assignments that are available to the professional appraiser.

## Job Market

Lending institutions, government agencies, or small independent appraisal firms typically employ appraisers. It is also common for experienced appraisers to be self-employed.

Opportunities for appraisers can vary. The number of available assignments is highly dependent on interest rates and the general economic conditions that affect all types of real estate activity. Over the last several years, extremely low interest rates created an enormous demand for appraisals because of the increase in mortgage refinancing along with purchases of residential and commercial properties. In periods of high interest rates or economic difficulty, real estate activity usually drops and there are fewer assignments available. In general, government positions are less sensitive to economic fluctuations, but there are not many of these positions available.

An appraiser's license or certification level affects the job opportunities available to him or her. For almost any appraisal job, at least a trainee license is necessary. With more experience and higher certification, there are even more opportunities available.

# Opportunities for Trainees

As a trainee, you must work under a supervising appraiser. This affects the number of positions and assignments that are available to you. Many companies prefer appraisers who already have experience and can work independently.

To obtain a position with a government agency or a lending institution, a bachelor's degree is usually necessary. Some lending institutions will hire high school graduates if they have experience in related fields like real estate, construction, building inspection, or architecture.

Many companies provide training for their beginning appraisers. Due to licensing and certification requirements, as well as the need for competency, a long training period is usually necessary in order to become skilled at appraising more complex types of real estate.

When looking for a position, trainees can apply to companies with appraisal departments such as banks, savings and loan institutions, utility companies, and insurance companies. Professional associations often provide a place for job listings on their website or in their newsletter. Applicants can also look at civil service openings. In addition, numerous independent appraisal firms may have openings. These firms often do not advertise, so calling local appraisers is an important step for a trainee who is seeking employment. Additionally, you should be able to get local appraisers' business information from your state's appraisal agency. You can use this information to mail resumes with a cover letter.

# Salaried Positions

Lending institutions, government agencies, and the larger appraisal firms may offer salaried positions. The experience of coming up through the ranks as an employee of one of these organizations is good training for the beginning appraiser.

Employers of this type usually offer benefits including paid vacations, sick leave, holidays, retirement, and health plans. Some also offer discounted life insurance, profit-sharing plans, and paid education and association fees. Employers may also furnish a car or reimburse the appraiser for using his or her personal vehicle.

Salaried appraisers usually work a normal 40-hour week. However, evening and weekend work is often necessary during busy times.

Promotions depend primarily on the individual appraiser gaining advanced training and experience. Experienced appraisers in advanced positions take on more difficult appraisal assignments and are often expected to supervise beginning appraisers as well.

The most common appraisal assignment is to appraise a single-family residence for lending purposes (either a purchase money loan or a refinance). Most salaried appraisers spend the bulk of their time doing this type of work.

Experienced appraisers are also hired as reviewers or may perform review appraisals as part of their duties. **Review appraisers** develop opinions as to the quality of another appraiser's work and check for issues relating to property value. When performing appraisals day in and day out, it is easy to lose sight of the fact that tens of thousands, even millions of dollars, may be riding upon the value estimates of the subject property. It just makes good business sense to have another qualified appraiser double-check the original appraisal to make sure that no significant mistakes have been made. Sometimes reviews are cursory in nature while at other times the review may be much more in-depth.

Appraisers may also review other appraisers' work to ensure compliance with guidelines issued by government agencies, as well as USPAP compliance. Review appraisers are hired to examine reports where fraud is suspected. Lenders and attorneys are major sources for this kind of work.

Working for the city, county, or state government as an assessor is another opportunity for a salaried position. County assessors are responsible for determining the value of all real property and taxable personal property in order to distribute tax liabilities fairly to taxpayers in various districts. They may hire independent appraisers to assist them. On the other side, owners who are disputing what the assessor thinks their property is worth need to hire an appraiser to assist them.

## Independent Appraisers

After receiving training and achieving a certain level of licensure, many appraisers branch out on their own as independent, self-employed appraisers.

Unlike real estate brokers, appraisers do not work on commission. A real estate broker's role is to get the best possible price for his or her client, and the broker makes more money if he or she is successful in doing so. An appraiser's role is to be an independent, objective third party. Therefore, appraisers charge a set fee based on the difficulty of the assignment. This pay arrangement helps to ensure that appraisers will not value a property higher than its worth in order to make more money.

Independent appraisers experience many of the same advantages and disadvantages encountered by other small business owners and self-employed individuals. They do not have the benefit of company-paid vacation, sick time, etc. However, an independent appraiser can set his or her own schedule and can even base the office at home. The independent appraiser is the boss, accepting or rejecting assignments, deciding how far to travel, setting the fee schedule, choosing the equipment to use, and choosing the supporting service providers to employ.

Through continuing education requirements, the appraiser will experience many opportunities to expand his or her horizons within the industry. Some of the most valuable lessons will come because of experiences in the field. An appraiser will grow in knowledge and experience as he or she performs ever-increasingly complex assignments.

There are a wide variety of assignments that appraisers may accept or even specialize in. To run a successful appraisal business, it is important to learn what those assignments are and who offers them.

## Typical Assignments

Appraising single-family residences for lending purposes is the most typical appraisal assignment. The appraisal may be for a purchase money loan or for a refinance. Banks, savings and loans, credit unions, thrifts, mortgage bankers, and mortgage brokers are all sources for this type of assignment.

## Specialty Assignments

While most real estate appraisers choose to specialize in appraising single-family residential properties for lending purposes; there is a whole range of services that an appraiser may provide. Assignments not only differ according to the kind of property but also according to the valuation issues involved. Mortgage brokers, mortgage bankers, banks, thrifts, credit unions, government agencies, utility companies, insurance companies, attorneys, accountants, and property owners are just a few of the many clients needing the services of real estate appraisers.

An appraiser may decide to specialize in different types of property such as single-family homes, commercial buildings, condominiums, apartment buildings, shopping malls, industrial sites, oil fields, bridges, skyscrapers, or farms.  An appraiser may work locally or may elect to travel and accept specialized appraisal assignments in a number of states or even in other countries.

Appraisers who only appraise single-family houses for lenders are often very busy when interest rates are low.  Once interest rates climb, there is more competition for this type of assignment.  An appraiser who chooses a niche, such as appraising for litigation purposes, appraising easements and partial interests, or appraising special-use properties such as wineries, hotels, airports, or casinos can become practically indispensable.  Many of these niches are resistant to the up-and-down cycles associated with work for lenders.  Appraisers having the ability and expertise to appraise numerous kinds of properties, and to analyze those properties under various scenarios are in the greatest demand.

## Taxes

Appraisers are needed to determine the value of property for tax purposes.  Working as an assessor is typically a salaried position; however, owners who are disputing what the assessor thinks their property is worth need to hire an appraiser to assist them.

## Mortgage Insurance

**Private Mortgage Insurance (PMI)** is insurance required by conventional lenders and is paid for by a borrower to protect a lender against loss if a property is taken back through foreclosure.  PMI is typically required if the real estate loan is greater then 80% of a property's value.  In many instances, when the loan balance falls to less then 80% of a property's value, the PMI insurance policy may be cancelled.  Cancellation of the policy can save the borrower hundreds of dollars a month.  In these cases, appraisers are hired to establish the value of the real estate.  Homeowners and lenders are usually the source for this kind of assignment.

Similar to PMI, **Mutual Mortgage Insurance** (MMI) is a requirement for loans written under the Federal Housing Administration program (FHA).  MMI is charged by the FHA-approved lender and protects the lender in case of default by the borrower and is actually how the FHA funds its loan program.  In case of default, or when the borrower surpasses 20% equity in the property, an appraiser is hired to establish current value of the property in question.

## Hazard Insurance

When lending money to purchase a house, the lender typically requires that the house be insured against loss due to fire and other hazards. A fire insurance policy usually covers an amount not less than the loan on the house. In some cases, the insurance company may need an appraisal to determine the value of the improvements. If a fire does occur and there is damage to the property, both the homeowner and the insurance company may need to hire an appraiser if there is any disagreement about the dollar amount of the damage.

## Lawsuits

Attorneys hire appraisers when there are lawsuits involving real estate. Properties that are have been damaged physically, affected by external influences, or stigmatized, often need to be appraised to determine the amount of the loss. **Stigmatized** properties are ones that have a negative judgment about them, whether real or perceived. Estimating the loss in value, if any, due to construction defects, hazardous waste contamination, mold, asbestos, flood and fire damage, access rights, ownership and title issues, below market rents, or nearby noxious influences are just a few of the reasons properties may need to be appraised for legal purposes.

## Estate and Probate

In addition, appraisers are sometimes hired by estate attorneys to appraise a property for estate and probate purposes. **Probate** is the legal process to prove that a will is valid. Probate proceedings are held in the superior court to determine creditors' claims and beneficiaries' interest in an estate upon the owner's death.

## Condemnation

When the government chooses to exercise its right of eminent domain and condemn private property, the government must pay fair market value for the condemned property. **Eminent domain** is the right of government to take privately owned real property for some necessary public use. **Condemnation** is the act whereby private property is acquired by the governing authority. Appraisers determine the fair market value of the real estate involved. Real estate attorneys, as well as government agencies, utility companies, school districts, redevelopment agencies and other agencies having the power of eminent domain, are potential clients for this kind of work.

## Partial Interests

Sometimes properties have multiple owners, each of whom who have a partial interests in the ownership of that property. **Partial interest** include concurrent ownership, tenancy in common, joint tenancy, and easements, among others. The appraisal of these ownership interests may involve some very complex analysis. A property may be crossed by a roadway, driveway, hiking or other trails. If these are not owned by the same person who owns the remainder of the property, how does that affect value? Appraisers experienced and knowledgeable in these kinds of assignments are often in demand.

## Other Legal Issues

Other times, appraisers are asked to appraise properties when the owners are in the midst of a divorce and the courts need to determine how the real estate assets are to be divided. In many different types of cases, appraisers may be called upon to give expert testimony in court.

## Businesses

Oftentimes, appraisers choose to specialize in business-related appraisals. While most of these assignments go beyond just analyzing property value, the value of a business entity's properties comprises a significant portion of the business' worth.

### Net Worth

Business owners may need an appraisal of real property to establish his or her net worth for various business or investment purposes. Business owners may also need appraisals for income tax purposes. Therefore, accountants are another good potential source of business for the appraiser.

### Feasibility Analysis

Experienced appraisers may be called upon to act as consultants. For example, a developer may know that he can build a certain number of homes on his land but he wants to determine what kind of homes would maximize his profit. Would it make sense to build only three-bedroom homes in his development? Would it be more profitable if he were to build three, four, and five-bedroom homes? Should the homes be 1,500 to 2,200 square feet in size, or should he build homes ranging from 2,800 square feet to 3,500 square feet in size? The developer also needs to know what base price to ask for each of the individual homes he is building. Appraisers performing consulting services are often in high demand.

### *Miscellaneous*

Bail bondsmen are also potential clients. When posting bail, real property is often pledged as security for the bond, and value must be established. In serving the needs of bail bondsmen, time is of the essence.

## Professional Appraisal Organizations

Affiliation with one or more of the professional appraisal trade associations is a way for appraisers to find employment, gain knowledge and expertise, keep up with changes in the profession, and network with fellow appraisers. Professional associations offer seminars and classes conducted by leaders in the field.

There are a wide variety of professional associations ranging from large organizations like the Appraisal Institute, the National Association of Real Estate Appraisers, the Foundation of Real Estate Appraisers, and the American Society of Appraisers to specialized groups like the American Society of Farm Managers and Rural Appraisers, the International Association of Assessing Officers, and the Association of Online Appraisers.

# Technology

Professional appraisers also need to understand the importance of technology. The field of appraisal has always been on the cutting edge of technology. This was brought about by the necessity of gathering information from the marketplace quickly and efficiently, and transmitting that information to clients rapidly and in an easy-to-understand format.

## Office Tools

Appraisal offices may be located in office buildings but often they are located within the appraiser's home. Many appraisers who are employees of institutional lenders or large appraisal firms "telecommute" from their homes. Few industries can offer the freedom to set your own hours or work in your pajamas! The appraisal profession is well-suited to telecommuting and it is one of the many reasons people are drawn to this industry. The following tools are items any appraiser needs to consider when setting up an office.

## Computer and Peripherals

Starting mostly in the early 1980s, the personal computer has been adopted by the appraisal industry and has significantly changed the way real estate appraisers perform their job. Advances in technology, software, data sources, and the Internet have given appraisers tools to aid in the analysis and preparation of reports.

### *Software*

Virtually all appraisers rely upon software of some kind to help in generating their appraisal reports. Before choosing a computer, it is important to know what software you expect to use on that computer.

Appraisers specializing in residential appraising for lenders have many options available to them. Companies such as alamode (www.alamode.com), ACI (www.appraiserschoice.com), Bradford Technologies (www.bradfordsoftware.com), Day 1 Software (www.day1.com), Software for Real Estate Professionals (www.sfrep.com), and Homeputer (www.homeputer.com), all provide software used by appraisers for generating residential real estate appraisal reports. For additional fees, most of these companies offer their software bundled with additional features such as sketch processors, mapping options, and electronic data interchange (EDI) capabilities for electronically transmitting reports.

Specialized software geared to the needs of commercial appraisers is also available.

All appraisers should have good word processor software such as Microsoft Word®, Lotus Word Pro®, or WordPerfect® by Corel. Additionally, spreadsheet applications such as Microsoft Excel®, Corel QuatroPro®, and Lotus 1-2-3® are useful to appraisers. If the appraiser is working independently, bookkeeping and accounting software such as Quicken® or QuickBooks® is needed.

While there are literally hundreds of other software options available to appraisers, the software programs listed above are usually enough to get an office started.

## Hardware

For appraisers, the next step in choosing a computer is deciding how they want to work. Most appraisers use desktop computers in their offices. Some appraisers prefer the mobility of a laptop computer. Many appraisers end up having both kinds in order to have the flexibility to work in the most productive manner under any given circumstance.

Most appraisers choose Personal Computers (PCs) since the overwhelming majority of appraisal software is designed to run on PC systems (apologies to Macintosh® fans). When buying a computer for an appraisal office, appraisers often find it worthwhile to buy a system with the fastest processor and the highest capacity hard drive they can afford. They find that, though it is more expensive to purchase computers this way, these kinds of machines will last longer before newer technology or updated software makes the system obsolete.

Computers in appraisal offices should be equipped with an effective back-up system. Currently, CD-ROM burners, and Flash and Jump Drives seem to be the best way to back up appraisals, photos, and other files. In the past, other storage media such as tape back-ups, floppy disks, and Zip disks have been used.

Since appraisers spend hours looking at their computer monitors, quality is important in this area also. A large screen with a clear image is easier on the eyes, so it is usually a worthwhile investment.

## Printer

A reliable, high capacity printer is one of the most important pieces of equipment in an appraiser's office. The printing capabilities in an office are extremely important as appraisers generate many printouts when researching market data.

The properly equipped appraisal office should also have the ability to generate color pages for use in appraisal reports. Most clients require color photographs when they receive printed copies of a report. Since most photographs used in appraisal reports are now digitally generated, a good-quality color printer is necessary.

## Internet Access

If it is available, high-speed Internet access is a must. Appraisers today rely heavily upon the Internet. Advanced software applications now allow the appraiser to accept, complete, and submit appraisal assignments on-line.

Many providers of real estate data have online capabilities, sometimes with the ability to download information directly into a report. Sales and listing information, demographic information, title information, assessor's and zoning data are available for many areas nowadays through the Internet. Maps such as topographic, zoning, street, flood, and assessor's plat maps are often obtained online as well. Photographic resources showing sales, as well as aerial and satellite photos, can also be obtained through the Internet as well. Highly integrated geographic information systems (GIS) are becoming more and more common allowing an appraiser to research a vast amount of information in one location on the web.

In order to speed up the process, many clients currently request the appraiser to transmit appraisals over the Internet electronically. Some electronic appraisal report files can be quite large and transmitting these files over dial-up services is often just too slow. DSL, cable-based, and some satellite Internet providers work well for appraisers.

## Phone System

Another of the most important items in an appraisal office, and one that is often given little thought, is the office phone system. It is vital that an appraiser have a reliable phone system that includes a good message retrieval system.

For small appraisal offices, the answering system can aid in presenting a professional appearance to all callers. Easy retrieval of voice messages is important for the success of an appraisal firm.

A call-waiting option on a phone line may cause annoying interruptions to what may be an important call. A busy call-forwarding option is available from most telephone companies and alleviates the nuisance of being interrupted in the middle of a conversation.

## Other Office Machines

Appraisal request forms are often faxed to appraisers. In fact, a good portion of the appraiser's business is transacted over fax machines, so appraisal offices need some kind of fax capability. Some appraisers prefer a stand-alone fax machine. Other appraisers prefer to use the fax capabilities of their PC.

Additionally, the appraisal office should have a flatbed scanner in order to scan information to be included in reports. A scanner is also necessary if you plan to use the computer to send faxes.

# Field Tools

Since appraisers must frequently leave the office to inspect properties, there are other tools they also need.

## Camera

In the process of performing appraisals, the appraiser takes photos of both the subject property and the comparable properties used in the report. Photos of other salient items, such as views, pools, and upgrades are taken during the inspection of the subject.

In the past, appraisers took Polaroid® photos that were included in the report. While this was an easy way to take pictures, it was expensive and cumbersome. The Polaroid photos eventually gave way to 35mm photography, a less burdensome and cheaper way to take photos, but development costs were still high. In addition to the cost of the film, there were the added burdens of finding some place to develop the film, making sure to get the proper number of prints, and keeping track of the negatives. Sometimes, a photo did not turn out necessitating a return to the subject or comparable sale to take another photo.

With the advent of digital photography, appraisers were in the position to take and store many more photos than ever. With no film developing costs and the ability to instantly preview photos while still at the property, digital photography quickly became the standard in the industry. Additionally, with the low cost of digital storage media, the cost-per-photo has become minuscule. A good quality, rugged, digital camera is a necessary item in an appraiser's set of tools.

With a digital camera, the appraiser either plugs the camera into a USB port at the rear of the hard drive, or extracts some sort of removable storage media from the camera, such as a CompactFlash™ card. Then, the photos can be downloaded into any particular appraisal file and included on the appropriate pages of the appraisal report. They can be transmitted electronically with the appraisal report as simply as sending an e-mail, and the photo card is reusable for the next appraisal.

## Measuring Devices

Appraisers, especially residential appraisers, are often required to measure the size of the buildings on a property to determine the total size of the improvements. The appraiser needs to have some kind of measuring device to use when inspecting properties.

Historically, appraisers used measuring tapes ranging from 50' to 100' in length. Some appraisers prefer to use a type of rolling-wheel measuring device that measure distances when rolled along the ground. There are also some inexpensive electronic measuring devices that rely upon reflected sound to estimate distances. While these items are all still in widespread use, appraisers are beginning to use a more high tech way to measure properties.

There are currently devices available that use laser beams to measure distances. While these devices are much more expensive than the other options, they are extremely accurate, and in many situations save the appraiser significant amounts of time when measuring a property.

## Hand-Held Devices

One of the latest trends is for appraisers to start using portable hand-held electronic devices, such as hand-held computers, Personal Digital Assistants (PDAs), or tablet computers to input information directly into an appraisal program while in the field.

In years past, an appraiser took all his or her field notes on a tablet of paper attached to a clipboard. Once the appraiser returned to the office, he would then manually enter the information into the computer program. These hand-held devices eliminate the step of manually writing down the information and re-entering it into the computer later.

Some of these devices are equipped with digital cameras where the photos are instantly sorted, labeled, and stored. Look for the use of these small electronic devices to become more widespread in the future.

# Summary

Once licensed, an appraiser has multiple career options from which to choose. While lender-based residential work dominates the appraisal landscape, there certainly are many more specialties to consider.

Appraisers can strive to gain higher classes of license, which would legally permit them to appraise higher-priced properties and/or specialized properties. Additionally, if an appraiser chooses, he or she can join any of the different appraisal organizations that grant their own designations, most of which are recognized by potential employers.

Whichever path an appraiser chooses to follow, education and experience will ease the way. Check with your local state appraisal office to find out your state's specific minimum education and licensing requirements.

Whichever niche an appraiser carves out for himself, he will need to be familiar with appraisal-related software as well as more general programs like word processors and spreadsheets. Other tools are requisite for the diligent appraiser as well, including a digital camera and measuring device.

# Appendix B

# Answer Key

## Chapter 1 – The Appraisal Industry

### Answers – Matching

| | | | | | | | |
|---|---|---|---|---|---|---|---|
| 1. | E | 5. | U | 9. | C | 13. | S |
| 2. | B | 6. | L | 10. | P | 14. | D |
| 3. | G | 7. | M | 11. | K | 15. | F |
| 4. | O | 8. | T | 12. | J | | |

### Answers – Multiple Choice

1. (c) An appraisal is an unbiased estimate or opinion of a specific property's value on a given date. The work done by an appraiser is called appraisal. An appraiser is a person who is expected to value property in a competent, objective, and impartial manner. Page 2

2. (a) Lenders need to be sure that the value of the real estate being used as collateral for a loan is enough to cover the amount of the loan and thus protect investors. Page 3

3. (d) A prospective appraisal looks at the value of a property at a future point in time. For example, a lender who is providing a construction loan might ask an appraiser to determine if houses should be built for sale in a particular area. Part of the appraiser's work would be to value the houses as if they were finished. Page 4

4. (b) Cost represents expenses in money, labor, material, or sacrifices in acquiring or producing something. Remember that the cost or price of a property is not always the same as its value. Page 5

5. (b) The eight U.S.-based appraisal associations that had helped create USPAP founded a private, non-profit organization called The Appraisal Foundation (TAF). The Appraisal Foundation includes two independent boards: the Appraiser Qualifications Board (AQB) and the Appraiser Standards Board (ASB). Page 7

6. (b) In examining the causes and consequences of the S& Loan Crisis, many of the loans that defaulted were based on inflated real estate values. In some cases, this overvaluation was due to appraiser incompetence or as a result of appraisers yielding to pressure from lenders to manufacture values high enough to make the loan work. Page 8

7.  (c)   The Appraisal Subcommittee's mission is to ensure that real estate appraisers are sufficiently trained and tested since real estate appraisers play such an important role in the economy.  Page 10

8.  (c)   Most states have the following four levels of real estate appraiser licensing: Trainee License, Residential License, Certified Residential, and Certified General.  No states have a "certified trainee" level.  Page 11

9.  (d)   Although each state may vary somewhat in what is required for different license levels, no state that has a trainee license requires experience in order to obtain that license.  Pages 11 & 12

10.  (d)   Starting January 1, 2008, 300 hours of education along with a bachelor's degree or 30 units in specified college courses is the required education for the Certified General level.  Page 13

# Chapter 2 – Real Property Concepts and Characteristics

## Answers – Matching

| | | | |
|---|---|---|---|
| 1.  C | 5.  A | 9.  O | 13.  K |
| 2.  M | 6.  L | 10.  U | |
| 3.  E | 7.  F | 11.  T | |
| 4.  D | 8.  B | 12.  J | |

## Answers – Multiple Choice

1.  (d)   Property rights are the rights someone has in something and are known as the bundle of rights.  This important package includes the right to own, possess, use, enjoy, borrow against, and dispose of real property.  Page 22

2.  (d)   Real property includes four things: the land, anything permanently attached to the land, anything appurtenant to the land, and anything immovable by law. Airspace is a part of the land, and the land is part of real property.  However, choice d. is the most correct.  Page 22

3.  (c)   Land includes airspace, surface rights, mineral rights, and water rights.  Riparian rights are a type of water right.  Page 23

4.  (b)   The owner of property bordering a stream or river has riparian rights.  Owners of land bordering a lake possess littoral rights.  Page 23

5.  (c)   Any growing thing attached by roots (trees, shrubs, and flowers) are real property and established trees are considered immovable by law.  By definition, a fixture is real property that used to be personal property.  When the nursery sold the tree sapling, it was personal property at that time, but became a fixture once it was planted.  Page 24

6.  (b)   Crops ready for harvest are emblements and are personal property.  Page 24

7.  (a)   The sprinklers are permanently attached and custom-made for the property. There is no expressed intention or clear agreement that the tenants would take the sprinklers, so they are real property.  When tenants move out, they take personal property with them.  Real property remains with the landlord.  Page 27

8.  (a)  Each section is one mile by one mile and contains 640 acres. 640 acres times ¼ times ½ times ½ = 40 acres.  Pages 31 – 32

9.  (b)  A metes and bounds description of land delineates boundaries and measures distances between landmarks like trees, boulders, creeks, fences, etc.  This method describes the dimensions of the property as measured by distance and direction.  Page 34

10.  (d)  The Recorded Map System is another name for the Lot and Block system and is most common in metropolitan areas.  Page 28

# Chapter 3 – Legal Considerations in Appraisal

## Answers – Matching

| | | | | | | | |
|---|---|---|---|---|---|---|---|
| 1. | T | 11. | NN | 21. | N | 31. | E |
| 2. | B | 12. | CC | 22. | P | 32. | I |
| 3. | X | 13. | H | 23. | KK | 33. | MM |
| 4. | FF | 14. | LL | 24. | XX | 34. | GG |
| 5. | DD | 15. | Q | 25. | F | 35. | Y |
| 6. | II | 16. | EE | 26. | TT | 36. | K |
| 7. | R | 17. | G | 27. | WW | 37. | BB |
| 8. | PP | 18. | L | 28. | AA | 38. | RR |
| 9. | JJ | 19. | M | 29. | S | 39. | U |
| 10. | D | 20. | OO | 30. | O | 40. | VV |

## Answers – Multiple Choice

1.  (a)  Since an owner of a fee simple estate may dispose of it in his or her lifetime or after death by will, it is also known as an estate of inheritance or a perpetual estate.  Pages 42 – 43

2.  (c)  A fee simple qualified estate is a fee simple estate with conditions that control certain aspects of the owners' use of the property.  If the owners violate these conditions, they will lose title to the property, based on a forfeiture clause in the granting of title.  Page 43

3.  (b)  A life estate is one that is limited in duration to the life of its owner or the life of another designated person.  Page 43

4.  (c)  A less-than-freehold estate is an estate owned by a tenant who rents real property.  Page 42

5.  (b)  The owner of the leasehold estate (the lessee) has exclusive possession and use of the rented property for a fixed period of time.  Page 44

6.  (d)  When there is no written agreement between the landlord and tenant, the tenancy is known as an estate at will.  There is no agreed-upon termination date and either party must give 30 days notice before ending the tenancy.  Page 45

7.  (d)  A triple-net lease, also known as a net-net-net lease or absolute-net lease, indicates the tenant is paying rent and virtually all of the expenses.  Page 46

8. (a) $3,217 - $2,500 = $717.
$717 \times .08$ (8%) = $57.36 overage rent.
$57.36 + $900 = $957.36. Page 46

9. (c) Tenancy in common allows a tenant to will his or her share. Due to the right of survivorship, a joint tenant may not will his or her share. Ownership in severalty is not concurrent ownership. Common interest developments are a special ownership form that blends concurrent and separate ownership. Pages 47 – 48

10. (c) A joint tenant may sever his or her interest in the joint tenancy by selling it. The new co-owner would become a tenant in common with the remaining joint tenants. Pages 48 – 49

11. (a) Income derived from separate property is considered separate income. If separate income is used to purchase property, that property is also separate property. Page 50

12. (c) In an undivided interest, the land itself is not divided but the ownership is. The buyer receives an undivided interest in a parcel of land as a tenant in common with all the other owners. All owners have the nonexclusive right to the use and occupancy of the property. A recreational vehicle park with campground and other leisure-time amenities is an example. Page 51

13. (a) An encumbrance is an interest in real property that is held by someone who is not the owner. Page 53

14. (d) Any lien is considered an encumbrance. A specific lien is one that is placed against a certain property, such as a trust deed or mortgage. Trust deeds and mortgages are also voluntary liens. Page 53-54

15. (b) A non-money encumbrance is one that affects the use of property such as an easement, a building restriction, an encroachment, or a lease. Page 55

16. (d) Restrictions are known as CC&Rs (covenants, conditions, and restrictions). Page 55

17. (c) A condition precedent requires that a certain event, or condition, occur before title can pass to the new owner. It is a condition that must be taken care of preceding the transaction. Page 56

18. (b) The servient tenement is the land one person owns that is being used by someone else. The servient tenement is encumbered by the easement. The other person's land receives the benefit of the easement and is known as the dominant tenement. Page 57

19. (b) Easements not appurtenant to a specific parcel are known as easements in gross. Typically, these are owned by utility companies. Page 58

20. (b) Police power is the authority of the state to enact laws within constitutional limits to promote the order, safety, health, morals, and general welfare of our society. Page 59

21. (a) Rezoning an area can create nonconforming uses. Page 61

22. (b) Aesthetic zoning is zoning that is used to regulate the appearance of buildings in the area. Page 62

23. (a) A quitclaim deed contains no warranties and transfers any interest the grantor may have at the time the deed is signed. Page 63

24. (d)  Condemnation is the process by which the government acquires private property for public use, under its right of eminent domain.  Page 66

25. (c)  In order for a contract to be legally binding and enforceable, there are four requirements: (1) legally competent parties, (2) mutual consent between the parties, (3) lawful objective, and (4) sufficient consideration.  Page 67

26. (d)  Parties entering into a contract must have legal capacity.  To be considered legally competent, a person must be at least 18 years of age (unless married, in the military, or declared emancipated by the court).  When it has been determined judicially that a person is not of sound mind, that person is not considered legally competent.  Someone who is intoxicated or under the influence of legal or illegal drugs is not considered legally competent at that time.  Pages 67 – 68

27. (b)  Any person may give another the authority to act on his or her behalf.  The legal document that does this is called a power of attorney.  The person holding the power of attorney is an attorney-in-fact.  Page 68

28. (b)  When the person unknowingly provides wrong information, innocent misrepresentation occurs.  Even though no dishonesty is involved, a contract may be rescinded or revoked by the party who feels misled.  Page 69

29. (d)  Mutual rescission occurs when all parties to a contract agree to cancel the agreement.  Page 73

30. (d)  Generally, when using preprinted forms: specific information takes precedence over general information; typed clauses and insertions take precedence over the pre-printed material; and handwritten clauses and insertions take precedence over the typed and pre-printed material.  Page 71

# Chapter 4 – Value and Economic Principles

## Answers – Matching

| | | | |
|---|---|---|---|
| 1.  X | 6.  L | 11.  B | 16.  Q |
| 2.  V | 7.  W | 12.  T | 17.  G |
| 3.  R | 8.  S | 13.  U | 18.  K |
| 4.  J | 9.  Y | 14.  N | 19.  M |
| 5.  C | 10.  H | 15.  F | 20.  A |

## Answers – Multiple Choice

1. (d)  The four elements that create value are "DUST": demand, utility, scarcity, and transferability.  Page 87

2. (a)  Demand is the desire OR the ability to purchase a commodity.  Effective demand implies possession of both.  Page 87

3. (b)  While this particular property may be missing other elements that create value, from the information provided, its utility is negatively impacted by the contamination.  Page 88

4.  (c)   Assemblage is the act of putting several smaller, less valuable parcels together under one ownership interest so that the value of the combined parcels may increase.  Page 94

5.  (b)   A lot that contains 2,500 square feet and is 50 feet deep has a width of 50 feet. (2,500 square feet ÷ 50 feet = 50 feet).  Front foot is the width of a property along a street or other boundary, and is most widely used as a measurement for properties located on beaches and lakeshores.  $850,000 ÷ 50 feet = $17,000. Page 91

6.  (d)   The south and west sides of business streets are usually preferred by shopkeepers because customers will seek the shady side of the street and window displays will not be damaged by the sun.  Page 91

7.  (c)   An unearned increment is a term used in real estate appraisal to indicate that an increase in value was not the result of anything the owner did.  Factors like inflation, in the economy or just in the regional or local real estate market, can cause an increase in value.  Page 96

8.  (a)   A stigma is a lingering effect in the minds of people regarding the desirability or usefulness of a property, whether real or imagined.  Page 101

9.  (b)   Price is the amount a purchaser agrees to pay and a seller agrees to accept under the circumstances surrounding their transaction.  Page 86

10. (a)   When appraisers indicate the value of property, they are usually indicating an estimate of its monetary worth.  Page 86

11. (d)   By definition, value is the price an object or service would bring in a fair, open market.  Pages 86 & 102

12. (d)   An arm's-length transaction refers to a transaction where all parties involved are knowledgeable, acting in their own self-interest, and are under no undue influence or pressure from other parties.  Page 103

13. (a)   The overwhelming majority of appraisals performed are concerned with estimating the market value of a property, which is the same as its value in exchange.  Page 101

14. (a)   The principle of substitution is the foundation for all of the appraisal process. Page 109

15. (b)   Increasing supply or decreasing demand will reduce the price in the market. Reducing supply or increasing demand will raise the price in the market.  Page 109

16. (b)   Opportunity cost is the highest valued alternative investment that was NOT chosen.  Page 110

17. (c)   Progression and regression only affect properties of the same type.  Leonard's mansion is clearly defiant of the principle of conformity, which holds that when land uses are compatible and homes are similar in design and size, the maximum value is realized.  Page 110

18. (d)   The principle of contribution is the concept that the worth of a particular component is calculated in terms of its contribution to the value of the whole property, or as the amount that its absence would detract from the value of the whole.  Page 113

19. (a)  The four agents of production (land, labor, capital, and management) may be increased in varying amounts to increase the value and/or income attributable to a property.  Page 114

20. (c)  Property goes through four distinct changes called a neighborhood lifecycle: Growth, Stability, Decline, and Revitalization.  Page 112

# Chapter 5 – Real Estate Markets and Analysis

## Answers – Matching

| | | | |
|---|---|---|---|
| 1.  Z | 8.  M | 15.  CC | 22.  R |
| 2.  O | 9.  F | 16.  C | 23.  L |
| 3.  HH | 10.  S | 17.  B | 24.  A |
| 4.  GG | 11.  E | 18.  T | 25.  J |
| 5.  X | 12.  Y | 19.  W | |
| 6.  AA | 13.  P | 20.  I | |
| 7.  N | 14.  U | 21.  H | |

## Answers – Multiple Choice

1. (c)  The Federal Reserve System is the central bank of the United States.  It is an independent banking system designed to manage money and credit and to promote orderly growth in the economy.  Page 125

2. (c)  A trust is a legal arrangement in which the trustor gives fiduciary control of property to the trustee who holds title on behalf of the beneficiary.  Page 126

3. (d)  Partnerships are arrangements in which two or more partners jointly own an asset and share in any profits or losses.  General and limited partnerships are the two types of typical partnerships.  The limited partners have a passive role and their liability is limited only to the amount of capital invested.  Page 127

4. (b)  Typically, equity investors are active in the management of real estate.  They have an ownership interest, and assume a relatively higher risk.  Debt investors have a relatively passive role in the operation and management of the real estate.  They seek conservative investments, with relatively little risk.  Pages 126 & 128

5. (a)  Mortgage brokers bring together borrowers and lenders.  Mortgage brokers usually do not have the money themselves to fund the loans, but serve as facilitators in that they find the borrower(s), process the application, and submit the loan package to a wholesale lender who ultimately makes the loan.  Page 130

6. (a)  Low-risk investments typically provide a lower yield to the investor than high-risk investments.  Page 133

7. (d)  Government-issued bonds are considered very safe investments since they have the backing of the government entity issuing the bond.  The CD is backed by the credit of the issuing lending institution and is usually insured by the FDIC, which makes these kinds of deposits very secure.  U.S. Treasury Bills have the full faith and credit of the U.S. government.  Therefore, they are considered a very safe investment as well.  Page 135

8. (b)  The fee for renting money is called interest and the amount borrowed is called the principal.  Page 137

9. (d) The trustee (neutral third party) holds the trust deed as security for payment of a debt on behalf of the beneficiary (lender). The trustor (borrower) has equitable title and the trustee has bare or naked legal title to the property. Page 138

10. (c) The two parties in a mortgage are mortgagor (borrower) and mortgagee (lender). The three parties in a trust deed are trustor (borrower), beneficiary (lender), and trustee (neutral third party). Unlike a trust deed, under a mortgage both title and possession remain with the borrower. Page 139

11. (d) When the borrower makes lower payments than what should be made on a fully amortized loan, negative amortization occurs. The difference between what should be paid and what is actually paid is added to the principal balance of the loan causing the principal to increase. Page 140

12. (c) A balloon payment is the single, large payment that pays the remaining balance due. It is much larger than the previous payments because it includes all of the remaining principal and interest. This type of repayment schedule may have extra risks because the borrower may not be able to pay the balloon payment and may need to refinance the property, possibly at a higher rate. Page 142

13. (c) When the loan exceeds 80% of the value of the property, lenders usually require private mortgage insurance (PMI) on conventional loans. This means Jane will have to pay a 20% down payment of $67,000 in order to avoid PMI. Page 144

14. (a) Conforming loans have terms and conditions that follow the guidelines set forth by Fannie Mae and Freddie Mac and are called "A" paper loans, or prime loans. Page 144

15. (c) Appraisers are reprimanded if they do not use FHA guidelines when preparing appraisals for FHA loans. If an appraiser intentionally misrepresents the subject property's value on an FHA loan appraisal, and the inaccurate appraisal subsequently causes a loss, the appraiser could be fined and face legal action. Page 146

16. (a) The Federal National Mortgage Association (FNMA), the Federal Home Loan Mortgage Corporation (FHLMC), the Government National Mortgage Association (GNMA), and the Federal Agricultural Mortgage Corporation, are among the major organizations operating in the secondary market. The Federal Housing Administration (FHA) insures mortgages, but does not purchase them. Pages 131 & 146

17. (d) Some of the causes of these inefficiencies include: the unique nature of real property, its illiquidity, uninformed buyers and sellers, its relatively high cost, the immobile nature of real estate, and the inflexible supply of real estate. Page 150

18. (a) The five broad categories of real estate markets are residential, commercial, industrial, agricultural, and special-purpose. Page 152

19. (b) Real estate is not liquid, which means that real estate assets cannot be quickly sold for full market value. Page 155

20. (b) Between the two phases, there are 60 more units to sell.
    Year 1 sold 60 units.
    Year 2 will sell 40 units (two-thirds of 60), and
    Year 3 will sell the last 20 units (two-thirds of 40 is 26.67).
    So, it will take approximately two more years to sell the remaining 60 units.
    Page 158

# *Chapter 6 – Ethical Appraisal Practice*

## Answers – Matching

| | | | |
|---|---|---|---|
| 1. O | 4. L | 7. I | 10. D |
| 2. C | 5. K | 8. F | |
| 3. M | 6. A | 9. H | |

## Answers – Multiple Choice

1. (b)  Currently the USPAP document contains the Definitions, Preamble, Rules, Standards, Standards Rules, Comments, and Statements on Appraisal Standards.  In addition, the USPAP document also includes the Advisory Opinions (AOs), but these are not technically part of USPAP.  Page 168

2. (a)  The three sections precede the Standards because the information is  relevant and required for understanding and following the Standards.  Page 168

3. (b)  When USPAP was developed, its creators decided to encompass all appraisal disciplines, but Standards 1 & 2 are the ones that a beginning real estate appraiser will need to use.  Page 169

4. (c)  Advisory Opinions are issued to illustrate the applicability of Standards in specific situations and to offer advice from the ASB for the resolution of appraisal issues and problems; they are for guidance only and are not considered an integral part of USPAP.  Page 170

5. (b)  Real Property Appraisal          (Standards 1 and 2)
          Appraisal Review                  (Standard 3)
          Appraisal Consulting            (Standards 4 and 5)
          Mass Appraisal                    (Standard 6)
          Personal Property Appraisal  (Standards 7 and 8)
          Business Appraisal              (Standards 9 and 10)
          Pages 170 – 174

6. (c)  When reporting a real estate appraisal, the appraiser must "clearly and accurately set forth the appraisal in a manner that will not be misleading". Page 171

7. (a)  In addition to the rules that govern report clarity and content, Standard 2 also provides three reporting options: Self-Contained, Summary, and Restricted Use.  Page 171

8. (d)  Standard 3 gives the review appraiser the option to develop his or her own value opinion based on the information in the original workfile.  However, once the appraiser does this, the assignment becomes two-fold: a new appraisal as well as a review assignment, producing two reports.  Page 173

9. (d)  Personal property includes all tangible assets that are not real property, such as jewelry, autos, boats, etc.  The appraiser must be fully competent in the type of property he or she is appraising, or take the steps necessary to gain competency.  Pages 174 & 177

10. (c)  Nora is appraising the building — not the intangible assets of the business such as a logo or copyright.  This assignment is a real property appraisal.  Page 174

11. (d)  The Ethics Rule is divided into four sections: Conduct, Management, Confidentiality, and Record Keeping.  Page 175

12. (d)  The Conduct section forbids an appraiser to act as an advocate.  Many appraisers are also real estate salespeople, real estate brokers, lawyers, etc. and are required to be advocates as part of their non-appraisal duties.  Advocacy is acceptable within those roles.  Page 175

13. (b)  The Management section prohibits accepting an assignment where the fee is contingent on a predetermined or future result.  Page 175

14. (d)  An appraiser must keep his workfiles for at least five years or two years after final disposition of any judicial proceeding involving the file.  Page 176

15. (c)  Some of the most common fraud schemes include flipping, packed sales, bogus sales, and lender pressure.  Pages 181 – 183

# Chapter 7 – Valuation Process

## Answers – Matching

| | | | | | | | |
|---|---|---|---|---|---|---|---|
| 1. | A | 6. | U | 11. | J | 16. | I |
| 2. | X | 7. | E | 12. | T | 17. | P |
| 3. | Y | 8. | W | 13. | F | 18. | R |
| 4. | V | 9. | Q | 14. | B | | |
| 5. | M | 10. | L | 15. | H | | |

## Answers – Multiple Choice

1. (c)  Valuation services are services that pertain to some aspect of property value whether those services are performed by an appraiser or by someone else. A competitive market analysis is a comparison analysis that real estate brokers use to help determine an appropriate listing price for the seller's house and are also known as Broker Price Opinion.  Although they appear similar on the surface, there are many differences between a competitive market analysis and an appraisal report, mainly that appraisals follow more stringent guidelines.  Pages 194 – 195

2. (a)  If there are any significant differences between the seller's house and the comps, the broker adjusts the selling prices of those properties to derive a market value range and an appropriate list price for the house.  Page 195

3. (d)  In a CMA, which is also referred to as a Broker Price Opinion (BPO), brokers collect and analyze data, apply a version of the sales comparison approach, and report the results to their client.  Page 194

4. (b)  If a house is priced significantly higher than its appraised value, it can be very difficult to get a loan, since lenders do not want to lend on a house that is priced higher than it is worth.  A buyer should think twice before purchasing a home if its price is higher than its appraised value.  Page 196

5. (c)  The step called "define the problem" includes identifying the client and other intended users, the type and definition of the value sought, and the effective date of the appraiser's opinions and conclusions, among others.  Page 196

6. (a)  When collecting and analyzing information, appraisers gather general data including social, economic, physical, or governmental forces that may impact the value sought.  Page 196

7. (d) Often clients order an appraisal with the intention that other parties will rely upon the report generated by the appraiser. Parties intending to use an appraisal are called intended users by USPAP. Page 198

8. (b) In most instances, the effective date of an appraisal is the date of inspection. In some instances however, the date of value is at some point in the past, which makes it a retrospective appraisal. Page 200

9. (c) A prospective appraisal looks at the value of a property at a future point of time. Page 200

10. (d) A hypothetical condition is that which is contrary to what exists but is supposed for the purpose of analysis, which is what Jaime is doing for the purpose of this insurance appraisal. Also, a hypothetical condition is a type of limiting condition. Since she is appraising the property as it was before it burnt down, this also becomes a retrospective appraisal. Page 201

11. (a) Sometimes, information obtained from one data provider conflicts with data obtained from another source. Appraisers need to determine which data sources are the most reliable and deserve more credence. Page 206

12. (d) When choosing comparable properties for analysis, select comps that are arm's-length transactions because non-arm's-length transactions do not truly reflect the market. Also, select properties that are as similar to the subject as possible to minimize the need for adjustments. Page 207

13. (b) The cost approach is used most often to appraise new buildings and special-purpose or unique structures. A post office, library, and hospital are all classified as special-purpose and famous architectural buildings are considered unique. Page 210

14. (c) Two simple calculations are the basis of the income approach: (1) Gross Income $\times$ Gross Income Multiplier = Value and (2) Net Operating Income $\div$ Capitalization Rate = Value. Page 211

15. (a) Though the definition of reconciliation refers to the analyzing of the three value approaches, it also includes revisiting the scope of work, the quantity and quality of the data collected in each approach, the inherent strengths and weaknesses of each approach, and the relevance of each approach to the subject property and market behavior. These steps should be taken in every assignment even if only one approach is used. Page 212

# Chapter 8 – Highest and Best Use and Site Valuation

## Answers – Matching

| | | | |
|---|---|---|---|
| 1. H | 5. B | 9. C | 13. K |
| 2. N | 6. A | 10. F | 14. E |
| 3. Q | 7. L | 11. G | 15. J |
| 4. R | 8. P | 12. T | |

## Answers – Multiple Choice

1. (a) The highest and best use of a property, more than anything else, is what determines its value.  Page 222

2. (b) Highest and best use is defined as the use, from among reasonably probable and adequately supported alternative uses, that meets these four factors: physically possible, legally permitted, financially feasible, and maximally productive. "Most profitable" implies both financial feasibility and maximal productivity. Page 222

3. (c) Legally-permitted uses are normally defined by current zoning and other land use regulations.  An area zoned for residential use would not typically permit a business use.  Page 225

4. (b) Gas station sites are contaminated and therefore cultivating any type of crop is physically impossible without expensive soil cleaning.  Page 229

5. (c) An interior lot is surrounded by other lots, with frontage on the street.  It is the most common type of lot and may or may not be desirable, depending on other factors.  Page 233

6. (c) A site is a piece of land that either has been built on already or is ready to build on.  Page 230

7. (c) Assemblage is the process of combining two or more small sites into a larger one. The added value that results from this process is called plottage value.  Page 232

8. (a) A retaining wall is an on-site improvement.  While aspects of the other choices may exist on-site, their origins are off-site, and therefore they are classified as off-site improvements.  Page 235

9. (d) Ingress (access to the property) or egress (exit from the property) as well as noise and air pollution most likely will be negatively affected by heavy traffic volume.  Page 238

10. (a) Most zoning ordinances allow the local zoning authority to issue conditional use permits or variances, which permit certain uses that are not otherwise allowed in a certain zoning district, but which are beneficial to the community.  Page 226

# Chapter 9 Property Inspection and Description

## Answers – Matching

| | | | |
|---|---|---|---|
| 1. B | 4. G | 7. O | 10. M |
| 2. C | 5. N | 8. F | |
| 3. A | 6. H | 9. E | |

## Answers – Multiple Choice

1. (c) Two-story floor plans offer the most living space within a set perimeter.  They also can cost less to heat, cool, and build because the plumbing and other interior fixtures can be aligned.  Page 245

2. (a) A common style in the Southwest is the Spanish/Mediterranean style. This style utilizes white or light colored stucco on the exterior and an orange or brown clay tiled roof. Additionally, the Spanish style of home usually employs a courtyard and wrought iron trim and fencing. Page 247

3. (c) The precut home is like a house in a box. All the materials are delivered unassembled, but precut to fit exactly in place. Therefore, each component is in its smallest form. Page 246

4. (b) Usually a building inspection is divided into two parts: exterior inspection and interior inspection. Page 244

5. (c) Gross living area (GLA) is the total finished above ground habitable space. Usually attics, crawlspaces, and basements are not counted in this measurement. The backyard would never be counted since it is not part of the building at all. Therefore, subtract the attic and backyard areas from the total area to determine the GLA. Page 261

6. (c) The foundation is the support for the entire structure and its purpose is to transfer the weight of the building to the ground. Page 257

7. (d) Foundation problems can cause a multitude of other problems including plumbing leaks, squeaky and un-level floors, sticking doors, and cracked walls. Page 257

8. (a) In the colder parts of the country where the frost line may be five or six feet deep, many homes are built with basements. This minimizes the movement associated with the cyclical freezing and thawing of the soil during the winter. Page 260

9. (d) Monolithic, floating, screeded, and post-tension slab are the four major types of foundations. Page 258

10. (c) The three types of wood framing used in residential construction are platform frame, balloon frame and post and beam frame construction. Pages 256 – 257

## Chapter 10 – Sales Comparison Approach

### Answers – Matching

1. A    4. M    7. I    10. H
2. G    5. K    8. D
3. F    6. C    9. J

### Answers – Multiple Choice

1. (b) This valuation approach relies heavily upon the principal of substitution, which states that a typical buyer in a market will pay no more for a property than what he or she could pay for a reasonable substitute. Page 276

2. (b) If the perception is that there is little or no difference between two competing brands, consumers usually purchase the least expensive brand. Page 276

3. (a) Comparable Property Sales Price ± Adjustments = Adjusted Value Page 277

4. (d) The sales comparison approach is most applicable in situations where there are a sufficient number of reliable, arm's-length sales, and when appraising property types that are bought and sold on a regular basis. It is the predominant approach used when appraising single-family residences, multi-residential properties, and vacant land. Page 278

5. (c) The sales comparison approach is best suited for appraising single-family esidences (including condominiums, small multi-residential properties, and vacant land). It is also applicable anytime sufficient sales data is available. Page 278

6. (a) Although the "Analyze market data" step is missing, the remaining four steps are in correct order. The other choices are missing steps and out of order. Page 281

7. (d) In order to minimize discrepancies, inaccuracies, and incomplete records, appraisers should consult multiple data sources that provide quality data because inaccurate or incomplete data is much more susceptible to inaccurate analysis. Page 281

8. (d) The Multiple Listing Service (MLS) is a service is provided by local real estate boards for its members and is designed as a tool for marketing real estate. Listings are input into the MLS system to notify real estate licensees of properties available for sale. Listings include information such as the asking price and the total days the property has been on the market. Page 282

9. (a) $335,000 \times 36\% = \$120,600$ (assessed value)
$120,600 - \$2,000 = \$118,600$ (assessed value after exemption)
$118,600 \times .026 = \$3,083$ ($3,100 rounded) Page 284

10. (b) $1.30 \div 100 = .013$ or 13 mills. A mill equals one-thousandth of a dollar and is numerically expressed as $0.001$. Ten mills equal one cent, one-hundred mills equal ten cents, and one-thousand mills equal one dollar. Page 284

11. (a) $4,125 \div 0.03 = \$137,500$ (assessed value)
$137,500 \div 0.4 = \$343,750$ (property value)
Page 284

12. (a) Parties to the transaction are buyers, sellers, and their brokers. Page 286

13. (c) Sales information for like properties to the subject will provide the most credible, reliable, and appropriate market data for an appraisal. Page 290

14. (b) The geographic area an appraiser would typically search for comparable sales data depends upon the nature of the real estate being appraised. If similar properties are commonly bought and sold within a neighborhood, such as single-family residences, an appraiser would typically limit the search for sales data to similar properties located within that area. On the other hand, the market for some kinds of properties may be national or even worldwide in scope. Page 288

15. (d) Most clients require a minimum of three comparable closed sales to be included in their reports. However, the more comps an appraiser can analyze, the more sound and supportable his or her conclusions will be. Therefore, an appraiser should utilize as many comps as necessary to arrive at his or her conclusion. Page 289

16. (c) The cash equivalency technique is a procedure whereby the sale prices of comparable properties selling with atypical financing are adjusted to reflect financing that is typical in a market. Page 291

17. (b) 5% ÷ 12 = .4167% per month
.4167% × 9 months = 3.75% (rounded)
$268,000 × 3.75% = $10,050 (10,000 rounded) adjustment value.
Page 293

18. (d) Locational adjustments may be based on changes in neighborhood (zoning, zip code, school district, et al), proximity to negative or positive influences, street orientation, and market perceptions. Pages 294 – 296

19. (a) If the subject property has a feature that the comparable sale lacks, add the value of that feature to the comparable. Page 301

20. (d) Adjustments may be made solely on the basis of percentage or dollars, or adjustments may be made by using a combination of both. The manner in which the adjustment is extracted from the market determines which way the adjustment is applied. Page 302

21. (a) Comparables are always adjusted to mimic the amenities of the subject.
The sequence of adjustments should read as follows:
Financing:                  $200,000 – 5%    =  $190,000
Conditions of sale:         $190,000 – 8%    =  $174,800
Market conditions:          $174,800 + 20%   =  $209,760
Location adjustments:   $209,760 – 15%   =  $178,296
Physical characteristics: $178,296 + 5%    =  $187,210
Round the number        $187,000
Page 303

22. (d) The proper sequence of adjustments is financing, seller motivation, time, location, and physical. Page 309

23. (a) The paired-sales analysis identifies the amount of an adjustment when at least two sales are found that are virtually identical in all aspects except one. The one differing item between the sales equals the difference in value between the two properties. For the pool, the difference between Sale 1 and Sale 2 equals the value of a pool. $235,000 – $200,000 = $35,000. Page 303

24. (d) The difference between Sale 1 and Sale 3 equals the value for an extra garage space. $200,000 – $190,000 = $10,000. Page 302

25. (c) To determine the value of the subject, select any one of the comparables and apply the proper adjustments to it. Select the comparable that is as similar as possible to the subject, in this case, either Sale 2 or Sale 3 would work. If we use Sale 3, the only difference is that the subject has a pool and the comparable does not. To account for the difference, add $35,000 (the value of a pool) to the comparable, answering the question, "What would this comparable sell for if it had a pool like the subject?" If you select any of the other two comparables and apply the adjustments correctly, you will arrive at the same conclusion. Page 302

26. (c) The difference between the sales prices is $50,000. Divide that figure by the original price ($500,000) to calculate the total percentage the market has declined, 10%. It has been two years, however, and the question is asking for a yearly rate. Divide the total rate by 2 to calculate the annual rate of 5%. Pages 307 – 308

27. (d) Fannie Mae has a guideline that states a single line item adjustment should not exceed 10% of the sales price of the comparable. In this problem, the $12,000 adjustment for physical differences equals 12%. Page 313

28. (a) This comparable does not have a single adjustment that exceeds Fannie Mae's 10% single line adjustment guideline, nor does the gross adjustment value of $36,000 exceed the 25% guideline for gross adjustments. Pages 313 – 314

29. (b) When determining the gross adjustments, ignore the positive or negative aspects of the adjustment. When applying the adjustments, pay close attention to if they are positive or negative adjustments. After the listed adjustments are applied, the adjusted value of this comparable property is $170,000. Page 314

30. (d) It is the appraiser's job at this point to identify which of the comparable sales is given most weight in this analysis and the reasoning why it is the one most heavily weighted. It is not proper appraisal practice simply to average the adjusted sale prices together. Sound reasoning and judgment, not mere mechanical calculation, must be used on the part of the appraiser in order to reconcile the individual value indicators into a value estimate. Page 315

# Chapter 11 – Income Capitalization Approach

## Answers – Matching

| | | | |
|---|---|---|---|
| 1. O | 5. S | 9. H | 13. R |
| 2. F | 6. Q | 10. C | 14. D |
| 3. K | 7. B | 11. G | 15. A |
| 4. N | 8. M | 12. T | |

## Answers – Multiple Choice

1. (a) The principle of anticipation is the main principle behind the income approach, since the amount a buyer will typically pay for a property is directly proportional to the future income benefits the buyer expects to derive from that property. Page 326

2. (d) The most obvious income a property produces is the rent paid by tenants of a property. Sources of additional income include laundry and vending machines, parking fees, interest earned on security deposits, and possibly, income resulting from government programs. Potential gross income encompasses all of these possible sources. Page 327

3. (b) The purpose of performing a rental survey is to identify, with reasonable certainty, the amount of income the subject property can be expected to generate. Page 329

4. (a) 10 units multiplied by 12 months = 120 months of rent due. 2 units times 1 ½ months vacant = 3 months of rent lost due to vacancy. 3 months divided by 120 months = .025 or 2.5%. Page 330

5. (c) Fixed expenses are incurred by the owner whether or not the property is occupied. Property taxes, insurance premiums, and licenses typically fall into this category. Page 331

6. (c)  Accountants record expenses in a different manner from that of appraisers. Items such as financing expenses, income taxes, book depreciation charges, and capital improvements are all expenses that property owners incur. When compiling an appraisal operating statement, appraisers omit these expenses since they vary from owner to owner and are not based on the property itself. Of the expenses listed, the mortgage is the only expense that an appraiser would not count. $2,150 + $1,075 + $3,000 + $4,000 = $10,225. Page 333

7. (a)  $1025 multiplied by 240 = $246,000. Page 337

8. (b)  $92,250 divided by .09 (9%) = $1,025,000. Page 338

9. (b)  If an investment is safe, the odds are it will have a relatively low return on investment. However, a property with a low risk is generally worth more than one with a high risk where investment loss is more likely. Low risk = Low capitalization rate = High value. Page 339

10. (c)  The operating expense ratio is calculated by dividing the property's operating expenses by its effective gross income. $15,000 divided by $100,000 = .15. To calculate net operating income, an appraiser deducts operating expenses from effective gross income. $100,000 minus $15,000 = $85,000. A net operating income ratio is the ratio between the net operating income of a property and its effective gross income. $85,000 divided by $100,000 = .85. Because these two ratios are complementary, adding them together will result in 1.0 or 100%. .15 + .85 = 1.0. Pages 340 – 341

11. (d)  The mortgage constant is the ratio of the loan amount (principal) to the annual sum of the individual loan payments. Page 341

12. (b)  The building residual technique is used when the land value is known (or easily estimated). Page 344

13. (d)  When performing yield capitalization, the appraiser completes certain steps: 1. Project the holding period of the investment. 2. Estimate and forecast all the future cash flows associated with the investment. 3. Identify an appropriate discount rate. 4. Convert the future benefits into a present value estimate for the property. Page 347

14. (b)  Column 3 will tell the investor how much must be invested each year to accumulate a specific amount at the end of the stated period. Page 332 & 349

15. (d)  Column 5 is the one real estate appraisers use most frequently, and it is used to estimate the present value of an annuity. Page 351

# Chapter 12 – Approach: Reproduction of Improvements

## Answers – Matching

| | | | |
|---|---|---|---|
| 1.  B | 3.  H | 5.  E | 7.  I |
| 2.  C | 4.  G | 6.  J | |

## Answers – Multiple Choice

1. (b)  The cost approach recognizes there are two major components in real estate; land and improvements. Page 361

2. (d) The cost approach to value is not applicable to every appraisal assignment. Cost approach is inapplicable for condominiums. The cost to build an item rarely equals its value. It is difficult to apply this approach to older buildings, specifically because of its reliance on depreciation. Page 363

3. (a) The market-data approach (also known as the sales comparison approach) is nearly identical to the sales comparison method used to determine the value of vacant land. Pages 364 & 366

4. (c) If an improved property is $300,000 and the land to improvement ratio is 2:1, then the land is worth $200,000 and the improvements are worth $100,000. Remember to account for both parts of the ratio: 2 to 1 means 3 parts total. Pages 367 – 368

5. (b) The extraction (or abstraction) method derives the land value of a comparable property by deducting the depreciated costs of the improvements on that property from its known sale price. Page 368

6. (b) Reproduction cost is the dollar amount required to construct an exact replica of the property being appraised. This cost estimate assumes the cost of using like kind and quality of materials, identical construction and workmanship standards, as well as identical design and layout. Page 371

7. (c) The unit-in-place method is a more in-depth cost estimate that provides more detail than the square-foot or index method. The quantity survey method is the most in-depth of the commonly used methods for estimating costs; however, it was not given as a choice. The like-quality method does not exist. Page 375

8. (a) Divide the current index by the historical index (378 ÷ 220 = 1.718) and then multiply the result by the historical (or original) cost (1.718 × $65,000 = $111,682). Rounded, the best answer is $112,000. Page 376

9. (b) A 2,000 square foot building that cost $300,000 to build has a cost per square foot of $150 ($300,000 ÷ 2,000 = 150). Page 377

10. (a) The math is as follows:

| | | |
|---|---|---|
| Base above grade × above grade area | $81 × 978 | = $79,218 |
| Base garage × garage area | $23 × 168 | = $3,864 |
| Total before regional multiplier | $83,082 | |
| Total after regional multiplier | $83,082 × 1.19 = $98,868 | |

The land value is not part of the reproduction cost. Page 371

11. (c) The unit-in-place method breaks down the cost of a building into the cost of its component parts. The individual costs estimated for each of the building components required in this method are in terms of the standardized units typically used for the individual building component. Pages 380 – 381

12. (c) Direct costs include all the costs directly involved with construction including any costs associated with maintaining a construction site. Page 373

13. (c) Indirect costs are costs that are part of the overall process of building a project, but are not directly linked to construction. Page 373

14. (b) Entrepreneurial profit reflects the amount developers expect to receive for their efforts and it is based upon the principle of anticipation. Page 383

15. (d) Items like pools, fences and landscaping that are not part of the main primary structure but still add value are called site improvements. Typically, these items are not depreciated. As the final step in the cost approach section on the URAR form, they are added to the depreciated value of improvements and land value to create the overall property value. Page 384

# Chapter 13 – Cost Approach: Depreciation of Improvements

## Answers – Matching

| | | | |
|---|---|---|---|
| 1. A | 4. H | 7. B | 10. C |
| 2. D | 5. E | 8. O | 11. F |
| 3. I | 6. N | 9. L | 12. M |

## Answers – Multiple Choice

1. (c) Accrued depreciation is a loss in value to a property due to any cause as of the effective date of the appraisal. It is the difference between the market value of the improvements and the cost-new of the improvements. Page 400

2. (a) Curable depreciation is a loss in value that is economically feasible to correct. Roof repair or replacement, painting, building maintenance, floor covering replacement, and forced air heater replacement are examples of curable physical deterioration. If spending $15,000 to improve the home returns a value of $20,000 then it is economically feasible, and thus curable. Page 394

3. (b) Incurable depreciation refers to items of depreciation that either are physically impossible to cure or are too expensive to be of any worth. Moving a property away from an airport is impossible. Page 395

4. (c) A furnace typically lasts 20 – 30 years and may never need to be replaced. If it does need replacement, it is usually a curable item. Pages 394 & 400

5. (d) The age/life method uses the ratio of the building's age (or component) to its expected life. 24 divided by 80 = 30%. If 30% of the life has been used, 70% remains. To convert this to value, multiply the cost-new by 70% to get $350,000. Page 401

6. (a) Superadequacies are features that are too large or of a higher quality than needed for a property and have a negative effect on property values. Having a home over-insulated for an area qualifies as consisting of higher quality than needed. Page 398

7. (c) Lack of modern facilities most often is curable, but the cost to cure must be measured against the benefit to property value. When adding modern facilities that are valued in the marketplace, they must add equal or greater value than the cost to add in order to be considered curable. From the information given, converting the garage would cost $15,000, but would only add $10,000 to the property's value. Page 398

8. (b) External obsolescence takes place when influences that are external to the property adversely affect that property. External obsolescence is almost always incurable. Page 398

9. (d)  While certain physical, functional, and external forces can cause land to lose value, losses attributed to these factors will already have been reflected in the market value estimate of the land.  Page 400

10. (b)  The cost-to-cure method, while simplistic, only allows for a 100% depreciation of any item.  When an item like a roof is not brand new, but still has years left before it needs to be replaced, the cost to cure method is not very useful.  Page 401

11. (d)  The effective age accounts for improvements that appear younger or older than the structure's actual age due to quality maintenance, or lack thereof.  40 years actual age plus 20 years equals 60 years.  Page 392

12. (c)  The difference between the structure's estimated economic life and its effective age is its remaining economic life.  (99 – 25 = 74 years.)  Page 401

13. (c)  Using the economic age/life method, divide the effective age by the economic life (20 ÷ 95 = 21%).  Then multiply the result by the replacement cost of $450,000 to calculate the amount of accrued depreciation.  450,000 × 21% = $95,000 (rounded).  Page 401

14. (a)  Depreciation may be extracted from the market by performing sale-resale analysis, by paired-sales analysis, and by extraction.  Page 406

15. (a)  If the property is losing $4 per square foot per month then: $4 × 28,000 × 12 (months) equals the total loss per year of $1,344,000.  Page 399

# Chapter 14 – Reconciliation

## Answers – Matching

| | | | |
|---|---|---|---|
| 1. F | 4. I | 7. B | 10. E |
| 2. A | 5. G | 8. J | |
| 3. H | 6. C | 9. D | |

## Answers – Multiple Choice

1. (d)  Each approach has so many variables that there is a miniscule chance that one value approach will ever match another if performed on the same property.  In fact, if it does occur, it should be considered a major red flag.  Page 416

2. (c)  One example of when an approach is inapplicable to the assignment is appraising vacant land.  There is no physical way of using the cost approach since this method requires the valuing of improvements.  Page 416

3. (d)  If the sales comparison approach was used in the assignment, the appraiser should re-verify that the comparables are comparable to the subject property; there is an adequate amount of sales data; the sales data is both accurate and reliable; the logic of adjustments made between subject and comps is in good order; the adjustments are mathematically correct; and the value conclusion drawn from the adjusted comparables is legitimate.  Page 418

4. (b)  If all three approaches were applied to a property, the value derived by the cost approach analysis would probably be the highest, and not entirely represent what that property may sell for on the open market.  Page 420

5. (c)  The income approach is the best indicator of value for income-producing properties; however, if a property is not currently producing income, this approach can convert its potential income into a current value.  Page 419

6. (b)  The final value estimate should be rounded to the nearest thousand to emphasize the fact that it is indeed an estimate.  If an estimate were too distinct, it would cease to be an estimate of market value and become too exact for the marketplace.  Page 421

7. (d)  While reconciling, appraisers should never limit themselves to a mathematical equation, should never bend values to fit preconceived notions, and never make changes to data or values unless truly warranted.  Page 422

8. (c)  Reports will vary on amount and detail of information disclosed, but the type of report used should never affect how much effort is put into the actual appraisal.  Page 423

9. (c)  The Self-Contained Report is the most elaborate report and contains the most detailed information.  Page 423

10. (d)  An appraiser should always keep his or her workfiles in case he or she must revisit the appraisal or defend his or her appraisal.  Pages 426 – 427

# Chapter 15 – Appraisal Statistical Concepts and Appraisal Mathematics

## Answers – Matching

| | | | |
|---|---|---|---|
| 1. C | 5. P | 9. H | 13. N |
| 2. Q | 6. F | 10. I | 14. M |
| 3. A | 7. B | 11. K | 15. L |
| 4. O | 8. G | 12. D | |

## Answers – Multiple Choice

1. (c)  The period that sets apart a whole number from a fractional part of that number is called a decimal point.  Page 432

2. (c)  Any numerals to the right of the decimal point are less than one and the 10th position is the first position to the right of the decimal point.  Page 432

3. (b)  To convert a percentage to a decimal, move the decimal point two places to the left and remove the percentage sign.  Page 434

4. (b)  To convert a fraction into a percentage is a two step process.  First, divide the numerator (top) by the denominator: $5 \div 2 = 2.5$.  Then, convert the resulting decimal into a percentage by moving the decimal two places to the right and adding a percent sign.  Pages 433 – 434

5. (a)  If the number is greater than or equal to half of the place you are rounding to, round up; if it is lower, round down.  Since the thousand place is being rounded to, $574,511 is rounded up to $575,000; $499,996 is rounded up to $500,000; and $525,444 is rounded down to $525,000.  Page 435

6. (b) The problem states that the unknown original price plus 30% is equal to the current price of $390,000. It asks you to solve for 30% of the unknown price. Using the Whole × Percent = Part problem, the calculations are as follows:
$x$ × 1.3 (100% original price + 30% rise in value) = $390,000
$x$ = $390,000 ÷ 1.3
$x$ = $300,000 (price one year ago)
$390,000 − $300,000 = $90,000 accrued equity
Page 439

7. (c) The problem is asking what percentage of the original price is the rebate. Using the Whole × Percent = Part problem, the calculations are as follows:
$210,000 × $y$ = $30,000
$y$ = $30,000 ÷ $210,000
$y$ = 0.1428 or 14.3%
Pages 437 − 439

8. (c) Sherri's total expenditure for the investment would be $100,000: Lot 1 + Lot 2 + Cost to Demolish ($30,000 + $55,000 + $15,000) Sherri would earn $15,000 in profit ($115,000 − $100,000) once the project was sold.
Using the Whole × Percent = Part problem, the calculations are as follows:
$100,000 × $y$ = $15,000
$y$ = $15,000 ÷ $100,000
$y$ = 15%.
Pages 438 − 440

9. (b) Since it is an interest only loan, all the payments up to the final one were only interest payments.
Using the I = P × R × T formula, the solution is as follows:
I = $10,000 × 9% × 1
I = $900 a year, $75 a month ($900 ÷ 12)
11 payments of $75, 1 payment of $10,075 (loan balance + last month of interest)
Page 441

10. (b) To compute an area or square measurement, one simply needs to multiply two linear measurements together. Page 444

11. (d) The perimeter is the linear measurement around a shape. Add the linear measurements that compose four sides of the rectangular house (42' + 42' + 24' + 24' = 132 feet). A linear measurement cannot be square. Page 444

12. (a) To compute an area measurement, one simply needs to multiply two linear measurements together: 24' × 42' = 1,008 square feet. Page 444

13. (b) To properly calculate the volume for this structure it must be separated into two separate geometric shapes: the rectangular prism that makes up the bottom floor and the triangular prism that is the second floor. Once these two volumes are calculated separately, add them together to compute the total volume.
Rectangular Prism:     24' × 42' × 10'       = 10,080 cubic feet
Triangular Prism:     ½ × 24' × 42' × 8'  =   4,032 cubic feet
Total volume:          10,080 + 4,032        = 14,112 cubic feet.
Page 447

14. (c) Make the figure a rectangle then subtract the dotted-line sections:

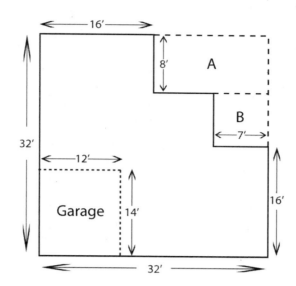

| | |
|---|---|
| Square: | 32' × 32' = 1,024 square feet |
| Section A: | 8' × 16' = − 128 square feet |
| Section B: | 7' × 8' = − 56 square feet |
| Garage: | 12' × 14' = − 168 square feet |
| Floor plan square footage: | 672 square feet |

Page 446

15. (d) To solve this problem, convert all of the measurements to the same unit of comparison. Once all the measurements have been converted to square feet, they can be easily compared. Choice (d) is clearly the largest.

   a. There are 43,560 sq ft in 1 acre.
      3 × 43,560 = 130,680, so 3 acres equals 130,680 square feet.
   b. There are 9 sq ft in 1 sq yd. (9 sq ft × 15 sq yds. = 135 sq ft)
      15 square yards equals 135 square feet.
   c. We have to apply two conversion factors.
      First, there are 640 acres in 1 section.
         640 acres divided by 128 = 5 acres
      Second, there are 43,560 sq ft in 1 acre.
         5 acres × 43,560 sq ft = 217,800 square feet.
   d. Pay careful attention to the wording here. "A 1/2 mile square" means a square that is 1/2 mile on each side. One mile is 5,280 feet, therefore 1/2 mile equals 2,640 ft. (5,280 x 1/2 = 2,640 ft.)
   To find the square feet, multiply length times width:
   2,640 sq ft. × 2,640 sq ft. = 6,969,600 square feet.
   Page 448

16. (a) 6 acres equals 261,360 square feet. If her lots are 2,640 square feet each (60 feet × 44 feet), then she can subdivide the parcel into 99 equal lots: 261,360 sq, ft, ÷ 2,640 sq.ft. = 99. The lots sell for $20,000 each or $1,980,000 total: 99 × $20,000 = $1,980,000. Pages 448 – 449

17. (c) First, convert measurements to feet (300 ft W, 525 ft SE, and 432 ft N). Then, draw the figure from the description.

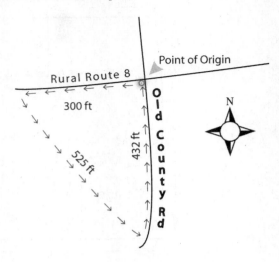

The formula for a triangular shape is 1/2 × base × height, so the area for this lot is 1/2 × 300 × 432, which equals 64,800 square feet. The question wants it converted into acreage, so divide this number by 43,560. This gives an answer of 1.49 acres, or 1.5 rounded. Pages 443 – 448

18. (b) First, calculate the perimeter of the home. The cost of a foundation is typically measured in linear feet, so add the four sides of the rectangle 36.33 ft. + 38.83 ft. + 36.33 ft. + 38.83 ft. to get the linear measurement of 150.32 feet. Multiply 150.32 linear feet by the cost per linear foot. 150.32 times $18.63 equals $2,800.46 for the cost of the foundation. Page 444

19. (a) Use the formula for a cylinder and plug in the provided dimensions. The formula is $R^2 × \pi × H$, so 81 square feet × 3.14 × 41 feet = 10,428 cubic feet. At $15.00 per cubic foot with a regional multiplier of 0.98 the cost-new for the silo will be $153,291. Using the time age/life method (90 ÷ 100), the structure has approximately 90% of its life remaining, so apply that percentage to the cost-new to get $138,000 rounded. Page 443

20. (a) Add all the variates together and divide by the number of variates. 649,300 ÷ 9 = $72,144. Page 452

21. (b) Organize the figures into an array from lowest priced to highest priced and then find the variate in the middle. Since there are nine variates in this sample, the fifth variate in the array will be the median. Page 453

22. (d) The most frequently occurring variate is $95,000. Page 454

23. (c) Subtract the lowest-priced home from the highest-priced home to calculate the range of the sample. $103,000 – $15,000 = $88,000. Page 455

24. (c) Subtract each variate from the population's mean.

| Variate | Deviation |
|---|---|
| $15,000 | $57,144 |
| $103,000 | $30,856 |
| $99,900 | $27,756 |
| $67,500 | $4,644 |
| $95,000 | $22,856 |
| $95,000 | $22,856 |
| $66,000 | $6,144 |
| $33,000 | $39,144 |
| $74,900 | $2,756 |

Then, add those figures together (ignoring if they are positive or negative), and divide the sum of the differences by the number of variates: $214,156 ÷ 9 = $23,795. Pages 455 – 456

25. (d) Subtract each variate from the population's mean and then square them.

| Variate | Difference |
|---|---|
| $15,000 | $3,265,436,736 |
| $103,000 | $952,092,736 |
| $99,900 | $770,395,536 |
| $67,500 | $21,566,736 |
| $95,000 | $522,396,736 |
| $95,000 | $522,396,736 |
| $66,000 | $37,748,736 |
| $33,000 | $1,532,252,736 |
| $74,900 | $7,595,536 |

Find the total of the squared differences ($7,631,882,224), divide by 9 ($847,986,914), and then take the square root of this figure ($29,120). Pages 456 – 457

# Appendix C

# *Glossary*

## A

**above-grade improvements**
Improvements above ground level.

**absorption analysis**
A study of the number of units of residential or nonresidential property that can be sold or leased over a given period of time in a defined location.

**absorption period**
The estimated time period required to sell, lease, place in use, or trade the subject property in its marketing area at prevailing prices or rental rates.

**absorption rate**
The rate at which a type of property is either bought or leased, i.e., *absorbed* by the market.

**abstraction method**
*See* extraction method.

**acceptance**
An unqualified agreement to the terms of an offer.

**accrued depreciation**
Depreciation that has already occurred. It is the difference between the cost to replace the property and the property's current market value.

**acknowledgment**
A signed statement, made before a notary public, by a named person confirming the signature on a document and that it was made of free will.

**acquisition**
The act or process by which a person procures property.

**acquisition appraisal**
A market value appraisal of property condemned or otherwise acquired for public use, to establish the compensation to be paid to the owner.

**acre**
A measure of land equaling 43,560 square feet, or 4,840 square yards, or 160 square rods, or a tract about 208.71 feet square.

**actual age**
The chronological age of a building.

**actual depreciation**
That depreciation occurring as a result of physical, functional or economic forces, causing loss in value to a building.

**ad valorem**
A property tax based on assessed value from a Latin prefix meaning "according to value". (Pronounced "ad-va-LO-rem")

**adjustment**
In the sales comparison approach, a dollar or percentage amount that is added to or subtracted from the sale price of a comparable property, to account for a feature that the property has or does not have which differentiates it from the subject property.

**adjustment grid**
Lists important items affecting value such as site area, location, design and appeal, quality, condition, gross building area, basement area, room count, view, age, amenities, etc. Also called a matrix.

### Advisory Opinions

The Appraisal Standards Board (ASB) issues Advisory Opinions to illustrate the applicability of USPAP in specific situations and to offer advice for the resolution of appraisal issues and problems.

### aesthetic value

Relating to beauty, rather than to functional considerations.

### aesthetic zoning

Regulates the appearance of buildings in the area.

### affirmative easement

One that requires the owner of the servient estate to do something to benefit the dominant estate.

### age/life method

*See* economic age/life method.

### agents of production

Land, labor, capital, and management. *See* principle of increasing and decreasing returns and principle of surplus productivity.

### aggregate

(1) In statistics, the sum of all individual variates. (2) A surfacing material or ballast for a roof system. Aggregate can be rock, stone, crushed stone or slag, water-worn gravel, crushed lava rock or marble chips.

### air rights

The rights in real property to the reasonable use of the air space above the surface of the land.

### airspace

The interior area which an apartment, office or condominium occupies. Airspace is considered real property to a reasonable height. For example, an owner or developer of condominiums may sell the airspace as real property.

### allocation method

The allocation of the appraised total value between land and improvements. Allocation may be made using a ratio comparing building value to the total price (or value).

### allowance for vacancy and collection losses

The percentage of potential gross income that will be lost due to vacant units, collection losses, or both.

### amenities

Features that add value to a property.

### Americans with Disabilities Act

Federal law passed in 1990 that prohibits discrimination against individuals with disabilities.

### amortization

The liquidation of a financial obligation on an installment basis.

### annuity

A sum of money received at fixed intervals, such as a series of assured equal or nearly equal payments to be made over a period of time. The installment payments due to a landlord or a lender under a lease is a type of annuity.

### annuity capitalization

An income capitalization method, providing for "annuity" recapture of invested capital. Discounts the future income to an estimate of prevent value. Also referred to as yield capitalization.

### annuity method

A method of capitalization that treats income from real property as a fixed, regular return on an investment. For the annuity method to be applied the lessee must be reliable and the lease must be long term.

### anticipation, principle of

*See* principle of anticipation.

### appraisal

An unbiased estimate or opinion of the property value on a given date.

### appraisal consulting

The act or process of developing an analysis, recommendation, or opinion to solve a problem, where an opinion of value is a component of the analysis leading to the assignment results.

**appraisal methods**
The approaches used in the appraisal of real property: cost approach, income capitalization approach, and sales comparison approach.

**appraisal process**
An orderly systematic method to arrive at an estimate of value.

**appraisal report**
A written statement where an appraiser gives his or her opinion of value.

**appraisal review**
The review of an appraiser's analysis, research and conclusions by another appraiser.

**Appraisal Standards Board (ASB)**
Part of The Appraisal Foundation, the ASB develops, interprets, and amends USPAP.

**appraised value**
An appraiser's estimate of the amount of a particular value, such as assessed value, insurable value, or market value, based on the particular assignment.

**appraiser**
A person qualified by education, training and experience who is hired to estimate the value of real and personal property based on experience, judgment, facts, and use of formal appraisal processes.

**Appraiser Qualification Board (AQB)**
Part of The Appraisal Foundation and responsible for establishing minimum requirements for licensed and certified appraisers and licensing and certifying examinations.

**appreciation**
An increase in the worth or value of property over time.

**approaches to value**
Any of the following three methods used to estimate the value of real estate: sales comparison approach, cost approach, and income capitalization approach.

**appurtenance**
Anything used with the land for its benefit. (Pronounced ap-pur-te-nance).

**appurtenant**
Belonging appended or annexed to. Appurtenant items transfer with the land when property is sold.

**area**
The space or size of a surface that is defined by a set of boundaries.

**arm's-length transaction**
A transaction, such as a sale of property, in which all parties involved are acting in their own self-interest and are under no undue influence or pressure from other parties.

**aseptic system**
The "clean water" system.

**assemblage**
The process of putting several smaller, less valuable lots together under a single ownership.

**assessed value**
Value placed on land and buildings by a public tax assessor as a basis for use in levying annual real estate taxes.

**assessment**
The valuation of property for the purpose of levying a tax or the amount of the tax levied.

**assessment roll**
A list of all taxable property showing the assessed value of each parcel; establishes the tax base.

**assessor**
The official who has the responsibility of determining assessed values.

**asset**
Real or personal property that is owned and has value, such as cash.

**assignee**
Party to whom a lease is assigned or transferred.

**assignment**
The transfer of entire leasehold estate to a new person.

### assignor
The person transferring a claim, benefit, or right in property to another.

### attachment lien
The process by which the court holds the real or personal property of a defendant as security for a possible judgment pending the outcome of a lawsuit. Also known as writ of attachment.

### attic
The open area above the ceiling and under the roof.

### automated valuation models
Computer software programs that analyze data using automated systems, such as regression analysis and/or so-called artificial intelligence.

### average deviation
In statistics, the measure of how far the average variate differs from the mean of all variates.

### averaging
*See* mean

### avigation easement
An easement over private property near an airport that limits the height of structures and trees in order to keep the take off and landing paths of airports clear.

# B

### balance, principle of
*See* principle of balance.

### balloon frame construction
A type of wood framing in which the studs run from the floor of the first level to the ceiling of the second story uninterrupted.

### balloon payment
Under an installment loan, a final payment that is substantially larger than any other payment and repays the debt in full.

### band of investment technique
Method of estimating interest and capitalization rates, based on a weighted average of the mortgage interest rate (or other cost of borrowed funds) and the rate of return on equity required.

### bankruptcy
A court proceeding to relieve a person's or company's financial insolvency.

### bare legal title
Title conveyed using a trust deed; however, it does not actually convey possession.

### base rent
*See* minimum rent.

### baseline
A survey line running east and west, used as a reference when mapping land.

### basement
A building's lowest story which is partially or entirely below ground.

### below-grade improvements
Improvements below ground level.

### beneficiary
The lender under a deed of trust.

### bilateral contract
An agreement in which each person promises to perform an act in exchange for another person's promise to perform.

### bond
(1) An obligation under seal. Real estate bonds are issued on the security of a mortgage or deed of trust. (2) A certificate representing a contract for the payment of money, often used to repay certain loans or held as security to ensure the performance of a stated act.

### book depreciation
An accounting concept which refers to an allowance taken to provide for recovery of invested capital.

### bracketing
When using the sales comparison approach, selection of market data so that the subject is contained within a range of data.

**breach of contract**
A failure to perform on part or all of the terms and conditions of a contract.

**breakdown method**
A method of computing depreciation in which the appraiser estimates the loss in value for each type of depreciation separately.  Also known as observed condition method.

**brownfield**
An abandoned commercial or industrial site or under-utilized neighborhood where redevelopment is complicated by actual or perceived contamination.

**building capitalization rate**
The sum of the discount and capital recapture rates for a building.

**building code**
Municipal ordinance that regulates the type and quality of building materials and methods of construction permitted.

**building line**
Often called a setback line; a building line runs a certain distance from the street, in front of which an owner cannot build.  These lines are set by law.

**building residual technique**
Technique of income capitalization where the net income to the building (after deducting the income required for the land) is capitalized into an estimated value for the building.

**building restrictions**
Restrictions that limit the way a property can be used.  They may appear in building codes or title documents.

**bulk zoning**
Controls density and prevents overcrowding.  Bulk zoning regulates setbacks, building height, and percentage of open area.

**bundle of rights**
An ownership concept describing all the legal rights that attach to the ownership of real property.

**business appraisal**
The appraisal of business entities including a business' intangible assets, like a logo or copyright.

**business opportunity**
Any type of business that is for lease or sale.

**buyer's market**
A market containing more supply than demand.

# C

**capital**
Money and/or property owned or used by a person or business to acquire goods or services.

**capital improvement**
Any permanent improvement made to real estate for the purpose of increasing the useful life of the property or increasing the property's value.

**capital recapture**
The return of an investment.

**capitalization**
The process that can be employed to convert income to value.

**capitalization method**
*See* income capitalization method.

**capitalization rate**
The rate of interest which is considered a reasonable return on the investment, and used in the process of determining value based upon net income.  It may also be described as the yield rate that is necessary to attract the money of the average investor to a particular kind of investment.

**capitalized income approach**
*See* Income Approach.

**cash dividend**
Cash payment to a corporation's stockholders, usually based on profitability

**cash equivalency technique**
Method of adjusting a sales price downward to reflect the increase in price due to assumption or procurement by buyers of a loan at an interest rate lower than the prevailing market rate.

**cash-equivalent sale**
A sale where the financing does not affect the price; a sale with typical financing.

**CC&Rs**
*See* covenants, conditions and restrictions.

**certificates of deposit**
Financial instruments representing time deposits with banks and other lending institutions.

**Certified General appraiser**
An individual who has met specific education, experience, and examination requirements. May appraise any property. *See* appraiser.

**Certified Residential appraiser**
An individual who has met specific education, experience, and examination requirements. May appraise any 1-4 unit residential property. *See* appraiser.

**change, principle of**
*See* principle of change

**characteristics**
Distinguishing features of a property.

**chattel**
(1) Personal property. (2) This term is sometimes used in a law to describe any interest in real or personal property other than a freehold.

**chattel real**
Personal property which is connected to real estate; for example, a lease.

**cladding**
Any external protective skin or device for the exterior surfaces of the home.

**client**
The person who employs an agent to perform a service for a fee.

**collateral security**
(1) Something of value given as security for a debt. (2) A separate obligation attached to a contract to guarantee its performance.

**collection loss**
A loss incurred if tenants do not pay their agreed-upon rents.

**Comments**
Extensions of USPAP DEFINITIONS, Rules, and Standards Rules that provide interpretation, and establish context and conditions for application.

**commercial acre**
The area remaining from an acre of newly subdivided land after deducting the area devoted to streets, sidewalks, alleys, curbs, etc. Also known as a buildable acre.

**common area**
An entire common interest subdivision except the separate interests therein.

**common interest development (CID)**
A common-interest development combining the individual ownership of private dwellings with the shared ownership of common facilities of the entire project. The common areas are usually governed by a homeowners association. Also called common interest subdivision.

**community property**
All property acquired by a husband and wife during a valid marriage (excluding certain separate property).

**comparable sales (comps)**
Sales which have similar characteristics to the subject property and are used for analysis in the appraisal process. Commonly called "comps", they are recently sold properties similarly situated in a similar market

**comparative market analysis**
A comparison analysis that real estate brokers use while working with a seller to determine an appropriate listing price for the seller's house.

**comparative unit method**
A method for estimating reproduction or replacement cost, using typical per unit costs for the type of construction being estimated. *See* also square-foot method.

**comparison approach**
A real estate appraisal method which compares a given property with similar or comparable surrounding properties. Also called sales comparison approach or market comparison approach.

## COMPETENCY RULE
Per USPAP, identifies requirements for experience and knowledge both when completing an appraisal and prior to accepting an appraisal assignment.

### competition, principle of
*See* principle of competition.

### competitive market analysis
A comparison analysis that real estate brokers use while working with a seller to determine an appropriate listing price for the seller's house.

### complete appraisal
The act or process of estimating value or an estimate of value, performed without invoking the Departure Rule of the Uniform Standards of Professional Appraisal Practice. *See* appraisal.

### composite rate
A capitalization rate composed of interest and recapture in separately determined amounts.

### compound interest
Interest paid on original principal and also on the accrued and unpaid interest which has accumulated as the debt matures.

### comps
*See* comparable sales

### concurrent ownership
When property is owned by two or more persons or entities at the same time. Also known as co-ownership

### condemnation
The process to exercise the power of the government to take private property from an owner for the public good, paying fair market value.

### condition
Similar to a covenant. The penalty for breaking a condition is return of the property to the grantor.

### condition precedent
A condition which requires something to occur before a transaction becomes absolute and enforceable.

### condition subsequent
A condition which, if it occurs at some point in the future, can cause a property to revert to the grantor; for example, a requirement in a grant deed that a buyer must never use the property for anything other than a private residence.

### conditional use permit
Allows a land use that may be incompatible with other uses existing in the zone. Also called special use permit.

### conditional use
A use that does not meet the current use requirements but may be allowed by obtaining a special permit.

### conditions of sale
Circumstances of the sale such as exposure time, marketing process, and buyer motivation. Unusual conditions may affect the final purchase price of a comparable sale and cause the sales price to reflect the market improperly.

### conditions, covenants, and restrictions (CC&Rs)
Recorded deed restrictions that run with the land, usually initiated by the original subdivider.

### condominium
A housing unit consisting of a separate fee interest in a particular specific space, plus an undivided interest in all common or public areas of the development. Each unit owner has a deed, separate financing and pays the property taxes for their unit

### Conduct
The section of the USPAP ETHICS RULE that identifies issues regarding appraisers' conduct.

### Confidentiality
Per USPAP, the section of the ETHICS RULE which states that the appraiser must protect the confidential nature of the appraiser-client relationship and is obligated to obey all confidentiality and privacy laws.

### conforming loans
Loans which conform to Fannie Mae guidelines, which sets loan limits to a certain amount.

**conformity, principle of**
*See* principle of conformity.

**consistent use, principle of**
*See* principle of consistent use.

**contingent**
Conditional, uncertain, conditioned upon the occurrence or nonoccurrence of some future event.

**contingent valuation methodology**
A method used to identify how a particular feature affects the value of a property by asking those who are knowledgeable about that market, i.e. other appraisers and agents; used when there is no sales data available.

**contour**
The surface configuration of land. Shown on maps as a line through points of equal elevation.

**contract**
A legally enforceable agreement made by competent parties, to perform or not perform a certain act.

**contract date**
The date the contract is created which is the date the final acceptance was communicated back to the offeror.

**contribution, principle of**
*See* principle of contribution.

**conventional loan**
Any loan made by lenders without any governmental guarantees (FHA-insured or VA-guaranteed).

**cooperative (co-op)**
(1) Ownership of an apartment unit in which the owner has purchased shares in the corporation that holds title to the entire building. (2) A residential multifamily building.

**corner influence**
The effect on a property's value due to its location on or near a corner.

**correlation**
A step in the appraisal process involving the interpretation of data derived from the three approaches in value (cost, market and income) leading to a single determination of value. Also called reconciliation.

**cost**
The expenses in money, labor, material, or sacrifices in acquiring or producing something.

**cost approach**
An approach to value in which a value estimate of a property is derived by estimating the replacement cost of the improvements, deducting the estimated accrued depreciation, and then adding the market value of the land. Also known as the summation method.

**cost basis**
Original price paid for a property.

**cost index**
Figure representing construction cost at a particular time in relation to construction cost at an earlier time, prepared by a cost reporting or indexing service.

**cost multiplier**
Regional or local factor used in adjusting published construction cost figures to estimate local costs.

**cost services**
Companies who collect and provide information regarding cost trends.

**cost to cure method of depreciation**
Method of estimating accrued depreciation based on the cost to cure or repair observed building defects.

**covenant**
(1) A promise to do or not do certain things. (2) An agreement written into deeds and other instruments promising performance or nonperformance of certain acts or stipulating certain uses or non-uses of property.

**crawlspace**
An unfinished accessible space below the first floor of a building with no basement.

**cubic-foot method**
Similar to the square-foot method, except that it takes height as well as area into consideration. The cubic contents of buildings are compared instead of just the square footage.

**cumulative zoning**
Zoning laws that allow so-called higher uses (residential) to exist in lower use zones (industrial), but not vice versa.

**curable depreciation**
Items of physical deterioration and functional obsolescence which are economically feasible to repair or replace.

**curb appeal**
A phrase implying an informal valuation of a property based on observation and experience.

# D

**data**
Information pertinent to a specific appraisal assignment.  Data may be general (relating to the economic background and the region), local (relating to the city and the neighborhood), or specific (relating to the subject property and comparable properties in the market).

**data services**
The numerous companies engaged in the business of selling data to real estate appraisers.

**data sources**
Any of a variety of sources used by appraisers when collecting general, local, and specific information.

**debt capital**
The amount borrowed by the buyer to purchase a property.

**deed**
A formal legal document used to transfer title from one person to another.

**deed of reconveyance**
Document used to transfer legal title from the trustee back to the borrower after a debt secured by a trust deed has been paid to the lender.

**deed restrictions**
Limitations in the deed to a property that dictate certain uses that may or may not be made of the property.

**deferred maintenance**
Building maintenance that has been postponed or neglected.  A type of physical deterioration.

**define the problem**
Part of the appraisal process, includes identifying the client and other intended users, the intended use of the appraiser's opinions and conclusions, the type and definition of the value sought, and the effective date of the appraiser's opinions and conclusions.

**DEFINITIONS section**
The first section of USPAP; it contains definitions of terms specific to USPAP.

**demographic profile**
A profile of a specific area that contains general demographic information such as employment, education, average age, average salary ranges, gender, occupation, number of children, etc.

**demographics**
The statistical characteristics of human populations.

**demography**
The statistical study of human populations.

**DEPARTURE RULE**
This USPAP rule allows appraisers to "depart" from certain Standards Rules in particular situations.  Replaced by the SCOPE OF WORK RULE in 2006 USPAP.

**depreciated cost method**
Method for adjusting comparable sales where adjustments are calculated from an analysis of the depreciated replacement cost for each differentiating feature.

**depreciation**
(1) In appraisal, a loss in value from any cause.  (2) A tax advantage of ownership of income property.

**depth table**
A statistical table that may be used to estimate the value of the added depth of a lot.

**depth**
Distance from the front lot line to the rear lot line.

**diminished utility**
A loss in the usefulness of a property resulting in a loss in property value. *See* accrued depreciation.

### direct capitalization method

Income capitalization technique where value is estimated by dividing net operating income by the overall capitalization rate.

### direct costs

All of the costs directly involved with the construction of a structure, including labor, materials, and equipment, design and engineering, and subcontractors' fees.

### direct market comparison approach

*See* sales comparison approach.

### direct market method

*See* paired sales analysis.

### discharge of contract

The cancellation or termination of a contract.

### discount rate

The interest rate that is charged by the Federal Reserve Bank to its member banks for loans.

### discounted cash flow

(1) Estimated future investment returns mathematically discounted to their present value. (2) Technique of income capitalization. *See* yield capitalization.

### dominant tenement

The land receiving the benefit of an easement.

### downzoning

A zone change from a high-density use to a lower density use. For example, a commercial zone to a light industrial zone.

### drainage

The removal of excess surface water or groundwater from land by means of ditches or drains.

### dry rot

A wood fungus that thrives in damp conditions and turns wood fibers into powder.

### drywall

Gypsum panels used in place of wet plaster to finish the inside of buildings.

### duress

The use of force to get agreement in accepting a contract.

### DUST

The mnemonic for the four elements that create value: **D**esire, **U**tility, **S**carcity, and **T**ransferability.

# E

### easement

A non-possessory right to enter or use someone else's land for a specified purpose.

### easement appurtenant

An easement that is connected to a particular property and is transferred along with that property. Each easement appurtenant involves two properties — the servient tenement and the dominant tenement.

### easement in gross

An easement that is not appurtenant to any one parcel; for example, public utilities to install power lines.

### eaves

The horizontal, lower edge of a sloped roof that hangs over the exterior walls.

### economic age

Estimated age of a building based on its condition and usefulness.

### economic age/life method

A method of computing accrued depreciation in which the cost of a building is depreciated at a fixed annual percentage rate. This is the method most frequently used by residential appraisers. Also known as the straight-line method or the age/life method.

### economic base

The companies that provide jobs for a community or defined geographic area.

### economic life

The estimated period over which a building may be profitably used. Also known as useful life.

**economic obsolescence**
Depreciation caused by changes in the economy that negatively affects the subject property's value.  *See* external obsolescence.

**economic rent**
What a leased property would be expected to rent for under current market conditions if the property were vacant and available for rent.  Also known as market rent.

**economic trend**
Pattern of related changes in some aspect of the economy.

**economically feasible**
Financially possible, reasonable, or likely.  One of the tests of highest and best use.

**effective age**
The age of a building based on its condition and usefulness.  The number of years of age that is indicated by the condition of the structure, distinct from chronological age.

**effective date**
The specific day the conclusion of value applies whether it is a present, past, or future date.

**effective demand**
Demand or desire coupled with purchasing power.

**effective gross income**
The amount of income that remains after vacancy and credit losses are deducted from gross income.

**egress**
A way to exit a property.

**element of comparison**
Any aspect of a real estate transaction or any characteristic of the property that may affect the property's sales price.

**elements of value**
Four prerequisites that must be present for an object to have value: demand, utility, scarcity, and transferability.

**elevation sheet**
A labeled diagram or cutaway of a home detailing its features and building components, both interior and exterior.

**emblements**
Growing crops that are cultivated annually for sale.

**eminent domain**
The right of the government to take private property from an owner, for the public good, paying fair market value.

**encroachment**
The unauthorized placement of permanent improvements that intrude on adjacent property owned by another.

**encumbrance**
An interest in real property that is held by someone who is not the property owner.

**entrepreneurial profit**
A market-derived figure that represents the compensation the owner or developer expects to gain from developing the property.

**entry-level home**
A type of home for first-time buyers.

**equitable title**
The interest held by the trustor under a trust deed.

**equity**
The difference between the market value of a home and the loan amount.

**equity build-up**
The gradual increase of the borrower's equity in a property caused by amortization of loan principal.

**equity capital**
The amount a buyer invests into a property.

**equity capitalization rate**
(1) Factor used to estimate the value of the equity in the band of investment method of capitalization and other mortgage and equity techniques.  (2) The equity cash flow divided by the equity value.

**equity investors**
Investors using venture capital to take an unsecured and thus relatively risky part in an investment.

**erosion**
The gradual wearing away of land by natural processes.

**escalator clause**
A clause in a contract providing for the upward or downward adjustment of certain items to cover specified contingencies, usually tied to some index or event. Often used in long term leases to provide for rent adjustments and to cover tax and maintenance increases.

**escheat**
A legal process where property reverts to the state because the deceased left no will and has no legal heirs.

**escrow**
A small and short-lived trust arrangement used to close real estate transactions.

**estate**
The ownership interest or claim a person has in real property. A legal interest in land; defines the nature, degree, extent, and duration of a person's ownership in land.

**estate at sufferance**
A tenancy created when one is in wrongful possession of real estate even though the original possession may have been legal.

**estate at will**
A tenancy that may be ended by the unilateral decision of either party. There is no agreed-upon termination date, and either party must give 30 days notice before ending the tenancy.

**estate for years**
A leasehold estate with a definite end date; must be renegotiated; commonly used for commercial leases.

**estate from period to period**
A leasehold estate that is automatically renewed for the same term; does not need to be renegotiated upon each renewal; commonly a month-to-month rental.

**estate in fee**
*See* fee simple estate.

**estate in remainder**
An estate that has been conveyed to take effect and be enjoyed after the termination of a prior estate. Also known as remainder estate. *See* also future interest.

**estate in reversion**
An estate that comes back to the original holder, as when an owner conveys a life estate to someone else, with the estate to return to the original owner on termination of the life estate. *See* also future interest.

**estimate**
(1) A preliminary opinion of value. (2) To appraise or determine value.

**ETHICS RULE**
Per USPAP, identifies the requirements for "integrity, impartiality, objectivity, independent judgment, and ethical conduct".

**evaluation**
An analysis of a property and/or its attributes in which a value estimate is not required.

**excess land**
Surplus land beyond that which is needed to support the property's highest and best use.

**excess rent**
The amount by which the total contract rent exceeds market rent.

**execute**
(1) To perform or complete. (2) To sign.

**executed contract**
All parties have performed completely.

**execution sale**
The forced sale of a property to satisfy a money judgment.

**executory contract**
A contract in which obligation to perform exists on one or both sides.

**expense ratio**
*See* operating expense ratio.

**express contract**
Parties declare the terms and put their intentions in words, either oral or written.

**external obsolescence**
A type of depreciation occurring because of negative influences outside of the specific property site (i.e. an airport flight pattern). *See* economic obsolescence and locational obsolescence.

**externalities**
Outside influences that may have a positive or negative effect on property value.

**extraction method**
A method of determining the land value of a comparable property by deducting the depreciated costs of the improvements on that property from the property's known sale price. The remaining value represents value attributable to the land. This method is a variation on the allocation method and is based on the same principles. Also known as abstraction method.

**extraordinary assumption**
Per USPAP, "an assumption, directly related to a specific assignment, which, if found to be false, could alter the appraiser's opinions or conclusions."

# F

**facade**
The face of a building, especially the front face.

**factory-built housing**
Housing built in a factory instead of on site. Includes manufactured, modular, panelized, and precut homes.

**fair market value**
*See* market value.

**feasibility study**
An analysis of a proposed subject or property with emphasis on the attainable income, probable expenses, and most advantageous use and design. The purpose of such a study is to ascertain the probable success or failure of the project under consideration.

**Federal Emergency Management Agency (FEMA)**
A government agency involved with all the different aspects of emergency management from preparation to recovery and prevention.

**Federal Housing Administration (FHA)**
A government agency that insures private mortgage loans for financing of homes and home repairs.

**Federal National Mortgage Association (FNMA)**
Fannie Mae; a quasi-public agency converted into a private corporation whose primary function is to buy and sell FHA and VA mortgages in the secondary market.

**federally related transaction**
Any real estate transaction involving federal insurance or assistance. *See* also Financial Institutions Reform, Recovery, and Enforcement Act.

**fee simple absolute**
An estate in fee with no restrictions on its use. It is the largest, most complete ownership recognized by law.

**fee simple estate**
The most complete form of ownership of real property; a freehold estate that can be passed by descent or by will after the owner's death. Also known as estate of inheritance or estate in fee.

**fee simple qualified**
An estate in fee with any limitation on property use that could result in loss of the right of ownership. Also known as fee simple defeasible.

**fiduciary**
A relationship that implies a position of trust or confidence.

**final value estimate**
The appraiser's estimate of the defined value of the subject property, arrived at by reconciling the estimates of value derived from the sales comparison, cost, and income approaches.

**Financial Institutions Reform, Recovery, and Enforcement Act (FIREEA)**
A federal law passed in 1989 to provide guidelines for the regulation of financial institutions. One part of the law requires a state license or certification for the performance of federally related real estate transactions (with de minimus exceptions).

**finished area**
The enclosed area in a home that is suitable for year-round use.

**fixed expenses**
Operating costs that are more or less permanent and that vary little from year to year regardless of occupancy.

**fixture**
Personal property that has become affixed to real estate.

**flashing**
Sheet metal or other material that keeps the water from seeping into a building.

**flipping**
Buying a property at one price and quickly selling it to another at an inflated price.

**floating slab**
A type of foundation that is composed of one section for the floor and another for the foundation wall, each poured separately.

**floor plan**
A two-story offers the most living space within a set perimeter.

**foreclosure**
The legal procedure by which mortgaged property is sold to satisfy a debt when the borrower has defaulted on the loan. Proceedings are typically started by a lender when a borrower does not pay the loan on time; may also be started if borrower fails to pay property taxes or insurance or keep other promises.

**form report**
Written appraisal report, presented on a standardized form or checklist.

**foundation**
The base of a house, usually concrete.

**fraud**
An act meant to deceive in order to get someone to part with something of value.

**freehold estate**
An estate in real property which continues for an indefinite period of time. It differs from a leasehold estate, which allows possession for a limited time.

**frequency distribution**
The arrangement of data into groups according to the frequency with which they appear in the data set.

**front foot**
Measurement in feet of the width of a property on the side facing the street.

**frontage**
The width of a property on the side facing a street.

**functional obsolescence**
A type of depreciation stemming from poor architectural design, lack of modern facilities, out-of-date equipment, changes in styles of construction or in utility demand.

**functional utility**
The combined factors of usefulness with desirability.

**future benefits**
The anticipated benefits the present owner will receive from the property in the future.

**future interest**
An interest in real property that will take effect at a future time. *See* also estate in remainder and estate in reversion.

**future value**
The estimated lump-sum value of money or property at a date in the future.

# G

**gift deed**
Used to make a gift of property to a grantee, usually a close friend or relative.

**going concern value**
The value existing in an established business property compared with the value of selling the real estate and other assets of a concern whose business is not yet established. The term takes into account the goodwill and earning capacity of a business.

**good consideration**
Gifts of love and affection. Some type of consideration is required to create a contract.

**government survey system**
A method of specifying the location of a parcel of land using prime meridians, base lines, standard parallels, guide meridians, townships, and sections. Also known as the rectangular survey system, or the U.S. Government Section and Township survey.

**grade**
Ground level at the perimeter of the building.

**grading**
A process used when the level or elevation of the ground has to be changed or altered using bladed machines that scrape the earth.

**graduated lease**
A long-term lease that provides for adjustments in the rental rate on the basis of some future determination.

**grandfather clause**
The continuation of a use or business to proceed because the current law denies permission.

**grant**
A technical legal term in a deed of conveyance bestowing an interest in real property on another. The words "convey" and "transfer" have the same effect.

**grant deed**
A deed in which the grantor warrants that he or she has not previously conveyed the property being granted, has not encumbered the property except as disclosed, and will convey to the grantee any title he or she may acquire afterwards.

**grantee**
The person receiving the property, or the one to whom it is being conveyed.

**grantor**
The person conveying, or transferring, the property.

**gross building area (GBA)**
All enclosed floor areas, as measured along a building's outside perimeter.

**gross income**
Total income from property before any expenses are deducted.

**gross income multiplier (GIM)**
A figure which, when multiplied by the annual gross income, will equal the property's market value. The amount of the GIM must be obtained from recent comparable sales since it varies with specific properties and areas.

**gross leasable area**
Total space designed for occupancy and exclusive use of tenants, measured from outside wall surfaces to the center of shared interior walls.

**gross lease**
A lease agreement where the tenant pays an agreed-upon sum as rent and the landlord pays any other expenses such as taxes, maintenance, or insurance. Also called a flat, fixed, or straight lease.

**gross living area (GLA)**
Total finished, habitable, above-grade space, measured along the building's outside perimeter.

**gross rent**
Income (calculated annually or monthly) received from rental units before any expenses are deducted.

**gross rent multiplier (GRM)**
A figure which, when multiplied by the monthly rental income, will equal the property's market value. The amount of the GRM must be obtained from recent comparable sales since it varies with specific properties and areas.

**ground lease**
A lease of land only on which the lessee usually owns the building or is required to build as specified by the lease. Such leases are usually long-term net leases.

# H

**highest and best use (HBU)**
The use, from among reasonably probable and adequately supported alternative uses, that is physically possible, legally permitted, economically feasible, and maximally productive. This is the starting point for appraisal.

**historic cost**
Cost of a property at the time it was constructed or purchased.

**historic zoning**
Zoning laws enacted to protect historic buildings within a specified area referred to as a historic district.

**HUD**
US Department of Housing Urban Development/Settlement statement of all costs and fees in closing escrow.

**hybrid loans**
Loans that offer features from various loan types.

**hypothetical condition**
Defined in USPAP as "that which is contrary to what exists but is supposed for the purpose of analysis".

# I

**implied contract**
An agreement shown by acts and conduct rather than written words.

**improvements**
Additions made to property to enhance value or extend useful life. This term is typically used to refer to buildings and other structures that are permanently attached to the land.

**incentive zoning**
Allows a developer to exceed the limitations set by a zoning law if the developer agrees to fulfill conditions specified in the law.

**income approach**
An appraisal method that estimates the present worth of future benefits from ownership of a property to determine that property's value. Also known as income capitalization approach.

**income capitalization method**
Method for estimating depreciation by comparing the subject's capitalized value to its replacement cost new or by determining loss in rental income attributable to a depreciated item and applying a gross rent multiplier to that figure.

**income forecast**
Gross or net income estimate.

**income property**
Property that is purchased for its income-producing capabilities.

**income stream**
Actual or estimated flow of net earnings over time.

**increasing and decreasing returns, principle of**
*See* principle of increasing and decreasing returns.

**incurable depreciation**
Building defects or problems that would cost more to repair than the anticipated value increase from such repair.

**index method**
Method for estimating construction costs that adjusts the original costs to the current cost level by a multiplier obtained from a published cost index.

**indicated value**
Value estimate calculated or produced by an appraisal approach.

**indirect costs**
All of the time and money costs involved in a construction project that are not directly involved with construction itself. Examples are loan fees, interest, legal fees, and marketing costs.

**inflation**
The increase in the general price level of goods and services.

**ingress**
A way to enter a property.

**instrument**
A formal legal document such as a contract, deed or will.

**insulation**
Any material used in building construction that slows down the transfer of heat.

**insurable value**
The highest reasonable value that can be placed on property for insurance purposes.

**intangible property**
Rights to something other than tangible, physical property.

**intended users**
Per USPAP, parties intending to use an appraisal.

**interest**
(1) The charge for the use of money. (2) A legal share of ownership in property.

**interest rate**
The percentage of interest charged on the principal.

**interim use**
A short-term and temporary use of a property until it is ready for a more productive highest and best use. Occurs when the highest and best use is expected to change.

**intestate**
A situation where a person dies without leaving a will.

**inverse condemnation**
An action brought by a private party to force the government to pay just compensation for diminishing the value or use of his or her property.

**investment value**
The value of a particular property to a particular investor.

# J

**joint tenancy**
A type of ownership interest where two or more parties own real property as co-owners, with the right of survivorship.

**judgment**
The final legal decision of a judge in a court of law regarding the legal rights of parties to disputes.

**JURISDICTIONAL EXCEPTION RULE**
Part of USPAP, preserves the remainder of USPAP if one portion is contrary to a jurisdiction's law or public policy.

**just compensation**
Fair and reasonable payment due to a private property owner when his or her property is condemned under eminent domain.

# L

**land**
The surface of the earth including airspace, surface rights, mineral rights, and water rights.

**land capitalization rate**
The rate of return in investment and return of investment for the land only.

**land residual technique**
Income capitalization technique where the net income remaining to the land (after income attributable to the building has been deducted) is capitalized into an estimate of value for the land.

**landlocked**
Property surrounded by other property with no access to a public road or street.

**landscaping**
The art of arranging plants, rocks, and lumber around the outside of a property for aesthetic or practical purposes, such as to prevent erosion or provide parking areas.

**lease**
A contract between landlord (owner/lessor) and tenant (lessee) which gives the tenant an interest in the property. Also known as a rental agreement.

**leased-fee estate**
The property owner's interest in the leased property.

**leasehold estate**
The tenant's interest in the leased property during the term of the lease. This type of estate only has value if the agreed-on rent is less than the market rent. Also known as a less-than-freehold estate.

**legal description**
A land description recognized by law which can be used to locate a particular piece of property. Lot, block, and tract, government survey, and metes and bounds are types of legal descriptions.

**legally permitted**
Land uses that are allowed under current zoning and other land use regulations. One of the tests of highest and best use.

**lender pressure**
A lender directly or indirectly pressuring an appraiser to estimate a property's value at a certain amount.

**lender**
A company or person that makes mortgage loans, such as a mortgage banker, credit union, bank, or savings and loan.

**lessee**
Tenant or renter.

**lessor**
The person (landlord or property owner) who signs the lease to give possession and use to the tenant.

**less-than-freehold estate**
*See* leasehold estate.

**lien**
A claim on the property of another for the payment of a debt. A type of encumbrance.

**life estate**
An estate that is limited in duration to the life of its owner or the life of another designated person.

**limited appraisal**
An appraisal developed under and resulting from invoking USPAP's Departure Rule.

**limited liability company**
A type of business that has characteristics of both a corporation and a limited partnership.

**limited partnership**
A partnership of at least one general partner and one limited partner.

**linear regression**
Statistical technique used to calculate adjustment value or estimate sales price.

**liquidation value**
The value that can be received from the marketplace when the property has to be sold immediately.

**lis pendens**
A recorded notice that indicates pending litigation affecting title on a property.

**listing**
A contract between an owner of real property and an agent who is authorized to obtain a buyer.

**littoral**
Land bordering a lake, ocean, or sea — as opposed to land bordering a stream or river (running water). (Pronounced li-TORE-al)

**locational obsolescence**
Depreciation caused by the physical location of the subject property and its proximity to a negative influence. *See* external obsolescence.

**long-lived**
Structural components that need replacement infrequently, and sometimes never.

### lot, block, and tract system

A type of legal description that is created when developers divide parcels of land into lots. Each lot in a subdivision is identified by number, as is the block in which it is located, and each lot and block is in a referenced tract. Also known as lot and block system, subdivision system or recorded map system.

# M

### maintenance expenses

Costs incurred for day-to-day-upkeep, such as management, employee wages and benefits, fuel, utility services, decorating, and repairs.

### Management

The section of USPAP that discusses the disclosure of certain fees and commissions, identifies prohibited compensation arrangements, and discusses certain prohibited advertising and solicitation issues.

### manufactured home

A home built in a factory after June 15, 1976 which must conform to the U.S. government's Manufactured Home Construction and Safety Standards.

### MARIA

The mnemonic for the five tests of a fixture: **M**ethod of attachment, **A**daptation, **R**elationship of the parties, **I**ntention, and **A**greement of the parties.

### marital property

A general term for property owned by married people. Married people may have a special status as property owners; forms of ownership vary from state-to-state.

### market

A place or condition suitable for selling and buying.

### market analysis

To identify, research, and analyze the particular market in which the appraised property operates.

### market comparison approach

*See* sales comparison approach.

### market exposure

Making a reasonable number of potential buyers of a property aware that the property is available.

### market extraction

(1) General term for collecting information from the market. (2) Method of estimating depreciation where building values abstracted from sales are compared to current costs new.

### market price

The price paid regardless of pressures, motives, or intelligence.

### market rent

The rent a property should bring in the open market.

### market segmentation

The process of identifying and analyzing submarkets within larger markets.

### market value

The price a property would bring if freely offered on the open market, with both a willing buyer and a willing seller. Also known as objective value or value in exchange. *See* arm's-length transaction.

### mass appraisal

Appraising more than one property using standard computerized techniques (statistical analysis, regression, automated valuation models, etc.).

### master plan

A city or county's overall plan for physical development. *See* zoning.

### matrix

*See* adjustment grid.

### maximally productive

The property use that produces the greatest return on investment. One of the tests of highest and best use.

### mean

A measure of central tendency which is calculated by adding the average prices or numeric values of a statistical sample and dividing that by the number of values in the sample. Also known as the average.

**mechanic's lien**
A lien placed against a property by anyone who supplied labor, services, or materials used for improvements on real property and did not receive payment for the improvements.

**median**
A measure of central tendency that equals the middle value in a statistical sample. For example, the median home price in an area is the price that is midway between the least expensive and most expensive homes sold in that area during a given period of time.

**meridian**
A survey line running north and south, used as a reference when mapping land.

**metes and bounds**
A type of legal description that delineates boundaries and measures distances between landmarks to identify property.

**mile**
A linear measurement of distance. Equals 5,280 feet.

**mill**
Equals one-thousandth of a dollar and is numerically expressed as $0.001.

**millage rate**
Expresses the property tax rate in terms of tenths of a cent per dollar of property value. The rate varies from district to district and county to county.

**mineral rights**
The legal interest in the valuable items found below the surface of a property (i.e., gold and coal).

**minimum rent**
The fixed minimum rent amount paid under a percentage lease. Also known as base rent.

**mobile home**
A factory-built home manufactured prior to June 15, 1976, constructed on a chassis and wheels, and designed for permanent or semi-attachment to land.

**mode**
A measure of central tendency that equals the most frequently occurring price or value in a statistical sample.

**modified age/life method**
A method of calculating depreciation. Curable physical and functional items of accrued depreciation are identified. The cost to cure all these items is deducted from the reproduction or replacement cost of the improvements. The ratio derived from the age/life method is then multiplied by the remaining cost to arrive at an estimate of accrued depreciation from all other causes.

**modular home**
Building composed of modules constructed on an assembly line in a factory.

**monolithic slab**
A slab foundation poured in one piece.

**monument**
A fixed landmark used in a metes and bounds land description.

**mortgage**
A legal document used as security for a debt. The mortgage is the instrument which secures the promissory note.

**mortgage constant**
The annual debt payment divided by the loan amount (principal).

**mortgage yield**
The amount received or returned from an investment expressed as a percentage.

**mortgagee**
The lender under a mortgage.

**mortgagor**
An owner of real estate who borrows money and uses his or her property as security for the loan.

**multiple listing service (MLS)**
A cooperative listing service conducted by a group of brokers (usually members of a real estate association) to provide an inventory of all available properties in an area.

**multiple regression analysis**
A statistical technique for estimating a particular variable, such as probable sales price, using more than one other known variables.

**mutual consent**
An offer by one party and acceptance by another party. Also known as mutual assent or "meeting of the minds".

**mutual funds**
Investment vehicles operated by investment companies.

**mutual mortgage insurance (MMI)**
A fee for an insurance policy charged the borrower to protect the lender under an FHA loan in the event of foreclosure on the property.

**mutual rescission**
When all parties to a contract agree to cancel an agreement.

# N

**narrative appraisal report**
A detailed, formal written report of the appraisal and the value conclusion.

**negative amortization**
Occurs when monthly installment payments are insufficient to pay the interest, so any unpaid interest is added to the principal due.

**negative cash flow**
When monies will flow from the investor toward the investment.

**negative easement**
Prohibits a property owner from doing something on his or her estate because of the effect it would have on the dominant estate.

**neighborhood cycle**
The process of neighborhood change, including four phases of change: development, maturity, decline, and renaissance.

**neighborhood**
An area whose occupants and users share some common ties or characteristics. A neighborhood may be defined by physical boundaries, a change in land use, or intangible factors like school district boundaries.

**net income**
Gross annual income, less income lost due to vacancies and uncollectible rents, less all operating expenses.

**net income ratio**
Net income divided by the effective gross income.

**net lease**
The tenant pays an agreed-upon sum as rent, plus certain agreed upon expenses per month (e.g., taxes and insurance).

**net operating income (NOI)**
The income remaining after deducting operating expenses from effective gross income.

**non-conforming loan**
A loan that does not meet the standards of Fannie Mae and Freddie Mac. Jumbo loans and sub-prime loans are types of non-conforming loans.

**nonconforming use**
Legal use of property that was established and maintained at the time of its original construction but no longer conforms to the current zoning law.

**non-economic highest and best use**
A type of highest and best use that focuses on contribution to the community and community developmental goals rather than income-production.

# O

**observed condition method**
*See* breakdown method.

**obsolescence**
Loss in value due to reduced desirability and usefulness of a structure because its design and construction became obsolete or due to factors outside the property itself. May be functional or economic.

**occupancy rate**
The percentage of total rental units occupied and producing income.

**offer**
A presentation or proposal for acceptance to form a contract.

**offeree**
The party receiving an offer.

**offeror**
The party making an offer.

**operating expense ratio**
Relationship of a property's expenses to income, found by dividing total operating expenses by effective gross income.

**operating expenses**
Expenses required to run a property (i.e., to maintain its income). Includes fixed, variable, and reserves for replacement.

**operating statement**
Written record of a property's gross income, expenses, and resultant net income for a given period of time.

**opportunity cost**
The value differential between alternative investments with differing rates of return. *See* principle of opportunity cost.

**oral report**
An appraisal report that is communicated to the client verbally, rather than in writing.

**orientation**
The placement of a building on its lot in relation to exposure to sun, prevailing wind, traffic, and accessibility from the street.

**overage rent**
The amount paid over and above the base rent, under a percentage lease.

**overall capitalization rate**
*See* capitalization rate.

**over-improvement**
An improvement which is not the highest and best use for the site on which it is placed by reason of excess size or cost. Also called superadequacy.

**ownership**
(1) The right of one or more persons to possess and use property to the exclusion of all others. (2) A collection of rights to the use and enjoyment of property.

**ownership in severalty**
Property owned by one person or entity.

# P

**packed sale**
A type of mortgage fraud in which excessive points, fees, and interest rates are charged to unsuspecting buyers.

**paired sales analysis**
A method of estimating the amount of adjustment for the presence or absence of any feature by pairing the sales prices of otherwise identical properties with and without that feature. A sufficient number of sales must be found to allow the appraiser to isolate the effect on value of the pertinent factor. Also known as paired data set analysis, matched pairs analysis, and direct market method.

**panelized home**
A type of factory-built housing. A panelized home arrives at the construction site in small units, usually as completed walls with all the wiring and plumbing intact.

**parameter**
A statistical term for a single number or attribute of the individual things, persons, or other entities in a population.

**parcel map**
Map showing a parcel of land that will be subdivided into less than five parcels or units, and shows land boundaries, streets, and parcel numbers.

**partial interest**
An interest in real estate that represents less than the fee simple estate (i.e., a leased fee or leasehold estate).

**partial taking**
The process by which a governmental agency acquires only a portion of a property through condemnation.

**partition action**
A court action to divide a property held by co-owners.

**partnership**
A form of business in which two or more persons join their money and skills in conducting the business.

**PEPS**
The mnemonic for the four forces influencing value: **P**hysical and environmental characteristics, **E**conomic influences, **P**olitical (Governmental) regulations, and **S**ocial ideals and standards.

**percentage adjustment**
Type of sales adjustment where the estimated difference between the comparable sale and the subject is first calculated as a percentage of the sale price of the comparable, and then applied as an upward or downward adjustment to the price.

**percentage lease**
A type of lease in which the tenant pays a percentage of gross monthly receipts in addition to a base rent.

**personal property**
Anything movable that is not real property.

**physical deterioration**
Depreciation that comes from wear and tear, negligent care, damage by dry rot or termites, or severe changes in temperature. Also known as deferred maintenance.

**physical life**
The length of time a structure can be considered habitable, without regard to its economic use.

**physically possible**
A use for the property that is not prevented by any physical issues such as poor access, steep topography or unusable soil. The first test for highest and best use.

**pier and beam foundation**
A type of foundation using wood or concrete piers which rest on support beams or girders, which support the structure.

**planned unit development (PUD)**
A planning and zoning term describing land not subject to conventional zoning to permit clustering of residences or other characteristics of the project which differ from normal zoning. Also known as a planned development.

**plat map**
Map of a subdivision indicating the location and boundaries of individual lots.

**platform frame construction**
A type of framing used in residential construction. It is the most prevalent type for one- and two-story residences.

**plottage**
The value added by combining two or more parcels together into one large parcel.

**point of beginning**
Starting place for a legal description of land using the metes and bounds method.

**points**
Charges levied by the lender based on the loan amount. Each point equals one percent of the loan amount; for example, two points on a $100,000 mortgage is $2,000.

**police power**
The power of the state to enact laws within constitutional limits to promote the order, safety, health, morals, and general welfare of our society.

**population**
(1) The total number of people inhabiting a specific area. (2) In statistics, the entire set of data from which a statistical sample is drawn.

**positive cash flow**
When income generated by the property flows toward the owner.

**potential gross income**
A property's total potential income from all sources during a specified period of time.

**precut home**
A type of factory-built housing. A precut home is like a house in a box. All the materials are delivered to the construction site unassembled, but precut to fit exactly in place.

**prescriptive easement**
Using someone else's property without their permission.

**price**
The amount of money requested or paid.

**primary mortgage market**
The term for the market made up of lenders who make mortgage loans by lending directly to borrowers.

**principal**
(1) In a real estate transaction, the one who hires the broker to represent him or her in the sale of the property. (2) The amount of money borrowed.

**principal meridian**
One of 35 north and south survey lines established and defined as part of the U.S. government survey system.

**principle of:**

**anticipation**
States that value is created by the anticipation of benefits derived in the future.

**balance**
States that the greatest value of a property will occur when the type and size of the improvements are proportional to each other as well as to the land.

**change**
Holds that it is the future, not the past, which is of prime importance in estimating value. Real estate values are constantly changed by environmental, economic, political, and social forces.

**competition**
States that real estate values are affected by supply and demand because of competition. Typically follows three steps: (1) Market demand generates profits. (2) Profits generate competition. (3) Competition stabilizes profits.

**conformity**
States that maximum value results when properties in a neighborhood are relatively similar in size, style, quality, use, and/or type.

**consistent use**
Requires that land and improvements be appraised on the basis of the same use.

**contribution**
Calculates the worth of a particular component in terms of its contribution to the value of the whole property, or an item's worth is calculated as the amount that its absence would detract from the value of the whole.

**increasing and decreasing returns**
The idea that income and other benefits available from real estate may be increased by adding capital improvements only up to the point of balance in the agents of production, beyond which the increase in value tends to be less than the increase in costs. Also known as law of increasing and decreasing returns.

**opportunity cost**
The economic principle that recognizes competing investments, usually in different industries, that may have a greater return.

**progression**
States that the worth of a lesser valued residence tends to be enhanced by association with higher valued residences in the same area.

**regression**
States that higher-valued properties tend to suffer when placed in close proximity with lower-valued properties.

**substitution**
Affirms that the maximum value of a property tends to be set by the cost of acquiring an equally desirable and valuable substitute property, assuming no cost delay is encountered in making the substitution. The foundation for the appraisal process.

**supply and demand**
States that market value is affected by the intersection of supply and demand forces in the market as of the appraisal date. Prices and rent levels tend to increase when demand is greater than supply and tend to decrease when supply exceeds demand.

**surplus productivity**
States that the net income that remains after the ownership expenses of labor, capital, and management have been paid is surplus income that is attributable to the land. This is also called land rent and is used as the basis for the residual land valuation techniques.

**private grant**
The granting of private property to other private persons.

**private mortgage insurance**
Mortgage guarantee insurance required by conventional lenders on the first part of a high risk loan.

**private restrictions**
Created at the time of sale or in the general plan of a subdivision.

**progression, principle of**
*See* principle of progression

**promissory note**
The evidence of the debt, which states the amount of the money borrowed and the terms of repayment.

**property**
Anything that may be owned and gained lawfully.

**proprietary lease**
The lease used in co-op apartment buildings.

**public dedication**
When private property is intended for public use. There are three types of public dedication: common law dedication, statutory dedication, or deed.

**public grant**
The transfer of title by the government to a private individual.

**PUD**
*See* planned unit development.

# Q

**quantity survey method**
The most in-depth and detailed method used to estimate reproduction or replacement cost. This method requires a detailed estimate of all labor and materials used in the components of a building. Items such as overhead, insurance and contractor's profit are added to direct costs of building. This method is time consuming but very accurate.

**quiet title action**
A court proceeding to clear a cloud on the title of real property. Also known as action to quiet title.

**quitclaim deed**
Transfers any interest the grantor may have at the time the deed is signed with no warranties of clear title.

# R

**radon**
Colorless, odorless, gas that is a carcinogen detected by a spectrometer.

**range**
A land description used in the U.S. government survey system consisting of a strip of land located every six miles east and west of each principal meridian.

**range lines**
Imaginary vertical lines six miles east and west of the meridian to form columns. Used in the U.S. government survey system.

**rate**
*See* interest rate.

**ratio capitalization**
Describes any capitalization method that uses the typical ratio of income to value to convert projected income into a value estimate for the property (or property component) under appraisal. Includes direct capitalization, as well as land, building, and equity residual capitalization methods when sales price-income ratios are used.

**real property**
Land (air, surface, mineral, water rights), appurtenances, and anything attached, and immovable by law. Also included are the interests, benefits, and rights inherent in owning real estate, i.e., the "bundle of rights". Current usage makes the term real property synonymous with real estate.

**recapture**
The recovery by an owner of money invested. Known as return of investment, not to be confused with interest, which is a return on investment. Also known as capital recapture.

**reconciliation**
The adjustment process of weighing results of all three appraisal methods to arrive at a final estimate of the subject property's market value. Also known as correlation.

**reconstruction of the operating statement**
The process of eliminating the inapplicable expense items for appraisal purposes and adjusting the remaining valid expenses, if necessary.

**Record Keeping**
Per USPAP, this section of the ETHICS RULE identifies the record keeping requirements appraisers must follow.

**recorded map system**
*See* lot, block, and tract system.

**recording**
The process of placing a document on file with a designated public official for public notice.

**rectangular survey system**
*See* government survey system.

**refinancing**
The paying-off of an existing obligation and assuming a new obligation in its place. To finance anew, or to extend or renew existing financing.

**regression, principle of**
*See* principle of regression.

**rehabilitation**
The restoration of a property to its former or improved condition without changing the basic design or plan.

**remaining economic life**
The number of years between the structure's estimated economic life and its effective age.

**remodeling**
Changes the basic design or plan of the building to correct deficiencies.

**rent**
Payment for the use of a property, generally under a lease agreement.

**rental survey**
An analysis of competitive rents used to identify the amount of income the subject property might generate.

**replacement cost**
Cost of constructing a building or structure that would have a similar utility to the subject improvement, but constructed with modern materials and according to current standards, design, and layout.

**replacement reserves**
Funds set aside by the property owner to pay for the replacement of certain building components and fixtures that periodically wear out. Also known as reserves for replacement.

**replacement value**
The amount of money required to replace any improvements that have been lost to fire, flood, wind or other natural disasters.

**reproduction cost**
The current cost of building a replica of the subject structure, using similar quality materials.

**residential lease**
A lease used for single-family homes and duplexes.

### Residential License appraiser

An individual who has met specific education, experience, and examination requirements. May appraise any non-complex 1-4 unit residential property with a transaction value less than $1 million and any complex 1-4 unit residential property with a transaction value less than $250,000. *See* appraiser.

### residual

In appraising, the income or value remaining after all deductions have been made.

### residual techniques of capitalization

Capitalization techniques that attribute income to a component of the property, such as land or building, or debt or equity, to analyze its value contribution to the total property.

### Restricted Use Appraisal Report

This is the briefest presentation of an appraisal and contains the least detail. It is called restricted-use because the client is the only intended user of the report.

### restriction

A limitation placed on the use of property. A restriction may be placed by a private owner, a developer, or the government.

### retaining walls

Walls constructed to hold back soil and prevent erosion.

### retrospective appraisal

An appraisal that looks at the value of a property at a point of time in the past.

### retrospective value

The value of the property as of a previous date.

### return

*See* return on investment.

### return of investment

Recapture or conversion of the investment in real estate to cash or other valuable assets. *See* recapture.

### return on investment

The interest earned by an investor on an investment (or by a bank on the money it has loaned). Also called return or yield.

### reversion

The right to future possession or enjoyment by a person, or the person's heirs, creating the proceeding estate.

### reversionary interest

A future interest. For example, the right of a landlord to reclaim the property at the end of the lease.

### riparian rights

The rights of a landowner whose land is next to a natural watercourse to reasonable use of whatever water flows past the property.

### row house

*See* townhouse.

### Rules

The five rules in USPAP: the ETHICS RULE, the COMPETENCY RULE, the DEPARTURE RULE (or SCOPE OF WORK RULE), the JURISDICTIONAL EXCEPTION RULE, and the SUPPLEMENTAL STANDARDS RULE.

### R-value

A rating that measures how well insulation resists heat.

# S

### sale-resale analysis

A method for determining adjustment or depreciation amounts that is useful when a property sells and is resold in a relatively short period of time. Assuming both sales are arm's-length, open market transactions, and assuming that there have been no significant changes to the property during the time between the two sales, the difference in price could be a basis for a time adjustment.

**sales comparison approach**
An appraisal method based on the principles of substitution that compares similar properties, which have recently sold, to the subject property. Also called the market data approach, market approach, or comparison approach.

**sales price**
The actual price that a buyer pays for a property.

**salvage value**
For income tax purposes, the anticipated fair market value of the property at the end of its useful life.

**sample**
A defined group within the whole that appraisers work with when analyzing statistical data.

**sandwich lease**
A lease agreement in which a tenant sublets the property to another person, thus creating a sublessor-sublessee relationship.

**savings and loan association (S&L)**
A lending institution created as a mutual organization or as a stock institution. Deposits are insured by the Federal Deposit Insurance Corporation (FDIC).

**scarcity**
A lack of supply of some type of real property resulting in increased value when demand exceeds supply.

**scheduled rent**
Rent paid by agreement between lessor and lessee. Also called contract rent.

**SCI**
The mnemonic for three approaches to value: **S**ales comparison approach, **C**ost approach, and **I**ncome approach.

**scope of work**
The type and extent of research done and the type and extent of analysis applied.

**secondary mortgage market**
The buying and selling of existing mortgages.

**section**
An area of land that is one square mile or 640 acres; 1/36 of a township.

**Self-Contained Appraisal Report**
Contains the most detailed information. Self-contained means that everything the user of the report needs to fully understand it is contained within the report.

**seller's market**
The market condition in which demand exceeds supply.

**separate property**
Property owned by a married person in his or her own right outside of the community interest including property acquired by the spouse: (a) before marriage, (b) by gift or inheritance, (c) from rents and profits on separate property, and (d) with the proceeds from other separate property.

**septic system**
The waste removal system.

**septic tank**
A watertight sewage-settling tank designed to accommodate liquid and solid waste.

**servient tenement**
The property that is burdened by an easement.

**setback**
The distance a building must be set back for the lot line; usually front, back or side setback.

**short-lived**
Structural components that are expected to be replaced or repaired on a consistent basis throughout the life of the structure.

**siding**
Used to protect the interior and framing from temperature and weather. Types of siding include wood, masonry, stucco, steel/aluminum, and vinyl.

**sinking fund**
A fund set aside from a property's income which, with accrued interest, will eventually pay for replacement of the improvements.

**site**

(1) Land that has been prepared for use with grading, utilities, and access. (2) The position, situation, or location of a piece of land in a neighborhood.

**slab-on-grade**

A type of foundation where the structure sits directly on the ground. Monolithic slabs, floating slabs, screeded slabs, and post-tensioned slabs are all types of slab-on-grade foundations.

**special assessments**

Taxes used for specific local purposes.

**special flood hazard area**

Flood-prone area identified by FEMA; if the subject property is within a flood hazard zone, it needs to be noted in the appraisal report.

**special-purpose property**

Property that has unique usage requirements, such as a church or a museum, making it difficult to convert to other uses.

**special-use permit**

*See* conditional-use permit.

**square-foot method**

A method for calculating reproduction or replacement cost by multiplying the cost per square foot by the building's area in square feet. The most common method used by appraisers and real estate agents to estimate the cost of construction.

**standard depth**

The most typical lot depth in the neighborhood.

**standard deviation**

A measure of the extent of variability in a sample, that is, whether the observations are clustered near the mean or scattered throughout the range. Standard deviation is calculated by taking the square root of the sum of the squared differences between each observation and the mean of all observations, divided by the total number of observations.

**standards**

There are ten standards within USPAP, and each Standard includes a series of Standards Rules.

**Standards Rules**

A series of rules within USPAP that specify what the appraiser must do.

**Statements on Appraisal Standards**

Part of USPAP, they clarify, interpret, explain, or elaborate on a Rule or Standard.

**statistics**

The science of collecting, classifying, and interpreting information based on the number of things.

**stigmatized property**

Property which buyers or tenants may avoid for reasons which are unrelated to its physical conditions or features. For example, properties in which there have been murders, suicides, or criminal activity are typically stigmatized properties. Also known as psychologically impacted property.

**stock cooperative**

A corporation formed for the purpose of owning property.

**stock dividend**

A dividend paid out in stock, rather than cash.

**stocks**

Shares of ownership in a company or corporation.

**straight lease**

Lease agreement in which rent is a fixed amount that stays the same over the entire lease term.

**straight-line method**

*See* economic age/life method.

**subdivision**

A tract of land divided by the owner into building lots and streets by a recorded subdivision plat.

**subdivision development method**

A method of valuing land used for subdivision development. It relies on accurate forecasting of market demand, including both forecast absorption (the rate at which properties will sell) and projected gross sales (total income that the project will produce). Also called the land development method.

**subdivision system**
*See* lot, block, and tract system.

**subject property**
The property that is being appraised.

**subjective value**
Value based on personal reasons.

**substitution, principle of**
*See* principle of substitution.

**substructure**
Refers to all the below grade improvements.

**Summary Appraisal Report**
The most commonly used report option. It fulfills the minimum requirements for lenders to process their loans.

**sump**
A pit or tank that catches liquid runoff for drainage or disposal. A sump pump is used to pump the liquid out of the pit or tank.

**superadequacy**
A feature that is too large or of a higher quality than needed for a property. Also called an over-improvement.

**superstructure**
Refers to all the above-grade improvements.

**supply**
The total amount of a given type of property for sale or lease, at various prices, at any given point in time.

**supply and demand, principle of**
*See* principle of supply and demand

**surface rights**
The rights to use the surface of land, including the right to drill or mine through the surface when subsurface rights are involved.

**surplus productivity, principle of**
*See* principle of surplus productivity

**survey**
The process by which a parcel of land is measured and its area is ascertained.

# T

**tangible property**
Physical objects and/or the rights thereto.

**tenancy**
A mode or method of ownership or holding title to property.

**tenancy by the entirety**
The joint ownership, recognized in some states, of property acquired by husband and wife during marriage. On the death of one spouse the survivor becomes the owner of the property.

**tenancy in common**
When two or more persons, whose interests are not necessarily equal, are owners of undivided interests in a single estate.

**tenancy in partnership**
Ownership by two or more persons who form a partnership for business purposes.

**term**
The period of time during which loan payments are made. At the end of the loan term, the loan must be paid in full.

**The Appraisal Foundation**
An entity created by the appraisal profession to regulate its own industry. Empowered by the Financial Institutions Reform, Recovery, and Enforcement Act of 1989 to set minimum standards and qualifications for performing appraisals in federally related financial transactions.

**time adjustment**
A term usually applied to adjustments made because of changing market conditions (not merely the passage of time).

**TIMMUR**
The mnemonic for fixed operating expenses: **T**axes, **I**nsurance, **M**anagement, **M**aintenance, **U**tilities, and **R**eserves.

**title**
Evidence that the owner of land is in lawful possession.

**title plant**
The storage facility of a title company in which it has accumulated complete title records of properties in its area.

**topography**
Nature of the surface of land; topography may be level, rolling, mountainous, sloped, etc.

**townhouse**
One of a row of houses usually of the same or similar design with common side walls or with a very narrow space between adjacent side walls. Also known as a row house.

**township**
Used in the government survey system, a area six miles by six miles (36 square miles) described by its location relative to the intersection of the baseline and meridian.

**township lines**
Imaginary lines drawn every six miles north and south of the base line to form a horizontal row or tier of townships.

**tract**
A piece of land in an unimproved state — it does not have utilities, sewer lines, etc.

**trade fixture**
An item of personal property, such as a shelf, cash register, room partition or wall mirror, used to conduct a business.

**Trainee License appraiser**
In some states, this is the lowest level of appraisal license. The education, experience, and exam requirements to obtain a trainee license vary widely by state. Trainees must be supervised and may appraise any property that the supervising appraiser is permitted to appraise. *See* appraiser.

**transferability**
The ability to transfer ownership of an item from one person or entity to another.

**Treasury bill**
*See* U.S. Treasury Bill.

**triple-net lease**
A type of lease where the tenant is paying rent and virtually all of the expenses. Also known as a net-net-net lease or absolute net lease,

**trust deed**
A security instrument that conveys naked legal title of real property.

**trustee**
Holds naked legal title to property as a neutral third party where there is a deed of trust.

**trustor**
The borrower under a deed of trust.

**T-TIP**
The mnemonic for the four unities of joint tenancy: **T**ime, **T**itle, **I**nterest, and **P**ossession.

# U

**under-improvement**
An improvement which, because of a deficiency in size or cost, is not the highest and best use of the site.

**undivided interest**
(1) An interest that allows all owners to use the entire property even if ownership interests are unequal. (2) A special ownership form where the land itself is not divided but the ownership is. The buyer receives an undivided interest in a parcel of land as a tenant in common with all the other owners.

**unearned increment**
An increase in real estate value that comes about from forces outside the control of the owner(s), such as a favorable shift in population.

**unenforceable contract**
A contract that was valid when made but either cannot be proved or will not be enforced by a court.

**unfinished areas**
The areas of a home that do not have flooring, insulation, etc., that is similar to the rest of the house.

**Uniform Residential Appraisal Report (URAR)**
An example of a summary report. It is probably the most widely used form.

**Uniform Standards of Professional Appraisal Practice (USPAP)**
A set of standards and ethics, originally developed by nine appraisal associations to guide members in the development and reporting of appraisals. Now developed, published, interpreted, and amended by the Appraisal Standards Board of the Appraisal Foundation.

**unilateral contract**
A contract where one party promises to perform without expectation of performance by the other party.

**unilateral rescission**
Legal action taken by one party to repeal a contract when the other party has breached the contract.

**unit of comparison adjustment**
Sales analysis tool, wherein the sales prices of the comparables are converted to price per physical or economic unit that is found to be closely related to selling price or value. The value of the subject property is suggested by multiplying its number of units by the price per unit of comparison found to be typical or appropriate.

**unit-in-place method**
A method of determining reproduction or replacement cost. In this method, the costs of the various building components, as installed, are computed and added together to determine the structure cost. Also known as the segregated cost method.

**unit of measurement**
The particular measurement being used. The two most commonly used are square foot (area) and cubic foot (volume).

**urban property**
City property; closely settled property.

**urban sprawl**
The unplanned and often haphazard growth of an urban area into adjoining areas.

**U.S. Treasury Bill (T-Bill)**
Short-term debt incurred by the U.S. government.

**usable area**
The portion of the site that is suitable for building.

**use value**
(1) The subjective value of an item or object to a particular user. (2) The value of a property under a given use. Also known as value-in-use.

**useful area**
That portion of the gross area of a site that can be built on or developed.

**useful life**
*See* economic life.

**utility**
The ability of a property to satisfy a need or desire, such as for shelter or income.

# V

**vacancy loss**
Loss of potential income because of a vacant unit.

**valid contract**
A binding and enforceable contract that has all the elements required by law.

**valuable consideration**
Something of value such as money, property, or personal services. Each party to a contract must give up something to make the agreement binding.

**valuation**
The process of estimating value.

**value**
The present and future anticipated enjoyment or profit from the ownership of property. Also known as worth.

**value conclusion**
*See* final value estimate.

**value in exchange**
*See* market value.

**value in use**
*See* use value.

**variable expenses**
Operating expenses that vary with occupancy level or intensity of use of a property (e.g., utility costs and maintenance).

**variance**
An exception granted to existing zoning regulations for special reasons.

**variate**
In statistics, a single random variable with a numerical value within a particular sample.

**vendee**
The buyer under a contract of sale (land contract).

**vendor**
The seller under a contract of sale (land contract).

**verification**
Sworn statement before a duly qualified officer to the correctness of an instrument's contents. *See* instrument.

**void contract**
A contract that has no legal effect due to lack of capacity or illegal subject matter.

**voidable contract**
An agreement which is valid and enforceable on its face, but may be rejected by one or more of the parties.

**voltage**
The amount of pressure at which electricity is delivered.

**volume**
Measurement of the amount of space that a three-dimensional object occupies. In real estate, volume is normally measured in cubic feet or cubic yards.

# W

**warranty deed**
A deed used to transfer title to property, guaranteeing that the title is clear and the grantor has the right to transfer it.

**workfile**
Appraiser's records that contain all the documentation necessary to support the appraiser's analyses, opinions, and conclusions conveyed in the appraisal report.

# X

**xeriscape™**
A patented name for landscaping that conserves water by using a wide variety of plants appropriate for the natural environment.

# Y

**yard**
A unit of measurement three feet long.

**yield**
*See* return on investment.

**yield capitalization**
Capitalization method that mathematically discounts future benefits at appropriate yield rates, producing a value that explicitly reflects the income pattern, value change, and yield-rate characteristics of the investment.

# Z

**zero-lot-line home**
House built without a side yard.

**zeroscaping**
The use of rock and hardscape with only a few sparse plants to create low water landscaping.

**zone**
The area set off by the proper authorities for specific use; an area subject to certain restrictions or restraints.

**zoning**
The regulation of structures and uses of property within selected districts.

**zoning law**
(1) Type of law used to execute master plans and control the mix of properties in a particular area. (2) A particular law used to execute master plans and control the mix of properties in a particular area. Also known as a zoning ordinance.

**zoning variance**
An exemption from a zoning ordinance or regulation permitting a structure or use that would not otherwise be allowed.

# ENDNOTES

Illustrations
Eric Sharkey, Allied Business Schools, Inc., Laguna Hills, California

Figure:        2.7, 2.10, 2.11, 2.12, 10.1.

Chapter 9:     One and a Half Story graphic, Row graphic, Cape Cod graphic,
               Contemporary graphic, Colonial graphic.

Chapter 15:    Area and Volume graphic, Area vs. Perimeter graphic, Irregular
               Lot graphic, Irregular Lot Solution A graphic, Irregular Lot
               Solution B graphic, Number line graphic.

# Index

## A

"A" paper loans, 144
above grade improvement, 245
absorption analysis, 158, 160
absorption rate, 158
abstract of judgment, 55
abstraction method, 392
acceptance, 68, 69
access, 238
accrued depreciation, 392
acknowledgement, 67
actual age, 392
ad valorem, 173-174
adaptation, 26
Adjustable Rate Mortgage (ARM), 141
adjustment grid, 289, 299
adjustment guidelines, 313
adjustments, 277
Advisory Opinions, 168,170
advocate, 175
aesthetic zoning, 62
affirmative easement, 57
after-acquired title, 63
age/life method, 401
agency, 68
agents of production, 114
aggregate, 451
agreement of the parties, 26
agricultural properties, 154
airspace, 23, 52
allocation method, 366-369, 385
amenities, 89, 106, 110, 112, 237
amortization, 140
annuity, 351
anything appurtenant to the land, 25
anything immovable by law, 25
anything permanently attached to the land, 24
apply adjustments, 298
appraisal, 2, 14
appraisal associations, 7
appraisal consulting, 173
Appraisal Foundation, The (TAF), 14
appraisal licensing and certification, 11
appraisal process, 193, 214
appraisal report, 2, 14
Appraisal Review, 169, 170, 172, 178
Appraisal Standards Board (ASB), 7
Appraisal Subcommittee (ASC), 10, 15
appraiser, 2, 14
Appraiser Qualifications Board (AQB), 7, 14
appreciation, 96

appurtenance, 25
architectural styles, 247
arm's-length transaction, 103, 207
aseptic system, 266
asphalt composition shingles, 251
assemblage, 94, 232
assessed value, 103
assignee, 73
assignment, 73
assignor, 73
associate's degree, 13
attachment lien, 54
attic, 264
attorney-in-fact, 68
average deviation, 455
averaging, 422
avigation easement, 58
awning, 254, 255

## B

bachelor's degree, 13
balloon frame construction, 257
balloon payment, 142
band of investment method, 341, 354
bankruptcy, 64
bare legal title, 138
baseboard, 256
baselines, 29
basement, 260
bay window, 204, 254, 255
below grade improvements, 245, 260
beneficiary, 126, 138
bilateral contract, 72
bill of sale, 25
blighted area, 96
bogus sale, 182
bonds, 134
book depreciation, 334
book value, 106
bounds, 34
bracketing, 315
breach of contract, 74
breakdown method, 403
broker price opinion (BPO), 194
building codes, 98
building residual technique, 344
building restrictions, 55
built-up roofing, 251
bulk zoning, 62
bundle of rights, 22
Business Appraisal, 170, 174

# C

cabinets, 268, 404
Cape Cod, 248
capital, 114, 159
capital improvements, 334
capitalization rate (cap-rate), 211, 338, 353, 458
carports, 269, 379
casement windows, 254, 255
cash dividend, 134
cash equivalency technique, 291
cash equivalent sale, 291
casing, 254
ceilings, 263
central bank, 125
central cooling system, 265
certificates of deposit (CDs), 136
Certified General, 11-13
Certified Residential, 11-13
chain of title, 66
chattel, 25
chronological age, 392
cinder block, 258
circuit breakers, 267
cladding, 252
client, 198
climate, 92
cloud on the title, 63, 65
collateral, 3
collecting market data, 214
collection loss, 330
colonial, 248
commercial banks, 128
commercial properties, 153
common areas, 52
common facilities, 51
common interest development, 51
common law dedication, 64
community property, 49
comparable properties, 109, 157, 203-205, 208,
    211, 275-277, 281, 288-290, 294-299, 302,
    315, 328-329, 339, 419
comparable sales, 195
comparable sales method, 339
comparative unit, 375-378, 381, 418
COMPETENCY RULE, 183
competition, 109
competitive market analysis (CMA), 194
Complete Appraisal, 178
complex 1-4 unit residential property, 12
comps, 195
concrete masonry unit (CMU), 258
concurrent ownership, 47
condemnation, 66, 472
condition, 56
condition precedent, 56
condition subsequent, 56
conditional use permits, 61, 226
conditional uses, 59

conditions of sale, 289-291, 309
condominium, 52
conduct, 28, 64, 72, 169, 175
confidentiality, 175-176, 287, 373
conforming loans, 144
consideration, 70
construction cost data, 373
contemporary style, 248
contingent valuation methodology, 308
contract, 67, 72
contribution, 113
contributory value, 367
conventional loan, 144
co-ownership, 47
corner lot, 233
cornice, 256
corporate bonds, 135
cost, 5, 87
cost approach, 197, 209
cost services, 376
cost to cure method, 400-401
counteroffer, 69
covenant, 55
covenants, conditions and restrictions (CC&Rs),
    55-56, 226, 448
crawlspace, 235, 248, 258, 260-261
credit reporting bureaus, 149
credit unions, 129
crops, 24
cubic foot, 303, 377, 448
cul-de-sac, 233
cumulative zoning, 62
curable depreciation, 394

# D

data services, 285
data sources, 281
debt capital, 341
debt investors, 128, 159
decimal point, 432
decline, 112
deed of reconveyance, 64
deed of trust, 64, 138
deferred maintenance, 396
define the problem, 196, 214
demand, 87, 108
demographics, 160
demography, 158
denominator, 433
density, 59
Department of Veterans Affairs (DVA), 147
Departure Rule, 174, 177-178
depreciation, 209
deregulation, 228, 229
designated person, 43
diamond-paned windows, 248
direct costs, 373-375, 381-383

shape of the parcel, 94
shellac, 252
short-lived, 396
siding, 248, 252, 371
sill, 254
single-hung windows, 254-255
site, 197, 230
size, 231
size of the land, 94
skylights, 254-255
slab-on-grade, 258
slate, 251
smart houses, 397
social ideals and standards, 99
soffit vents, 251
soft costs, 373
softwood, 256
soil, 234
solar energy, 268
solar panels, 237, 267-268
spa, 271
space heaters, 265
Spanish style, 247
special assessments,
Special Flood Hazard Areas, 234
special purpose properties, 155
special-use permit, 61
specific data, 196, 204-206, 214
specific lien, 54
split-foyer, 246
split-level, 246
square, 381
square foot, 367, 377, 448
square-foot method, 375, 377
square root, 457
squaring, 456
stability, 112
stain, 252
staircases, 263
standard deviation, 456
standards, 169
Standards Rules 1-4, 183
Statements on Appraisal Standards, 169
statistics, 451
Statute of Frauds, 70
statute of limitations, 74
statutory dedication, 64
steel, 150, 252, 256, 258, 263
stigma, 101
stock cooperative, 52
stock dividend, 134
stocks, 134
straight line method, 401
street address, 28
stucco, 252
Subdivision Development Analysis, 369, 385
subdivision map, 28

subdivision system, 28
subject property, 201
subjective value, 106
sub-prime loans, 145
substitution, 109
substructure, 245, 257
subterranean lines, 267
Summary Appraisal Report, 172, 425
sump, 260
sump pumps, 260
superadequacies, 398
superstructure, 245
supply, 108
supply and demand, 100, 108-110, 157, 227, 228, 293, 366
surface rights, 23
survey method, 308
surviving joint tenant, 48
suspended ceilings, 263
swimming pools, 270
syndication, 127

**T**

t-bars, 263
T-Bills, 136
T-intersection lot, 233
TAF (The Appraisal Foundation), 7
tangible assets, 174
Tax Reform Act of 1986, 8
tenancy, 47
tenancy by the entirety, 50
tenancy in common, 47
tenancy in partnership, 50
termites, 258
textured ceilings, 263
thermostats, 266
things attached by roots, 24
threshold, 254
thrifts, 128
tier of townships, 30
tile, 251
time adjustment, 292
time-share, 53
title, 47
title plants, 287
topography, 92, 234
townhouse or row house, 248
township lines, 30
townships, 30
tract, 230
trade fixtures, 28
traffic flow, 238
traffic volume, 238
Trainee License, 11-13
transaction value, 9
transfer, 62
transferability, 89